MW00770563

ALEXANDER OF APHRODISIAS

Supplement to On the Soul

Alexander of Aphrodisias

Supplement to On the Soul

Translated by
R. W. Sharples

BLOOMSBURY

LONDON • NEW DELHI • NEW YORK • SYDNEY

Bloomsbury Academic
An imprint of Bloomsbury Publishing Plc

50 Bedford Square	1385 Broadway
London	New York
WC1B 3DP	NY 10018
UK	USA

www.bloomsbury.com

Bloomsbury is a registered trade mark of Bloomsbury Publishing Plc

First published in 2004 by Gerald Duckworth & Co. Ltd.
Paperback edition first published 2014

© R.W. Sharples, 2004

R.W. Sharples has asserted his right under the Copyright, Designs and
Patents Act, 1988, to be identified as Author of this work.

All rights reserved. No part of this publication may be reproduced or transmitted in
any form or by any means, electronic or mechanical, including photocopying,
recording, or any information storage or retrieval system, without prior
permission in writing from the publishers.

No responsibility for loss caused to any individual or organization acting on or
refraining from action as a result of the material in this publication can be
accepted by Bloomsbury Academic or the author.

British Library Cataloguing-in-Publication Data
A catalogue record for this book is available from the British Library.

ISBN HB:	978-0-7156-3236-9
PB:	978-1-4725-5773-5
ePDF:	978-1-4725-0109-7

Library of Congress Cataloging-in-Publication Data
A catalog record for this book is available from the Library of Congress.

Acknowledgements
The present translations have been made possible by generous and imaginative funding from
the following resources: the National Endowment for the Humanities, Division of Research
Programs, an independent federal agency of the USA; the Leverhulme Trust; the British
Academy; the Jowett Copyright Trustees; the Royal Society (UK); Centro Internazionale A.
Beltrame di Storia della Spazio e del Tempo (Padua); Mario Mignucci; Liverpool University;
the Leventis Foundation; the Arts and Humanities Research Borad of the British Academy;
the Esmée Fairbairn Charitable Trust; the Henry Brown Trust; Mr and Mrs N. Egon; the
Netherlands Organisation for Scientific Research (NWO/GW). The editor wishes to thank
Pamela Huby, Inna Kupreeva, Alan Lacey, Jan Opsomer, and Robert Todd for their comments.

Typeset by Ray Davies
Printed and bound in Great Britain

Contents

Introduction[1]

This *Supplement* to Alexander of Aphrodisias' book *On the Soul* is transmitted in the MSS as the second book of that work. In fact it consists of a series of short and more or less independent pieces. Its description as a *Mantissa* – literally 'makeweight' – or *Supplement* is due to Freudenthal,[2] and was adopted by Ivo Bruns who edited the Greek text in 1887.

Subsequently Bruns argued (1892, xii-xiii) that the *Mantissa* contained texts of two types. One, the majority, consists of list of arguments – or sometimes just indications of how one might develop an argument – against specific theses, often identifiably those of rival philosophical schools. Into this category fall §§3, 4, 6, 14, 20 (against the Stoics), §7 against a view held by Numenius, and §§9-13 against non-Peripatetic theories of vision. §8 too may be directed against the Stoics, though the issue to which it relates had been controversial within Aristotelianism; §18 and perhaps §19 (which differs in arguing for a thesis rather than attacking one) relate rather to discussion of the interpretation of Aristotle within the Peripatetic school. That the context of these collections was a practical one of live debate is suggested, as Bruns notes, by such passages as 113,28, 114,6-9, 118,7-8 and 122,21.

Bruns 1892, xii regards the remaining sections as forming a single group, 'comments completed by Alexander himself and published separately'. In fact they are more heterogeneous than this might suggest. §§1 and 25 are reworkings in condensed form of themes treated at more length by Alexander elsewhere; §1 gives a general account of the soul, treated at much greater length in Alexander's *D(e) A(nima)*, and §25 appears to be a reworking of material from his *(De) Fat(o)* into what is at least superficially a more organised and positive exposition of his own distinctive

---

[1] This Introduction is an abridgement of material discussed more fully in Sharples (forthcoming, 2).

[2] Bruns 1887, v.

doctrine of fate. §23, an account of responsibility ('what depends on us', *to eph' hêmin*), also draws on and develops arguments in *Fat.* and can be seen as a development of one particular aspect of that work; it relates to several of the *Quaestiones* and *Ethical Problems* attributed to Alexander. §§15 and 16 set out aspects of the Aristotelian theory of vision and colour, showing a close relation to discussions in Alexander's *DA* and also in his commentary on Aristotle's *De sensu*; no doubt if we possessed Alexander's commentary on Aristotle's *DA*, of which commentary Accattino and Donini (1996, vii-viii) have suggested Alexander's own *DA* is an abridgement, parallels would be apparent there too. The latter part of §15 is an attempt to explain the perception of distance and movement within the Aristotelian theory of vision, and can plausibly be seen as a reaction to criticisms such as those made by Galen. The theme of §16 is also discussed in *Quaestio* 1.2 attributed to Alexander.

§§5 and §21 are arguments for particular points of interpretation within Aristotelian doctrine, which differ from texts like §§8 and 19 chiefly by not being cast in the form of a sequence of arguments. (§5 shows some affinity to such a sequence, but also to the form of a problem in the narrow sense of that term.) §5 is linked by subject-matter both with Alexander, *DA* 14,24-15,5, and with *Quaest.* 1.8, 1.17 and 1.26. The starting-point of §21 is a remark in Aristotle's *Metaphysics*. §24 is an orthodox exposition of the Aristotelian doctrine of chance, disregarding rather than developing difficulties raised by *Fat.*; it may be connected in some way with Alexander's lost *Physics* commentary. (I do not however wish to suggest that these texts are simply extracts from the commentaries; their form is too self-contained to suggest that they have been taken from the commentaries without any recasting.)

Accattino 2001 persuasively argues that §2, *On Intellect*, which has historically been the most influential of the entire collection, is an early work by Alexander. It is composed of three originally separate sections, of which the first (A) is an exposition of Alexander's doctrine of intellect, developed and in important respects modified in his later *DA*, while the second and third sections (B and C) record treatments of the topic which he heard in school discussion, probably from one of his teachers, followed in B by his own development of the argument and in C by his rejection of it.

§17 is a criticism of earlier attempts to formulate an Aristotelian view on the characteristically Stoic topic of 'the first appropriate thing'; §22 is the report of an eccentric defence of non-determinist reponsibility within the Aristotelian system, which it is difficult to believe expresses views Alexander himself ever held, though he may have recorded them. (See however below, 205 n.683).

Connections in subject-matter cut across these distinctions by literary form. §§9-16 form a sequence relating to the theory of vision, and may have a connection to Alexander's lost work *On How We See* (see below, introduction to §9) and to the treatise *On Vision* of his teacher Sosigenes. This leads to the broader question of the thematic unity of the collection as a whole. Bruns 1892, xiii took the minimalist view that it was labelled 'On the Soul' simply because that is the theme of its first section; and indeed in the primary MS, V (Venetus Marcianus gr. 258), §1 has no separate title of its own. (See below, 88-9.) However, the collection does seem to constitute a series of texts which have been arranged, without regard to their literary form, approximately in the sequence in which topics are discussed in Aristotle's *DA* and, following it, Alexander's. Thus §1 sets out the general doctrine of soul; §§3-6 relate to general issues concerning the hylomorphic theory, with implications for the relation between body and soul, and §2 could have been placed where it is because of its denial of individual immortality to the human intellect (an issue which is raised early in Aristotle's *DA* at 1.1 403a3-10, 2.1 413a6-7), even though the principal discussion of intellect comes toward the end of that work). §§7 and 8 could be seen as having implications, not indeed spelled out, for nutrition and respiration respectively; §§9-16 on vision follow them, as the account of sensation follows the general account of soul and that of nutritive soul in Aristotle, *DA* and Alexander, *DA*; and §§17-20 and 22-25 are in the broadest sense concerned with ethics, which could be loosely linked with the account of the appetitive faculty in Aristotle, *DA* 3.9-11 and Alexander, *DA* 73, 14-80,15.

The fit is indeed a loose one, but the arrangement of sections does seem to have an internal logic, and one bearing at least some relationship to Aristotle, *DA*. And such an arrangement would not be without parallel in the collections of minor texts attributed to Alexander; for Moraux 1942, 23 observed that those of the

Quaestiones that relate to identifiable passages in Aristotle's *DA* follow each other in the sequence of that work, regardless of their literary form, and – strangely – with other discussions interrupting the sequence on no discernible principle, presumably as the result of a somewhat chaotic later editing process. It may also be significant that there are no texts in the *Quaestiones* similar to the lists of arguments which form the bulk of the *Mantissa*, although texts of this type *are* found in the *Ethical Problems*; for this raises the possibility that at an early stage in the compiling of these collections material relating to the soul, specifically, was distributed into two separate groups at least partly on the basis of its perceived literary form. (Thus, if *Mant.* §§9-16 on vision already formed a group, the fact that the earlier sections of this group are in the form of lists of arguments may have been sufficient to cause the *entire* group to be placed in the *Mantissa*.) The editing procedure that gave us the *Quaestiones*, at least, in the form in which we have them was less than perfect (Bruns 1892, xi).[3]

We do not know when this editing took place, and this raises the question of the authenticity of the pieces that were included. It has already been indicated that some sections express views it is difficult to suppose Alexander ever held (§22) or that conflict with his views in other works (aspects of the view argued for positively in §2A). But neither of these rules out his authorship, since in the former case he may have recorded views he rejected, and in the latter he may have changed his mind; and beyond this reasons for doubting authenticity relate to the relatively pedestrian nature and lack of acuteness in argument of some of the sections (particularly

---

[3]   One possible trace of a stage before the compilation of the *Mantissa* as we now have it may be preserved in a strange feature of the orthography of the primary ninth-century MS V; there is a marked preponderance of forms of *gignesthai* in *gign-* rather than *gin-* in the last four sections of *Mant.*, by contrast with the rest of *Mant.* and with all the other works of Alexander in this MS, and there are signs that the copyist of V only realised this after copying several lines. The most obvious explanations would seem to be either that at some earlier stage in the tradition the last four sections were copied by a different hand following a different convention, or that, being connected in subject matter, they originally circulated in a separate MS tradition (as they were to do so again in 15th century copies). See further Sharples (forthcoming, 2).

§§8 and 21). However, any writer will show some variation in depth of analysis and degree of insight from one context to another, and this seems a dubious ground for denying authorship. Statistical analysis of the language of the texts might provide some pointers, but there are problems in its application to texts which are relatively short and which, in the case of the collections of arguments, may bear traces of the varied sources from which they came.[4]

Bruns did not introduce a numbering system for the sections of the *Mantissa*, possibly because the sections are numbered in the MSS, but in an erroneous way. What Bruns rightly treats as the second section, *On Intellect*, is divided in the MSS into §§2-4 of the whole, §3 starting with the description of intellect *in habitu* (*en hexei*) at 107,20, and §4 with that of creative or active intellect at 107,29. Ironically *On Intellect* is indeed a composite text, as indicated above, but the new sections start not where V places them but, unnoticed by V and presumably by its source, at 110.4 and 112.5.[5] The result is that what I have treated as §3, that starting on page 113 of the Berlin edition, is numbered 5 in the MSS, and so on thereafter. Rather than splitting *On Intellect* into three sections, albeit at different points from the MSS, and thus preserving the MSS numbering of the rest of the collection, I have followed Bruns in presenting it as a single text, so as not to give the false impression that the breaks at 110,4 and 112.5 are present in the MSS tradition. Consequently all subsequent sections here have a number two lower than that in the MSS.

As already noted, the majority of the sections of the Mantissa are characterised by a rapid succession of numerous short arguments for the same point, often introduced by *eti,* 'moreover'. In some of the Greek MSS attempts have been made, with varying degrees of consistency and success, to number these arguments in the margin of the text. It seemed desirable not only to number the arguments in this translation, but also to reproduce the numbering of the MSS where possible. Argument numbers from the primary

---

[4] See 190 n.641. Some analysis of the vocabulary of §25 in comparison to that of *Fat.* was undertaken in Sharples 1980.

[5] The inappropriateness of V's division is shown by the fact that its sections 2 and 3 amount to 34 and 7 lines respectively in the Berlin text, while section 4 amounts to six pages.

MS V are placed between round brackets; where V does not provide numbering, numbers from later MSS have been placed between {braces}; and numbers I have supplied myself are placed, as are words supplied in the translation, between square brackets. Material between angle brackets in the translation indicates supplements to the Greek text.

I have endeavoured to translate Greek terms consistently into English as far as possible, but the requirements of readability and comprehensibility impose restrictions. Particular issues of translation arise in §2, *On Intellect*. I have used 'intellect' and 'intelligibles' for *nous* and *noêta*, but 'think' for the cognate verb *noein*. This risks obscuring the connection between them, but the alternative was either to use the unlovely verb 'intelligize' or to turn the doctrine of the Productive Intellect into a doctrine of the Productive Thought; references to Alexander's doctrine of intellect and its influence are so widespread in modern literature that to follow the latter course would have created obscurity of another sort. Furthermore, since I believe A.C. Lloyd[6] was right to argue that for Aristotle we think (e.g.) a horse when we have the form of horse in our mind, that the form in our mind just *is* the thought, and that the expression 'to think *of* a horse' suggests a potentially misleading distinction between thought and its (internal) object, I have used 'think' as a transitive verb with the thing thought as its direct object. This has one potentially confusing result, in that the grammatical distinction between 'thought' as a noun and as a passive participle is no longer apparent in referring to 'things that are thought' (rather than to 'things that are thought *of*); but the ambiguity is on the level of grammar rather than of philosophical doctrine, for thoughts just *are* the things that are thought.

For *diaphanês* I have adopted the conventional translation 'transparent', which fits the way in which the term is used in the *Mantissa*, except in §16 where I have transliterated it. As indicated in the notes to that section, the discrepancy originates in a similar difference in the use of the term by Aristotle in his *DA* on the one hand and *De sensu* on the other. For *aporrhoia*, usually rendered by the technical 'effluence', I have used 'streaming off', simply because this offers a convenient translation of the verb *aporrhein*.

---

[6] Lloyd 1980, 10-17.

Another problematic term is *korê*, conventionally translated (in relation to the eye) as 'pupil'. Richard Sorabji has shown that for Aristotle the term refers rather to the more or less fluid contents of the eye, the 'eye-jelly'. It is presumably applied to these because the pupil is the point at which the contents of the eye can be seen from outside and affected by what is outside. Even in §15, where Alexander is explaining (and developing) Aristotle's own theory, 'pupil' is sometimes the more appropriate translation; still more so in the sections where he is criticising rival theories. I have therefore used whichever translation seemed more appropriate at each point, with explanatory notes where necessary. For *hairetos* I have used 'to be chosen' rather than the unlovely 'choiceworthy'; an anonymous referee suggested 'may be chosen', but that seems to me to give too weak a sense, and Chrysippus' distinction between *hairetos* and *haireteos* in *SVF* 3.89 and 91 is not between what 'may be chosen' (if that implies 'but need not be') and what is 'to be chosen' but between goods and the possessing of them.

The present translation is based upon a new edition of the Greek text, for which I have collated all MSS known to me, either by direct inspection or from photographs. That edition of the text, together with a fuller discussion of the MSS evidence, is to be published by Les Belles Lettres, Paris, in the Budé series. That publication will also include a French translation, introduction and notes, and I am grateful to Les Belles Lettres and to Duckworth for agreeing to this arrangement. My thanks are also due to the British Academy (grant no. BA-AN1718/APN1984) and the A.G. Leventis Foundation, for funding which enabled Sophia Kapetanaki and myself to catalogue the MSS of the minor works of Alexander; to the British Academy, for a Small Grant (no. SG-30033) which enabled me to obtain further prints and microfilms of the *Mantissa* MSS; to the Arts and Humanities Research Board (grant no. AN 1718/APN 12007) and to University College London, for the research leave which enabled me to complete work on the editing of the Greek text; to University College London and to Carlo Natali of the University of Venice for facilitating my travel to Venice to consult MSS V and B; to the Librarian of the Institute of Classical Studies, London, for study facilities during my research leave; to Silvia Fazzo, for transcribing for me the notes in one copy of the Aldine edition in Milan and alerting me to the existence of those in another; to Inna Kupreeva, for showing me her own draft translations of §§ 1-14 (for §§1-8 cf. Kupreeva 1999, 288-333); to Sylvia Berryman for reading through sections of drafts; to Pat Easterling for reading through the Introduction to the edition of the Greek text. I am also grateful to the staff of the Institut de Recherche et d'Histoire des Textes, and of all the libraries which supplied me with microfilms or prints of MSS. The *Thesaurus Linguae Graecae* CD-ROM "E" has been of considerable assistance, especially in locating parallel texts.

Parts of the translation and notes to §20 appeared in Sharples 2000b, published by the Cambridge Philological Society. The translations of §§22-25 are revised versions of those in Sharples 1983, published like the present volume by Duckworth, and that of §22 had previously appeared in Sharples 1975b, published by the Institute of Classical Studies. I am grateful to the respective publishers for permission to re-use this material. Excerpts from the translations, and some material from the notes, to §§15 and 19 will also appear in Sharples (forthcoming, 1 and 3 respectively) in volumes to be published by Oxford University Press.

I am also grateful to many colleagues for discussion and correspondence concerning matters palaeographical, philological and philosophical, especially Paolo Accattino, Han Baltussen, Sylvia Berryman, István Bodnar, Edwin Brandon, Sarah Broadie, Charalambos Dendrinos, Wolfgang Detel, Pat Easterling, John Ellis, Silvia Fazzo, David Gallop, Todd Ganson, Elias Giannakis, Kerstin Hadjú of the Bayerische Staatsbibliothek in Munich, Fritz-Gregor Hermann, Harry Hine, Pamela Huby, Richard Janko, Inna Kupreeva, Alan Lacey, Alain Lernould, Walter Leszl, Francesco Montarese, Danielle Muzerelle of the Arsenal library in Paris, Carlo Natali, Jan Opsomer, Anthony Price, David Robertson, Christopher Rowe, Hans-Jochen Ruland, Ricardo Salles, David Sedley, Anne Sheppard, Richard Sorabji, Carlos Steel, Bob Todd, Julius Tomin, and the editorial teams of the Aristotelian Commentators Project and the *Commentators Sourcebook*. Above all, my thanks are as ever due for the support shown to me by my wife Grace and daughter Elizabeth.

University College London   R.W. Sharples

Alexander of Aphrodisias, *Supplement to* On the Soul: chapter-headings.[7]

1	[On the Soul.]
2	On Intellect.[8]
[3]	That the soul is incorporeal.
[4]	That the capacities of the soul are many and not one.
[5]	That the soul is not in a subject.
[6]	That qualities are not bodies.
[7]	Against those who say that none of the four bodies which we call elements subsists on its own.
[8]	That air is by nature hot.
[9]	Against those who say that seeing comes about through rays.
[10]	Against those who explain seeing through the tension of the air.
[11]	Against those who say that seeing comes about through the entry of images.
[12]	Against those who say that seeing <comes about> through streamings off from both [the one seeing and the thing seen].
[13]	That light is not a body.
[14]	That it is impossible for body to extend through body.
[15]	How seeing comes about according to Aristotle.
[16]	That colour is the limit of the *diaphanes.*

[7] There is no table of chapter headings in the primary MS V (by contrast with the *Quaestiones* and *Ethical Problems* in the same MS). Bessarion compiled one for MS B, and gave it the heading 'Alexander of Aphrodisias, *On the Soul* 2 and some enquiries in ethics: chapter-headings'. The present table has been compiled from the headings as they appear in the following translation, rather than reproducing differences (which are trivial) in the readings adopted by Bessarion in his table.

[8] §§2-4 in the MSS. See above, Introduction p.5.

Alexander of Aphrodisias

Supplement to On the Soul

Translation

Alexander of Aphrodisias, *On the Soul* 'book 2'.   101,2

1. [On the Soul].

In the primary MS V this piece has no individual title. In Bessarion's table of contents in MS B it is described as a 'preface' to the
collection.[9] It is in fact an account of Alexander's doctrine of soul,
covering in a much shorter space the same general ground as his
treatise *On the Soul* (*D*(*e*) *A*(*nima*)), going into considerable
detail on the general hylomorphic theory but only giving a very
summary account of the individual soul-faculties. Whereas Alexander's *DA* begins with general remarks on the subject's importance
and complexity, and then proceeds straight to the form-matter
contrast, our *Mantissa* text begins with the contrast between the
question of the soul's existence and that of its nature – a standard
move present in *On Fate* but also in *Mant.* §§24 and 25 – and next
proceeds to the ten categories, singling out substance and analys-
ing it as matter and form. The preliminaries to the *Mant.* discussion are thus much more scholastic than in *DA*, conforming to an
academic rather than to a rhetorical pattern.

   In this section I have found it necessary to translate *ousia*
sometimes by 'being', when it has a more general sense, and
sometimes by 'substance'. Instances of 'being' = *ousia* are identified in the text; 'substance' always renders *ousia*, and 'being',
where no specific indication is given, renders a part of *einai*.

   I am grateful to participants at the London seminar, especially
Sylvia Berryman, Anthony Price and Richard Sorabji, for helpful
comments on this section and on my draft translation.

Concerning soul, what it is, and what its being (*ousia*) is
and what its accidents are, is not able to be discovered
readily or most easily; consideration of these things is   5
among the most difficult, even though the existence of soul

---

[9]   Moraux 2001, 318-319 n.3 suggests that this section originally had the title 'On Soul' and that the transfer of this title to the
whole collection may explain the transmission of the latter as the
second book of Alexander's *On the Soul*. However, 'On Soul' is a
not inappropriate title for the *Mantissa* as a whole. See above,
Introduction, 3.

is most well-known and obvious. But there are many extant things whose existence is most well-known but whose being (*ousia*) is most obscure, such as motion and place, and still more, time. For of each of these the existence is well-known and indisputable, but what their being (*ousia*) is, is among
10   the most difficult things to observe. And soul is one of the things like this. For that soul is something is well-known and obvious, but what it is is not easy to discover.

If we were to start our account of it beginning further back, from the division of being into the primary kinds and to make it clear under which of the kinds soul falls, perhaps
15   when this had been established we would grasp its whole being (*ousia*). Well, being is divided into the ten primary and highest kinds,[10] and we say that one of these is substance, some of which is composite, and other [substances] those out of which what is composite has its being. Well, we say that composite substance is that of which we can predicate [that it is a] 'this-something', that which is perceptible and
20   exists in actuality and underlies all the other kinds of what is, for example this stone, this [piece of] wood, this gold, this fire and each of the things like this. For these and things like them are all composite substances: for there is in them something which underlies, which we call matter and which has the capacity to receive some form in itself, and the form, having received which into itself that which underlies, being indifferent in its own nature in all the
25   things in which it is, becomes differentiated and is now a this-something, in one case silver, in another gold, in another fire, in another something else. For all these things, being the same as each other in respect of the matter and what underlies, are differentiated according to form.[11]
102,1   For as it is with the products of craft, analogously so we must think it is with natural substances. In the case of craft – the [craft of] sculpture, let us say – the bronze underlies all the things that are made to come to be from it by the

---

[10] I.e. the ten categories.
[11] As Anthony Price points out to me, matter is here absolute and undifferentiated in itself; in other words, prime matter.

craftsman, but the forms which come to be in it according to the craft are the causes of the difference and of each of them being a this-something, one a discus-thrower, one a [boy] binding his hair,[12] and each of them is a composite made up of the bronze and of a shape of a particular sort. Just so must we think it is also in the case of composite substances. For in these too one thing is what underlies, and another the form according to which each of them is 'this-something', one water, one air, one something else...[13]

The living creature does <not> come to be by the soul <being destroyed>*[14] in its mixture with the body. Well, if it is in neither of these ways that the living creature is a composite substance, it remains that it is so in the third way.[15] This was that in which one part of what is composite is what underlies and matter, [while] the other [is] form. For it is not in the [same] way as with numbers; for what is composed of them is incorporeal, but the living creature is not like this. So the living creature is composed of soul and body, and it is by one of these being what underlies, and the other the form, that it is composed of these.

Well, what remains is either that the body should be the form of the soul, or the soul of the body. But to say that the body is the form of the soul is impossible; the body is what underlies. Moreover, each of the extant things is a 'this-something' in respect of its form, for example statue, house,

[12] A statue by Polycleitus: Pliny, *Nat. Hist.* 34.55.

[13] Aristotle at *Metaph.* 7.16 1040b8 argues that the four elements are not substances, and it may seem surprising that our text describes mass terms like gold, fire, water and air as 'this-something's. Cf. however ibid. 5.8 1017b10, 7.17 1041b14 (I am grateful to Walter Leszl for drawing my attention to the former passage) and Alexander, *In Metaph.* 115,10, 153,7; *DA* 6,8.27; *Quaest.* 2.24 75,10, with Sharples 1999.

[14] * indicates a variation from Bruns' printed text. See Notes on the Text, below 238.

[15] Similarly, as noted by Bruns, Alex., *DA* 12,6-7, from which it is clear that the first way, here missing in the lacuna, is the mere juxtaposition of soul and body.

20   ship, fire, water, earth.[16] And it is in respect of its soul that
the living creature is a living creature. So the soul is the
form. Moreover, when the form[17] is no longer present, and
not in what underlies, [this] has ceased to be the this-
something that it was before; and a living creature has
ceased to be a living creature when the soul is separated
from the body. The axe is an axe in respect of its shape, and
25   this is its form, and if it had soul, the shape rather than the
iron would be its soul. Just so the soul in the living creature
is analogous to the shape of the axe, for it is in respect of
this that the living creature is a living creature. So being
(*ousia*) in respect of form will be soul.*

Moreover, those things by which natural bodies differ
from one another are forms, and they differ by some having
soul and others [being] without soul; [so] soul will be
form.[18]

Moreover, that by which primarily we understand is
30   understanding (for it is in respect of understanding that we
understand), and understanding is not something that
underlies, but that [by] receiving which that which underlies is said to understand in a secondary way (and [what
underlies] is soul). That by which primarily we are healthy
is health, and this is not something that underlies; for it is
the body that underlies and receives health, and it is [the
body] that is healthy in a secondary way.[19] Well, that by
35   which primarily we live is soul, and soul is not something
103,1 that underlies, but that which what underlies receives and is
said to be alive, itself too, in a secondary way, just as the
body that has received health [is said] to be healthy and the

---

[16] Similarly, as Bruns notes – but of the elements only, and
without the reference to a 'this- something' – at Alex., *DA* 6,21-23.

[17] Literally 'If the form is that which, when it is no longer
present ... and a living creature ... (for the axe is an axe ... is a
living creature), [the being] in respect of form will be soul'.

[18] Cf. Alexander, *DA* 15,28-29: Papadis 1991, 202 n.253.

[19] The point being, as Richard Sorabji notes, that the body is
healthy because of health; this is made clear at Alex., *DA* 31,10-25,
of which the present argument is, as Bruns notes, a condensed
version. Cf. Aristotle, *Metaph.* 4.2 1003a34.

soul that has received understanding [is said] to understand. So, being (*ousia*) in respect of form will be soul.

Aristotle says that form is perfection and actuality. So it is reasonable for soul, which is being (*ousia*) in respect of form,[20] to be called actuality by him. For of the extant things some are said to be potentially, and some in actuality, and the things that are said to be in actuality are those that already have the form that they can have, and the shape. So it is reasonable that that, by the presence of which something that is potential comes to be actual, is actuality. But what is potentially a living creature, for example seed, comes to be a living creature in actuality by the presence of soul. So it will be shown in this way too that soul is form and actuality.

One [sort of] actuality is first [actuality], another second. For sciences, and crafts, and in general dispositions are first actualities, but the activities which come about in respect of them and from them are second actualities. The musician is such in actuality – for he possesses the art of music – but it is in respect of the first actuality that he is said to be a musician in actuality; [so] too is already the person who is actively playing music,[21] who has already acquired the second actuality in addition. So actuality is double, and soul is actuality in the way that disposition is. For the person possesses soul none the less who is not active in respect of it,[22] for example the one who is asleep. For he is not then active in respect of sensation, but he nevertheless has sensitive soul. So soul is first actuality.

Since every form and actuality is of something, it is clear that what comes next is to consider, of what [soul is the form and actuality]. Well, that it is of the body has more or

[20] I.e., soul is being (substance, *ousia*) in the way that form is, not in the way that matter or the form-matter compound is. Cf., with Bruns, the longer argument at Alex., *DA* 15,29-16,7.

[21] Literally: 'who is active in accordance with music'. Bruns suggests rather 'Already also actively playing music is the one who has already acquired ...': this gives more force to the *êdê* in 103,16, but seems hard to reconcile with the *ho* before *energôn*.

[22] Cf., with Bruns, Alex., *DA* 16,12.

less been shown already. For the living creature is a substance composed of what underlies and of form, and what underlies in it is body, the actuality is the soul. But
25   since of bodies some are [products] of craft, and others natural, of what sort of body is soul actuality? For it is not possible for soul to come to be in every [sort of] body. Well, it is not [the actuality] of any [body produced] by craft. For it would itself be a form [produced] by craft, like that of the statue, and living creatures would be produced by craft, like statues. But in this way it would not even be a substance; for a form [produced] by craft is not a substance.[23] So, soul is
30   the actuality of a natural body – and a natural body is one that has a principle of movement in itself –, for the living creature too, of which the soul is a part, [is] by nature.

But there are differences among natural bodies: some of them are simple, others compound. And the soul is not the actuality of any of the simple bodies, for soul is not the form
35   of fire or air or water, nor yet of earth, since none of these is a living creature. So what sort of body is the body of a living creature, of which soul is the actuality? Well, every body which has soul and is alive is nourished and grows by itself, for it is in this way that what is alive is different from what is
104,1   not. Nourishment and digestion and addition and growth require certain organs: some things make use of mouth and throat and belly and gut for these, others roots and pith and bark. As many living creatures as are more perfect require proportionately more organs too, and of the faculties of soul,
5   which all operate through certain organs proper [to each], as is clear in the case of the senses. So soul will be the first actuality of a natural body having organs.[24] For no body is able to live or possess soul if it does not have organs or have the parts* which will serve the faculties of soul.

Well, this will be the most general definition and account of soul. For it includes the soul of plants, too. But our
10   account is of soul which comes to be in mortal bodies.[25] For

[23] See below, §5 121,17.
[24] Aristotle, *DA* 2.1 412b5-6; Alex., *DA* 16,10.
[25] Cf., with Bruns, Alex., *DA* 28,25.

when we say that soul is of a natural body which potentially has life,[26] we are not then applying 'potentially' to the body in the way that we are accustomed to apply it to things that do not yet have something but are suitable to receive it. For it is not that this body first exists without soul, and subsequently receives it,[27] but what potentially has life is what is   15
able to live,[28] that is what possesses organs for the activities in life, and 'potentially having life' is equivalent to 'having organs'.[29]

But if the soul is the form and actuality of body, it is clear that it will be incorporeal.[30] For every form is incorporeal. For if the form too were itself a body, then either it will be without form and without quality – and [it is] matter [that] is like this – or, if it is going to possess form, and [that]   20
form, being body, [is going to possess] another form, this will go on to infinity. The soul, being actuality, [extends] throughout the whole body, for every part of what has soul has soul. And soul is actuality not in the way that shape is [the actuality] of things that have been shaped, nor as position and arrangement [is the actuality] of things that have been put together, nor as some disposition and being affected, nor as mixture or blending[31] (for pleasure and pain   25
are being affected or disposition, but soul is none of these). Certainly these come to be present in the body, for it is through these that [there exist] the organs which soul uses; but [soul] itself is some capacity and substance which supervenes on these.[32] The body and its blending are the

[26] Aristotle, *DA* 2.1 412a27-8. Cf. Alex., *Quaest.* 2.8, and Sharples 1992, 104 n.338.

[27] Cf. Alex., *DA* 15,3-5, *Mant.* §5 120,13-16, *Quaest.* 1.8 17,9-10. Papadis 1991, 97 n.314, 158 nn.42-43.

[28] Cf. Alex., *DA* 16,13. Papadis 1991, 97 n.313.

[29] Cf. Alex., *DA* 16,12-13. Shields 1993, 10 n.20; Accattino and Donini 1996, 131.

[30] Contrary to the Stoic view of soul. Cf., with Bruns, Alex., *DA* 17,10-11, and below §3.

[31] Or 'temperament' (*krasis*); the view of Galen, *Quod animi mores* 37,5-26, 44,18-45,3.

[32] Alex., *DA* 24,15-26,30. This was the view put forward by

cause of the soul's coming-to-be in the first place. This is
clear from the difference between living creatures in
30   respect of their parts. For it is not the souls that fashion
their shapes, but rather the different souls follow on the
constitution[33] of these being of a certain sort, and change
with them. For the actuality and that of which it is the
actuality are related reciprocally.[34] And that difference in
soul follows on a certain sort of blending in the body is
shown also by wild animals, which have an [even] more
different sort of soul deriving from the blending in their
body being of a certain sort.
35   What we call the activities of soul are not [activities] of

Andronicus: see Galen, *Quod animi mores* 44,12ff., with
Gottschalk 1987, 1113 and nn. See also below, §2 112,15-16, and
40 n.98, 53 n.148.

[33] *sustasis*; a Stoic technical term. Cf. Seneca, *Letter* 70. (I owe
this reference to Richard Sorabji.)

[34] Literally 'are of each other.' Cf. Accattino 1988, 87. Moraux
1942, 232 claims that this passage simply echoes Alex., *DA* 24,3-4,
which states that soul 'has its origin from the sort of mixture of the
primary bodies, as has been shown'; cf. also Alex., (*De*)
Princ(*ipiis*) §18 fin., p.53 Genequand 2001. At *DA* 7,24-5 Alexander
speaks of simpler forms, such as those of flesh and bone, as
contributing to more complex ones, such as the soul. But at 6,2-4
he insists that both form and matter are substances in their own
right; and at 7,4-8 he insists that it is the form of each thing that
determines its nature. He does indeed *subsequently* attribute
differences between natural kinds to their different material
composition (9,5-7) and speak of the capacity of different matter for
receiving different forms (10,26); but this is *after* the general
notion of form has been introduced. The question is whether the
reference back at 24,3-4 is to be read in the light of 7,4-8. See
Moraux 1942, 29-62; Donini 1971; Thillet 1981, 12; Papadis 1991,
226-7; Robinson 1991, especially 214-18, with my reply at Sharples
1993, 87-8; Sharples 1994,2; Accattino 1995; Caston 1997, 347-54.
For form supervening on material change in Aristotle cf. *Phys.* 7.3
246a4-9, 246b14-15, with Everson 1997, 269-73 (rightly arguing that
determination of form by matter is not inconsistent with hypothetical necessitation of matter by form but in fact supports it), and
Magee 2000, 316. Compare also Mirus 2001, especially 370-2.

soul in itself, but of what has it. For just as it is not the soul itself that walks or wrestles, but the person having it, just so what is pained and desires and rejoices and grows angry is what possesses soul, not the soul [itself]. For all the so-called movements of the soul are [actually] of the compound, that which is alive.[35]   105,1

The faculties of soul have a certain ordering in relation to one another. For one of them is first, another second, another after these.[36] A sign of this: what has the first is able   5 to have a share of the second, but it cannot have the second without the first.[37] The first is [the faculty of] nourishment and growth and reproduction, and plants too have this [sort of] soul. For this is not, as some people think,[38] nature, but the first faculty of soul, since the simple bodies too have nature, but we do not yet say that these are alive. For nature is a principle of movement. But plants have more than [just   10 what they would have] in accordance with [nature]; for they have the [ability] to be nourished and grow by themselves and to reproduce things like [themselves], and these are defined [as characteristics] of being alive.[39] And being alive is through the presence of soul.

The second faculty of soul is that of sensation, by which living creatures are defined; and it is not possible to have this without the first one. But plants, which have nutritive soul, do not have sensitive [soul]. In addition to these facul-   15 ties there is that of impulse, which is coupled with that of sensation. For there is no benefit to living creatures from sensation if impulse is not present in them; for this is the beginning of all action.

These are the three most necessary and primary parts of

[35] Cf. Aristotle, *DA* 1.4 408b11-15; Alex. *DA* 23,6-24,3, and below, §3 117,14-18. Papadis 1991, 188.

[36] Cf. Aristotle, *DA* 2.3 414b28-32, with the discussion in Alex., *Quaest.* 1.11 23,13-16, with Sharples 1992, 50 n.129; also, with Bruns, Alex., *DA* 16,19-17,1.

[37] Cf., with Bruns, Alex., *DA* 29,26-30,6.

[38] The Stoics: cf., with Bruns ad loc., Alex., *DA* 31,25-32,6; below, §4.

[39] Cf. Alex., *DA* 31,8-10.

the soul, common to all living creatures, the plant-like, the
sensitive, and the impulsive, each of them being useful for
20   some one of the things in which being for a living creature
consists. For the functions of a living creature are first to be
and to live, second the judgement of things that impinge
upon it, and in addition to these activity and action. Well,
the plant-like faculty of soul contributes to the living
creature's being and living, the sensitive to judgement, the
impulsive to acting. The action, strictly, of a living creature
25   is activity with use of the parts of the body which are
organs, [activity] such as walking or speaking.

The nutritive faculty is divided into nourishing, causing to
grow and reproducing, the sensitive into sensing and
imagining and remembering and assenting,[40] and the impulsive is as it were a certain end of imagination and assent; for
30   it is for its sake that these [exist]. For in every case assent
goes ahead of impulse, and imagination ahead of [assent].[41]
Of this [faculty] which is impulsive and concerned with
action one [part] is as leading and another as serving; the
[part] that leads is what is properly called impulsive and
appetitive, while the other pulls the puppet-strings,[42] and
includes the [power] of speech.[43] To the impulsive part
106,1   belong desiring and becoming angry and wishing; for these
are species of appetition.[44] Of these wishing already seems
to have a share also in reasoning; for it is appetition accompanied by deliberation. There is also another judging faculty
of the soul, the reasoning one, which is present in the more

---

[40] Assenting is attributed to the sensitive or perceptive part
because Alexander is here concerned with animals in general,
rational human animals not being introduced until 106,2. For
irrational animals assenting cf. Alex., *Fat.* 14 183,31; *Quaest.* 3.13
107,8.

[41] The terminology is Stoic. Cf. Alex., *DA* 72,13ff., *Fat.* 14
184,1ff.

[42] *neurospastikos*; cf. [Aristotle], *De mundo* 6 398b16. Inna
Kupreeva compares *kata to neurôdes* in *SVF* 3.473.

[43] The recognition of speech as a distinct soul-faculty is again
Stoic; LS 53H = *SVF* 2.836.

[44] Below, §5 119,9-10: Alex., *DA* 74,1-2.

perfect among living creatures, namely, the human being, whose deliberating and comprehending and opining belong 5 to this faculty.

The soul moves the body not by being moved itself and so moving it, for it is unmoved in itself, but as the cause for the living creature's movement, as the heaviness present in earth is the cause of its downwards movement.[45] For not all the things that cause movement do so in a similar way. It is in one way that the oxen move the waggon, in another that the good and the [object] of desire and the [object] of 10 appetition moves what desires it; for [it does so] without being moved [itself].[46] And that is why being moved by such things is characteristic of things having soul. The soul causes movement because it is in respect of it that we think and make choices; for what is good causes movement by being thought of, but the soul [does so] by thinking. For as craftsmen are moved on account of the crafts and in accordance with the crafts, and these are the causes of their moving in such a way, though they are not moved themselves, just so things having soul are moved in respect 15 of their soul although it is not moved itself.[47] And it is in respect of the impulsive and appetitive faculty of the soul that living creatures are moved; for this is the cause of living creatures' own proper movement.

[45] Cf. Alex., *DA* 22,7ff., *Princ.* §5, p.45 Genequand 2001, and Pines 1961, 42, 46 n.121.

[46] The text here seems to conflate the claims (a) that the soul is unmoved (for which cf. Aristotle, *Phys.* 8.6 259b2-3, 16-20; Alex., *DA* 21,24, 22,13) and (b) that the object of desire moves the soul, while itself being unmoved, for which cf. Aristotle, *DA* 3.10 433b15-17 (also *Phys.* 8.2 253a11ff., 8.6 259b6-16, with Furley 1978).

[47] Cf. Alex., *DA* 21,22-22,12.

106,18   **2. On Intellect.**

Discussion of this text has focused on three interrelated issues: whether it is a single text or a combination of several pieces originally more or less independent; whether the author or any of the authors, if there are more than one, can be identified with Alexander, and what the relation is between the views advanced here and those in the discussion of intellect in Alexander's *On the Soul*; and whether the 'Aristoteles' referred to at 110.4 is to be identified with Aristotle the Stagirite or with the second-century A.D Peripatetic Aristoteles of Mytilene. The text is here presented in three sections, [A], [B] and [C], each subdivided according to the structure of its argument; in the MSS, [A1] constitutes §3 of the *Mantissa*, [A2] §4, and all of [A3]-[C2] §5.

Greek text, Italian translation and commentary in Accattino 2001; translations into French in Moraux 1942, 185-94, and in Carrière et al., 1961; into English in Fotinis 1980, 137-53, and in Schroeder and Todd 1990, with commentary. The medieval Arabic version (no.21 in Dietrich 1964), is edited in Finnegan 1956, and in Badawī 1971, 31-42. From this Arabic version a Latin version was made by Gerard of Cremona, edited in Théry 1926, 69-83. I am particularly grateful to Inna Kupreeva, who has advised me on the implications of the Arabic version for the readings of the Greek text.

See also, in addition to other literature cited below in the notes, Freudenthal 1884, 24-7; Gilson 1929; Moraux 1942, 143-64, 1978, 301-5, 1984, 406-25 and 2001, 386-94; Gätje 1971, 70-71; Badawī 1972, 445; Bazán 1973; Donini 1974, 49-50, 60-61; Thillet 1981; Schroeder 1982, 1997; Gottschalk 1987, 1160-62; Sharples 1987, 1211-14; Papadis 1991, 313-82; Accattino and Donini 1996, xxvii-xxx; Rashed 1997.

[A1]

Intellect is according to Aristotle of three [types]. One is
20 material intellect. I say 'material' not because it is
something that underlies like matter[48] – for I say 'matter' of

---

[48] Accattino 2001, 39 well suggests that this is a response to Xenarchus' view that Aristotle identified intellect and prime matter, reported *by Alexander* ap. Philoponus *In DA* 15,65-9 Verbeke; cf. Moraux 1973, 207-8. The account of material intellect

something which underlies and is able to become a 'this-something'[49] through the presence of some form. Rather, since matter's being matter [consists] in its having the potentiality for all things, [it follows that] that in which there is potentiality and indeed that which is potential, insofar as it is such, is 'material'. And so the intellect which is not yet thinking, but has the potentiality to come to be like this, is 'material', and it is this sort of potentiality of the   25 soul that is the material intellect, not being in actuality any of the extant things, but having the potentiality for becoming all of them, if indeed it is possible for there to be[50] thinking of all the extant things. For that which is going to apprehend all things must not be any of them in its own proper nature in actuality; its own proper form would appear incidentally in the apprehending of external things and become a hindrance to thinking of them.[51]

For the senses, too, do not apprehend those things in   30 which they have their own being. It is for this reason that sight, which apprehends colours, has the organ, in which it is and through which it apprehends, without colour; for water is without colour as far as its own proper colour is concerned. [The sense of] smell, too, [comes] from air   107,1 which is without smell, and it apprehends smells; and touch does not sense those things which are hot or cold or hard or soft in a similar way to it, but rather those which differ [from it] by being more or less [so]. And this is so because it was impossible for it, being a body, not to possess these contrarieties. For every natural and generated body is   5 tangible.

In the case of the senses, then, it is impossible for that

---

in [A1] is closely parallel to that in Alex., *DA* 84,14-85,10, as Moraux 2001, 387 n.314 notes. For the background of the concept see further Accattino and Donini 1996, 271.

[49] I.e a particular instance of a definite type. See above, 15 n.13.

[50] Literally: 'to come to be'.

[51] With this and the subsequent argument cf. Aristotle, *DA* 3.4 429a18-27; Alex., *DA* 44,3, 84,14-22. Bruns 1887, 84,16 n., 106,28 n.; Papadis 1991, 316-20, 342-3; Gannagé 2002, 148 and n.47.

which possesses some [attribute] to apprehend and judge what it [itself] possesses. And in this way, since intellect is an apprehending and judging of intelligibles, it is not possible for it to be any* of the things which are judged by it, either. But it apprehends all extant things, if it is possible to think all things. So [intellect] is not in actuality any of the
10   extant things; but it is all of them potentially. For this is what it is for it to be intellect. The senses, which come about through bodies, are not [themselves] the things that they apprehend, but are certain other things in actuality, and [their] potentiality is [the potentiality] of some body. Because of this the apprehending of sensible things involves the body being affected in some way. For this reason not every sense apprehends every thing; for it is
15   already itself some [sense] in actuality.[52] But intellect does not apprehend extant things through body; it is not a potentiality of a body, and it is not affected. It is not in actuality any of the extant things at all,[53] nor is what has the potentiality a this- something,[54] but it just is without qualification a potentiality for an actuality and soul of this sort, capable of receiving forms and thoughts. So this intellect, which is
20   material, is in all the things that have a share in complete [perfect] soul, that is, human beings.[55]

[A2][56]

107,21   Another [type of intellect] is that which is already thinking and possesses the disposition of thinking, and is able to apprehend the forms of intelligible things by its own power.

---

[52] Translating Bruns' *tis ... energeiâi*. MS M has *tis ... energeia* ('some actuality'), but this may be either a simple error or a mistaken correction to give a superficially easier sense.
[53] Cf. Alex., *DA* 84,21-22.
[54] I.e., a specific thing. Above, 25 n.49.
[55] Cf. Alexander, *DA* 81,26-8: Papadis 1991, 317 n.23.
[56] The MSS here have a new heading and section number, 3. On Intellect with the Disposition (*en hexei*; sc. the disposition for thinking). This is what became known in medieval discussions as 'intellect *in habitu*', from the Latin rendering of *en hexei*.

being analogous to those who possess the disposition of craftsmen[57] and are able to perform the actions of the craft by themselves. The first [type of intellect] was not like these, but more like those who are able to take up the craft and become craftsmen. And this [second type of intellect] is   25 the material [intellect] when it has already acquired the disposition and actual thinking.[58] This sort of intellect is in those who are already more perfect and are thinking.[59] So this is the second [type of] intellect.

[A3][60]

The third [type of] intellect besides the two already   107,29 mentioned is the productive,[61] on account of which the   30 material [intellect] comes to have the disposition, this productive [intellect] being analogous, as Aristotle says[62], to light. For as light is the cause for colours that are potentially visible of their becoming visible in actuality, so this third [type of] intellect makes the potential and material intellect

---

[57] Cf. Aristotle, *DA* 3.4 429b5-9, Alex., *DA* 86,1-5; Papadis 1991, 376 n.302; Geoffroy 2002, 205 n.38. – The Greek word order might rather suggest 'those of craftsmen who possess the disposition'. But this is illogical; those who do not (yet) possess the disposition are not (yet) craftsmen. And in Greek of this period the repetition of *tên* before *tôn tekhnitôn* is not to be insisted upon.

[58] Literally, 'the thinking and being actual/active'. – Why is actual intellection referred to here, rather than just the first actuality, the developed ability to think? (I owe this question to Alan Lacey). Presumably because, when the ability develops, it is exercised, even if it is not continually exercised thereafter; someone who becomes a competent geometrician does not first become competent and only do actual geometry some time later.

[59] Cf. Alexander, *DA* 82,1-3.

[60] The MSS here have a new heading and section number, 4. On the Productive Intellect.

[61] Commonly known as the 'active intellect'. With the distinction of three types of intellect, the productive bringing the potential to actuality, compare Alcinous, *Didascalicus* 10.

[62] Aristotle, *DA* 3.5 430a15-17. Below, 42 n.106.

[become] intellect in actuality, by creating in it the disposition of intellection.

108,1   This [intellect] is what is intelligible in its own nature and is such in actuality; for it is this that produces thinking and leads the material intellect to actuality. This too is itself an intellect; for immaterial form, which alone is intelligible in its own nature, is intellect.

     For enmattered forms are made intelligible by the intellect, being intelligible potentially.[63] The intellect separates
5   them from the matter with which they have their being, and itself makes them intelligible in actuality, and each of them, when it is thought, then comes to be intelligible in actuality and intellect; [but] they are not like this previously or by their own nature. For intellect in actuality is nothing other than the form that is being thought, so that each of these things too, that are not intelligible without qualification, becomes intellect, whenever it is thought. As knowledge in
10   actuality is the same as what is knowable in actuality,[64] and

---

[63] Geoffroy 2002, 206 says that it is clear that the reference here is to the Active Intellect, and (208) that ambiguity in the Arabic version caused both this and the beginning of the preceding paragraph to be referred erroneously to the actualised intellect in the individual. But in the present paragraph Alexander is in fact speaking of abstraction by the human intellect (cf. Accattino 2001, 11 and 43, and Alex. *DA* 87,25; below, 35 n.80), as an argument for the preceding general claim that immaterial form is intellect and *hence* that the transcendent active intellect which is indeed referred to at the beginning of the preceding paragraph is both intelligible and intellect.

[64] It is odd that in the case of knowledge and its object the identity is only stated once, while in that of sensation which follows it is stated twice. The Arabic and Latin versions indeed add 'and what is known in actuality (i.e., knowable in actuality; the actuality of the knowable is its being known) is knowledge in actuality', followed in two of the Arabic MSS and the Latin by a further addition (in the Arabic: 'for one thing is knowledge in actuality and what is known in actuality, and the object of knowledge in actuality is knowledge in actuality'), perhaps a marginal variant incorporated into the text. (I am grateful to Inna Kupreeva for this suggestion and for information on the Arabic version

as sensation in actuality is the same as the sensible in actuality and the sensible in actuality [is the same] as sensation in actuality, so too intellect in actuality is the same as what is intelligible in actuality, and what is intelligible in actuality [is the same] as intellect in actuality. For intellect, apprehending the form of the thing that is thought and separating it from the matter, both makes it 15 intelligible in actuality and itself comes to be intellect in actuality.

If then there is any of the extant things that is intelligible in actuality in its own nature, and because it is immaterial possesses of itself the [property] of being such, not deriving it from an intellect that separates it from matter, such a thing is intellect in actuality always. For what is intelligible in actuality is intellect. This thing that is both intelligible in 20 its own nature and intellect in actuality comes to be the cause of the material intellect's, by reference to such a form,[65] separating and imitating[66] and thinking each of the

---

of the passage.)

[65] Conceivably inspired by Aristotle's reference to intellect as 'form of forms' at *DA* 3.8 432a1-3; cf. also, with Accattino 2001, 46, *DA* 3.4 429b3-4. But the implication that the productive intellect, i.e. God, is the first thing that we think of, and that it is this thought that enables us to think of other things, is bizarre. (Geoffroy 2002, 211, 218 interprets the present passage as saying that the material intellect is actualised by referring material forms to the immaterial forms which are the objects of the productive intellect's thought; but see 28 n.63 above.) In Alexander's *DA* the way in which the productive intellect is productive of our thinking is much less clearly indicated (cf. Sharples 1987, 1206-8). Moreover, as Moraux 2001, 390 and nn. points out, Averroes observed that Alexander's *DA* appears to hold that it is not intellect *in habitu* that apprehends transcendent, *per se* intelligibles, but the active intellect itself coming to be in us.

Moraux (1978, 304-5; 2001, 392-4), Accattino and Donini 1996 xxx, and Accattino 2001, 45-6 and 52, suppose that the present text is an authentic but early work of Alexander's, and that the views developed in his *DA* superseded those expressed here. This seems more plausible than that the present text is later than *DA*

enmattered forms as well, and making it intelligible. It is the intellect said to be 'from without',[67] the productive [intellect], not being a part or power of our soul, but coming to be in us from outside, whenever we think of it, if indeed thought comes about in the apprehending of the form, and
25 (if indeed) it is itself immaterial form, never being accompanied by matter nor being separated from matter when it is thought.

Being like this it is, reasonably, separate from us, since its being intellect does not come about in its being thought by us, but it is such in its own nature, being in actuality both intellect and intelligible. Form of this sort and substance separate from matter is imperishable. For this reason the productive intellect, which is in actuality a form of this sort
30 being from without, is reasonably called immortal intellect
109,1 by Aristotle. For each of the other forms that are thought, too, is intellect when it is thought, but it is not intellect from without or from outside,[68] but comes to be [intellect] when it is thought. But this intellect, being [intellect] even before it is thought [by us], is and is said to be 'from without', reasonably, when it is thought.

The intellect which [possesses] the disposition [for intellection] and is active is able to think itself [as its object]. For
5 it [does] not [do so] in that it is an intellect – for [in that case] it will possess thinking and being thought at the same time and in the same respect – but, first, in the way in which intellect in actuality is the same as things that are thought in actuality. Thinking these it thinks itself, if the things

---

and represents either Alexander's own development of that work (Bazán 1973, especially 476-8) or a misunderstanding of *DA* by someone other than Alexander (Moraux 1942, 132-42, a view which Moraux later abandoned; Schroeder and Todd 1990, 13-14, 19-20). Cf. p.2 above, and below, 37 n.87, 44 n.115.

[66] Accattino 2001, 45 well suggests that 'imitating' here should be understood in the sense of 'reproducing'.

[67] Cf. Alex., *DA* 90,19; Aristotle, *GA* 2.3 736b28; and below 112,6.

[68] Because it is only in the mind that the abstraction of form from the perceived form-matter compound takes place.

which it thinks, in being thought of, come to be intellect. For if the things that are thought are intellect in actuality, and it thinks these, it comes to think itself. For in thinking it comes to be the same as the things that are thought, but when not thinking it is other than they. In this way sensa-tion too may be said to sense itself, since it senses the things which in actuality become the same as it. For as we said,[69] sensation in actuality, too, is the thing that can be sensed. For both sensation and intellect apprehend their proper [objects] by grasping the forms separately from matter.

Moreover, intellect may be said to think itself not in that it is intellect, but in that it is intelligible. For it is as intelligible that it apprehends [itself], just as [it does] each of the other intelligibles too, [and] not as intellect. For it is an attribute of intellect that it is also intelligible; for since it too is one of the extant things, and it is not perceptible by the senses, the remaining [possibility] is that it be intelligible. For if it was as intellect and in that it is intellect that it was thought by itself, it would not think anything else that is not intellect, and so it would think only itself. But [as it is], in thinking the intelligibles which are* not intellect before they are thought, it also thinks itself as [being] of this sort, as one among the intelligibles. So this intellect incidentally comes to think itself, advancing from the material intellect.

And the primary intellect, intellect in actuality, also thinks itself in a similar way and for the same reason. But it has something more than this [human intellect]; for it does not think anything other than itself. For by being intelligible it is thought by itself; and, by being intelligible in actuality and in its own nature, it will always be thought; and clearly [it will be thought] by what is <always>[70] thinking in actuality. But it

10

15

20

25

[69] At 108,10 above: so Bruns, ad loc.
[70] Added by Freudenthal 1884, 26, followed by Bruns, from the text of pseudo-Alexander, *In Metaph.*, as edited by Bonitz (673,21 = 699,4 Hayduck). The word appears in one MS of pseudo-Alexander but not in others, and though accepted by Bonitz was rejected without comment by Hayduck. It does not appear in the Greek MSS of the *Mantissa*; the Arabic and Latin versions are

is itself the only intellect that is always thinking in actuality;
so it will always think itself. [It will think itself] alone,
inasmuch as it is simple. For intellect that is simple thinks
what is simple, and nothing else is a simple intelligible except
30   itself. For it is unmixed and immaterial and having nothing
in potentiality in itself. So it will think itself alone. Thus in
110,1   that it is intellect, it will think itself as intelligible; in that it is
in actuality both intellect and intelligible, it will always think
itself; in that it alone is simple, it will think itself alone. For
itself alone being simple it is able to think something simple,
and it itself alone among the intelligibles is simple.

[B1]

110,4   I also heard, about the intellect from without from Aristotle,
[things] which I preserved:[71]
5   The things that prompted Aristotle to introduce the intellect from without were said[72] to be these: the analogy from

---

here compressed and so do not provide a sure guide. (I am grateful to Inna Kupreeva for clarification of this point.) Nevertheless,
'always' does seem to be required here by the argument.

[71] For this translation of this notorious sentence, which I owe to
Jan Opsomer, see Opsomer and Sharples 2000. If it is instead translated 'I also heard from Aristoteles things about the intellect from
without, which I preserved', the reference will probably be to Aristoteles of Mytilene, a second-century A.D. Peripatetic mentioned by
Galen. This was proposed by Moraux 1967 (cf. id., 1984, 399-401;
1985, 2001, 393 n.334a), and is adopted by Papadis 1991, 334;
Accattino and Donini 1996, xxvii and nn.77-8; Accattino 2001, 13-15.
That the reference in this sentence is rather to Aristotle the Stagirite has been argued by Moraux 1942, 148; Thillet 1984, xi-xxxi,
especially xv-xix; Schroeder and Todd 1990, 23-4, 28-31; Opsomer
and Sharples 2000. (The suggestion of Zeller 1903, 815 n.3, followed
by Trabucco 1958, 117-26, that the text should be emended to refer
to Aristocles of Messene is not supported by anything we know of
Aristocles' doctrines.) In the next sentence the reference is on any
view to Aristotle the Stagirite.

[72] Although the position adopted in [B2] below is broadly
similar to that in [A], [B] as a whole differs from [A] in making

things perceptible by the senses, and that applying to all things that come to be. For in all things that come to be there is something that is affected, something that produces, and thirdly, from both of these, what comes to be. It is similar in the case of sensible things; for what is affected is the sense-organ, what produces is the sensible [object], and what comes to be is the apprehending of the   10 sensible thing through the sense-organ. In the same way in the case of the intellect too [Aristotle] supposed that there must be some productive intellect, which would be able to lead the potential and material intellect to actuality; and actuality is making intelligible to itself all the extant things. For as there are sensible things which are themselves* in actuality and produce sensation in actuality, so there must also be things which produce intellect, being intelligible in   15 actuality themselves. For it is not possible for anything to be productive of anything if it is not itself in actuality.

But none of these things which are thought by us is intelligible in actuality. For our intellect thinks the sensible things which are intelligible potentially, and these are made intelligible by the intellect. For this is the activity of intellect, by its own power to separate and abstract the things which are sensible in actuality from those things in the company of which they are sensible, and to define   20 (them) in themselves.[73] If then this is the activity of the intellect that previously existed potentially, and what is brought to be and is led from potentiality to actuality must

---

the issue of 'the intellect from without' its starting-point and moreover in doing so in the context of an earlier tradition. This may suggest that it is earlier than [A] and has perhaps been attached by an editor to [A], the latter being the later and more complete version.

[73] Bruns suggests reading *kath' hauta <ta eidê autôn>, ei dê hautê*, which would give the sense 'and to define their forms in themselves'. The reference is certainly to forms (cf. Alex., *DA* 87,24-5); but it can perhaps be understood rather than added in the Greek. Inna Kupreeva points out that the Arabic seems to have construed *ei dê* as *eidê*.

be brought to be by something that exists in actuality, there must also be some productive intellect which exists in actuality, and will make that, which at one time existed potentially, able to be active and to think[74]. And this is what the [intellect] that comes in from without is like. These then are the things that prompted [Aristotle].

[B2][75]

110,25   There will then be something that is intelligible in actuality, being such by its own nature, just as [there is] also what is sensible, not being made to be so by the sensing. This is intellect, a certain nature and substance, not knowable by anything other than intellect. For it is not perceptible by the senses; nor yet do all the things which are thought by our intellect come to be intelligible not being intelligible in their

30   own nature, but there is also something which is intelligible in itself, being such by its own nature. This then [is what] the potential intellect, when it is being perfected and has developed,[76] thinks.

    For just as the power of walking, which a human being has as soon as he comes to be, is led to actuality, as time advances, by being perfected itself and not by being

111,1   affected in some way, in the same way[77] the [potential]

---

[74] Cf. Alex., *DA* 88,23-4; Papadis 1991, 352-3.

[75] I have marked a new section here in order to emphasise, following Accattino 2001, 10-11, that only the first part of [B] is presented as an explanation of Aristotle's position derived from an earlier source. In [B2] Alexander proceds to develop the interpretation further himself.

[76] 'has developed' translates the aorist participle *auxomenos*. To avoid a conflict with the implication at [A3] 108,20ff. (above, n.65) that the productive intellect is the first thing that the material intellect thinks, it would be necessary to understand 'has developed' proleptically; it is the very fact of thinking of the productive intellect that brings about the development. Cf. Schroeder 1997, 112.

[77] At Alex., *DA* 82,5-10, walking and intellect are rather contrasted, in that the development occurs naturally in the case of

intellect too when it has been perfected both thinks the things that are intelligible by nature and makes sensible things intelligible to itself, as being productive. For intellect is not in its own nature such as to be affected, so as to be brought about by something else and affected, like sensation.[78] The reverse is the case. For sensation is by being affected, for it is [a thing] that can be affected, and its apprehending is through being affected; but intellect is [a   5 thing] that is productive. For in the case of most things, being able to think them, it at the same time[79] comes to be their producer too in order that it may think them – unless someone might want to say that the intellect too is subject to being affected in this respect, that it apprehends the forms. For to apprehend seems to be to be affected. And this indeed it shares with sensation; but since each of them is characterised and defined not by what it shares with   10 something else but by what is peculiar to it, this too that [intellect] shares with sensation will be characterised by what is peculiar to it. So, if it shares with sensation the fact that it is able to apprehend forms, even if not in the same way, but it is peculiar to it that it produces these forms which it apprehends, it will rather be defined by producing.[80] Accordingly intellect will be [a thing] that is

---

the former but not in that of the latter, where it requires practice: cf. Accattino and Donini 1996, 273, and Accattino 2001, 52.

[78] In fact Aristotle denies (*DA* 2.5 417b2ff.) that either thinking or perceiving is being affected in the ordinary sense of the term. Cf. Alex., *Quaest.* 3.2-3, and on the distinction between alteration and perfecting Burnyeat 2002, especially 63 n.92 on the usage of the Aristotelian commentators.

[79] More literally, 'being able to think most things it at the same time...'. But I have translated in this way to avoid any implication that there are some things which intellect cannot think at all. I am grateful to Inna Kupreeva for raising this issue.

[80] This is our intellect, intellect *in habitu*, not the primary, divine productive intellect; compare 111,21 below, and for the description of our intellect as producing intelligible forms cf. Alex., *DA* 87,25. At Sharples 1987, 1212 n.135, I described the use of *poiêtikos* 'productive' here as 'confusing': I did not thereby

productive, rather than one that can be affected.

15   Moreover, its producing is prior and [part of] its substance. First it produces by abstraction [something] intelligible, and then in this way it apprehends some one of these things which it thinks and defines as a this-something. Even if it separates and apprehends at the same time, nevertheless the separating is conceptually prior;[81] for this is what it is for it to be able to apprehend the form. We say that fire is productive in the highest degree, because it consumes all

20   matter that it gets hold of and provides [it as] nourishment for itself; and yet, in that it is nourished it is affected. In the same way[82] we must consider that the intellect that is in us is productive; for it itself makes intelligible the things that are not intelligible in actuality. For nothing is intelligible other than the intellect that is in actuality and in itself. And the things that are made intelligible by what thinks them, and the activities of this, [are] also themselves intellect

25   when they are thought. So, if intellect did not exist, nothing would be intelligible, neither what is naturally [so][83] – for it itself was alone of this sort – nor what is brought about by this;[84] for if it did not exist, it would not produce.

The intellect that is by nature and from without will assist that in us, because other things too would not be

---

intend, as Accattino 2001, 11 supposes, to suggest that Alexander is himself confused here, only that the reader might be.

[81] I.e., a necessary condition? (I owe this suggestion to Anne Sheppard).

[82] Though the change involved here is hardly as drastic as that involved in fire's burning its fuel.

[83] Cf. 111,29 below.

[84] Accattino 2001, 54 interprets both 'if intellect did not exist' and 'this' in 'what is produced by this' as referring to our intellect. This certainly fits the overall argument better – there is no suggestion in *On Intellect* that the divine intellect produces intelligibles directly, as opposed to enabling our intellects to do so by abstraction; see above, 29 n.65 – but it requires, as Accattino says, understanding 'nothing would be intelligible' as 'nothing would be intelligible to us'.

intelligible, though being [so] potentially, if there did not exist something that was intelligible by its own peculiar nature. This, being intelligible by its own nature,[85] by being thought comes to be in the one who thinks it; it is intellect   30 that has come to be in the one who thinks, and it is thought 'from without' and [is] immortal, and implants in the material [intellect] a disposition such that it thinks the things that are intelligible potentially.[86] Light, which is productive of sight in actuality, is itself seen[87] as are also the things that go with it,[88] and through it colour [is seen]; just so the intellect from without comes to be the cause of our thinking, being thought itself as well; it does not make [our intellect] intellect,[89] but by its own nature perfects the intel-   35 lect that exists [already] and leads it to the things that are proper to it.[90]

So intellect is a thing which is intelligible by nature;[91] the other things are those that are intelligible by

[85] Because it is not enmattered, and so not only potentially intelligible.

[86] It is not made clear here whether the productive intellect is one and the same for all human beings, nor whether it is divine. Bruns, followed by Moraux 1942, 19, regards the words 'and immortal' as an intrusion into the text, anticipating 112,5ff.; but even if this anticipation is a convincing objection in itself, it loses its force if 112,5ff. is an originally independent text. See below, 40 n.99.

[87] Alan Lacey points out to me that it is the source of light that is seen, rather than the light that it produces. – Against the arguments of Schroeder 1997, especially 113-17, that the present passage draws on Plotinus' account of divine intellect and so is evidence for section [B] of *On Intellect* being later than Alexander himself see Accattino 2001, 52.

[88] I.e., the things which it illuminates.

[89] Presumably because it is already potential intellect. See 112,2 below.

[90] Presumably both transcendent, immaterial forms and those separated from matter by the process of abstraction; cf. 111,1-2, 112,3-4.

[91]The sequel shows that the intellect discussed in this sentence is our intellect (so Accattino 2001, 54-5). The divine intellect too is

112,1   its craft and are produced by it. The potential [intellect]
produces them not by being affected and brought about by
something, for it was intellect even before it was active, but
by having developed and being perfected. When it has been
perfected it thinks both the things that are intelligible by
nature and those that [are so] in accordance with its own
proper activity and craft. For being productive is peculiar to
intellect, and its thinking is being active, not being affected.

[C1]

112,5   He[92] wanted to show that the intellect is immortal, and to

---

indeed intelligible by nature; perhaps for this reason Alexander
only says here that intellect is intelligible by nature, not that it is
intelligible by *its own* nature. I am grateful to Inna Kupreeva for
discussion of this passage.

[92] In [C1] the views of an unnamed person are reported by the
writer who goes on to criticise them in [C2]. Whether the person
whose views are reported in [C1] is also the person whose views
on Aristotle's motives are reported in [B1] is not immediately
clear. The opening of [C1] is abrupt: Schroeder and Todd 1990, 26
and 31 suppose that [C] is a disjointed fragment and, like Moraux
1942, 149, that the identity of the proponent of the views
expressed in [C1] has been lost in a lacuna. The view of the
relation of the productive intellect to our intellect in [C1] is very
different from that in [B] (cf. below, 42 n.106). Trabucco 1958,
120-123, followed by Moraux 1967, 175 and Sharples 1987, 1212,
explained this as the report of a single individual first expounding
a general tradition in [B] and then going on to develop an
argument on a specific issue in [C1] (n.b. *kat' idian epinoian* in
112,8); but this is scarcely tenable (cf. Opsomer and Sharples
2001, 252-3). Accattino 2001, 10-15 argues that [C1] and [B1]
reflect the views of the same person, the report in [B1] being
followed by the development in [B2] before returning in [C1] to
further views of the person reported in [B1]. Rashed 1997, 192
n.28 notes the unusual use of the first-person singular (rather than
the 'editorial' plural) in 110,4 and 113,12 as suggesting that the
authors of [B] and [C] are the same, and Accattino 2001, 15 points
out that the past tense in both passages is appropriate for a

avoid the difficulties which they bring against the 'intellect
from without',[93] which must necessarily change its place but
cannot, if it is incorporeal, either be in place or change its
place and be in different places at different times.[94] So,
following his own individual idea, he said things like the
following about the intellect that was said to be in every
mortal body. He said that intellect is in matter as one   10
substance in another substance[95] and [is so] in actuality,[96]
and always performs its own activities.[97] When, from the

---

recording of the author's introduction to the subject through the
views of his teacher. Nevertheless, the abrupt transition from
[B2] to [C1], and the fact that [B2] is a development while [C2] is
a refutation, may justify us in regarding [B] and [C] as in some
sense originally separate pieces of writing.

[93] Above, 30 n.67.

[94] The objection was probably raised by the Platonist Atticus.
Cf. Atticus, fr. 7.75ff. des Places; Donini 1974, 51; Rashed 1997,
189-91; Accattino 2001, 55. – Schroeder and Todd (1990) 31, 74
suggest transposing 113,18ff. below to here. But this seems
unnecessary; 113,18ff. give the solution approved by [C2], which
naturally follows the rejection, in the first part of [C2], of the
solution in [C1]. Whereas the proposer of [C1] says that intellect
need not move because it is everywhere, [C2] 113,18ff. argues
that one should rather respond to the problem by saying it is not
in place at all.

[95] Whether this is the original formulation of the person whose
views who are being reported, or that of the reporter who will go
on to criticise them in [C2], is not certain. (I am grateful to
Pamela Huby for raising this point.) Since divine intellect is for
[C1] incorporeal, the paradox of two bodies being in the same
place, raised by Alexander against the Stoics at *Mixt.* 5 218,15, 11
225,4, 12 227,4, is not mentioned either here or in the objections
in [C2] below.

[96] So Moraux 1942, 192. The Greek could also mean 'as one
substance in another substance and actuality.'

[97] Here and in what follows 'activity' and 'actuality' translate the
same Greek word, *energeia*. What the activities of the active intellect are when it is not operating through our intellects as its
instruments is not entirely clear; 113,6-12 below suggest that it
has a providential or organising role in relation to the physical

body that was blended, there comes to be fire or something of this sort as the result of the mixture, which is able to provide an instrument for this intellect, which is in this mixture – for it is in every body, and this too is a body –,

15   then this instrument is said to be intellect potentially, super-vening on this sort of blending of bodies as a suitable poten-tiality for receiving the intellect that is in actuality.[98] When [the intellect that is in actuality] takes hold of this instru-ment, then it is active as through an instrument and in relation to matter and through matter, and then we are said to think. For our intellect is composed of the potentiality, which is the instrument of the divine[99] intellect [and] which

20   Aristotle calls intellect in potentiality, and of the activity of that [divine intellect].[100] And if either of these is not present it is impossible for us to think.

For straight away, at the first depositing of the seed, the intellect which is in actuality is there, going through all things and being [there] in actuality, as also in any other body whatsoever. But when it is also active through our potentiality,[101] then this is said to be our intellect and we

---

world, but how much detail [C1] himself provided is unclear (see below, 42 n.107). I am grateful to Inna Kupreeva for raising this issue.

[98] Accattino 2001, 57, notes the similarity between [C1]'s expression here and Alexander's own definition of soul at *DA* 24,3ff., 26,21ff. (cf. 24,21-3 and above §1 104,28ff.), while also noting that [C1], unlike Alexander, does not regard the potentiality as distinct from its corporeal basis.

[99] Papadis 1991, 363 notes that in *On Intellect* 'divine' is applied to the productive intellect only in the reporting of the theory in [C1] and in the refutation in [C2] (113,13, below): it is not quite true however that it is not used of the productive intellect at all in Alexander's *DA*, for it is once so used by implication, at 91,5.

[100] There is a less sharp distinction here than in [A] and [B] between *three* types of intellect; intellect *in habitu* is here the combination of productive and potential intellect rather than the development of the latter with reference to the former. Cf. Accattino 2001, 12, noting also [C2]'s complaint at 113,16 below.

[101] Or: 'capacity'.

think; just as if someone thought of a craftsman who   25
sometimes is active in accordance with his craft without
instruments,[102] and sometimes with instruments when his
activity in accordance with the craft is in relation to the
matter. In the same way the divine intellect, too, is always
active – which is why it is in actuality –; and it [is also active]
through an instrument when, from the combination of
bodies and their satisfactory blending, an instrument of this
sort comes to be.[103] For then [the divine intellect] is active   30
with a certain activity involving matter, and this is our
intellect.

And it departs in the [same] way as it enters. It does not
change place being somewhere else, but, since it is everywhere, it remains also in the body which is broken up as a
result of its departure,[104] [though] the instrumental [intellect]   113,1
is destroyed; just as the craftsman who has cast away his
instruments is active then too, but with an activity which is
not concerned with matter or by means of instruments.[105]

---

[102] E.g. a doctor who is thinking about how to cure the patient
but has not yet started the treatment? Cf. Aristotle, *Metaph.* 7.7
1032b6ff. (I owe the explanation, and the Aristotle reference, to
Inna Kupreeva). Or, with Accattino 2001, 58, a painter planning
his picture rather than executing it?

[103] The idea that human intelligence depends on physical
blending is Aristotelian: *GA* 2.6 744a27ff. Preus 1990, 80 n.26.

[104] The use of 'departure' here is paradoxical: the point is not
that the intellect becomes separated spatially from the dead body,
but that while it is still present in it, as it is everywhere, it is no
longer in the same relation to it as previously. It is strictly speaking the departure of soul, rather than of intellect, which causes
the corruption of the body.

[105] Accattino 2001, 58 suggests a painter who can continue to
think about his painting even when his brush has broken; Philoponus, in *GC* 271,10 (cited by de Haas 1999, 31 n.38) has the
example of a builder who has no materials. Plotinus employs the
musician who first uses a lyre and then sings without one as an
analogy for the soul's concern for but independence of the body
(1.4 [46], 16.23-9), and may well be dependent on Alexander here
(Movia 1970, 67-8; cf. Fotinis 1979, 157 and nn.5-6); but if so
Plotinus (characteristically) improved the image, for a singer is

So, he said that, if one should suppose that intellect is divine and imperishable according to Aristotle at all, one must consider [that it is so] in this way, and not otherwise.

5 And, fitting the passage in the third book of [Aristotle's] *On the Soul* to this [theory], he said that both the 'disposition' and the 'light' must be applied to this [intellect] that is everywhere.[106]

This intellect either [1] organises things here [in the sublunary region] on its own, in relation to the movement of the heavenly bodies above,*[107] and combines and separates them, so that it is itself the craftsman [producing] the intellect that is potentially, as well; or else [2] [it organises things here] along with[108] the orderly movement of the heavenly bodies. For it is by this that things here are

10 brought about, chiefly by the approach and withdrawal of the sun: either [2a] they are brought about by [the sun] and by the intellect here, or else [2b] it is nature that is brought about by these things [the heavenly bodies] and their movement, and it [nature] organises individual things along

---

more obviously independent of musical instruments (apart from his own voice) than other craftsmen are of their tools.

[106] Aristotle, *DA* 3.5 430a14-15: 'one sort of intellect is by becoming everything, the other by making everything, as a certain disposition, like light'. Accattino 2001, 12 (cf. 58) notes that this connection of the 'disposition' referred to by Aristotle with the divine intellect is in conflict with [A] 107,29-34 and [B2] 111,29-34 above, and also with the treatment of *nous en hexei* in Alexander's own *DA.* It is however perhaps the more natural reading of Aristotle's actual words. Donini 1995, 126-9, cited by Accattino, suggests that Alexander reacted against his teacher's interpretation of Aristotle.

[107] See Notes on the Text. 113,15-16 below implies that [C1] himself connected sublunary coming-to-be with the heavens (see 43 n.113 below); whether the detailed alternatives are due to [C1] or to Alexander himself is less clear (Moraux 1984, 419-20; Accattino 2001, 59). Alex., *Quaest.* 2.3 48,19-22 may refer back to this passage; Moraux 1967, 163 n.2 (cf. Sharples 1992, 95 n.311).

[108] I.e., 'with the assistance of'.

with intellect.[109]

[C2]   113,12

It seemed to me to be an objection to this [theory] both that intellect, [though] it is divine, is in even the basest things, as the Stoics thought,[110] and in general that there should be intellect and some sort of primary[111] providence in things here (and yet[112] providence over things here comes   15 about [according to this theory] in accordance with their relation to the divine [heavenly bodies]);[113] also that thinking would not depend on us and would not be our task, but as soon as we come to be there would naturally be present in us both the composition of the potential and instrumental

---

[109]   Both [2a] and [2b] treat both intellect present in the sublunary world, and the movement of the heavens, as causes; the difference is that in [2a] the heavens act directly, whereas in [2b] – as elsewhere in the writings attributed to Alexander; cf. *Fat.* 6 169,23, *Mant.* §23 172,17, *Quaest.* 2.3 47,30, 49,29, *In Meteor.* 7,9, *Prov.* 77,12 Ruland – their influence is identified with nature, here regarded as an intermediary cause. But, as Accattino 2001, 60 notes, [2b] would still be unacceptable to Alexander himself, because it denies the transcendence of divine intellect.

[110]   113,12-14 = *SVF* 2.1038.

[111]   Alexander himself rejects the notion that sublunary beings are a primary concern of the gods, and seeks to establish a way in which concern for the sublunary can be neither primary nor accidental. See Sharples 1987, 1216-18; Sharples 2000, 365-8.

[112]   The reference to 'some sort of primary providence' may suggest that the term 'providence' was not used by the proponent of [C1] himself, and that it is Alexander himself who is interpreting [C1]'s view in these terms, and finding in it a theory of providence like that of the Stoics which he himself considers objectionable.

[113]   This is Alexander's own view too, at least as far as sublunary species are concerned; but the accusative and infinitive shows that it is here reported as a view of the proponent of [C1]. The point is presumably that the direct involvement of the divine in the sublunary makes reference to the heavens unnecessary (I am grateful to Inna Kupreeva for this suggestion).

[intellect] and the activity [brought about] through the [intellect] that is from without.[114]

20 Rather, what comes to be in something through being thought does not change place. For neither do the forms of things perceived by the senses come to be in the sense-organs as their *places* when we sense them.[115] The intellect from without is said to be 'separate' and is separated from us not as going away somewhere and changing its place; rather, it is separate because it exists in itself and without matter, and it is separated from us by not being thought [by us], not by going away. For that is how it came to be in us, too.

113,25 **[3]. That the soul is incorporeal.**

This is the first of the texts in the *Mantissa* to take the most characteristic form in the collection, that of a "battery" of arguments for a specific thesis. It is directed against the Stoics (Moraux 1942, 28; Mansfeld 1990, 3136), They are similarly not named where their views are the primary target in *Fat.* and in *Mant.* §1.[116] Many of the arguments are in the form of *modus tollendo tollens* characteristically employed by the Stoics

---

[114] Though the theory advanced in [C1] need not, and surely should not, suggest that the combination and the activity are fully developed as soon as we are conceived (and 112,21-3 above need not imply this).

[115] The parallel does not seem exact; the sensible form is, arguably, localised in the *object* of sensation, while the intelligible form is not localised anywhere. (I am grateful to Anthony Price for discussion of this issue.) Rashed 1997, 189 and 193-4 argues that the present argument disregards the distinction between being in a place and moving with respect to place indicated by a more sophisticated discussion of the same issue in Alexander's *Physics* commentary (cod. Parisinus suppl. gr. 643, fol. 101r, on *Physics* 6.4 234b10-20, reflected – inaccurately, as Rashed shows – in Simplicius, *In Phys.* 964,9-23) and hence is likely to be an early work by Alexander himself.

[116] They are however named in Alex., *DA* 17,16, 26,16, *Mixt.* 3 216,5 (and Chrysippus by name at 1 213,7, 3 216,8, etc.) and *Prov.* 9,2 Ruland; see also *Mant.* §2 113,13, §17 150,28 and §20 160,5.

themselves (cf. below, 73 n.231).

See Wurm 1973, 181-93; Mansfeld 1990, 3075 n.62, 3109 n.220, 3135-6; Papadis 1991, 171-78; Annas 1992, 38-41; Accattino and Donini 1996, 133.

That the soul is incorporeal is sufficiently shown by the argument by which in Aristotle the soul is shown to be a form;[117] for no form is a body. Nevertheless, that it is incorporeal could also be shown from the following arguments.   113,26

(I) If the qualities of every body can be perceived by the senses, and the qualities of soul cannot be perceived by the senses – for virtues and vices are not like this – then soul is not a body.   30

(II) Moreover, if soul were a body, and every body in its own nature can be perceived by at least one sense (I am speaking of bodies that exist in actuality and have, as they themselves[118] say, been qualified), soul too would be perceptible by the senses (for they will not say that it is a body without quality, for [then] it will be matter). But it isn't; so it isn't body. For it is not non-perceptible in the [same] way as bodies that are imperceptible because of their smallness.   35

(III) Moreover, every body is perceptible either actually or potentially. But soul is not perceptible either actually or potentially. So [soul] is not a body.   114,1

(IV) Moreover, if soul perceives itself as being perceptible, it will also perceive another [soul]. But it does not perceive another [soul]; so it does not perceive itself as being perceptible.

(V) Moreover if the soul is a body, it is either ensouled or without soul. But it is bizarre for it to be without soul. If it is   5

---

[117] Aristotle, *DA* 2.1. – At this point the discussion might seem to be over, at least for those who accept Aristotelian principles. What follows pursues the topic on the basis of Aristotelian assumptions, providing ammunition against opposing views but not on the opponents' own terms; that is to say, the arguments are unnecessary for Aristotelians, and may not persuade non-Aristotelians. (I am grateful to Verity Harte for pressing for clarification on this issue.)

[118] The Stoics. See below, 46 n.121. 113,31-4 = *SVF* 2.794.

ensouled, then it will be a living creature and again that*
soul will be either ensouled or without soul, and so *ad
infinitum*.[119] If they resist the division of bodies that says
that some of them are ensouled and some without soul,
saying that it is not a sound division because some are
ensouled, some without soul, and some are souls, one must
say that, when things are divided according to a contradic-
10   tion, that which is denied is never [itself] divided in opposition to them. For example, if dividing we were to say that
some bodies are coloured and some colourless (for in the
same genus, which admits the [positive] state (*hexis*), the
privation is equivalent to the denial) we do not however also
say: 'and some are colours'. For being coloured or colourless is a differentia of bodies, but colours [are] not. And
15   again of bodies some have an odour, and some do not and
are odourless, but we do not go on to say 'and some are
odours'. And some things have quality, others do not have
quality and are without quality; but not also: and some are
qualities.[120] Or of bodies* some are composite, some are not
composite; but not also: and some are compositions. For
composition is not a body. Similarly of living creatures some
20   are mortal, others are not mortal and are immortal; but not
also: and some are deaths. For death is not a living creature.
Again of living creatures some are rational, others are not
rational and are irrational; but not also: and some are
reasons. For living creatures are not reasons. In the same
way we will say that of bodies some are ensouled, others are
not ensouled and are without soul; but not also that some
are souls. For souls are not bodies.
     (VI) Moreover, if the soul is a body, it is held together
25   either by something [else] or by itself.[121] But it is not

----

[119] Cf. the arguments combining dilemma and infinite regress
at §5 121,7-15, §6 123,4-13, 123,36-124,9 below.

[120] For the Stoics the items in the second 'category' are indeed
not qualities but 'qualifieds'. Cf. *SVF* 2.369, 371, 383; LS vol.1, 172.

[121] The Stoics in fact held that fire and air, which constitute
pneuma and hence soul, hold other bodies together (are *sunek-
tika* of them) and 'hold' themselves (are *hektika*): cf. SVF 2.444;
Rieth 1933, 67-9 and 141; Sharples 1983, 153-4; LS vol.1, 282, 287.

Mantissa §3   47

possible [for it to be held together] by itself because it is
single and similar throughout. For it is impossible for the
same thing in the same respect both to hold together and to
be held together. So it remains for part of it to hold
together, and part to be held together. But if so, the part
that holds together, and not that which is held together,
would be the soul;[122] and this [the soul], if it is also itself a
body, will either be held together by [something] else, or
by itself, and so ad infinitum. For if they should say that it   30
itself holds together and is held together as a whole, being a
single and [self-]identical thing, something will be able both
to hold and be held by itself, and to do and undergo the
same thing.[123] Not even the hand that rubs [the other hand],
and undergoes [this experience] in return, acts and undergoes [action] in respect of the same capacity. And in
general none of the things that [other] things possess also
itself possesses [itself]: not heat or sweetness or shape or
colour or health or attunement, and not virtue or knowledge   35
either. But the soul is a thing of this sort.[124]

(VII) Moreover, if the soul, being some rare body, itself
holds the body together and is in return held together by it,
this very dense body too will be soul, if what holds together
is soul. So the body will be the soul's soul, if it holds it
together. For that nothing holds itself together is clear from
the fact that not even the things that seem to be of this sort   115,1
are so. For neither does glue hold together itself and the
things glued by it. For it is one [part] of it that holds
together and another that is held together. As much [of it]
as is bodily is held together, but what holds together is the

---

[122] Cf. Aristotle, *DA* 1.5 415b10-15; Papadis 1991, 172 n.113.

[123] That 'holding oneself' (*ekhein*) or 'holding oneself together'
(*sunekhein*) constitute *acting* is debatable; but the Stoics
themselves defined body as what can act or be acted on (below,
53 n.152. I owe these points to Anthony Price and Jan Opsomer).
For the argument in the next sentence cf., with Steel 2003, 85-6,
Philoponus, *In DA* 12,26-30, and Ammonius and Numenius ap.
Nemesius, *Nat. hom.* 2 17-18 Morani; and for nothing acting upon
itself cf. Aristotle, *Physics* 8.5 257b6.

[124] I.e. one that other things possess.

quality and capacity, which is incorporeal.[125] At any rate,
5   when this sort of quality is destroyed, the material and
bodily [part] that remains can no longer hold together
either itself or the pieces of wood.

(VIII) Moreover, if the soul is a body, it is either fire or a
rare breath (*pneuma*, spirit) extending through all of the
ensouled body.[126] If so, it is clear that they will not say that it
is unwrought[127] or in just any condition. For not every fire or
every breath has this capacity. So it will be combined with
10 some peculiar form and rational principle and capacity and,
as they themselves say, 'tension'.[128] But if so, it will not be
the breath or the fire that is the soul, but the form and
capacity and tension in these, according to which they differ
from other things of similar type.[129]

(IX) Moreover, it is reasonable that, as matter* is body
without form, so form should be without matter and incorporeal. For it is from these that the compound [of matter
and form is made up].

(X) Moreover, if body is without soul, why is not also soul

---

[125]   This begs the question; but if the opponent claimed that the
capacity is corporeal the way would be open to a regress
argument: what holds this body together … and so on.

[126]   The first view being that of Heraclitus and Democritus, the
second that of the Stoics, as is noted by Mansfeld 1990, 3109
n.220, comparing 115,15-16 below and noting that our text is
employing for dialectical purposes theories about the soul listed in
Aëtius, 4.3. *diêkein* 'extending throughout' is the term regularly
used in Peripatetic criticisms of the Stoics for making 'body
extend through body'; see §14 below.

[127]   This translation of *argos* is suggested by Kupreeva ; cf. LSJ
s.v. II. To describe fire as inactive, the more common meaning,
would seem odd. In any case the point is that the fire or *pneuma* is
fire or *pneuma* in a particular state.

[128]   'tension' is the Stoic term; 'form' is Aristotelian. 115,6-10 =
SVF 2.785.

[129]   The conclusion is overstated; that soul is not just breath or
fire does not mean that it cannot be breath or fire in a certain
state, and there is no reason – at least until we come to the
argument of (XIX) below – to argue that soul is the state rather
than the breath or fire.

without body?

(XI) Moreover, if the soul is a body, it is either simple or a   15
compound. If it is simple, it is either earth[130] or fire or air or
water. But if soul is one of these in itself, everything of this
sort will be soul – for example, all fire or all air – and everything surrounding this will be an ensouled body. So if the
soul is the air, the wind-pipe and the lung and the inflated
wineskin will be a living creature, and so will every body
that has air in itself. If it is water, the jar full of this [will be a   20
living creature]. But these things are absurd.

[XIa] Moreover, if the soul is some one of the simple
bodies, every compound in which this body is present will
be ensouled and a living creature. But if the soul is a
compound from the simple bodies, our <body>* too will be
soul.

(XII) Moreover, every body [has] some proper movement
of its own, simple of what is simple, of what is composite
mixed, or according to the [part] which predominates;[131] but   25
no spatial movement is proper to soul as its own. So it will
not be one either of simple or of composite bodies. For
neither the [movements] in sensation or imagination or
being affected, which aɪe in respect of alteration, nor* the
spatial [movements], are movements of the soul in itself,
but [rather] of the compound [of soul and body].

(XIII) Moreover, if the soul is a body, how does the body
have a share in soul? And how is the soul present in it? For
either it will be [present in it] as a part, and in this way none   30
of the other parts of the body will be ensouled, or rather
nothing of it altogether [will be] ensouled, but soul and
body [will be] by themselves. Nor will soul be in body as in
a vessel. For in this way too the body [as a] whole will not
be ensouled. Nor by juxtaposition; for not in this way either
will the whole body be ensouled, or rather it will not be

---

[130] Mansfeld 1990, 3075 n.62 notes that earth is only included
here for rhetorical effectiveness, and that the same applies at
Plotinus 4.7[2], 2; no-one actually held that soul was made of
earth.

[131] So also Alexander, text 35 in Van Ess 1966, as summarised
by Endress 2002, 49.

35   ensouled at all. For in a heap [of mixed grain] the wheat is
not *in* the barley.[132] But if [it is present] as a whole throughout a whole, since all the body is ensouled, it needs to be
shown how body extends through body.[133] For indeed also,
since the qualities of the soul[134] and of the body are bodies
according to them, there will be many bodies in the same
[body][135] and different ones extending through each other
116,1   and in the same place;[136] and this is in need of explanation
and demonstration.

   (XIV) Moreover, when these [qualities which are bodies]
are added and depart, how will they not increase or diminish the body?[137]

   (XV) Moreover, when the qualities change, the former
ones,[138] being separated and being bodies, will be destroyed
into not-being; for they are not anywhere. And in this way
they will also [come to] be from not-being.

5   (XVI) Moreover, if the soul is in* the body in such a way
as to extend through it as a whole through a whole, and to
be blended with the body, it will no longer be the case that
one [aspect] of the living creature is soul, the other body,
but it will be some single other thing from both of them,
they being destroyed and altered together,[139] as in the case

---

[132]   Cf. Aristotle, *GC* 1.10 328a2. (I owe this reference to Verity
Harte). Alexander at *Mixt.* 13 228,33 speaks rather of a heap of
wheat and *beans*.

[133]   Cf. Alex., *DA* 20,6-8, and *In Top.* 173,14-16; Calcidius, *In
Tim.* 221. Todd 1976, 82 and 84-5; Papadis 1991, 171 n.107, 174
n.123.

[134]   von Arnim, *SVF* 2.797 conjectures *epei kai* in place of *kai
epei*: 'for indeed, since the qualities of the soul also and of the
body ...'.

[135]   I owe this interpretation to Inna Kupreeva.

[136]   115,32-4, 115,35-116.1 = *SVF* 2.797 (a). That qualities are,
contrary to the Stoic view, not bodies is argued in *Mant.* §6. For
'body passing through body' cf. below, §14.

[137]   See below, §6 123,13-18.

[138]   Literally 'those that are first'.

[139]   In blending the distinct powers of the ingredients are
replaced by the new properties of the blend; but Alex., *Mixt.* 14
230,17 (cf. Aristotle, *GC* 1.10 328b18) makes clear that this is not

of the diluted honey.[140] And no longer* will one [aspect] lead and the other serve, or one [aspect] be more honourable, the other less so, nor will body possess soul, or soul be in body. Nor in the first place will one [aspect] of the living   10 creature be soul, the other body, but the only thing that will be a living creature will be the blend of these, a single thing and altogether like itself, like the [mixture of] honey and wine: which is absurd. For one [aspect] of the living creature is soul, the other body, so that they are different from each other, and therefore they are separated.[141]

(XVII) Moreover, if both virtues and crafts are bodies, how, when these are added to someone, will they not either cramp the body or increase it?[142]   15

(XVIII) Moreover, if that, according to which something [possesses] being-what-it-is-said-to-be, is form, and it is according to soul that a living creature [possesses] its being a living creature, soul is form. And that soul is form is clear from the fact that one cannot in another way show that a living creature is composed of soul and body.

(XIX) Moreover, if body does not differ from body in any way *qua* body, but it does differ by possessing soul, soul is not body. For things that are the same in kind have a   20 common nature; and things that have a common nature are

---

complete destruction, as the ingredients are still present in the blend. However, this is in the context of his own theory; he argues that the *Stoics* are, against their will, committed to the view that total blending when one body extends through another does involve the joint destruction of both (*Mixt.* 7 221,20-3; cf. [Galen], *Qual. incorp.* 471,2-15 Kühn = 7,20-8,7 Westenberger = 14,139-151 Giusta. Todd 1976, 203).

[140] *melikraton*; honey mixed either with water or with milk. Cf. Alex., *DA* 11,7-20, 15,5-8; Papadis 1991, 173 n.121.

[141] The Greek could also mean 'it [the soul] is separated'. The separation in question is probably conceptual (as Inna Kupreeva suggest to me) rather than physical separation in death. Or is the argument *ad homines* against the Stoics, who did accept a (limited) survival of the individual soul after the death of the body (below, 126 n.425)?

[142] 116,13-15 = *SVF* 2.797(b). See below, §6 123,13-15, 124,16-20.

without difference in respect of what is common. So the things which are common in kind are without difference in respect of their kind, and their kind is body; so bodies do not differ qua bodies. So body does not differ from body, qua body;[143] so the things by which bodies differ from one another are not bodies. But incorporeals are not the same in kind; so they are not without difference [from each other] qua incorporeal. For 'incorporeal' is an ambiguous (*homônumos*) term. Some incorporeals are in [the category of] substance, some in quantity, some in the other categories.

But if someone should say that body does not differ from body in respect of common body, but [that each of them differs] in that it is a certain body,[144] one should say that each body has its being from its proper differentiae and proper species, which are different from one another, and that these are incorporeal: so that the things by which certain bodies differ from one another are not bodies.[145]

(XX) Furthermore, if soul is primarily breath or in breath or in the fire within us,[146] it will be possible for it to be in these even when separated.[147] For when separated from the living creature they continue to be breath and fire. But if so, both breath and fire will be living creatures. If this is impossible, it is impossible for soul to be in any of these, but rather in what is mixed from the four [simple bodies], what

---

[143] Cf. Alcinous, *Didascalicus* §11.1 (below, 79 n.255); Wurm 1973, 188.

[144] I.e., as is shown by what immediately follows, a body of a certain *type*; we are not here dealing with the question what individuates, for example, two bronze spheres. I am grateful to Anthony Price for pointing this out.

[145] Compare the argument of Aristotle, *DA* 2.1 412a17: body is not predicated of a subject but is a subject.

[146] Literally: 'if primary soul is ...'.

[147] How significant is the distinction, which is made but immediately dropped, between soul being breath (*pneuma*) and its being in breath? For, as Pamela Huby points out to me, if the latter is taken to mean that soul is breath (or fire) characterised in a certain way, the argument that even outside the body these will be soul is weakened.

is mixed and composed in the way that the body of living
creatures is mixed.[148]

What they say trying to show that the soul is a body is not   117,1
sound. {1} For[149] the fact that similarity is predicated of it
does not make it a body.[150] For similarity does not apply to
bodies. For similarity is present in lines and shapes and
surfaces, and still more in colours and qualities, and these
are not bodies.[151] In general body is substance, and it is   5
peculiar to substance that it is spoken of as the same in
respect of itself, not just similar. But [it is peculiar] to
quality, which is incorporeal, [that it is spoken of] as
'similar', so that even if anything else is spoken of as similar,
it is in that it has a share of quality that it will be said to be
similar. And soul, then, is similar to soul, [but] not qua soul.
For it is not qua soul, but in that it shares in some similar
quality and disposition [that it is similar].

{2} The argument is also false that says that what is incor-   10
poreal is not affected along with body, so that the soul is not
incorporeal.[152] For neither is it true that what is incorporeal
is not affected along with body – for when bodies are

---

[148] According to Alex. *DA* 24,15-26,30, soul is the power that
supervenes on the mixture of the bodily elements; Andronicus'
theory, rejected by Galen who wanted the soul to be the mixture,
simply(*Quod animi mores* 44,12ff,; above, 19 n.32). Here, if *einai en*
is translated 'be in', we have Alexander's view; if 'consist in', Galen's.

[149] Numbers in {braces} are marginal numbers added by MS
B, not present in V.

[150] As Cleanthes had argued (*SVF* 1.518): Papadis 1991, 176
nn.131-3; Annas 1992, 40. Parts of 117.1-30 form *SVF* 2.792.

[151] This might seem to show that similarity does not apply *only*
to bodies, rather than that it does not apply to them at all. But the
sequel shows that being the same and being similar are treated as
mutually exclusive; bodies are (not just similar but) the *same* in
that they are bodies (cf. 116,18ff. above). In Greek 'similar'
(*homoios*) is cognate with 'of a certain quality' (*poios*). I am grateful to Anthony Price for the explanation of this passage.

[152] For the Stoics nothing except bodies can either act or be
acted upon: *SVF* 1.90, 1.518, 2.363 = LS 45ABC. The parallel with
SVF 1.518, concerned with soul, is particularly close: Todd 1976,
84 n.243.

affected what is incorporeal in them is also affected along
with them, in most cases accidentally, but in some also
without qualification, as with the surface of the body which
is crushed; nor is the soul affected along with the body as
15   something which is other and separate, as friends are said
to be affected along with [each other], but what is affected
is the compound, for example the living creature, composed
of soul and body, which is cut in respect of its body, but
feels pain in respect of its soul. And what feels pain is the
living creature, as also what walks and sees and desires and
loves and hates;[153] but there are [ways of] being affected
that are peculiar to body, like being heated and being cut,
20   but do not also apply to soul, because body exists also
without soul,[154] but not soul without body; for [soul] is the
actuality and form of [body].

{3} The argument is not sound either which says that
nothing incorporeal is separated from body, but soul is
separated from body, and that [soul] is therefore not
incorporeal.[155] For separation is of two [kinds], one in
existence, when each of the two things having been
separated survives, the other [is] by the destruction of one
25   of the two things, as when white is 'separated' from the
body which has become black.[156] It is in the second sense
that what is incorporeal is separated from body, and in this
way that soul [is separated] from body. There are also
certain incorporeal things which can be separated from
body in terms of the account [given of them], as form from
matter and body from place.

[153] Cf. above, §1 104,35-105,2, and 21 n.35 there.
[154] Accattino and Donini 1996, 133 compare this passage with
Alex., *DA* 17,11ff.; the body is itself a form-matter compound, and
so can exist without soul, though not as an ensouled or organic
body.
[155] Attributed to Chrysippus in *SVF* 2.790 (Nemesius). Todd
1976, 84 n.243; Mansfeld 1990, 3135 and n.374; Annas 1992, 40-41.
[156] The use of the quality white as an analogy for soul should
not perhaps be pressed, but it does highlight the doubts that have
been felt about Alexander's commitment to the substantiality of
soul. See above, 20 n.34.

{4} Nor is it true to say that [only] those things are separated from one another which are in contact with each other. For all accidents can be separated, but they are not in   30 contact.

{5} Moreover, it is not true that we are ensouled in virtue of that by which[157] we breathe.* {6} For even if living creatures   118,1 cannot exist without their connate breath, that is not, for this reason, soul. For there are other things too without which it is not possible for a living creature to exist, which not even they say are soul. For creatures with blood [cannot exist] without blood, or in general without moisture.

[4]. That the capacities of the soul are many and not one.[158]   118,5

This discussion is directed against two doctrines of the Stoic Chrysippus: his denial that lack of self-control is to be explained by a conflict between the reasoning faculty and the emotional faculty (LS 65GHI), and his view that the functioning of plants, and the plant-like functions in animals, are to be attributed to nature but not to soul (LS 47NP = *SVF* 2.716, 458). In fact Chrysippus too recognised a plurality of parts of the soul, distinguishing (in humans) between the five senses, the powers of speech and reproduction (but not growth and nutrition, which are due to nature), and the 'ruling principle' (*hêgemonikon*), which is reason (LS 53H = *SVF* 2.836); the issue between Stoics and Peripatetics is not so much whether the soul has a single capacity, as where the distinctions are to be drawn. Alexander, following Aristotle (*DA* 2.2-3) insists on the plurality of soul-faculties or capacities similarly at *DA* 27,4ff. (where the doctrine is attributed to 'Democritus and certain others'), 28,3ff., 30,2-3 (Papadis 1991, 117 n.406). At *DA* 27,4ff. the principal argument used is that a single capacity would conflict with the principle that nature does nothing

---

[157] Or, (taking *hôi* as resulting from attraction of the accusative relative into the dative), just 'that which we breathe in'? (I owe this suggestion to Inna Kupreeva).

[158] A copy of the Aldine edition in the Ambrosiana library, Milan (S.Q1. VII.25) has at this point a note referring to Plato, *Republic* 4. (Information from Silvia Fazzo). One might think also of Aristotle, *EN* 1 1102b17, though the term *pathos* is not there used.

in vain (for which see below, 169 n.570), since not all creatures with souls can perform all the activities due to soul; this argument does not appear in the present text.

Inwood 1985, 35, with 266 n.80, argues that the present text misrepresents the Stoic position in various respects, in particular confusing the issues of parts of mind and of parts of soul, and introducing non-Stoic notions such as a distinction between contemplative and practical intellect (below, XIII) and the suggestion that the perceptive power as such is not concerned with action. (See also below, n.168). He therefore argues that our text either is directed against an unorthodox Stoic position, or else has introduced Aristotelian presuppositions of its own. The latter in general seems the more likely explanation. The value of the present text as evidence for Stoic views is defended against Inwood by Alesse 1994, 208 n.92.

118,6   That there is not [just] one capacity of the soul, so that the same [capacity, through] being in a certain state [on each occasion], at one time thinks, at another grows angry,[159] and another desires in turn, is to be shown [I][160] from the conflict of the emotions (*pathê*) against reason that there is in the self-controlled person and in the one lacking self-control. For it is not the same thing that is both victorious and defeated in these.[161]

[159] 'being in a certain state' (*pôs ekhon*) is Stoic terminology; but I am not aware of any evidence that Chrysippus actually used it to explain the passions. *SVF* 2.826 refers to imagination, assent, impulse and reason differing 'by individuality of quality' (*idiotêti poiotêtos*); 2.849 to reason and sensation each having a different 'constitution' (*kataskeuên*. I am grateful to Inna Kupreeva for these references and for discussion of this issue.) For Chrysippus moreover, as Richard Sorabji points out to me, anger and thinking are not distinct; emotions are judgements, but incorrect ones. 118,6-7 = *SVF* 2.823.

[160] The numbering of arguments in this section is seriously disrupted in the MSS: V, followed by A, preserves elements of three different sequences in different styles of lettering, two of the sequences lacking their early members, and B has two sequences and is inconsistent with VA at various points. I have therefore introduced my own numbering.

[161] A point that Chrysippus might find difficult to answer,

[II] Next, if one [part] of the soul is worse, the other   10
better, it is reasonable that each of them should be
different, and then that the capacities should be separated,
and not all present in each. For what is vegetative is soul
and a part and capacity of the soul, and its parts are the
nutritive and the [part] concerned with growth and the
reproductive [part]; it is not, as some[162] say, nature [as
opposed to soul]. We will show this first from the fact that
not all things which possess a nature and are in accordance
with nature possess these capacities. For the simple bodies   15
exist by nature and possess a nature, but they are not
nourished through themselves and do not grow or reproduce.[163]

[III] Moreover, if nutrition and growth and reproduction
[belong to] nature rather than soul, but perception belongs
to soul, either it must be said that we are not alive when we
are not perceiving,[164] or that there are two lives present in

---

except by claiming that in such cases bad reason defeats good.
Cf., with Bruns, Alex., *DA* 27,7-8.

[162] I.e. the Stoics. Cf. above, §1 105,7ff., and 21 n.38 there.
118,12-14 = *SVF* 2.711.

[163] Cf., with Bruns ad loc., §1 105,8 above. One might object
that fire in a sense feeds on its fuel and nourishes itself. But
Richard Sorabji suggests that the point is that it does not grow in
a way that involves development of itself into an organised whole,
comparing Aristotle, *DA* 2.4 416a15. There was also a widespread
ancient belief that rocks grow (cf. Plotinus 4.4 [28] 27.9-11 and 6.7
[38]11.24-30, and Origen in *SVF* 2.989: Sharples 1998b, 182 n.529
and further references there). Themistius, *In DA* 41,34, argues
that the growth of stones is not growth in the proper sense if it is
by addition rather than growth in every part.

[164] For Aristotle soul is the first actuality of a natural body
potentially possessing life, the capacity to perceive (for example)
rather than the actual activity of perceiving. But just because soul
is the potential for life, living itself can be identified with the activity. (And for such a distinction between soul and life cf.
Alexander, *Quaest.* 2.8 54,15ff., though the end of that paragraph
is problematic. I am grateful to Richard Sorabji for discussion of
this issue.) In reality we do not either lose perceptive soul, or

us, which is bizarre.

[IV] Moreover, if life [results from] the presence of soul,
20   and even things that have only the vegetative capacity
live,[165] the vegetative capacity will be soul. For nourishment
and growth through oneself is life.[166]

[V] Moreover, if making use of nature is to live, the
simple elements, moving in accordance with nature, will
live.

[VI] Moreover, if the things that make use of soul live,
but those that make use of nature do not, nature is not soul.

[VII] Moreover, if the things that make use of soul live,
and the things that have the vegetative and nutritive [part]
25   live, the vegetative and nutritive [part] is soul.[167]

[VIII] Moreover, if they say that the reproductive part
belongs to the soul, but [classify] this under the vegetative,
all the vegetative [part], too, will belong to soul.[168]

Showing this is useful most of all with a view to demonstrating that the differentiae of soul are not [a matter of][169]
the things concerning which soul is active; rather, the
capacities of the soul themselves differ from one another,

---

cease to be alive, when we are not actually perceiving, but the
reason we do not cease to be alive is that other soul-functions –
those of nutritive soul – continue.

[165] There does not seem to be any evidence that the Stoics
themselves spoke of plants as 'living'.

[166] Cf., with Rovida (below 238) Alex., *DA* 92,18.

[167] The argument is not logically cogent as it stands; we need to
understand 'only things that make use of soul live' and 'the things
that have only the vegetative and nutritive part live'.

[168] For Chrysippus reproduction was a faculty of the soul, but
growth and nutrition were not. Plants, which lack soul for the
Stoics, do indeed reproduce, but they do so in ways which are
apparently very different from those of animals, so this might well
not have been felt as an objection. (I am grateful to Richard
Sorabji for discussion of this issue.) Panaetius, however (fr. 86 van
Straaten) held that the reproductive faculty (*to spermatikon*) too
was a part of nature rather than of soul; cf. Inwood 1985, 35, and
above, 56. 118,25-26 = *SVF* 2.873.

[169] Following Bruns' interpretation ad loc.

and it is not possible [to do different things] with the same capacity,[170] for example to think with the [capacity] of sense-   30
perception or to perceive by sense with the [capacity] of thinking. [IX] For if the vegetative [part] too belongs to soul, and it is impossible to act in several different ways simultaneously with the same capacity, and the nutritive [part] is always active in living things, then either we will perform no other activity in respect of our soul, if the capacity of soul is single, or else, if we do perform other activities, for example perceiving and feeding at the same [time], then the capacity of soul is not single, and neither is the ruling   35
(*hêgemonikon*) principle active concerning each group of things [because] it is in a certain state.[171] For neither do the crafts differ because of the difference of their instruments, nor in virtue of what they are concerned with and their [products],[172] but the difference between them is first due to their own proper capacities.

[X] Moreover, we perceive with several senses simultaneously.[173]

[XI] Moreover, if action is activity with use of the organic   119,1
parts of the body, for example speaking, walking, performing some activity with one's hands, then observation (*theôrein*)[174] and thinking will not be acting, so that neither will the discerning [part] be productive of action

---

[170] This claim appears as a premiss in the following argument, at 118,31. It must therefore be included here as an indication of the basis on which the conclusion 'the capacities of the soul themselves differ from one another' will be argued for, not as part of the conclusion itself.

[171] 'ruling principle' and 'in a certain state' are again Stoic terms.

[172] Literally 'that of which they are'. At *In Top.* 2,16-19, compared by Rovida, Alexander says that crafts differ in respect of their matter and the way they employ it, while not differing *qua* crafts.

[173] Presumably the five senses, seeing, hearing and the rest.

[174] Not 'contemplation', for as 119,3 ff. shows we are here concerned with observation, as opposed to action, at every level down to that of perception.

(*praktikon*).[175]

[XII] Moreover, if the end (goal, *telos*) of the perceptive [part] is concerned with observation (for it is concerned with discernment, taking place indeed through the body[176] and for this reason accompanied by being affected),[177] but
5   the end of the impulsive [part] is concerned with action and is the actions, these [parts] too will differ in respect of their end, and also by the fact that they are not implied by each other and do not both become present simultaneously, and that the perceptive part leads, and that impulse does not always follow upon perception but impulse always, whenever it occurs, occurs after a perception. It is to the appetitive and impulsive [part] that desiring and becoming
10 angry and wishing [belong].[178]

Moreover, the rational [part] too discerns, and does so as the leading (*hêgemonikon*)[179] [part]. For the discerning [part] is led by the rational [part], which we also call the thinking [part]. The perceptive [part] follows and is subordinate; to this [belong] imagining and assenting and remembering.[180] And that the common sense, too,[181] is

[175] Deliberation is one of the activities of the rational capacity, which is in turn a subdivision of the discerning faculty (§1 106,4); so to interpret *praktikon* as denying that the discerning part is 'concerned with action' would be overstated.

[176] I am grateful to Inna Kupreeva and to Richard Sorabji for clarifying this passage for me.

[177] Or 'accompanied by emotion (*pathos*)'; but for sensation involving being affected, see above at 35 n.78. Even if Aristotle in *DA* 2.7 417b14 puts the matter more cautiously, he endorses the use of this term if properly understood: 418a5.

[178] Similarly above at §1 105,34, and at Alex., *DA* 74,1-2 (noted by Rovida).

[179] Translated above as 'ruling'; but in the present context 'leading' seems more appropriate.

[180] So too above at §1 105,27-28: cf. Alex., *DA* 76,9-12, 78,13-21 (noted by Rovida).

[181] For the 'common sense' cf. Aristotle, *DA* 3.1 425a14-30. It is there introduced as perceiving sensibles which are not the proper objects of specific senses, such as movement, shape, size and number: but cf. the next note.

different from the individual ones is clear from the fact that [our] seeing can be perceived, but is not visible.[182] And similarly with the other [senses] too.   15

[XIII] Moreover, the contemplative intellect is not concerned with things that are to be done,* nor with things to be chosen or avoided.

[XIV] Moreover, what depends on us is a matter of acting and of choice, not of exercising impulse or assenting or imagining or perceiving,[183] and not of the vegetative [part] either.

[XV] Moreover, it is in respect of the appetitive [part] that we are moved by soul, not in respect of any other capacity: 20 so this is different from those.

[5]. That the soul is not in a subject.   119,21

A number of statements by Simplicius indicate that Alexander found difficulty in statements by Aristotle implying that form (and the soul is the paradigm case of sublunary form) is in a subject.

Simplicius, *In Phys.* 270,26-31 cites Alexander as noting the discrepancy between the claim in Aristotle, *Cat.* 5 3a7 that no substance is in a subject (also cited at the start of the present section) and the statement at *Phys.* 2.1 192b34 (cf. 120,33 below) that nature is 'in a subject' (both our present text and Alexander as cited by Simplicius taking it for granted that nature is form). And at *In Cael.* 279,5-14[184] Simplicius similarly reports Alexander as observing a discrepancy between *Categories* 5 3a7 and the statement at Aristotle, *Cael.* 1.9 278b1-3 that material things have their *ousia* in some underlying (*hupokeimenê*) matter. Our

---

[182] Aristotle, *DA* 3.2 425b12-25 suggests rather that it is by sight that we perceive that we see; so too Alex., *Quaest.* 3.7. However, that it is by the common sense that we perceive that we see is also, as Rovida notes, the view of Alex., *DA* 65,2-10. Accattino and Donini 1996, 234 suggest that Alexander bases this position on Arist. *De somno* 2 455a15ff., and that he has misunderstood *prôtês* in Aristotle, *DA* 3.2 425b17 as referring to the *prôton aisthêtêrion* as the common sense.

[183] Cf. Alex., *Fat.* 14 183,21ff.

[184] Cf. Sharples 1987, 1201 n.63; Accattino and Donini 1996, 128.

present text at 121,2-6 also notes a similar discrepancy between
the *Categories* passage and Aristotle, *DA* 2.1 412a18.

Further, Simplicius, *In Phys.* 552,18-24, cites Alexander as
noting a discrepancy between the claim at *Categories* 2 1a24-5
that what is 'in a subject'[185] is not itself a part of that subject, and
Aristotle's apparent conflation at *Physics* 4.3 210a20-1 of the way
in which form is in matter and that in which health is in a
subject.[186] For form, Alexander insists, *is* a part of the form-matter
composite; and this implies that it cannot be in matter as in a
subject.[187] The example of health is suggestive; for though Alexander as cited by Simplicius does not develop the point, what
Aristotle actually says is that health is 'in' hot and cold, suggesting
that it is in them in the sense that it depends on them and results
from them – precisely the point at issue where Alexander's own
view of the relation between soul and body is concerned (above,
n.34).

The issue is also discussed at Alex., *DA* 14,24-15,5 (briefly: see
below, 66 nn.201, 70 n.216), and in *Quaestiones* 1.8, 1.17 and 1.26.
Of the latter 1.8 and 1.26 appear to develop the argument of the
present section further (below, 64-6 nn.196, 199). It is is funda-
mental for our understanding of Aristotelianism, because it
highlights in the clearest possible way the danger of misunderstanding if we approach Aristotle from the perspective of a view
that regards form as simply a qualification of an independently
existing matter – as we may be tempted to do, from within ancient
philosophy itself, both by Plato's analysis of sensible objects as
transient semblances of the Forms in a Receptacle which was
frequently, even if not by Plato himself, understood as matter, and
by the Stoic analysis of individuals as qualifications of substance
(below, 72 n.227), and more insidiously by the familiarity of more
recent 'bundle-of-qualities' theories. For Aristotle a soul or a form
is not as it were something added to a reality that exists

---

[185] 'Subject' throughout this discussion is a translation of
hupokeimenon, 'that which underlies'.

[186] I am grateful to Silvia Fazzo for drawing my attention to this
passage of Simplicius. See below, 65 n.197.

[187] Simplicius then cites Aristotle's immediate pupil Eudemus
as already noting that affections (*pathê*) and dispositions (*hexeis*)
are in matter 'in a different way', and that the question how shape
(*morphê*) is in matter requires consideration: Simplicius, *In Phys.*
552,24-6 = Eudemus fr.77 Wehrli. Cf. Wehrli 1969, 105; Algra
1995, 249; Sharples 2002a, 122.

independently of it. Socrates is not the result of a soul being present in a human body in the way that one thing can be present in another, for there are not in that sense two things there at all; there would not be a human body if soul were not present.[188] Even though we can *analyse* that human being by saying what material ingredients the form requires, the form is the starting-point, not an incidental addition. (Thus the differentia, too, cannot be in a subject: Aristotle, *Cat.* 5 3a22-28).[189]

The discrepancy between the *Categories* and other works of Aristotle which develop the form-matter analysis has been central to modern discussions of Aristotle's development, not least because the identification of substance with form in the *Metaphysics* has seemed to some incompatible with the *Categories* doctrine that primary substance is the individual.[190] The comment of Madigan 1994, 90, that Alexander reads the *Metaphysics* in the light of the *Categories* rather than vice versa, is very much to the point.

The latter part of the present section, from 121,7 onwards, is concerned with arguing first that soul is not body, and then that soul is substance: see below, 68-9 n.211, and §3 above. On the present section see, in addition to literature cited below for specific points, Wurm 1973, 184-6; Sharples 1994b; Papadis 1991,

[188] Cf. Anscombe and Geach 1961, 33-4. One might argue that there would be something, or rather some things, there; the ingredients that go to make up a human body have natures of their own. But it is less clear that even this is so if a dead hand is only homonymously a hand (Aristotle, *GA* 1.19 726b22-4), and perhaps dead flesh only homonymously flesh. (Cf. however below, 65 n.198). On the question whether this leads to circularity in Aristotle's definition of soul as the form of a body potentially possessing life cf. Alex., *Quaest.* 2.8 and 2.26, with Sharples 1994a, 124 n.155, and 1994b, 164 and n.8; and for the problems raised by this same issue for the distinction between body and soul in Aristotle himself compare Ackrill 1972-3, Williams 1986, Cohen 1992, Whiting 1992, Shields 1993, Lewis 1994, Wehrle 1994 especially 310-16, Mirus 2001.

[189] Woods 1991, 84, argues that the relation of the form to the individual is not different from the attribution of a property, but "a particular view of what the property of being a human being is". It seems to me that this understates an important distinction. See also de Haas 1997, 201-203.

[190] As to why this is not an insoluble problem for Alexander, cf. Tweedale 1984; Sharples 1987, 1200-2, 1992, 6, and (forthcoming, 4).

156-160; Ellis 1994, 76-80; Fazzo 2002a, 101-105. I am indebted to
John Ellis for discussion of this section, and have consulted a draft
translation of his in making my own; I am also indebted to Silvia
Fazzo for the opportunity to see her discussion in advance of its
publication. I have also, as elsewhere, benefited from discussion
with Inna Kupreeva, and from comparing my own translation with
hers.

119,22   Aristotle in the *Categories* says that no substance is in a*
subject.[191] So, if the soul is substance, it will not be in a
subject. But it can be said against this that in speaking
25   about the substances which he was mentioning in the
Categories (these being the individual and the species and
the genus) he was no longer[192] speaking about matter and
the substance which corresponds to form;[193] for he said
there that there was nothing opposite to substance,[194]
although he says that the natural form, which is a
substance, has as its opposite the privation,[195] while none of
those substances [under discussion in the *Categories*] has
30   any opposite. Well then, let us consider in its own right
whether it is possible for the soul to be in the body as in a
subject, or generally the form in the matter.
    May it not be that there is a way of being in something
different from being in a subject, [namely] the [way] in
which form is in matter?[196] For it is not possible for form to

[191] Aristotle, *Cat.* 5 3a7. See below, 68 n.210.
[192] 'No longer' must here have a logical, rather than a temporal
sense; Alexander is not claiming that the theory of the *Categories*
superseded that of the *Physics* and *Metaphysics*.
[193] Cf. Alexander cited by Simplicius, *In Cael.* 279,12-14 (above,
61 n.184) as arguing that Aristotle in the *Categories* is referring to
substance in the sense of the compound of matter and form; also
Boethus ap. Simplicius, *In Cat.* 78,5-20, and Porphyry, *In Cat.*
88,13-22, with de Haas 2001, 505 and n.37, 519-20 and n.90.
[194] Aristotle, *Cat.* 5 3b24.
[195] Aristotle, *Phys.* 1.7 191a14.
[196] Alex., *Quaest.* 1.26, 42.25-43,17, having rejected two ways of
form being in matter, (i) as an accident in a subject and (ii) as a
per se attribute of matter, suggests a third, (iii) that form belongs
per se to matter because reference to matter is required in the

be in matter as in a subject, if what is in a subject is 'what is in something not as a part and cannot be apart from that in which it is'.[197] For that, which is a subject to what is in a   35 subject, must be a 'this-something'; and with reference to   120,1 being in actuality, nothing without a form is a this-something, and that* in which [a thing] is said to be.[198]

At any rate, it is for this reason that matter, too, cannot have real existence (*hupostasis*)[199] just by itself, because the

---

account of enmattered form (cf. Aristotle, *An. Post.* 1.4 33a34ff.). It may be questioned whether the present text would be expressed in the way it is if the author were already familiar with *Quaest.* 1.26.

[197] Aristotle, *Cat.* 1a24-5. As is shown by Simplicius' quotation of Alexander at *In Phys.* 552,21-4, it is the first part of the definition that is relevant: form is regarded as a *part* of the form-matter compound that cannot exist without the whole.

[198] I.e., since a thing has to have form to be a subject (for qualities, etc.) at all, nothing can be a subject for form itself. I am indebted here to John Ellis for this general understanding of this passage, though his view on the reading in 120,1 is different (see below, Notes on the Text), and to the editors of the Commentators Sourcebook for the exact wording adopted here. The argument, it may be noted, disregards the point, emphasised by Alexander in his *DA* (notably at 8,8-13) that things characterised by less complex forms can be the matter for more complex ones, in nature as much as in the case of products of craft. Perhaps our text and the others related to it represent a reaction against a view that seemed to make complex forms too reductively the products of simpler ones. With the present passage one may indeed compare Alex., *DA* 4,22-5, where Alexander comments that, while prime matter cannot exist independently, proximate matter can, and immediately follows this by the statement that 'at any rate' (*goun*) the matter of products of craft can.

[199] Ellis 1994, 76 n.17 shows that the implied contrast is with potential existence. For the argument cf. *Quaest.* 1.8 17,8-12, 1.17 30,3ff. and 1.26 42,14ff. In *Quaest.* 1.8 it is followed by the objection that it could equally well be argued that body cannot exist without the accidents of shape and colour (17,12-17) and by a reply to this (17,17ff.): Ellis well suggests that the *Quaestio* is referring to the present discussion and developing it further (cf.

form is not yet in it. For it is with the form that each of the things that are is a 'this-something'; for it is according to the form that everything is what it is said to be. Accordingly the
5   natural form will not be in matter as in a subject. For the form which comes to be by craft is in a subject, in virtue of the subject's being a 'this-something' and having a form; it is in this*[200] that the craftsman produces and applies the form relating to the craft. But it is not possible also to say that the natural form is in the matter in this way; for the matter is not in itself a 'this-something' or a subject in actuality.
10   If then the natural form is not in a subject, and the soul is a natural form, neither will the soul be in a subject. For the soul does not come to be in body without qualification, since it would [then] come to be in every body, and so also in the simple [bodies], fire, air, water, earth; and this is impossible. Rather, what is its subject and is its matter is the organic body, which cannot be organic before it possesses a
15   soul, nor, when it has lost the soul, is it organic any more. For no body without soul is organic. So it is, for this reason, not possible to apprehend [sc. without reference to soul itself] what the soul is in. For it is [by] being along with [the soul] that [the body that soul is in] is organic,[201] as lead [is lead by being] along with weight.[202]

But fire [is like soul in that it] is not in coal as in a subject. For what is said to be fire in a primary and proper way is not in coal or in wood or in any other such matter (for its
20   existence is in itself, as is that of air and earth and water), but the fire which serves us, which needs the matter in our region,[203] is not itself either in logs or coal as subjects;

Ellis 1994, 81 and n.27: Sharples 1990, 110 and n.178).

[200] The bronze of which the statue is made was bronze before the statue was cast and will be after it has been melted down again. Cf. above, §1 103,29.

[201] Cf. Alex., *DA* 15,2-5; *Mant.* §1 104,14-17; *Quaest.* 1.8 17,9-10. Papadis 1991, 97 n.314, 158 nn.42-3.

[202] For the analogy between soul and weight cf. above, §1 106,5-8, and 23 n.45.

[203] The contrast is between the *hupekkauma* or 'fire-sphere'

rather, each of these is matter for the fire. For when it has come to be fire, it is no longer coal or wood, but then it is fire in actuality and coal in potentiality.[204] If it were coal [in actuality] at that time, the fire would be in it [as] in a   25
subject; but that it is not coal is clear from its not possessing the properties of coal. What possesses something [as] in a subject possesses it while preserving its own proper substance. For as air, produced by change from water, is potentially water but not actually – and this is why air is not in water as in a subject – just so neither does the coal which has become fire have the fire in itself as in a subject,   30
because it does not remain coal any longer. [The fire] will be [as] in a subject neither in that which has its being in the fire,*[205] nor in what was previously coal but, now that fire has come to be in it, no longer is but has been destroyed.[206]

---

immediately below the heavens, and fire as experienced by us here on earth. (For "serving", *diakonikos* fire cf. Gannagé 2002, 136.) See below, 81 and n.262, §16 148,21; Aristotle, *Meteor.* 1.3 340b23, 1.4 341b13, Theophrastus, *De igne 3-4* (where however the contrast is between fire that requires fuel and *heat* in the heavens); Nicolaus of Damascus fr. 40, pp.90 and 168-9 Drossaart-Lulofs 1965; Ocellus Lucanus 2.9, 17,16ff. Harder, cited by Drossaart-Lulofs; Alex., *In Meteor.* 14,25ff, *Quaest.* 2.17; Alex. ap. Simplic. *In Cael.* 439,14. Sharples 1990, 98-9, and 1994a, 114 n.59.

[204] When burning coal is extinguished the part that has burned does not however turn back to coal; it is the part that has not yet become fire that remains coal – the part that has become fire reverts not to coal but to ash. (Ancient 'coal' was often charcoal, sometimes mineral coal; this does not seem to affect the issue.) Comparison with Alex., *Quaest.* 2.20 would seem to suggest that this is because coal is not one of the simple bodies but already a compound formed from them.

[205] I.e. the coal which, having now become matter for fire, has its nature defined by the form of fire, rather than being coal in actuality any more.

[206] Similarly at more length at Alex., *Quaest.* 1.26 42,18-25, which makes clear that the problem with the first option here (the second there) is that the fire would then be an accident of itself. Cf. also *Quaest.* 1.17 30,9-12.

One should note that Aristotle says in the second book of
121,1   the *Lecture-Course on Physics* (2.1 192b34) that nature,
being a form, is in a subject. 'For [what has a nature][207] is
always a subject and nature is in a subject.' He also says at
the beginning of the second book of the *De Anima* (2.1
412a18) 'for body is not one of those things [that are] of a
subject,' on the one hand calling 'of a subject' (*kath' hupoke-
imenou*) what is in a subject (*en hupokeimenôi*),[208] but on
5   the other* saying that body is not like this, but soul is.[209] Or
rather: is it possible that he is now calling 'of a subject' not
what is in a subject, but rather what needs some subject for
its being?[210] And this is how the form is in the matter.

That this is how form is [in matter], one might show in
the following way.[211] If form is body, either it will be [body]

---

[207] These words are supplied from the context in the *Physics*,
with Fazzo 2002a, 103 n.223; the natural sense of the quotation as
our text gives it, without the context, would be 'for nature is
always a subject and in a subject'.
[208] Fazzo 2002a, 104 and n.225 well suggests that this clause reflects
an earlier stage of discussion utilising this passage of Aristotle to
argue that soul *is* in the body, the thesis which Alexander then rejects.
[209] Actually this is implied by Aristotle's argument, rather than
actually stated. Cf. Ross 1961, 213 ad loc.: "the missing but easily
supplied part of the proof is 'whereas soul (or besouledness) is, as
we have seen, not a substance but an attribute'." Wurm 1973, 184
and n.27.
[210] Alexander has answered the problem of the *DA* passage to
his own satisfaction, but has said nothing about the one from the
Physics that he quoted first. Simplicius, *In Phys.* 268,31-269,4,
interprets that text as claiming that (i) nature is inseparable from
body, and argues that (ii) this distinguishes nature from *Platonic*
soul; at 270,31-4 he repeats (i) as a solution to the problem of
inconsistency with the *Categories* raised by Alexander (above, 64
n.191). Here indeed Simplicius apparently presents (i) as his own
contribution rather than as derived from Alexander's commentary;
but at *In Cael.* 279,7-9 he attributes it, with approval, to Alexander
himself. Cf. Fazzo 2002a, 105 and n.227.
[211] It is natural to take *houtôs* 'this is how' in 121,7 as picking
up the same word at the end of the previous paragraph. But what
follows is an argument for form not being body, not for form

without form, or this body will [itself] possess form. Well, if
it is without form, form will be [just] matter [,which is
absurd]. If on the other hand form possesses form, then   10
either that [form] itself too will be body, and the same
argument will apply again to it, or, if it is incorporeal, the
form taken first will be incorporeal as well. Moreover, if that
form, which was a body, possesses a form, that form, the
one according to which [this] bodily form is soul, will
[itself] be either incorporeal or a body. If it is incorporeal,
but the body [i.e. the supposed bodily soul] possesses its
being soul in accordance with [its] form, the soul will be
incorporeal. If on the other hand this too is a body, the   15
argument will go on to infinity.

   But why is the soul, which is an actuality, a
substance?[212] Or rather: [the actualities] of all natural
things, which are substances in the proper sense, are
substances*. For products of craft too are substances, not
qua products of craft, but in that natural bodies underlie
them; the forms and actualities of things that exist by nature
are substances, in that each of them is a 'this-something',
for example earth or fire.[213] And a living creature too is a   20
natural substance and its form and actuality, *qua* living
creature, is its soul. So this too is a substance. For
substances [are] from substances; a substance could not

---

requiring matter. Alternatively, one might suppose – a suggestion
that I owe to Richard Sorabji – that the discussion of soul not
being in body as in a substrate is complete at 121,6, that 121,7
makes a fresh start considering the nature of soul more generally,
and that *houtôs* in 121,7 refers forward rather than back – comparing perhaps the way in which *Quaest.* 1.25 has been put together
from two originally separate discussions, as Bruns observed (cf.
Sharples 1992, 82 n.255). I am grateful to Richard Sorabji and
David Robertson for discussion of this issue.
   [212] For this claim cf. Alex., *DA* 6,2-3. Bessarion conjectured
'But why is the soul an actuality? Is it because it is a substance?' (I
am grateful to Charalambos Dendrinos for clarifying Bessarion's
marginal note in B for me.)
   [213] See above, 15 n.13.

come to be from non-substances.[214] So, since natural substances are [compounded] from matter and form, matter and form are substances.[215]

Moreover, natural substance is [composed] of form and matter which are natural; and those things of which natural substance is composed are substances. So the form and the
25   matter are natural substances.

Moreover, if it is a property of substance to be able to admit of opposites in turn,[216] and the soul is able to admit of opposites in turn (for [it is able to admit of] wickedness and virtue), it will be substance.

How then is it impossible for substance to come to be from non-substances, while body comes to be from things that are incorporeal?[217] For matter is not body, and neither is form, but body [comes] from these. Or rather: if body did come to be,[218] it would need to come to be from what is not
30   body, for everything that comes to be comes to be from what is opposite to it.[219] Similarly too, if there were coming to be of substance without qualification, it would come to be from what is not substance.[220] But since none of these things come to be without qualification, and [since] matter does not ever, itself by itself, and form, existing separately,

---

[214] Cf. Alex., *DA* 6,3.

[215] Cf. Alex., *DA* 6,1-4, and, with Wurm 1973, 185 n.29, Aristotle, *DA* 2.1 412a6-9, *Metaph.* 7.10 1035a2.

[216] Aristotle, *Cat.* 5 4a10ff.; Papadis 1991, 157 and n.38. Cf. Alex., *DA* 14,25-15,1.

[217] Cf. Alex., *DA* 6,6-20: Papadis 1991, 161 n.63; Accattino and Donini 1996, 111. Silvia Berryman compares Philoponus, *In GC* 31,7-24.

[218] Whereas in fact body does not come to be as such; rather, one body changes into another: below, 122,1-2. Cf. Aristotle, *Cael.* 3.2 301b33, Alex., *DA* 6,15-17. Accattino and Donini, loc. cit.; Papadis 1991, 161 n.64. (So too Philoponus, *In GC* 31,10ff.; cf. the previous note.)

[219] Cf., with Wurm 1973, 185 n.30, Aristotle, *Phys.* 3.5 205a6.

[220] One might object here that a horse, for example, is a substance and does come to be. But it does not come to be from nothing, rather from matter; and for matter as substance cf. Alex., *DA* 6,2-4 (above, 20 n.34).

come together and make body, but rather these things are separated in thought while [in fact] matter is always [characterised] by[221] some form, and there is no [time] when it is without form, and the coming-to-be of things that come-to-be is not from matter and form without quali- fication, but rather comes to be from this body to that in accordance with the change of form – for this reason some body comes to be from some body, not body from body without qualification.[222] Body would come to be without qualification, if it were ever the case that form and matter, separated in actuality, came together; and in this way [body would come to be] from what are not bodies.[223]

35

122,1

How then do we say that the parts of substance are substance, and for this reason we say that form and matter are substance, but not also that the parts of body are bodies, if these too are parts of body, [namely] matter and form? Or rather: form and matter are not parts [of a thing] *qua* body. For it is the things that complete body that are parts of body, but these do not complete the body.[224] But they are

5

---

[221] Literally: 'in some form'.

[222] Or '... in accordance with the change of form, so that some body comes to be from some body – [for this reason] body [does not come to be] from body without qualification' (so Bruns ad loc.)

[223] The problem that body can come from non-body, while substance cannot come from non-substance, has been solved by denying that body, just as such, ever comes to be, while substances do. But, if for 'come from' we substitute 'be composed of', the problem returns; the answer at 122,4ff. is that form and matter are not parts of *body* at all (cf. the next note). DA 6,12-17, compared by Rescigno 1999, 214-215 and n.25, has the claim that body does not come into being absolutely, but not (explicitly) the problem of the non-parallelism with substance, or the solution at 122,4ff.

[224] For the problem and its solution cf. Alex., *DA* 18,8-27, cited here by Rovida. We are told more here about why form and matter are parts of a substance than about why they are not parts of a body; the fuller version in Alex., *DA* makes it clear that the contrast is with parts of body in the sense of a part of a greater extension, as for example all four quarters into which a particular body may be divided are needed if it is to be complete. (Contrast

parts [of the thing] as a substance. For this reason, they [have]
10   the same nature as that of which they are parts, but they
are not the same as that of which they are not parts. That
they are parts [of the thing] as a substance is clear from the
fact that the compound substance is said [to be] substance
both in that it is a subject and in that the form[225] is a 'this-
something'. For substance is a subject; and it is not possible
for anything to be a subject if it is not a 'this-something'.
The substance is assisted in being a subject by the form.
15   Accordingly the things from which substance derives its
being a subject in so far as it is substance, are [themselves]
substance.[226]

122,16   **[6]. That qualities are not bodies.**

That qualities are bodies is a view widely attributed to the Stoics
(*SVF* 2.380, 383, 388, 389, 394 [= Alex., *DA* 18,7-10] 410, 467). It
may be interpreted as a deliberately paradoxical way of saying
that qualities do not exist except in the form of qualified bodies
(and the second Stoic 'category' consisted of 'qualifieds', *poia*,
rather than of qualities);[227] it may also be seen as an allusion to the
doctrine that it is the (bodily) *pneuma* present in each thing

---

the quite different use of 'completing' at Simplicius, *In Cat.*
48,1-34; Ellis 1994, 83ff.) The *DA* account uses not *sumplêrôtikos*,
the term translated here by 'completing', but *suntelein*, 18,16. It
also adds the point that the parts of body in this sense are parts
only of a body which is of a certain type, and that it is so because
of the form, the implication being that parts in this sense are
posterior to the form. Cf., in general, Aristotle, *Metaph.* 7.10-11;
Wurm 1973, 186.
   [225] Or (deleting *to eidos* in 122,12, which Bruns in his apparatus suggests is an interpolation, and which is also marked with
dots by Rovida) 'and in that it is a 'this-something'.
   [226] Cf. Porphyry, *In Cat.* 88,21, De Haas 2001, 520 n.90: above,
64 n.193.
   [227] Above, 45 n.118. [Galen], *Qual.*, vol.19 480,15-481,3 K(ühn)
= 16,6-12 W(estenberger 1906) = 21,308-13 G(iusta), indeed
allows that the doctrine might be acceptable if interpreted in this
way.

which gives it the qualities it has.[228] Our text however does not concern itself with such subtleties, but proceeds to assemble a battery of arguments against the doctrine interpreted in a straight-forward sense.[229]

The Stoic doctrine is also attacked by pseudo-Galen, *On incorporeal qualities* (henceforth: *Qual.*), and by Alcinous, *Didascalicus* ch.11.[230] Not surprisingly, there are points of similarity in the arguments of these three texts, but they are not close enough to suggest any dependence. As Westenberger notes (1906, xxiii-xxiv) the arguments are different, and the usage of the author of the pseudo-Galen work differs from that of Alexander in respect of hiatus and in various aspects of word-usage (and in the latter respect from that of Galen himself: ibid. xx-xxii).

Cf. Wurm 1973, 186-187.

(I) If quality is a natural body, and every natural body is a 122,17 substance, quality is substance. – Or rather: quality is different from the nature that underlies it (for water and the coldness that applies to it are not the same [thing]; for [in that case] everything that was cold would be water and all water would be cold), and it is the nature that underlies the 20 quality that is substance. Quality is not substance, for it [belongs to] a different nature. This should be confirmed by induction; for [in the case of] every substance the quality that applies to it is different [from it]. But the first; therefore the second.[231] So quality is different from substance; what is

---

[228] *SVF* 2.389, 449.

[229] Todd 1976, 85-86 rightly speaks of 'the mechanical application' of the view that qualities are bodies 'for polemical purposes', and suggests that this formulation 'may well have emerged ... solely within an anti-Stoic tradition'.

[230] Cf. Dillon 1993, 111-14, and Göransson 1995, 53. Orth 1947 attributed the [Galen] text to Albinus; but against this cf. Giusta 1986, 170-1, and Göransson, loc. cit.

[231] A formula in the terminology of Stoic logic, indicating an argument in *modus ponens*: '(if the first, then the second); but the first; so the second'. The argument sketched in the immediately preceding clause can thus be formulated as 'if the quality that applies to a substance is different from it, the quality is not substance; but the quality that applies to a substance is different

different from substance is not substance; so quality is not
substance. But if every body is substance, and quality is not
25　　substance, then quality is not body.

(II) Moreover, if whiteness is a natural body, and every
natural body is tangible, then whiteness [will be] tangible.
But it is not tangible. So it is not a body. For if whiteness
were tangible, touch would be affected by it. But it is not
affected. So [whiteness] is not tangible.[232]

[IIa] Moreover, touch is disposed and affected in opposite
ways by opposite things, hard, soft, hot, cold. So it would be
30　　affected in opposite ways both by whiteness and blackness,
which is the opposite of white, and also by sweetness and
bitterness. But it is not affected in opposite ways. So whiteness is not tangible.

(III) Moreover, every natural body that causes
123,1　change[233] as a body causes change in place and in the
manner of body, that is [by] touching, either pushing or
throwing or dragging or crushing or rotating or supporting
and carrying, or any other way there may be of causing
change in the manner of a body. But no quality causes
change in place by itself; so quality is not body.

(IV) <Moreover,> if quality is body, and every body either
5　　possesses quality or is able to admit quality, quality too will
either possess quality or be able to admit quality, which is
absurd. So quality is not body. For if it were to admit
[quality], [this would] go on to infinity.[234]

(V) Moreover, if quality is body, and every body that is in

---

from it; so the quality is not substance'. Cf. [Galen], *Qual.*
481,8-10K = 16,17-19W = 22,319-21G; Alcinous, *Didascalicus* 11.1.
　　[232] Cf. [Galen], *Qual.* 483,1-8K = 17,20-18,7W = 25,347-54G.
Westenberger 1906, 35.
　　[233] *kinoun*, which could also be translated by 'causes
movement'. But since the text goes on to specify *kinêsis* in place,
it seems appropriate to keep the more general term here.
　　[234] At [Galen], *Qual.* 474,8-10K = 10,10-12W = 14,196-8G a
similar regress is generated in terms of body and shape, specifically (cf. Westenberger 1906, 28-9).

actuality possesses quality (for matter is body potentially),[235] quality too will possess quality, which is absurd.

[Va] Moreover, the quality which [the quality] possesses either is or is not body. If then [the possessed quality] is not   10 body, quality is no longer body [in this case at least]; and what is the random principle[236] [by which] the quality preceding it is body but this [quality] is not? If however [the latter] itself also is body, it too will possess quality, and this [will go on] to infinity. Moreover, there would be many bodies in the same [place]; and that this is impossible we have shown elsewhere.[237]

(VI) Moreover, if qualities are bodies, how will bodies not be increased and diminished by their presence and absence?   15 If they[238] should say that it is because some arrive as others depart, it is worth raising the difficulty, how those that arrive are in every case[239] equal to those that depart.

---

[235]   [Prime] matter, matter as such, is without quality (cf. below 124,7; Alex., *DA* 17,17 and 18,2, *Quaest.* 1.15 24,7, 2.7 52,23, 2.15 60,27). If matter, which is potential body, is the only thing without quality, it follows that all actual bodies will have quality.

[236]   *apoklerôsis.* Alexander has in effect conflated two ways of making his point: with a question, 'What is the rational principle of decision?', implying that there is none and the choice is arbitrary, and with a statement, 'this is an arbitrary decision'. Or perhaps the question is an indignant one: 'What arbitrary decision is this?' (LSJ cite the same expression at Alex., *DA* 22,25 as indicating 'what is there unreasonable in ...?'; but this seems wrong both there and here, suggesting that the distinctions in question in the two passages are reasonable ones, whereas in fact the point is that they are arbitrary and objectionably so.) I am grateful to Inna Kupreeva for discussion of this passage.

[237]   Probably a reference to Alex., *Mixt.* chs. 5-6 (so Bruns, citing a similar reference at Alex., *DA* 20,18); but cf. also §14 below. With this argument cf. Alcinous, *Didascalicus* 11.1, and [Galen], *Qual.* 471,17-472,2K = 8,9-11W = 12,159-61G: Westenberger 1906, 26; Todd 1976, 85 n.247.

[238]   This is the first time opponents have been alluded to in this section in personal terms. 'They' could just be 'anyone who supports the view that qualities are bodies'; but Alexander may have definite, Stoic opponents in mind.

[239]   Literally 'all those that arrive are ...' Cf. [Galen], *Qual.*

(VII) Moreover, where do those that come come from, and where do those that are separated off depart to? For they must have a place, if they are bodies.[240]

(VIII) Moreover, in the case of things that possess odour, how is it that, as the odour is continually being given off, the thing that possesses it and from which it is being given off is not diminished? For indeed in this case there is not

20 another [odour] coming in to take its place.[241]

(IX) Moreover, some* bodies acquire qualities without losing any of those which they possess, as in the case of air that does not have a odour but then, when some one of the things that possess odour is brought up, comes to transmit the odour;[242] and [also] in the case of the person who acquires virtue or vice, not having previously been in a vicious [state].[243] How then will [these] not increase?

(X) Moreover, if quality is body, it is clear that the quality relating to the odour in the apple extends through the

25 whole body of the apple and occupies an equal place to it. But when the apple has been moved the surrounding air too has been filled with the fragrance, being many times as great; so the same quality extended through this too and

---

475,1-3K = 11,2-4W = 15,209-11G, arguing that it is absurd to suppose that the qualities make way for each other by agreement.

[240] Cf. [Galen], *Qual.* 474,1-9K = 10,3-12W = 14,190-98G, with specific reference to the problem of 'body going through body' (below, §14); id. 475,16-17K = 11,17-18W = 16,223-5G (Westenberger 1906, 29).

[241] Cf. Lucretius 3.221-7. An similar argument also appears to be used against the effluence theory of smell by Theophrastus, *De sensibus* 20; but the issue is complex (cf. Sedley 1985).

[242] Literally 'becomes transodorant (*diosmos*)'; a term for the medium (air or water) through which odour travels, coined by Theophrastus, as we know from Philoponus, *In DA* 354,12-16 (= Theophrastus, 277C FHS&G, q.v.), on the analogy of 'transparent'. Cf. Ellis 1990 (I am grateful to Alain Lernould for this reference).

[243] This argument would have no force against the Stoics, who reject the notion of an intermediate state between vice and virtue. Cf. Alex., *Ethical Problem* 3.

occupied a place equal to it. And if the apple is moved again [the fragrance] will again fill another [equal] amount of air. How then does a body equal [in size to the apple], remaining and extending through the apple too,[244] both remain occupying that place along with the apple and at the same 30 time [occupy] another place many times as great, and a different [place] at different times? For neither is the same fragrance transported along with the apple in the first [body of] air, nor is a new fragrance always being produced from the apple. For how could [a scent] many times as great [in volume] proceed from a little body, when nothing is being added to it?[245]

(XI) Moreover, no body perishes into not-being, but qualities do perish into not-being. So qualities are not bodies. For 35 whiteness does not persist and come to be blackness.[246]

(XII) Moreover, if quality is body, and every body is either matter or [composed of] matter and quality, one [or other of] these [options] will [apply to] quality too.[247] Well, [for it to be] matter is impossible;[248] so what is left is to say that quality is [composed of] matter and quality. But if so, 124,1 [then], first, quality [will] not [be] quality but matter and quality (for these[249] are different from each other), and

[244] The expression would be less awkward if the second *kai* ('too') in 123,29 were deleted, but the awkwardness may be Alexander's.

[245] See above, 76 n.241. The example of the apple is also used by [Galen], *Qual.* 469,15-472,2K = 6,17-8,11W = 9,114-12,161G, but rather to raise difficulties concerning the relation between whole and part within the apple.

[246] If a piece of wood which was white is repainted black, the *wood* remains and becomes black, but the whiteness of the wood does not remain and become blackness. Cf. Aristotle, *Phys.* 1.7 190a9-13.

[247] Literally: 'quality too will be one of these.'

[248] Quality cannot be just matter, because matter (matter as such, prime matter) is without quality; above, 74 n.235. Cf. Alcinous, *Didascalicus* 11.1.

[249] 'these' being the matter and the quality, or rather, the quality first assumed and the second quality which is one of its two ingredients? (I owe the latter suggestion to Inna Kupreeva).

moreover the quality [that is combined] with the matter will also itself be matter and quality, if [it is] a body, and so on to infinity, and there will be an infinite [number of] matters in each quality. For if matter is quality,[250] every body that is in
5 actuality will not be [composed of] matter and quality, but of quality and quality; that is of matter and matter, if matter and quality are the same thing. And there will be no difference between matter and body which is actual. But if this is so, and matter is without quality, body which is actual, too, will be without quality, and either quality will not even exist at all, or there will be no body other than quality.

10   (XIII) Moreover, if qualities are body, and light is a quality and, as they suppose,[251] a body, how does there proceed from a lamp, which is such a small body, so great a body that it becomes equal to the surrounding air which is so great, and, when [the lamp] has been moved, there will again proceed [from it] into other air another equally great [body]? Or how will the air not increase [in size] when so great a body is added to it? Or how does the light extend
15 through it, and [how] is it mixed with it, when it is full? Or, if [the light] is transported along with [the lamp], how is the light produced externally by the lamp united with [the lamp]?[252]

---

[250] It is not clear how this statement is justified by anything that has preceded. The conclusion that each quality will contain an infinite number of matters can in any case be derived more directly. For at stage n of the regress the quality will be composed of $matter_1$ + $matter_2$ + ... $matter_n$ + $quality_n$; $quality_n$ then itself decomposes into $matter_{n+1}$ + $quality_{n+1}$, and so on. The equation of matter and quality is however needed to derive the absurd conclusion which follows in the text, that there will be no difference between body in actuality and matter.

[251] See above, 75 n.238; and for the application of this argument to light, [Galen], *Qual.* 473,5-9K = 9,10-14W = 13,151-157G (Westenberger 1906, 27-8; Todd 1976, 198), and below, 138,25-7 and 140,38-141,4 (which are directed against the Stoics), also 128,34ff. and 129,24ff. (which are not); Todd, op. cit. 85. 124,9-10 = *SVF* 2.864.

[252] As it would have to be, in some way, to explain why it

(XIV) Moreover, how will the air in a room, when it takes on many qualities, not be increased? For in the same equal [place there are] both light and heat and odour and colour and sound. [If] all these are bodies and extend* through the whole of the air in the room, how will they not increase it, and how will they not burst the building? For the air in the   20
wine-skin, if it is increased by a little, bursts the wine-skin.

[XV] For it is clear from what follows that quality is different both in concept and in account from what possesses quality and is a qualified body. Body and qualified body are either the same or different. If they are different, it is clear that it is by some addition and difference that qualified body is different from body.[253] Well, that by which qualified body   25
differs from body is quality; so it is by the presence and addition of quality that body became[254] qualified body. What has acquired a share in something is different from what [it was] before acquiring it, and what is acquired is different from what acquires it. That by which qualified body differs from body is quality, [which] clearly is not body. For body   30
is common to body and qualified body, and qualified body does not differ from body by qualified body, but by quality. At any rate, when we define qualified body and body we make the difference between them in terms not of qualified body but of quality.[255]

[XVI] But if someone were to say that body and qualified body are the same, [then], first, the accounts of them will be the same, so that the same account will [apply to] white   35

---

should move around with the lamp when that is moved.

[253]   Bruns rightly brackets the sentence that follows in the MSS, "And it is clear that it is different; for their definitions* and accounts differ", which breaks the flow of the argument, as a marginal comment which has found its way into the text.

[254]   As Wurm 1973, 186 and n.21 notes, the past tense here is not to be taken literally, since body never actually exists without quality. The past tense is rather that of logical analysis.

[255]   Alcinous, *Didascalicus* 11.1 argues more generally that it is by quality that one body differs from another.

body, and again to body, and to black body.[256] And if so, the same account [will apply] both to white body and to black body; for each of [the accounts] will be the same as the [account] of body [simply].

125,1 [XVII] Moreover, if being a body and being a qualified body are the same,[257] the body that underlies what is white, and that which has already received whiteness and [is] white, will be the same; and when the [latter] is destroyed, so too the body which underlies what is white will be destroyed. But we do not see this occurring; for this thing, which was for a time white, persists and, being the same numerically,[258] admits the opposite [qualities].

125,5 [7]. Against those who say that none of the four bodies which we call elements subsists on its own.

The view attacked in this text claims (cf. arguments I, V, VI) that the elements cannot exist separately on the grounds that visibility derives from fire and tangibility from earth, as asserted by Plato at *Timaeus* 31b. As Falcon 2001, 128-34 points out, a similar argument was advanced by Numenius (fr. 51 des Places = Proclus, *In Tim.* vol.2 p.9,4-5 Diehl) and is criticised by Plotinus 2.1 [40], 6, on the grounds that it requires the presence of water in the fiery heavens. The same argument based on the *Timaeus* is reported by Philoponus, *In GC* 228,8ff., with the comment that if instead we follow Aristotle and characterise solid and fluid by definite shape and its absence, hot and cold by dissolution and coalescence (cf. Aristotle, *GC* 2.2 329b25-31), there will be nothing to prevent each element existing in isolation.[259] Although Philoponus does not cite Alexander for this particular point, he

---

[256] The argument equivocates on 'account of qualified body', first taking it to mean 'account of body *qua* qualified' and then 'account of body *qua* qualified in a specific way'.

[257] For the denial that this is so Wurm 1973, 187 and n.32 compares Aristotle, *Metaph.* 7.4 1029b13-1030a2.

[258] i.e. being the same individual, not just the same in species. Alcinous, *Didascalicus* 11.1 argues that qualities are opposite to one another but bodies are not; cf. Aristotle, *Cat.* 5 3b25, 8 10b13.

[259] I am grateful to Sylvia Berryman for drawing my attention to this passage.

makes frequent use of Alexander's lost *GC* commentary and may
well be doing so here. That the elements do not exist in isolation
is also implied by Galen, *De elementis ex Hippocrate* 1 454.1-3
Kühn (I owe this reference to Inna Kupreeva).

Aristotle himself distinguishes between the four simple bodies
as we experience them, and their pure types, at *GC* 2.3 330b21ff.;[260]
and at *De longitudine et brevitate vitae* 3 465b1-14 he allows that
there may be a region consisting exclusively of fire, but insists that
this fire will not be simply hot with no other attributes, and so will
be subject to change.[261] Alexander argues that pure fire does not
need nourishment (*Quaest.* 2.17 62,12-14, and cf. above at 120,18),
and also that, just because the fire immediately beneath the
heavens (the *hupekkauma*: cf. above 66 n.203, and Sharples 1994,
114 n.59) is not as hot as terrestrial fire, we need not suppose that
it is admixture of earth that makes it cooler. He consistently
regards the *hupekkauma* as the elemental form of fire.[262]

(I) [Some say that] the four bodies are always mixed with   125,7
one another and each of them is called a certain thing[263]

[260] Cf. Gannagé 2002, 134. That the sublunary elements are
mixed is suggested by Theophrastus, *De igne* 8, 352,2-10 Wimmer
1865, but with the suggestion that there are prior and pure principles (ibid. 9 352,10-11, accepting Gercke's addition of *mê*, and
comparing 4 351,23-24).

[261] I owe this reference to István Bodnár.

[262] While accepting, at least in his commentary on the *Meteorology* (14,25ff.), Aristotle's view (*Meteor.* 1.3 340b23; cf., with
Gannagé 2002, 139, *GC* 2.3 330b24) that it is terrestrial fire that is
properly called 'fire' (cf. Sharples 1990, 98-9). Gannagé 2002, 135ff.
notes that in his commentary on *GC* 2.3 (ap. Ǧābir ibn Ḥayyān,
Kitāb al-Taṣrīf 29) Alexander likens the pure type of fire to form,
and describes the fire familiar to us as mixed with matter; she
argues from this that Alexander has introduced an un-Aristotelian
distinction between fire as form and fire as form-matter compound,
and, following a suggestion of Denis O'Brien, argues that in revers-
ing Aristotle's view Alexander is moving closer to the position of
Plato, *Timaeus* 49d-52a which Aristotle had rejected.

[263] Literally 'a this-something', *tode ti.* See above, 15 n.13.
'[Some say that]' has been added to break up a complex sentence
in the original; the Greek simply has 'If the four bodies ...', the 'If'
being picked up by 'what will they [then] say' at 125,13.

from what predominates in it, but none of them can be
found on its own, because resistance is proper to earth,
10   visibility to fire,[264] and something else to each of the others;
and for this reason each of them is perceptible by several
senses, inasmuch as it shares in the other [elements] too.
For fire too is tangible and has resistance, because it has
earth in it, and earth is visible because there is fire in it.[265] –
[But] what will they [then] say is proper to body, and what
account will they give of body in general and natural [body],
15   just in so far as it is body? For if resistance does not
[belong] to every body, and the account of [body] is not
what is extended in three ways together with resistance –
for they say that this is proper to earth[266] – what is the
account of body in general? For there must be one, if there
is some account of genera which is different from that of
each of the species; for it is in this way that the genus

[264] Cf. Plato, *Timaeus* 31b, and Theophrastus ap. Taurus ap.
Philoponus, *Aet. mund. contra Proclum* 13.15 (520,4-521,6 Rabe) =
Theophrastus 161A FHS&G; Theophrastus ap. Proclus, *In Tim.* 2
6,1-28 = 161B FHS&G; Alcinous, *Didasc.* 12, 167,24-32 Hermann;
Galen, *PHP* 7.5.44 (462,8-10 De Lacy); Nemesius, *Nat. hom.* 6
56,6-8 Morani. (I am grateful to Inna Kupreeva for the latter three
references.)

[265] This is presumably still part of the opponents' argument,
rather than a claim Alexander would himself endorse. The
general claim that fire is tangible seems more plausible – for it is
touch that detects heat – than the specific claim that it has resistance. (I am grateful to Ricardo Salles for raising this issue.)

[266] The text is ambiguous as to whether those attacked explicitly reject the account of body as what is extended in three ways
together with resistance, or whether Alexander is rather claiming
that they are in fact committed to rejecting it, whether they realise
this or not, by their connection of tangibility with earth. The
definition of body as what is extended in three ways together with
resistance was adopted by the Stoics (*SVF* 2.357, 381) but was not
peculiar to them; cf. Todd 1976, 198; LS vol.1 273; Falcon 2001,
58-61, arguing that the definition was originally Epicurean. Inna
Kupreeva notes that [Galen], *Qual. incorp.* 464,2-4 Kühn = 1,12-13
Westenberger = 1,11-2,13 Giusta argues against the Stoics on the
basis of this definition of body, regarding it as common property.

differs from things that are said ambiguously.

(II) Moreover, if the reason why air is tangible is that it contains [a portion] of earth, and the reason why it does not   20 have much resistance is that it [contains] rather little earth, why then, when someone fills a wineskin with breath, does it have more resistance? For they must say that the breath has then acquired a larger portion of earth, if it is from earth that the resistance derives. But if the reason why it has resistance is that it is shut in and cannot be diffused, then its resistance does not come from having more or less of earth [in it], but from its own nature. For while remaining   25 the same it sometimes has more resistance and sometimes less; so [its] resistance derives from something else.[267]

(III) Moreover, if these bodies change into one another, with a common matter underlying them, and it is in form that they have opposition to one another, and what prevails always converts what is prevailed over into its own proper nature, why then [does it happen that] in the case of things   30 that are separated externally,[268] when they are placed alongside one another, the lesser [number] are destroyed by the greater [number], if they are opposites, while when the lesser are present *in* each body among the greater, which

---

[267] The expression of the whole argument seems awkwardly compressed. The claim is that the change in the air's resistance does not derive from a change in its material composition. 'from its own nature' is presumably shorthand for 'not as a result of a change in its nature, but because it is the nature of air to resist when shut in'. However, it is more natural to express this by saying that the resistance derives from something *other* than the air itself, i.e. the fact that it is shut in; and this is indeed the way the point is put in the following sentence, thus creating the appearance of a contradiction.

[268] I.e., separate masses of (e.g.) fire and water, as opposed to fire and water combined (according to the theory of Alexander's opponents) in a single body characterised by whatever predominates in it. If one body overcomes the other and transforms it into its own nature in the former case, why not in the latter? (The Aldine has 'in the case of other separated things', which would have to be understood, by a common Greek idiom, as 'other things, i.e. those that are separated.)

are for this reason said to be a certain thing,[269] they are not destroyed as far as their own nature [is concerned] by what predominates? For it will turn out for those who speak thus that, as with Anaxagoras' homoiomeries,[270] they will be saying that coming to be [takes place] by the combination and separation of the elements, not by [their] transformation.[271]

[IV] Moreover, if everything one takes has the four [elements] in it, and it is not possible to find anything pure, there will be a progression to infinity, since whatever one takes and whatever one removes will share in [all] four [elements]. For if they are going to say that it is when they escape perception through smallness that they are found [to be] pure, it will no longer be the case that all things are mixed.

[V]* Moreover, how will what is visible be [produced] from the juxtaposition of such things? For juxtaposition will not, from things that are unmixed, produce an [ad]mixture of something else; and if the juxtaposition of such things is going to be invisible because each of them is unmixed with fire, a body which is put together in this way will be able to increase in size indefinitely while remaining invisible; and

---

[269] I.e. what has more fire than anything else in it is called fire.

[270] For change being combination and separation cf. Anaxagoras 59B17 DK = Simplicius, *In Phys.* 163,20ff. The term 'homoeomeries' is here used in the plural to indicate Anaxagoras' elements, as at Aëtius 1.3.5 and Diogenes of Oenoanda fr. 6.II.6 Smith (I am grateful to Francesco Montarese for the latter reference); but ' ... the word *homoiomereia* had ... become a catchword that was almost automatically applied to Anaxagoras' physical theories' (Kirk, Raven and Schofield 1983, 377). Is Anaxagoras chosen here (rather than the Atomists, or Empedocles, for whom also change is rearrangement) because his doctrine that 'in everything there is a portion of everything' is particularly suitable in a criticism of those for whom no element exists in a pure form?

[271] This seems to suggest that *any* mixture of the elements, except one where there is an exactly equally balance, will necessarily be converted into the predominating element. Contrast Aristotle, *GC* 1.10 328a28-31.

similarly intangible, if it is put together from things that are
free from earth.   10a

[VI] Moreover, if even when [earth] is no longer seen it is   3b
still mixed with fire, it is not because it is visible that it
contains [a portion] of fire; for being no longer visible and
not being seen it [still] possesses a portion of fire then.   5a

[VII] Moreover, will they say that it is impossible for   10b
matter to admit warmth and dryness and become fire
without [also possessing] coldness and dryness, in which
the being of earth [consists]? Or [will they say] that it is
also possible to admit warmth without coldness? For if they
say that [this] is impossible, how is it not absurd that
[matter] should admit coldness and warmth in the same
respect, when these are opposites, [while] it is unable to   15
admit either of these on its own? But if, as is reasonable, it is
able to admit one without the other (for it is impossible [for
it to admit both] in the same respect), how then will what
underlies, which has warmth and dryness, not be tangible?
For if [they say it is not],[272] what is warm will not be perceptible in its own nature for them, if*[273] it is impossible for it,
subsisting in actuality, to be subject to perception[274] without
there being [something] of coldness also mixed with it. For   20
it is in this that the being of earth [consists], and it is by this
that it differs from fire.[275] So it will derive its perceptibility
from its own opposite. And similarly in the case of the other
things too; and in this way nothing that is unmixed with
[its] opposite, and pure, will be perceptible.

---

[272] So Bruns ad loc.: literally 'in this case', *houtôs*: if (i) heat can
exist without coldness and if (ii) what is hot and dry is *not* tangible. I
am grateful to Inna Kupreeva for this interpretation of the passage.

[273] In effect, what follows states condition (ii) in the previous note.

[274] Clearly what is hot cannot, on the opponents' view, be *tangible*
if it contains no earth; but why should it not be perceptible in the
sense of being visible? (I am grateful to Sylvia Berryman for raising
this question.) The answer is, presumably, that the *hot* is perceptible
in its own nature by touch, but by sight only *per accidens*.

[275] Earth is dry and cold; fire dry and hot.

126,24   **[8]. That air is by nature hot.**

This text is a straightforward exposition of orthodox Aristotelian theory, with no attempt to consider rival views. Air was hot for Aristotle but cold for the Stoics (*SVF* 2.430, 841) — though it was also cold for Theophrastus (*De igne* 26). Longrigg 1975, 221-2 points out that Theophrastus was building on the fact that, even for Aristotle, air has a cooling function in respiration: and indeed, the present text might have been more suitable for inclusion in a collection relating to living, ensouled beings if it had taken account of this fact.

25   [I] If fire, which is hot and dry, is by nature light, what is light [next] after it will be [so by] sharing with it in that by which it is light. But fire is light and hot;[276] at any rate dryness by nature is present in earth, which is heavy. So air, which is light in the second degree, is hot.

[II] Moreover, if the other elements that are adjacent to each other are adjacent in respect of something [they have

30   in] common, it is reasonable that air should have something in common with fire which corresponds;[277] and since it is

127,1   moist [whereas fire is dry], what else could it have in common with [fire] other than being hot? For earth and water have cold in common, water and air have moistness, so what is left for air and fire is heat.

[III] Moreover, if what are simple are hot, cold, dry and moist, and it is these that give form to the elements, the

5   things that differ from each other in kind will be those that differ by simple tangible difference. So if water and air differ in kind, they will differ by some simple difference. But their moistness is the same, so what is left is for their difference to be in respect of cold and heat.

[IV] Moreover, if things which differ from each other in

[276] Bruns proposes *kouphon katho thermon*, 'light insofar as it is hot'. That is clearly the point being made, but it is perhaps not clear that emendation is required.

[277] Literally, a *koinon sumbolon*; a tally or identity-token of which the two halves, broken apart, correspond when put together again.

respect of the more and the less[278] do not differ in kind, [then] if air too were cold and moist, it would not differ in kind 10 from water; for that too is cold and moist. And even if someone were to say that the one is more so, and the other less, even so they will not differ in kind; so both would be one, and the elements [would] no longer be four [in number].

[V] Moreover, if there are four combinations of dry, moist, hot and cold[279] and three [of them] give form to the other elements, it is reasonable that the pairing that is left should give form to air. For hot and dry give form to fire, 15 dry and cold to earth, cold and moist to water, so hot and moist will give form to air.

[VI] Moreover, that which comes to be through heat is hot in its own nature. But air comes to be from water through heat; for it is when water is heated that it changes to air. And as much from earth as changes to air turns and is 20 changed when it is heated.[280] So air is hot in its own nature.

[VII] Moreover, if the change of the elements into each other comes about more easily in respect of something which corresponds,[281] and the [other] three have something in common which corresponds, one to another, then air and fire will have something in common which corresponds.[282] And this cannot be anything other than heat. So air is hot. What is in common and corresponds for earth and water is 25 cold, for fire and earth dryness, for water and air moistness, for fire and air heat.

---

[278] As we might say: by degrees. Cf. however Simplicius, *In Cat.* 235,3-13 (= Theophrastus, 438 FHS&G), citing Theophrastus as arguing that difference in degree can constitute difference in kind, though Simplicius himself rejects this. Cf. Fortenbaugh 1985, 227 n.5; Lennox 1987; Meinwald 1998.

[279] Because the diametrically opposed pairs hot and cold, moist and dry do not combine; Aristotle, *GC* 2.3 330a30ff. For "give form to" (*eidopoiein*) as a term favoured by Alexander see Gannagé 2002, 142-3.

[280] For the production of air from earth cf. Aristotle, *GC* 2.4 331b9.

[281] Aristotle, *GC* 2.4 331b3 ff.

[282] Because air and fire easily change into each other.

[§§9-16: On Vision.]

§§9-16 are concerned with, or ancillary to, the theory of vision. (See below, 117.) There are signs that they constitute an editorial arrangement of texts some at least of which were originally independent, rather than a continuous original text: see below, 117 n.393, 120-1. Several of the sections are more or less closely parallel to discussions in Alexander's commentary on Aristotle's *De Sensu*: see below, 89, 107, 143.

Aëtius 4.13 (Diels 1879, 403-4) is devoted to the topic of vision, and a number of the theories discussed here are also mentioned there, as noted below. Sextus Empiricus mentions a number of theories of vision, very much in passing, at *Outlines of Pyrrhonism* 3.51, without identifying their proponents: the tensioning of a cone (of air: §10 here), the separating off and impinging of images (§11 here), and the sending out of rays (§9 here) or of colours (perhaps to be interpreted, with Bury 1933, 360 note (a), as an allusion to the Aristotelian theory, expounded here in §15, if the sending out of colours is interpreted as sending out by the thing seen).[283]

On these texts on vision generally see Zahlfleisch 1895-6, criticised by Hass 1907; Sharples 1998a, 394-403. Rose 1863, 375, followed by Moraux 2001, 365 n.216, suggested that these texts might be extracts from the work *On How We See*[284] referred to at

---

[283] §15 is at pains to insist that no actual movement takes place, but the Aristotelian position was neither uniform nor widely understood. For the change in Aristotle's own views from one involving emission from the eye to the distinctive theory of *DA* and *De Sensu* denying any physical movement at all cf. Preus 1968, 177-8; Lindberg 1976, 217-18 n.39; Simon 1988, 49; Berryman 1998, 184-6. Galen criticises Aristotle for inconsistency (*PHP* 7.7.10-15, 473,3-24 De Lacy); on the other hand Berryman 1998 notes that the surveys of theories of vision in Geminus ap. Damianus, *Optica* p.24, and Calcidius, *In Tim.* 238, do not mention the theory of Aristotle's *DA* at all. Cf. further Sharples 2003, 217-20, and references there.

[284] Which cannot, Moraux argues, simply be identified with §15 alone as we now have it, for that does not explain how certain things are seen in the darkness, as *DA* 43,17-18 indicates *On How We See* did; though it does *mention* them, at 144,21-3. See 135 n.456 below.

Alex., *DA* 43,16,18 (cf. Bruns' note ad loc.) and (in Moraux' view, following Rose, by a scholiast rather than by Alexander himself) at Alex., *In Meteor.* 141,11-12.

[9.] Against those who say that seeing comes about through   127,27
rays.

There are numerous parallels, noted by Bruns and Wendland, between this section and Alexander's commentary on Aristotle's *De sensu*, 28,16-31,18 Wendland.[285] The arrangement of the material is however different: in particular, whereas our text considers the possibilities that what is sent out from the eye is air (127,33-4), light or illuminated air (127,34-128,11) or fire (128,12-20), the commentary considers air (30,23-5, with the same argument as here) fire (30,25-31,9) and light (31,9-18), treating air and fire as the two corporeal possibilities (30,21-3) and only mentioning light subsequently as a separate hypothesis to be ruled out because it is in fact incorporeal and a relation (cf. below, 127). The main argument advanced in the commentary against light as what is sent out is found in a later part of the discussion here (130,6-11); and some of the arguments advanced against light (regarded as corporeal) here are advanced against fire in the commentary (below, 91 n.292). Two arguments here appear in a preceding section of the commentary, at 22,21-23,4 (below, 91 n.294, 93 n.300); one argument in the commentary is divided into two here (below, 96-7 n.318), which might suggest that the version in the commentary is primary (or reflects *On How We See* more accurately?).

The argument against air at 127,33-4 appears in the commentary (30,23-5) in a series of objections (28,16-31,18) which at first sight seem to be directed against the view that the eye is *fire*, which could suggest that material from the *Mantissa* has been incorporated into the commentary in a mechanical way. This is not in fact so. Aristotle at *De sensu* 2 438a25ff. contrasts [i] the theory that rays are sent out from the eye and [ii] the theory that [a] light from the eye is fused with [b] light outside – the theory of Plato (Alexander, *In De sensu* 28,7-15: cf. *Timaeus* 45bd, and Aëtius 4.13.11). Alexander, noting that Aristotle does not argue against [i], says that he argues against [ii] as a way of refuting those who say the eye is *fire* (28,12-15). But it is clear from 32,1-9

[285] Bruns cites this text from Thurot 1875: I have updated the references.

that what follows at 28,16-31,18 is not in fact directed against this view alone, but against [i] in general; that is, *ekeinous* at 28,16 refers back to 28,11-12 rather than to 28,13-14. [i] is attributed by Alexander (*In De sensu* 28,2) to 'mathematicians';[286] Crombie 1994, 173 suggests that *Mantissa* §9 is directed against their theory, but they are not actually mentioned here. See below, 91 n.293, 96 n.317.

Before proceeding to discussion of [b], the commentary argues, at 31,19ff., that the theory of something entering the eye (discussed in §11 below) is subject to approximately those difficulties that apply to the theory of rays leaving the eye, but also to others of its own, and then remarks that 'these topics have been discussed at greater length elsewhere'. Wendland ad loc. interprets this as referring to both theories, that of rays leaving the eye and that of bodies entering it, and so takes it as a reference to our present text. It is perhaps more likely that the reference is to §11, since the theory considered in the present section is discussed at length in the commentary too, but that in §11 only very briefly.[287] There are other reasons for regarding the commentary on *De sensu* as relatively late among Alexander's works.[288]

There is an Arabic version of this text, D13a, ed. Badawī 1971 no.3; cf. Gätje 1966, 267f., id. 1971, 71, and Badawī 1979, 7. I am most grateful to Inna Kupreeva for showing me her translation of the Arabic and for her advice on its implications for the Greek text.

127,28   If seeing is by the pouring forth and ejection of rays, it is clear that these are bodies. For it would not be possible for
30   them to move and proceed otherwise. Then is this body which [constitutes] the rays air or light or fire? And is it continuous, or divided? And if it is continuous, is it sent out like this, or is it divided when sent out, but after being sent out it coalesces and becomes continuous?[289] For all these

---

[286] Aëtius attributes [i] to 'certain of the Academics', at 4.13.2, and also to Hipparchus: see below, 93 n.303.

[287] Moraux 2001, 397 suggests the reference is to *On How We See*: above, 88-9.

[288] Though earlier than Alex., *DA*. See Moraux 2001, 395-7.

[289] [III][7] below suggests that the contrast is not between emission in a continuous stream and in successive 'packets' along the axis of emission; rather, the question is whether the ray is, as it were, solid in cross-section as it is emitted. Cf. also Alexander,

[possibilities] are strange.

[I] (1) If it is air, what need is there for it to be sent out, since there is air outside also?[290] If it is light and as it were illuminated air (for we think that light is something like this),[291] on this basis too the sending out is superfluous, 35 since there is light outside as well. And without the outside [light] it is not possible to see.

[I] (2) And then, why do we not see at night and in the dark? For the light sent out through the eyes would itself be sufficient to illuminate the air outside,[292] seeing that it is the 128,1 nature of [this light] to extend even as far as the stars;[293] for it is so strong. But if it is weaker than the light of mid-day, we ought to see so much the more at night and in the dark, but not in the day. For the lesser light is always weakened by the brighter light;[294] at any rate some things emit light in 5

In De sensu 28,9 (Wendland ad loc.).

[290] Cf., with Bruns, Alex., *In De sensu* 30,23-5 Wendland, and above, 89. – In §9 the primary MS V presents a series of successive numbered sequences, differentiated by the use of either a diagonal or horizontal stroke as the indicator of a numeral, keyed to marginal headings: for the sequence beginning here, 'That [it is] not air or light'. I have supplied Roman numerals (in square brackets) for the main sections, and reproduced the numbering of V within these in round brackets. The numbering in V ends at 128,34; thereafter I have introduced my own numbering, following the paragraph divisions in V. The later MS B has a different arrangement of numbered sequences; from 129,20 I have followed this, but placing the numbering of B in braces {}.

[291] See below, 129-31.

[292] Cf., with Bruns, Alex., *In De sensu* 31,4-5 Wendland, in the context however of the possibility that *fire* is emitted.

[293] Since we can see them, on this theory light from our eyes must reach them. Aristotle mentions the theory that light issues from the eyes and extends to the stars at *De sensu* 438a25, and Alexander ad loc. (*In De sensu* 28,2) refers to this as the theory of 'mathematicians': Johansen 1998, 58. Cf. also Philoponus, *In DA* 326.10 (I owe this reference to Sylvia Berryman).

[294] And the weak light from our eyes would be weakened by the brighter light of day, but not at night. Cf., with Bruns, Alex., *In De sensu* 22,23-23,4 Wendland, and for the general principle also

this way at night, but by day their light is darkened, such as certain bones and fish-heads and the so-called 'fire-tails' [glow-worms].[295]

[I](3) Moreover, if what is sent out is weak, why when many people come together in the same place in the dark, is the mixture of [what is sent out] from [them] all[296] not sufficient to give an amount of illumination that each was not sufficient for in itself, just as [the light] from a considerable number of lamps gives more illumination?[297]

[I](4) Moreover, if light is visible, why do we not see one another's seeings[298] either by day or in the dark?

[II] If what is sent out is neither air nor light, what is left is for it to be fire.

[II](1) If it is fire, it will be hot and burning. But it is not; so it is not fire. If it is not burning, they will [go] back to saying that it is light. What then is this light? It is not a streaming off of fire,[299] as they think; for indeed other things

---

Aristotle, *Insomn.* 3 461a1; [Aristotle], *Probl.* 3.5 871a35; Theophrastus, *De sensibus* 18, *De igne* 11.

[295] Cf. Aristotle, *DA* 2.7 419a2-5 (fungus, meat, and the heads, scales and eyes of fish): *De sensu* 2 437b5-7 (fish-heads and cuttlefish ink), with Alex., *In De sensu* 17,3-7 ad loc., and below, 135 n.456. The context in *De sensu* is the alleged flashing of the eye, and the explanation is in terms of the smoothness of the objects, so the phenomenon being described is not just phosphoresence due to decay, even though the *DA* examples of fungus and meat might suggest this.

[296] Taking *pantôn* as masculine. Alternatively, taking it as neuter, 'the combination of all [the emissions]', suggested to me by Inna Kupreeva.

[297] Cf. Alex., *In De sensu* 31,6-7; again, in the discussion of fire. This argument is numbered {2} in MS B.

[298] I.e. the rays from each others' eyes which on this theory explain our seeing. This argument is numbered {3} in MS B.

[299] The Greek could indicate either just 'from fire' or also 'constituted of fire'; probably the latter too is meant. For the contrast between fire and effluence from fire cf. 138,4 below (I owe this reference to Inna Kupreeva); that suggests that the description of light as an effluence from fire is Stoic, but cf. also

illuminate which are not fire.

[II] (2) Moreover, if what is sent out is fire, how will it not be quenched in water?[300] But we can see in water too,[301] and the animals in the water can see.

[II] (3) Moreover, if what is sent out is fire, movement upwards will be natural for it, so that we ought not to see similarly looking upwards and downwards, but more easily upwards, struggling and with difficulty downwards.[302]   20

[III] (1) Moreover, if seeing is by means of rays, sight will be some [sort of] touch, and the apprehension by the rays will be by touch. If the sight[303] that extends forth has the power of sensation, why does it not perceive hot and cold? For it would perceive the tangible differences more than colours.

[III] (2) Moreover, if the seeing body is sent out [as] continuous, first the whole pupil[304] must be a pore, which   25 clearly is not the case.

[III] (3) Next, even if it is sent out continuously, how is this flow of sight not scattered, split by the external air since

---

Plato, *Timaeus* 58c. – In MS V the present argument is numbered as the first under the heading 'Nor fire'; and so by implication in B.

[300] Cf., with Bruns, Alex., *In De sensu* 22,21-3. This argument is numbered {2} also in B.

[301] Cf., with Bruns, Alex., *In De sensu* 31,1-3.

[302] Cf., with Bruns, Alex., *In De sensu* 30,25-31,1. Numbered {3} also in B.

[303] Literally plural: *opseis*. On the term cf. Berryman 1998, 184-5; also Preus 1968, 177-8; Lindberg 1976, 217-18 n.39; Simon 1988, 49; Jones 1994, 60-71. The theory that vision by means of rays is by touch is attributed to Hipparchus by Aëtius 4.13.9. In MS V this argument is first in the sequence headed 'Why we do not see through rays'; MS B continues numbering from the previous argument with number {4}.

[304] 'Pupil' seems the required sense here; if the pupil contains several pores, the visual ray will be emitted separately through each one and so will not be a single continuous body. However, see below, 94 n.309. This argument is numbered (1) in MS B.

it is more rare than it?[305] Or if it is not scattered, how does it not contract [and become] narrow as it advances? For we see this happening to other bodies too as they proceed

30 forwards. Water when it proceeds forwards either runs away or narrows, as with that which flows from springs, although it is more solid than the rays; and a flame terminates in a sharp [point]. How then is the seeing body spread out into a cone, and greater the more it proceeds forwards, when this happens neither to denser nor to rarer bodies?[306]

[III] (4) Moreover, if it is body, it occupies place. So either

129,1 body passes through body[307] or there is a determinate void or mutual replacement occurs,[308] of air if the sending out is in air, of water if in water. Well, it is absurd to say that water is transferred by exchange into the jelly of the eye,[309] so we must enquire, into what. Not into [our] breathing; for the creatures that see in water do not breathe, nor do

5 water-[creatures] in general do so, apart from a few. [310]

[III] [5] Moreover, if it is transferred by exchange into the jelly of the eye, we will not send out [rays] from all of it, nor

---

[305] Cf. Alex., In De sensu 28,23-6. This argument is not numbered separately in B.

[306] Cf. Alex., In De sensu 29,8-12.

[307] Cf. Alex., Mixt. 3-9, with the discussion of Todd 1976, who notes (85 and n.245) that here and at 129,24-32 below the paradox, originating in polemic against the Stoics, is applied to a non-Stoic theory. See also below, §14.

[308] For mutual replacement as an alternative to body passing through body cf., with Todd 1976, 201, Alex., Mixt. 6 220,12 and In De sensu 29,12-30,1 (I am grateful to Inna Kupreeva for drawing my attention to Todd's discussion of this point.)

[309] At 128,25 above the sense seemed to require the translation of korê by 'pupil'; but in Aristotle and Alexander this word normally indicates rather the more or less fluid contents of the eye (below, 130 n.441). In the present passage (and at 129,6 below) either rendering seems possible.

[310] With this paragraph (numbered {2} in MS B) cf. Alex., In De sensu 29,12-21. Bruns includes in the comparison 29,21-30,1, which combines the issue of mutual replacement with the situation when several people look at the same thing. See also below, 98 n.325 .

see [with all of it], but there will be a space so that there will be room for what is being transferred by exchange inwards; so we will see in one part of [the jelly of the eye] and not in another.[311]

[III][6] Moreover, why will creatures that do not close their eyes in sleep not see, if they have the pores of the body[312] filled?

[III][7] If however this body from the jelly of the eye[313] does not go out continuously, but divided, then either 10 it coalesces and becomes continuous after it has been emitted, or else it remains divided. Well,[314] if it coalesces, how, when it coalesces, is it unfolded again into a cone, and [a cone] so large that the base of a[315] cone cuts off the greatest part of the sky? For it ought, when it has once begun to come together and coalesce, to be compressed and made narrow [even] more by the surrounding air. 15

---

[311] Numbered {3} in B. As Jones 1994, 47-76 points out, Philoponus, *In DA* 326,20-6 notes that if sight takes place by means of pores in our eyes continuous surfaces would be seen only in intermittent patches.

[312] I.e., of the jelly of the eye; or perhaps we should understand 'the pores/passages of the *pneuma*', in the sense of those that contain it. The argument (numbered {4} in B) is presumably that, if vision is by emission of *pneuma* from the eye, creatures without eyelids will see continuously because there is nothing to stop the emission. (I am grateful to Inna Kupreeva for this point.) The *De sensu* commentary has rather the argument (28,28-29,8; not found here) that, if the visual ray is very fine, we should be able to see even with our eyes closed.

[313] Literally, 'of the jelly of the eye'. This original reading of V was altered by Bessarion to 'this body does not go out continuously from the jelly of the eye', but was restored by Bruns. The parallels cited by Bruns, 'this body which constitutes the rays' at 127,29 and 'this flow of seeing' at 128,26, are not valid (neither says the external body is 'of' the eye-jelly): with some hesitation I have retained the original reading on the principle of *difficilior lectio potior*.

[314] MS B numbers {1} of a new sequence at this point.

[315] Translating the MSS *tinos*. But perhaps we should read *tou*, 'the base of the cone'.

[III][8] Moreover, if the cone is surrounded by rays which are divided and separated,[316] then, [i] if the [space] between the rays is greater [than that occupied by the rays themselves], what is not seen will be more than what is seen, and [ii] the circumference will be seen, where the straight lines[317] impact upon it, but the centre will not be. If it is equal, an equal area will not be seen. And how could the space [between] the straight [lines] be less [than that occupied by the rays themselves], when the straight [lines]
20   produce so large a base [of the cone]?

[IV]{1} Moreover, how can the rays be such dense bodies when they are sent forth from the jelly of the eye, a small body?[318]

---

[316] I.e., made up of such rays; the spokes of a closed umbrella without its covering, and with the tip at the eye, may provide a helpful analogy. This argument is numbered {2} in MS B.

[317] The rays making up the sides of the cone; so, if you look at a circular painting, you would see the frame but not the picture. It is not clear why there could not be rays within the cone as well as at its circumference, and indeed this is envisaged in the similar description at Galen, *Us. part.* 10.12, vol.2 p.96,14-22 Helmreich = vol. 3 817,9-17 Kühn (Lindberg 1976, 12-13). Point [i] is however independent of this, if we suppose that even a very large number of rays within the body of the cone will become further apart the further they proceed. A similar point is made by Ptolemy, *Optica* 2.50, noted by Lindberg 1976, 16. The power of our vision to resolve different parts of a distant object is indeed limited, and Berryman 1998, 183 rightly sees the ability of the ray theory to explain this as one of its strengths. The present paragraph clearly draws on the post-Aristotelian developments in philosophical discussions of vision prompted by Euclidean optics and documented by Lindberg and Berryman; characteristically for Alexander these developments are used in a polemical defence of the 'orthodox' Aristotelian theory of *DA* and *De Sensu*.

[318] V does not mark a paragraph break at the start of this argument at all: B starts a new numbering sequence. The reference of 'such' (*houtôs*) is not immediately clear. Bruns here compares Alex., *In De sensu* 28,23-8, where the point is that if the rays are so (*houtôs*) fine that they can be emitted from the eye without using it up, then they will be moved by the wind. This

[IV]{2} Moreover, why are the rays sent out not moved around by the winds or by moving water, but we always see in straight [lines] even when these [things] are [so], if the surface of the water remains in the same [place]?[319]

[IV]{3} Moreover, how do the rays pass through   25 transparent[320] solids? For if they should say that these have pores, then either they will have empty [pores] and there will be some determinate void, or else [they will be] full of air or some other body, and where will this withdraw to?[321]

[IV]{4} And how will several people see* through the same [transparent solid]? For several bodies will pass through the same pores.[322]

[IV]{5} Then, why are transparent things seen as continuous? For only their pores ought to be seen,[323] or their   30 surface should have interruptions, as [does that] of sieves. Similarly the things seen through them ought to be obscured where the transparent things do not have pores.[324]

[IV]{6} And from where does a body [come to be] in us so great that it can be sent out as far as the stars, this being in us before we see? How can this body move so quickly,   130,1 that as soon as we look up we see the sky?

[IV]{7} Moreover, how will those looking at each other

---

both states the argument of the present paragraph more clearly and combines it with that of the next paragraph. This may suggest that the present passage is derivative and that the awkwardness of *houtôs* is to be explained by this. Cf. above, 89, and Sharples 1998a, 396 n.67.

[319] Compare, with Bruns, below §10 134,9-10.

[320] *diaphanes.* See 6, 142.

[321] Above, 94 n.308. Cf., with Todd 1976, 85 n.246, below, §13 139,9-11, Alex., *Mixt.* 5 218,24-6, and Philoponus, *In DA* 344,7-8. Jones 1994, 66-7, raises similar difficulties for the theory of the visual ray implied in Theophrastus, *De vertigine* 6-9.

[322] No new paragraph for this argument in V, but a marginal number in B.

[323] One would rather have expected: only the solid part *between* the pores.

[324] Cf., with Todd 1976, 85 n.246, below §13 139,14-17, Alex., *Mixt.* 5 219,1-3, and Philoponus, *In DA* 326,20-6.

from opposite [directions] be seen, if the rays meet each
other in the same [place]?[325] For either they will come to a
stop in between and [the people] will not see each other, or
5   they will pass through each other and in this way again
body will go through body, or one will prevail and only one
person will see the other.

[IV]{8} Moreover everything that moves in place moves
in time, and it is impossible for something that moves
having the same speed across the same [interval] to move
twice as [far] in the same time.[326] But we see at the same
time things nearby and those [separated] from [us by] an
10   interval many times as great; at any rate, we see the stars,
which are a very great [distance] away, at the same time as
[we see] people standing next to us.[327] So seeing is not by
the movement of anything; and if it is not by movement, it is
not by the projection of rays [from our eyes], nor by the
streaming off of images [from the things seen], nor by
[movement] from both.[328]

130,13   [10.] Against those who explain seeing through the tension
of the air.[329]

The theory criticised here is that of the Stoics. This section does
not have any close parallels in Alexander's *De sensu* commentary:
the theory is post-Aristotelian, and Alexander does not choose to

[325] Bruns compares Alex., *In De sensu* 30,6-12, but the reference there is to several people looking at the same thing. The
parallel is rather to 30,18-21. Cf. also ibid. 30,12-18, of diagonally
intersecting lines of sight; 29,21-31, above 94 n.310; and below §15
147,16ff.

[326] Or, deleting *kata* (as suggested by Bruns in his apparatus,
by analogy with Alex., *In De sensu* 30,3), 'for the same thing that
moves at the same speed to move twice as far in the same time'.

[327] Or, taking *tois parestôsi* as neuter, 'the things next to us', a
suggestion I owe to Inna Kupreeva. Cf., with Bruns, Alex., *In De
sensu* 30,1-6, which refers to *ta ektos*.

[328] For the second and third possibilities see below, §§ 11 and
12. If this sentence is an original part of §9, it suggests that §§9, 11
and 12 may have been conceived as a unit.

[329] Literally: 'those who make seeing ...'.

introduce it into his discussion of Aristotle's text. Aëtius attributes
the theory to Chrysippus, but, oddly, does so not in his chapter on
vision but in that on the specific topic of whether darkness is
visible (for which see below, 149 n.505). Cf. Todd 1974.

In this section the primary MS V marks paragraphs but does
not number arguments. I have therefore reproduced the numbering in the secondary MS B, in {braces}.

There are some who say that seeing comes about 130,14
through the tension of the air. For the air which is in
contact with the pupil[330] is pierced by the sight and shaped
into a cone. When this is as it were stamped at its base by
the objects of sight perception comes about, as with contact
through a stick.[331]

Well, many of the same things can be said against these
too as have been said against those who explain seeing
through rays, but one might ask them individually about
this very tensioning of the air in contact with the pupil that   20
is brought about by sight, and about the stamping in the
other part by what is seen, and further about how the
pressure can be received when air is rare, especially as, if
anything like this were [the case], we would have awareness of some resistance [at the same time as seeing]. And,
when we move backwards, we see just as well; yet [on their
theory] we ought to see when pressing forwards, but not   25
when moving backwards. What pressure is there through
ourselves at that time? Or will they say that there is
pressure [at that time]?[332]

And if sight comes from the ruling principle [in the soul],
if the [effects] of tensioned motion apply to this too, as they

---

[330] See above, 94 n.309. Even if the intended reference is to
eye-jelly, the pupil is the point at which the contact will occur.

[331] Cf. Galen, *PHP* 7.5.41, 460,29-30 De Lacy; Diog. Laert. 7.157
= *SVF* 2.867; Plotinus, 4.5 [29] 4.40. Lindberg 1976, 10-11; De Lacy
1984, 679, and below 102 n.338. 130,14-17 and 130,26-131,5 = *SVF*
2.864.

[332] Supplying 'at that time' with Bruns: the implication being
that, if they do *not* say this, they will be left without an
explanation.

say, how do there not occur certain interruptions in seeing, since the tension does not apply continuously to the limits,[333] and for this very same reason neither does the
131,1 pressure? One might ask this about touch too, by which we touch other bodies; for neither in the case of this do interruptions in our apprehension occur, though there ought to be; for this is what the tensioned motion is like according to them. If it is just the *pneuma* which they call sight that is moved in the aforementioned motion, which they call tensioned, it is illogical to speak thus concerning this alone,[334] and yet they do not say [this].

In general, the theory of tensioned motion involves many difficulties.

{1} First of all something which is homogeneous will move itself, which is shown to be impossible by considering the individual motions.

{2} Next, if some one thing holds together the whole world at the same time as the things in it, and in each of the particular bodies there is something that holds it together, how is it not necessary for the same thing to move in opposite motions at the same time?[335] For when the motion of the penetrating *pneuma* is from the centre of the world towards its limits, then it is necessary for each of the particular bodies to be moved either away from the centre or towards the centre by the part of *pneuma* as a whole which passes through each. It makes no difference from

[333] Here and in the sequel the motion of Stoic *pneuma* seems to be interpreted as motion *alternately* in different directions, and hence as implying interruption, whereas in fact it was motion *simultaneously and continuously* inwards and outwards – as Alex., *Mixt.* 10 224,3ff. makes clear (= LS 47I; cf. Nemesius, *Nat. hom.* 2 18,2-10 Morani = LS 47J, and LS vol.1 p.288).

[334] Having constructed an objection to the claim that there are gaps in our vision, by appealing to the analogy with touch, Alexander now counters a possible attempt by his opponents to deny the analogy – before commenting that in fact they do not make this move. Von Arnim comments that one would rather expect 'if it is not just the *pneuma* ...'.

[335] 131,5-10 = *SVF* 2.448.

whichever direction we say it occurs. So, if this too is moved away from the centre – I mean, the *pneuma* in some one of   15
the particular bodies – the [*pneuma*] which passes through the parts of its constitution which are lower than its centre will move downwards and upwards at the same time. In so far as the whole of which this is a part [moves] upwards, [it will move] upwards, but in so far as what is lower than the centre moves from the centre of that in which it is towards the limits, it will clearly move downwards. So the same thing [will] at the same time [move] upwards and   20
downwards. But if it moves from the limits to the centre, the same will happen when the *pneuma* has passed through the parts of it which are above the centre.[336]

{3} But even if it were granted that seeing comes about in some way through pressure of the intervening air, still [it is] clear* that in this way apprehension occurs of hardness and softness and roughness and smoothness and liquidity[337] and dryness more than of colour. For we can recognise these   25
even through a stick, but not colours or shapes or how much or what size, and these are the things we see.[338] For colours and shapes and sizes are what we apprehend through sight. And in general sight will be a sort of touch. For things that can be touched fall under touch, so that either bodies will be visible *qua* bodies, or their accidental   30
affections [will be].

[336] If *pneuma* is moving inwards, that in the *lower* part of an individual thing, nearest the centre of the universe, will have to move simultaneously in opposite directions, towards the centre of the universe and towards the centre of the individual thing. But, apart from the questionable assumptions that the motions of *pneuma* relating to the whole universe and to individual things can be treated on the same level (cf. Todd 1974, 254-7), and that inwards motions in the two contexts will be synchronised, the very supposition that inward and outward motions alternate seems wrong; see the preceding note.

[337] Or 'moistness'; as in the case of soft mud which yields to the pressure of a stick more easily than does hard, dry earth.

[338] The same objection to the Stoic view at Galen, *PHP* 7.7.20, p.474,8-12 De Lacy.

{4} Moreover, why are things in the dark not seen from the light, but things in the light [are seen] from the dark?[339] To say that illuminated air, because it has been dispersed,[340] has more strength and can affect our perception by pressure, while what is unilluminated is slackened because* it cannot be tensioned by sight, even though[341] it is denser

35   than that which has been illuminated – how is this plausible? The opposite is reasonable, that what is denser can be tensioned more easily, especially as it is natural for this to happen to it, whenever things in the light are seen from the dark. But if what is in contact with the pupil, being unilluminated, is not of a nature to be tensioned, but only that which is illuminated, what difference does it make

132,1 whether the slackened part of the air is at this end or that, I mean adjacent to the one who sees or to what is seen? For it is reasonable that also when the [air] next to the pupil is unilluminated, and the illuminated [air] is next to the thing seen, the tension [which proceeds] from the sight should be undone again as it passes first through what is unillumi- nated and hard to move, and that, being undone, it should

5   no longer be able to tension the illuminated [air]* next to the thing seen. For [thus] things in the light should no more be seen by those in the darkness than vice versa.

{5} Moreover there are times when, two rooms being opposite [each other] and illuminated, but the air between the two rooms being dark, people see one another from the rooms none the less, although the air between is not

10   tensioned. How can this happen?

{6} Moreover, why do we not see the stars themselves in the day, but we do see them at night? For here we seem to be able to tension the dark and coalesced air as far as the

---

[339] For this problem in an Atomist context cf. Lucretius 4 337-52, and Sharples 2002b, 7-8.

[340] i.e. rarefied.

[341] I take it that 'even though' already reflects Alexander's own standpoint, developed in the next sentence, rather than that of his opponents. See also the Notes on the Text. I am grateful to Inna Kupreeva for extensive discussion of this passage. 131,30-5 = *SVF* 2.868.

stars, but what is dispersed and sunnier and for this reason has more strength, as they say, we cannot tension or press upon to so great a distance, but to a much shorter one. And yet, when the moon passes beneath the sun and produces a total eclipse of it, we become able to tension the coalesced and darkened air as far as the stars, though we were not able to do so before. And if we are in a shady wood or in a deep well we do the same. For the stars are visible to us from such places even by day.

{7} Moreover, when we see things in liquid, is the water too tensioned along with the air, or not? For if it is not tensioned along with it, seeing does not [come about] in this way. For things in water too, are seen. But if the water too is tensioned, it is much more reasonable that darkened air [should be]. For water is far denser than this. But if it is because it is *rare* that darkened air is not tensioned, illumi-nated [air], which is *much* rarer than water, [will] not be tensioned.

{8} Moreover, when we are in the water itself we sometimes see things at the bottom, even though no air is in contact with the pupil; so this too is false, to say that seeing comes about through the tension of the intervening *air*.

{9} Moreover, how is it possible for water [creatures] to see, since there is no air in the water? If they are going to say that there is air in these too, how is this not squeezed out[342] by the water, since its nature is to float upon it?

{10} Moreover, if they say that light, being a body, passes both through water and through other things, it is clear that, if light is shown not to be a body, the argument will be an empty one. For if it is because it is a body that pressure can occur in it, [then] if it is *not* a body, it is clear that it will not be pressed.

{11} Moreover, how does this light not coalesce through the coldness of the water and thus cease to be light, if it is by dispersal that it is light?

---

[342] Literally 'squeezed out like a pip'. Cf. Strato, fr.51 Wehrli. (I owe this reference to Inna Kupreeva.)

{12} Moreover, less light ought to occur in frosts, just as [there is also less] warmth. For that the *pneuma* should not coalesce when water coalesces and becomes ice is paradoxical, if light is dispersed air.[343] For it is paradoxical to say that, when the water coalesces and freezes, the air, which is more easily affected, does not coalesce. And we see flame being affected by frost. And against those who say that in snow some *pneuma* like light is trapped, and that this is the cause of its whiteness, we should say, how is this not made to coalesce by the cold?

{13} Moreover how is it that after bending, either from mirrors or from transparent things, the effect of the pressure is preserved? This is not possible with a stick; for all things that are bent are made ineffective for pressing, as maimed bodies are for their activities.

{14} Moreover, if we look into a deep and dark well, why do we not see the water, but do see our own reflection? For it is ridiculous to say that there is no pressure against the water, but that when what did not press against the water is bent [back] some pressure occurs after the bending with what has been bent. For it is like saying that, when a stick has been bent and doubled, the [part][344] at the bending causes no pressure perceptible to us, but that through the bending we can exert pressure with the other end.

{15} Moreover, if *pneuma* passes through all things, it is clear that it passes through walls too, just as through things that are transparent. So why do we tension the air in transparent things and see through them, but not tension that in things that are not transparent and not see through them? If they say that what is solid blocks the way, glass and horn and transparent stones are solid too. If they say that these are not solid, because they are easily broken, and that this

---

[343] 132,30-37 = *SVF* 2.432.

[344] Bruns *ad loc.* suggests understanding from the context, or adding to the Greek text, 'end' (*peras*). But although it makes sense in itself to speak of the break forming a new 'end' halfway along the stick, this makes the following reference to 'the other end' awkward, and it is better to leave the reference of *to kata tên klasin* vague.

is why we see through them, pottery is no less easily broken than these, so we ought to see through this too. What is it that blocks the way for such things, and why does air[345] pass through all things, while light, which is rarer than it, does not? For it ought to, and if that occurred the result would be that no shadow would occur anywhere, since light would pass through everything, like air.   25

[15a] And how do they say that air is stamped at the end when it strikes upon the things that are seen? For the most rare and most fluid of bodies cannot receive [an impression] marked upon them, like, on account of fluidity, water and fluid mud.[346]

{16} Moreover, even if it were granted that it is stamped and receives the impression, how can it receive anything else besides the shape? For no thing's colour is of a nature   30 as either to be marked on [anything] or to come to be present in the things that are stamped, so we ought not to see colour* but only shape. But perhaps not even shape. For as it is we recognise certain shapes through a stick, for example convex ones, because the stick slips round them, and concave ones, because it strikes their projections on each side, and straight things, because neither of these   35 [occurs]. But we would not recognise these through a stick, if it happened that the end of the stick were re-shaped when it touched any body, being as it were moulded round it, and this happens in the case of the air; so not even of shapes will apprehension occur in this way through it.

{17} Moreover, the stamping occurs at [one] end. So how do we see it at the other end? For neither in the case of   134,1 other things do stampings occur throughout. If they say that the air is transparent and that for this reason it is stamped throughout and that we see in this way, they will be saying that something else is the cause of seeing, that is

---

[345] i.e. *pneuma*, on the Stoic theory, rather than air in our ordinary experience.

[346] Following Bruns in deleting 'or air' from the MSS' 'water and mud or fluid air'; for the impossibility of stamping an impression on air is the conclusion of the argument by analogy, not a premiss.

the transparency, and not the pressing.

{18} Moreover it is remarkable how the things which are
5   most able to be stamped turn out not to be stamped deep
down, but in air, which is least like this, the stamping comes
to be present throughout.

{19} Moreover, if air is of a nature to be stamped like this,
why does the stamping not remain in it even when what
stamps it has departed, as in the case of other things, so
that we ought to see objects of sight even when they are no
longer present?

{20} Moreover, how are such stampings not confused –
10   [in] the same [way as happens] when water flows[347] – if
there is much *pneuma* in the air too?

{21} Moreover, some things that are seen [will] appear
the reverse of how they are, convex things as concave,
concave as convex, and in general what projects as recessed
and what is recessed conversely as projecting. For this is
how stamping occurs. If they say that what is convex is
judged by concavity in the base of the cone, and what is
15   concave by convexity, as also with touch by means of the
hands, [then] what happens in the case of painting will most
refute this. For although this is flat some parts appear to
project and others to be recessed, although they are judged
by the base of the cone which is flat.

{21a} Moreover, what will they say about the things
which are seen through reflection?[348] For in the case of
these the end of the cone is stamped by the surface of the
20   mirror, which may possibly be shaped in the opposite way
to what appears in [it], not in a similar way, but, for
example, when what appears in [the mirror] is convex or
straight, the mirror may be concave. It is remarkable, too,
that the stamping from [the mirror] does not block in
advance that which comes from what appears in [the
mirror], or prevent its shape from appearing in [it].

{22} Moreover the bending back and tensioning of the air

---

[347] Literally 'whenever water flows, the same thing'. I am grateful to Inna Kupreeva for discussion of this passage.
[348] MS B mistakenly repeats the number 21 for this paragraph.

from the mirror to the thing seen is problematic, as we have   25
said. For how, after the bending, is it possible for the pressing still to occur?

{23} Moreover, why do we not see the things that are
closest to the pupil? And yet we should; for the pressing is
over a short [distance] and the stamping is from close by.

[11]. Against those who say that seeing comes about   134,28
through the entry of images.

'Images' here translates *eidôla*, physical images emitted from the
objects of vision (and not images created by the perceiver's imagination). For the theory cf. Alex., *In Sens.* 31,19-29: above, 90.
Alexander returns to the topic in much fuller detail at *In Sens.*
56,10-58,22, in the context of the discussion of colour, and there
attributes the theory to the Atomists Leucippus and Democritus
and to Empedocles. Aëtius attributes the theory of vision through
images to Leucippus, Democritus and Epicurus (4.13.1) and also
says that Empedocles' view, while involving both rays (from the
eye) and effluences (from objects), falls more into the category of
explanation by means of images (4.13.4, in Stobaeus). See below,
114-15. Parallels between *In Sens.* and our text are noted by Bruns
and Wendland, and both our text and Alex., *In Sens.* 56,17-58,22
are analysed by Avotins 1980. Some of the parallels are verbally
much closer than in the case of §9.

In this section the primary MS V marks paragraphs but does
not number the arguments; I have therefore reproduced the
marginal numbering of MS B in {braces} as far as 135,5, after
which the numbering in B ceases, and thereafter I have supplied
my own numbering.

Text, English translation and commentary in Avotins 1980. On
this text cf. also Asmis 1984, 131-5.

Against those who say that seeing comes about through   134,30
images[349] first of all one might raise the difficulty, {1} how
each of the things that is seen is not swiftly used up when
so many [images] stream off from it. If they say that other

---

[349] The Epicureans, but probably the earlier Atomists too; see
below 113-14 n.381, and Avotins 1980, 430-1.

[particles] are added to them in exchange, then since the things that stream off and those that are added are not similar in shape to one another (for those that stream off are images and similar in shape, but those that are added are not added in this way), the things that underlie and are seen should not remain similar in shape, but have different sorts of shape at different times.[350]

{2} Moreover, when the streaming off [is] continuous and occurs everywhere and in every direction, how can the addition come about? For the things would hinder one another, those that are being separated off those that are being added, as the movement of both is continuous.[351]

{3} Moreover, how is it possible for apprehension of distance to occur, if it is the images that are seen?[352] For the air, which they say enters [us] first, is imperceptible, [though they say] that it is by its quantity that distance is measured. And what is it that measures this air?

{4} And how, moreover, is it that distant things too are seen as soon as we look up?[353]

[5] How is it possible for apprehension of shapes and magnitudes to occur through the images (this being what they want to preserve [when] they create the images), if the entry of [the images] into the eye occurs over a small [space]?[354] For the size of the pupil,[355] with which we see, is

35

135,1

5

---

[350] Cf. Alex., *In Sens.* 56,23-57,7.

[351] Cf. Alex., *In Sens.* 57,7-10.

[352] Cf. Alex., *In Sens.* 31,23-5, 57,11-12, and, with Wendland ad loc., Theophrastus, *Sens.* 36 509,20-21, 54 515,1 Diels; Baltussen 2002, 47-9.

[353] Cf. Alex., *In Sens.* 57,19-20.

[354] 'occurs a small section at a time', Avotins. See below, 109 n.356, 110 n.363, 114 n.382, and for the difficulty here raised against the atomic theory cf. Alex., *In Sens.* 32,25-7; Galen, *PHP* 7.7.8. Asmis 1984, 132 n.26 traces it back at least to Theophrastus, *Sens.* 36. Plotinus, 4.5 [29] 3.30-38, turns it against the Aristotelian theory that vision takes place by the affection of the intervening medium (for which cf. below, §15). Against the argument of Burkert 1977, 100 that Democritus already had an answer to this difficulty in terms of a contraction of the images, see Avotins 1980,

not greater than that of the image, which according to them   10
we receive into the pupil.[356] Even if someone conceded to
them that, because of the speed, different [images] are
received continuously, how [does it come about] that it will
get the next [part] of the image[357] and not often the same or
some other part, situated far from this, separated and then
put together?[358] How is it possible for the body of the thing
that is seen to be preserved? How for the proper size of   15
each thing? For it is possible for the [images] of other
things to be added to the first images and mixed with them
and not be seen each of them according to its own proper
outline, nor is there any sign that these are the images of
this thing and these not.[359]

[6] In general, what happens to the things that enter in
beforehand?[360] For to say that they are kept buried

443-4.

[355] See above, 94 n.310.

[356] One might rather expect: the image actually received cannot
be larger than the pupil. That our text states the opposite (if we do
not emend with Bruns to read *tou tês korês*; but then *to* would
also be required before *megethos*) can be explained either as an
example of polar error (for which cf. 118 n.395) or by supposing
that what is referred to is not the (partial) image that is actually
received (see below, 110 n.363) but the single image of the entire
object which cannot in fact be received; cf. Avotins 1980, 437 n.27.
'According to them' will then in effect mean 'if one explains vision
by means of images at all'. The point can be put more clearly by
substituting 'smaller' for 'not greater'.

[357] Cf. Avotins 1980, 437 n.29.

[358] Cf. Alex., *In Sens.* 58,1-5. Avotins' less literal translation
brings out the point: 'or a different part situated far from it yet
subsequently added on, misplaced though it be'. Cf. his 437 n.30.

[359] Cf. Alex., *In Sens.* 58,8-12; Avotins 1980, 434 n.19, 437 n.32.
Asmis 1984, 134-5 objects that Epicurus recognises that this may
happen; the combination of images with different origins is used
by him to explain such things as belief in Centaurs (cf. Epicurus,
ad Hdt. 48; Lucretius 4.129-42, 732-44).

[360] 'happens to' is Avotins' translation of *ginetai*: cf. LSJ s.v. II.1.

[within]^{361} and are put together in the eye is too much like a
20   fairy-tale. For where are they buried or do they remain,
what is it that enters in^{362} to build them up and put them
together?^{363} Or how, if each of them is positioned separately,
are continuity and size and shape apparent?

[7] How, if the images are so easily affected, do their
shape and convexity and concavity persist when they enter
the eye, without being confused?^{364} How does it receive
25   shaped images from smooth walls which do not have
convexities and concavities?^{365} How from mirrors or* water
shapes of the things* that appear in them, when they are
smooth?

[8] How, if what is in the mirror is an image, do so many
images again stream off from it, and why are the images in

---

^{361} Asmis 1984, 134 n.28 compares *katabussoumena* here with
enkatabussousthai attributed to Democritus at DK 68A77.

^{362} Avotins 1980, 437 n.34 notes that in both places where the
word *embadon* is cited by LSJ as an adverb, at Homer, *Iliad* 15.505
and Pausanias 10.20.8, it refers to wading, and suggests that the
usage here may be sarcastic (as it is in the Homeric passage).

^{363} This suggests that images of whole objects do not contract
to fit in the eye, but rather a picture of the whole is built up from
images of sections of the original received in a sort of scanning
process – an interpretation found also at Alex., *In Sens.* 58,1ff.,
and which Avotins argues may preserve genuine, and valuable,
information about the Atomists' theory. Cf. Asmis 1984, 128-37,
and 1999, 269 n.12. The question what assembles the images is
however a highly pertinent one; is it the mind, or the eye?

^{364} Cf. Alex., *In Sens.* 58,14-15: the verbal parallel is close, but
reference is made there only to convexity, not concavity, and for
'easily affected' the commentary has 'fine [*lepta*] and weak'.

^{365} Avotins 1980, 434 n.21, comparing Alex., *In Sens.* 58,12, well
argues that in this and the following sentence 'shape' refers
specifically to convexity and concavity; how can a two-dimensional
mirror transmit the appearance of a three-dimensional reflected
object? The smooth walls (presumably of polished stone) are
acting as mirrors: so Avotins 1980, 438 n.37, comparing Alex., *In
Meteor.* 141.34. Alex., *In Sens.* 58,12-13 is verbally parallel to
135,24-6, but omits 'walls' (referring only to 'smooth things'), and
'and concavities'.

mirrors denser, so that so much streaming off comes from them?[366] Why do these remain and not move? Why, since   30
they do remain, do they not also remain even for a short time when the person who sees them has gone away?[367]
Why are images not on the surface of mirrors, but in their depth?

[9] Why, if [the images] are so easily affected and moved, are they not swept aside, when a wind blows, with the air in which they are?[368] For to say that the other things which are carried along pass right through [the images][369] is not to preserve the continuity of the image, and in addition to   136,1
leave [the images] some solidity and resistance. For thus [the images][370] will remain, and the things that are carried

---

[366] Alexander is assuming that the images that travel to our eyes are emitted by an image which is stationary in the mirror, rather than, with Lucretius 4.98ff., that successive images travelling from the reflected object bounce off the mirror and into our eyes. Avotins 1980, 452-3 notes the conflict with Lucretius, and in general with references in Epicurus (*Ad Hdt.* 47, 49) and Lucretius to the speed of images, and regards the *Mant.* here as unreliable, though noting that something similar may be implied by Aëtius 4.14.2 (*DG* 405,10-15) and [Galen], *Hist. Philos.* 95 (*DG* 636,28-637,2). It may be added that the reflection's appearing behind the mirror is a problem only on the present theory, not on that in Lucretius.

[367] Cf. Alex., *In Sens.* 58,15-16. The reference there is to the thing seen rather than, as here, to the one who sees; as Avotins 1980, 438 n.39 rightly explains, the reference in the present passage must be to someone looking at his or her *own* image in a mirror.

[368] Cf. Alex., *In Sens.* 57,10-11, 57,25-7. Below, 113 n.380.

[369] Avotins 1980, 438 takes this to refer rather to the air and the wind, the images passing through them. But see the next note.

[370] Avotins loc. cit. again takes this to refer to the air and wind, 'the things that are carried along' referring to the images. But while this gives an easier transition to the next sentence, a certain degree of disjointedness is not unusual in these texts. It is more immediately obvious that the images are discontinuous if other things pass through them; and if 'some solidity and resistance' refers to the images it is easier to take 'will remain' to refer to

along will pass right through the empty [spaces]. But if [the images] are easily moved [because they are composed] of things like bark and like membranes,[371] as they say, and every impulse is sufficient to sweep them aside, people who look downwind[372] ought not to see.

[10] Moreover, if the images themselves are what enter in and are seen, why are the things that are seen clearly far away? For to say that the sight is stimulated by the images is to make seeing not [a matter] of images, but they need to look for another way in which sight, once stimulated, will see the object of vision and apply itself to it. For how is the image still the object of vision, if the image is useful only for preparing and awakening the actual sight?[373]

[11] To say that apprehension of distance comes about by the quantity of air between the [thing] seen, from which the images come, and the eye (for [the air] is pushed in front of it by the image and enters the pupil before the image) exceeds [all] absurdity.[374] For how is the image able to push

---

them as well.

[371] Or 'easily moved by things like bark and membranes', which is a more natural interpretation of the Greek. Cf. Lackenbacher 1910, 229; Avotins 1980, 438 n.40. For the terminology cf. Lucretius 4.31, 4.51, Plutarch, *Non posse suaviter* 1106a, Diogenes of Oenoanda 10.V.3 Smith 1993; Avotins, loc. cit., and Sedley 1998, 41 and n.18.

[372] So Avotins 1980, 438 and n.41.

[373] Cf. Alex., *In Sens.* 58,16-20; Avotins 1980, 435 n.25, Rosenmeyer 1999, 32 and n.25. Avotins 1980, 450-51 compares the notion of after-images in Lucretius 4.975ff. and Diogenes of Oenoanda 9.III.6-9.IV.2 Smith 1993, and notes that, whereas in those passages the entry of images prepares the way for subsequent images, here it is rather a matter of subsequent vision being explained by something other than images. The latter is however part of our author's objection to the atomist theory, not necessarily accurate reporting of that theory; Avotins 1980, 452. Císař 2001, 22 and 40-42, sees a connection with the idea that thought, and also sight, require active concentration on the images.

[374] Cf. Alex., *In Sens.* 57,21-58,1; Lucretius 4.250ff. The text in

in front [of it] the air in front of itself, if [the image] is so easily affected?[375] And how does the pupil admit this, and in addition will admit such an amount many times?[376] For it is not by the entering of one single image that seeing occurs.[377] So each of the [images] that enter in will send such an amount of air into the pupil before itself, unless indeed the images that travel from the [thing] seen do not travel[378] when somebody looks, but [are already] adjacent to   20 the eye. For it is not the case that, when the eye sees, [only] then do the images stream off. So how, if they are [already] adjacent, will they still push in front [of themselves] the air in between?[379] Moreover, if the images are not scattered by the winds because they are below [the level of][380] and finer and rarer in nature than the air which is carried by the winds, how at the same time will it be possible [for them] to push this air in front [of themselves]?

[12] Moreover, if the images are colourless and sight   25 receives them like this, how does it apprehend colours?[381]

---

fact has not 'exceeds all absurdity' but 'exceeds no absurdity'; a logical slip rather than an error in transmission of the text. Cf. Avotins 1980, 439 n.42, and for similar examples in the texts attributed to Alexander cf. below, 118 n.395, and Sharples 1994a, 123 n.134.

[375] Alex., *In Sens.* 57,25-6.

[376] Or 'receive many times [*pollakis*] such an amount': so Avotins 1980, 439.

[377] Cf., with Avotins 1980, 445 and Rosenmeyer 1999, 26 n.6, Lucretius 4.89, 105, 256-8; Alex., *In Sens.* 57,23-5.

[378] Cf. Avotins 1980, 439 n.44.

[379] Cf. Alex., *In Sens.* 57,18-19.

[380] sc. in size or visibility. Cf. Avotins 1980, 439 n.46; Lucretius 3.273-4, 284. For the argument cf. Alex., *In Sens.* 57,27-58,1.

[381] This objection occurs only in *Mant.* and not in Alexander's commentary on the *De Sensu*. Epicurus held that individual atoms were colourless but produced the sensation of colour by their combination – as Alex., *Quaest.* 1.13 indeed points out. But Epicurus, as Avotins 1980, 453 notes, did not hold that *images* were colourless (*Ad Hdt.* 49). Avotins therefore interprets this part, and perhaps more, of *Mant.* §11 as directed primarily against

How shapes, when it receives them over a very small [area]?[382] So sight would not be either of colours or of shapes, if one examines [the matter] accurately and does not grant them, everything they ask for. Then what will sight be of?

136,29   [12]. Against those who say that seeing [comes about] through streamings off[383] from both [the one seeing and the thing seen].

This was the view of Democritus, according to Theophrastus, *Sens.* 50.[384] There is however no mention of such a theory at Alexander, *In Sens.* 56,12, where Leucippus and Democritus are simply said to explain vision by images travelling from the thing seen to the eye.[385] The presence of §12 is therefore no objection to the interpretation of §11 as referring to Democritus - though if the texts are both by the same author the question remains to whom, if anyone, he thought the theory attacked in §12 belonged.

As at the close of §11, so here too the images are described as colourless (137,30-1). The reference to images shows that the reference cannot be to Plato's theory in the *Timaeus*, which involves interaction of effluence from the eyes and from objects seen (46ab, 67d); moreover the arguments here are different from those directed against Plato's theory at Alex., *In Sens.* 32,1-33,25.

---

the earlier atomism of Democritus; as he says, the denial that the images themselves have colour suits Democritus' treatment of sensations as subjective (cf. KRS pp.409-13).

[382] Cf. above, 108 n.354.

[383] I.e. effluences. See Introduction, 6.

[384] The reading of the Theophrastean text as implying a combination of the two effluences at a distance from the eye has been challenged by Baldes 1975, who argues that it is in fact referring to a process taking place close to the eye, and that in speaking of what is seen Theophrastus is referring not to the distant object but to the atomic image of it that arrives at the eye and is actually seen. I am grateful to Pamela Huby for this reference. Cf. also Burkert 1977.

[385] Burkert 1977, 105-6 argues that this is because Alexander is dependent on Hellenistic sources, Democritus' theory, rendered obsolete by developments in geometrical optics, having been long forgotten.

A theory combining rays emitted by the one seeing and images emitted by the objects seen is mentioned at Aëtius 4.13.5. The text of pseudo-Plutarch's *Epitome* there attributes it to Empedocles; that of Stobaeus on the other hand attributes it to Hestiaeus of Perinthus (no.7 in *RE* 8.2 [1913] col. 1314), having already discussed Empedocles' theory in 4.13.4 and concluded that it falls rather in the category of explanation by means of images. Diels (1879, 64) supposed that pseudo-Plutarch had conflated the two entries which Stobaeus presents as separate.

[1] Against those who say that seeing comes about from   136,30
both, a streaming off coming about both from sight and
from the things seen, and that apprehension by sight comes
about by the mixture of these – for some light is sent out
from our sight, and is mixed with what streams off from the
thing seen, which has the form of the thing seen, and,   137,1
taking up and imprinting on itself[386] the form from that
thing, reports it to our perception – well, against these one
must say first that, if it is absurd for some body to be sent
out from each individually, either from the sight or from the
thing seen, it is clear that it is also absurd to make the
streaming off come from both of them. For the absurdities   5
which [are encountered by] each of those will be encountered by these too: that the apprehension of things seen
nearby and things seen from a long way off must occur at a
different time,[387] and that both the things that see and those
that are seen will be used up and diminished in this activity,
each of them, when so great a streaming off comes about
from them.[388]

[2] One must also define up to what point what is sent out   10
travels before being mixed with what streams off from the
thing which is seen. Whatever proportion they make it, it
must [take] more time to see things a long way away than
those nearby, because what is sent out from us moves over

---

[386] *anamassomenon* in the middle voice. I am grateful to Inna Kupreeva for this explanation of the passage.

[387] Above, 130,6ff., 135,5f.

[388] Above, 134,30ff.

a greater [distance][389] when applied to the former, and
movement over a greater [distance][390] takes a greater
15 time.[391] For that what streams off should reach the sight
more quickly is not sufficient for what is sent out from the
sight not to be poured forth further in the case of* things
seen from a long way off. For in the case of things seen
nearby, if what is more striking is placed nearer, for
example fire, and what is not similarly striking further away,
for example a human being (for the colour of the latter is
less striking), for example the one a single cubit away, the
20 other two or four cubits, and then we look up [at them], we
see them at the same time, and not the striking one more
swiftly, even though it is positioned nearer. So whether a
thing is striking or not makes no contribution to the
distance travelled forth from the sight being less or greater.

[3] Moreover, if each of the things sent out travels in a
straight line, what is the need for a sending out from both?
25 That* from what is seen could have reached the sight, or
that from the sight what is seen.

[4] Moreover, what is the imprinting of the form, and how
does stamping come about of what is sent out from the
sight by what streams off from what is seen, rather than
alteration? This too needs to be defined.

[5] Moreover, of what sort is what travels from the thing
seen? For if it has both shape and colour similar to that from
30 which it travels, it will be nothing other than an image, or
rather something more than an image. For they say that
[images] do not have colour. If it has colour but not shape,
[they] ought to have said how the apprehension of shapes
comes about. If it has shape but not colour, sight will no
longer apprehend colours.

[6] And in what way, moreover, after what is sent out from
the sight has been affected, does it inform the sight [of this]?
35 [7] Moreover, if what is sent out from the sight is light, it
is clear that it is visible. So why, when we look up in the

[389] Literally, 'moves more movement'.
[390] Literally, 'more movement'.
[391] See above, 98.

darkness, do we not see one another's [emitted light]?[392]
For as in darkened rooms, if light enters even through a
tiny opening, it becomes visible and is at once seen, so too   138,1
what travels out from the eyes should be seen, whenever
we look up in the dark.

[8] Moreover, according to these people too light will be a
body.[393]

[13]. That light is not a body.   138,3

This rejection of the theory that light is a body forms part of the
general rejection of Stoic corporealist theories in the *Mantissa*: cf.
§§3,6,14, and below 121-2 n.406; Todd 1976, 82 and 84-5. The point
that light is not a body is indeed already made, as Todd 1976, 82
notes, by Aristotle, *DA* 2.7 418b14; and it is also made in Alexander's discussion of vision in his own *DA*, 43,11 – a fact which may
be significant for the inclusion of the present section in the
Mantissa.

If light is a body, it is either fire or a streaming off from   5
fire, which they call radiance and a third form of fire.[394]

[I] {1} Well, it will not be fire. For light can be more or
less, but fire is not more or less [fire]. So light is not fire.
Or, even if there could be [fire that was] more fire, it would
also be more light, if indeed fire and light are the same
thing. But it is agreed that flame is more fire than light is,
and it is not more light.

{2} Moreover, fire heats and burns, but light [does] neither.

{3} Moreover there is light also in water, but fire cannot be   10
in water, and {4} there is light in ice, but it is impossible for
fire [to be there], if indeed ice [consists] in excess of cold.

---

[392] Cf. §9 128,10.

[393] This sentence may have been added by an editor to form a
connection with §13. 138,2 (and 4-5 below) = *SVF* 2.432.

[394] The primary MS V does not number arguments in this
section, only marking paragraphs. I have therefore reproduced
the numbering of the later MS B in {braces}. B gives three
sequences of numbers, thus dividing the whole into three main
sections: I have supplied numbers for these in square brackets.

{5} Moreover if light is fire, movement downwards from above is contrary to nature for it and forced. But we see light travelling equally[395] naturally upwards from below and downwards from above.

[II] But if someone says that it is a streaming off from
15   fire, {1} how does light also come about not from fire? For many things give light which are not like this, such as the glow-worm.[396]

{2} Moreover, if it is a streaming off, why does it not remain even for a short time when the things from which it streams off are removed? For in the case of things from which there are streamings off, what has streamed off remains for some time even when they have gone away. If it is so easily destroyed as not to remain at all, but needs
20   some continuous supply in order to exist, why are things that give light not swiftly consumed when so great a streaming off occurs from them? For how great is the addition from nourishment? And how are [precious] stones, which give light but do not feed themselves, not consumed? How much supply and nourishment do glow-worms need?

[III] In general, if light is a body, it is clear that it will occupy a place and be somewhere. {1} What then is the
25   place of light? Either that of light and of transparent things will be the same, and either the latter will not be bodies or body will pass through body and two bodies will occupy the same place; or, if these things are absurd, light will not be a body. For it is ridiculous to say that transparent stone or glass is not a body, but to say that light [is].[397]

{2} Moreover, will they say that darkness too is itself a

---

[395] The text actually has 'we see light travelling no less naturally upwards from below than downwards from above', where one might have expected 'no more'; for this sort of polar error where two things are being rhetorically compared (hence my translation 'equally') cf. Alex., *Fat.* 9 175.17 and *Quaest.* 2.23 72,19-20; Sharples 1983, 242; 1994a, 123 n.134; above 112 n.374. Nor are such errors peculiar to Alexander or even to ancient Greek: see Gowers 1973, 231-2.

[396] Cf. above, §9 128,6.

[397] See above, §9 129,25.

body, or that it is incorporeal? But that we speak of body   30
when we speak of a shadow is absurd; if however
[darkness] is incorporeal it is reasonable to say that light
too is incorporeal, being the opposite to darkness.

{3} Moreover, if darkness is body, does it remain and
admit light, or does it withdraw before it? If it remains,
there will be not only two bodies in the same* [place], but
three, air and darkness and light. If it withdraws, where
does it withdraw to? Or is it clear that it is to the place from   35
which light enters? Then there will be darkness in the sun
and the stars and in fire. But this is altogether absurd.

{4} Moreover if darkness, being a body, remains and
admits light, [one] opposite will admit the [other]; and this
is impossible. For if someone says that what underlies is
altered, neither light nor darkness will be body.[398]   139,1

{5} Moreover if darkness is body, the air, in which light
comes to be, will either as a body admit light throughout,
and thus body will pass through body, or it will have pores,
through which the light will pass. These will either be full of
some other body when there is no light – what will they say
this is, or where will it be removed to? For it will need to be   5
rarer than air, and also than light itself, if it retreats before
this and is removed. But what body will according to them
be rarer than light? If they say that this is fire, [the air] will
be full of fire, which is most absurd, if it is [characteristic] of
fire to give light and to give heat, neither of which is
[present] in darkness. – But if the pores of the air remain
empty when there is darkness, first there will be some   10
actual void in the world according to them, which they do
not want,[399] and moreover the air will be rarer at night, since
it will have voids in itself – whereas it seems [in fact] to
become denser then – and moreover light will not disperse

---

[398] Because alteration is the replacement of one *quality* by
another in what underlies, and qualities are not bodies.

[399] This explicit reference to Stoic views (*SVF* 1.95-96, 2.424,
433, 502, 522-4, 528) is noted by Todd 1976, 84 n.243. See also,
with Todd 1976, 85 n.246, §9 129,9-11 above; and below, §14
139,33-4.

and rarefy the air, as they say, but the opposite.[400]

[5a] Moreover how will light be even[ly distributed] in
15 the air, when only the pores possess it, if where there is
light there is illumination (and this will be the pores), but
where there is air or some other of the transparent bodies,
there is not illumination?[401]

{6} Moreover if light is a body, how, when it enters from
some source of illumination through a small opening into a
room where there is darkness, if the opening is cut off
completely [the light] does not remain, although it has no
other exit?

{7} Moreover if light is a body, how is it able at the same
20 time to illuminate both what is distant and what is nearby,
[when] these can be illuminated from the same distance?
For the things that are further away should [take] more
time to be illuminated, since the movement in place of every
body [takes] time. That light comes to be at the same time
over the nearest and over the furthest interval that is able to
be illuminated, when what illuminates remains in the same
[place], is clear.

25 {8} Moreover if light, being a body, is [present] in the
pores of air or of water, how, when the water flows or the
wind changes direction, is it too itself not carried along and
moved with it, but always remains in the same [place]
though the things in which it is do not remain?[402]

139,29 **[14]. That it is impossible for body to extend through body.**

The problem of body extending through body, or two bodies
occupying the same place, was mentioned both at §9 128,34, 130,5
and at §13 138,25. However, the present text is not for the most
part concerned with the specific issues of light or vision (the
former is mentioned at 141,2-4, but only in passing), and it looks
very much as if an originally independent discussion has been
inserted into the sequence on vision in order to take up the

---

[400] 139.1-7 and 9-14 = *SVF* 2.432.

[401] See, with Todd 1976, 85 n.246, §9 129,29-32 above, and 97
n.324.

[402] Compare §10 129,21 above.

reference in §13. The selection and arrangement of material in relation to a particular theme can be parallelled by the inclusion of *Quaest.* 2.7 in the anthology of texts on the soul in MS Florence, Riccard. gr. 63 (cf. Sharples 1994a, 89), by the MSS which select texts on determinism from the *Quaestiones* and *Mantissa*[403] or which include certain of the *Ethical Problems* within the composite commentary on the *Nicomachean Ethics* (*CAG* 20),[404] or indeed by the inclusion of sections of the *Mantissa* in the editions of Alex., *Fat.* by Orelli 1824 and Sharples 1983.

The objections to body extending through body here are in their general approach similar to, but in detail different from, those in Alex., *Mixt.* 5-6; cf. Todd 1976, 77 n.217. There are also parallels between the present discussion and Alexander ap. Simplicius, *In Phys.* 530,16ff., on the basis of which Todd (loc. cit.) suggests that the present passage is 'an abstract' of Alexander's commentary, now lost, on Aristotle, *Phys.* 4.1 209a4-7. Cf. also Alex., *Quaest.* 2.12 and notes in Sharples 1992, 110-12; [Galen], *Qual.* (above 76 n.240); Todd 1976, 82-3.

With regard to body extending through body: if it is   139,30
because bodies contain voids[405] and it is through these that one [body] passes through the other, that is a different argument – it involves absurdities, and at the same time [what] comes about is not body extending through body, but body through void. But [suppose] it is not through voids (for those who hold this view say that there is not even any void in actuality within the world),[406] but [rather] some body

---

[403] Berlin, DSB, Phillipps 1558 (gr. 260), 25r-32v; Copenhagen, KB, Fabricius 88 57r-64r; Leiden, Univ., Scaliger gr. 51, 1r-105v; Madrid, cod. reg. 109 25ff.; Milan, Ambros. gr. F88 sup (V416/348), 1r-20v; Paris, BN, ancien gr. 1739, 272r-279r; Paris, BN, ancien gr. 1996, 5r-16r; Paris, BN, ancien gr. 2544, 104r-114v.

[404] Berlin, access. 1889, 304; Florence, Laurentianus gr. 85.1, 376v; Modena, MS gr. Alpha V.6.4 (II.G.4/gr.197), 209v-211r; Vatican, Barb. gr. 223, 215v-217v; Vatican, Vat. gr. 269 (187), 184r-185r; Vatican, Vat. gr. 1622, 213v-215v.

[405] Cf. Alex., *Mixt.* 5 218,24-219,9, on mixture by means of pores, and for an explicit reference to pores in the present discussion cf. 140,8-10 below.

[406] Cf. Alex. ap. Simplic., *In Phys.* 530,22, with Todd 1976, 77 n.217. The Stoics held that there was void outside the universe

35   which is full of itself admits in itself another body,* that too similarly being full, but is not at all increased, rather remains in the same place. Why then will one particular body admit another in itself, but another not,[407] if [one type of body] will admit the [other] body and be extended

140,1   equally with it[408] and made equal to it, for example fire, but water will not admit [it]? For it is not because fire is less dense[409] than water that the former will remain and admit more substance, while water, being denser, will not. For the rarest body and the densest are equally full, if there is no place for empty body.[410]

---

but none within it (cf. *SVF* 2.535-46). The view that body can extend through body, or that there can be two bodies in the same place, is attributed to the Stoics; Todd 1976, 73-88 argues that developments of the theme in fact reflect Peripatetic discussion developing passages in Aristotle (*Phys.* 4.7 214b5-9, *GC* 1.5 321a6-9) and have little directly to do with the Stoics. See also below, 123-4 nn. 411-12, 415.

[407] 139,30-31, 33-7 = *SVF* 2.477.

[408] On the view under attack, when (for example) wine is mixed with water, both are present in every part of the mixture, so that the volume of one is extended to equal the volume of the other, both being equal to the volume of the mixture as a whole. (Cf. Todd 1976, 32-3 and 51.) It may seem odd that this passage refers to fire admitting (e.g.) iron into itself rather than vice versa, but cf. argument {4} below. For the example of fire blending with iron (notably when it is red-hot) cf. *SVF* 2.471 (Arius Didymus; Todd 1976, 54) and Alex., *Mixt.* 4 218,1-2 ; but for Alexander's own analysis of such cases in terms of the iron being matter for the fire cf. *Mixt.* 6 220,8-9, 9 222,35- 223,6, 12 227,10-228,4 and *Mant.* §5 120,17-33; Todd 1976, 210-11 and 228. The phenomenon could be seen as calling into question whether fire is a body in the relevant sense at all (cf. Theophrastus, *De Igne* 3).

[409] Literally: 'more rare'. The translation above has the disadvantage of obscuring the characteristic ancient Greek expression in terms of two polar opposites rather than of varying degrees of a single property; but it makes the overall argument easier to follow for a modern reader.

[410] Or (less naturally from the Greek) 'no place for what is

{2} Further, if copper is denser than water, how is it that 5
copper mixes with gold, while water does not?[411] And tin
with copper, but oil not? And copper mixes with lead, while
wax does not? For as far as the argument is concerned,
either everything ought to mix with everything,[412] or the
latter more than the former, or – as is reasonable – nothing
with anything. For if they make pores responsible, no
longer is all extended equally to all, but there will be juxtaposition, and in this way they will be saying the void [is] the
cause.   10

{3} Further, if wholes are extended equally with wholes,
and the smallest things with the largest right up to their
extreme surface, then the place that is occupied by one
thing will be occupied by the combination of both.[413] For it
is reasonable for the parts of the whole, as long as they are
in the whole, not being circumscribed by limits of their
own, not to be in place in themselves; but each of the things
that are mixed is circumscribed by[414] limits in a similar way
to the whole [composed] of them both, if they have passed 15
through each other as wholes. For each of them will occupy
the whole place which the other one occupied before the
mixing and [which] the combination [occupies] after the
mixing. For what has been mixed in too, becoming equal to

---

empty of body'. One might rather have expected 'no place in body
for what is empty'. Does Alexander's expression contain a joke –
there is no place for what is empty, whereas usually what is empty
is what provides a place for body?

[411] The same example is used by Alex. ap. Simplic., *In Phys.*
530,25-6, as noted by Todd 1976, 77 n.217. – The primary MS V
does not number the arguments in this section, only marking
paragraphs: I have therefore reproduced the numbering in the
later MS B in {braces}.

[412] Cf., with Todd 1976, 77 n.217, Alex. ap Simplic., *In Phys.*
530,16-19.

[413] 140,10-12, 20-30, 31-33 = *SVF* 2.477.

[414] Bruns suggests deleting *hupo* here, comparing 140,12
above; but it helps to clarify that the sense of this dative is different from that of 'the whole', and the usage is one found in late
classical Greek (cf. LSJ s.v., B.4 ad fin.).

the other [constituent] itself, must necessarily occupy a
place [that is] the same and equal to that [other]. So there
will be several bodies in the same place, and each of them
20 will occupy the whole place.[415] But if things which [occupy]
equal place are also themselves equal, then (i) the things of
which the combination [is composed] will be equal to one
another, and (ii) the compound [will be equal] to each of
them. So the measure[416] of wine poured out into the sea will
be equal to the sea, and the sea along with the measure will
be equal to the measure alone. For to say that it is not equal
in power is irrelevant to the argument; it is sufficient, for
25 showing the point at issue, that they are equal in quantity.

{4} Further, the iron passes through the fire as much as
the fire through the iron; for the soul, too, [passes] through
the body, and nature through plants, and 'condition'
through the other bodies,[417] and conversely the latter
through the former.[418] For being more or less dense does
30 not contribute anything to this, if both alike are full. But if
this too should be conceded, then, in the case of wine and
water, which will pass through the other?[419]

[415] Cf., with Todd 1976, 77 n.217, Alex. ap. Simpl., *In Phys.*
530,26-30.

[416] *kuathos*: literally 'ladle', but also a liquid measure,
one-twelfth of a (UK) pint, or 5 centilitres (two standard modern
spirit measures). For the example of wine and water cf. Diogenes
Laertius 7.151 (*SVF* 2.479), Plutarch, *Comm. not.* 37 1078e (*SVF*
2.480), Alex., *Mixt.* 4 217,26-32, 6 220,13ff. Todd 1976, 31ff., 39,
and 87 n.253 (giving further parallels).

[417] This is a Stoic classification; the divine active principle
appears, in the form of *pneuma*, as soul in living creatures,
'nature' in plants, and 'condition' or 'state' (*hexis*) in other bodies.
Cf. Alex., *Mixt.* 4 217,32-218,1; *SVF* 2.458-60 and 1013, also 2.714
and 2.988. For Alexander himself, on the other hand, plants have
soul and not just nature: see above, 21 n.38, 57 n.162. – Literally
the text has 'the fire does not pass through the iron any more than
the iron through the fire.'

[418] Alexander uses the argument that two bodies cannot be in the
same place to prove the incorporeality of soul in his *DA* (20,6ff.); cf.
also *Mant.* §3 116.1-2 and *Mixt.* 6 220,7-8. Todd 1976, 198.

[419] The argument seems to suppose, wrongly, that wine and

{5} Further, what reason is there on account of which the bulk resulting from certain things when they are mixed is greater, while from others it remains the same? For to say that iron has become denser by the mixture of fire [with it][420] is paradoxical; things that become denser undergo compression, but [the effect] of fire on iron is to expand it.[421] Further, it is clear that [iron] is made less dense[422] by fire; for when it has been heated it can be forged, whereas previously it could not.

{6} Further, if what is liquefied by something is made less dense,*[423] and things that can be liquefied are liquefied by fire, fire will not make things denser. It will follow that one should say that charcoal too is denser than wood, and also illuminated air than that which is not; and yet [air] illuminated by the sun seems to be less dense[424] than that which is not.

{7} Further, if someone were to place many torches or light [many] lamps in a small room, the air would become denser, being blackened [by the smoke], and as many bodies as there were sources of light would at the same time pass through one another and occupy an equal place; but these things are absurd.

{8} Further, if the soul and the body together with [the soul] occupy an equal place, and when [the soul] has been separated [the place] occupied by the body is no smaller, what will be the place [occupied by] the soul? For either there will be [some] void which it will occupy, or of necessity there will be some other body of a living creature into which it will migrate; and in this way soul will never be

35

141,1

5

---

water are of equal density.

[420] The suggestion being that, if iron plus fire occupies the same space as iron alone, the mixture must be denser as there is more in the same space than with iron alone.

[421] The translations 'compression' and 'expand' are the suggestion of Richard Sorabji.

[422] Literally 'made rare'. See above, 122 n.409.

[423] Literally 'made rare'.

[424] Literally 'more rare'.

outside a body and a living creature.[425] And the same argument [will] also apply to the fire that is in the iron.

10 {9} Further, whenever a measure of wine is mixed with two measures of water,[426] the whole blend and mixture becomes three measures. But how is this possible on their [theory]? For if the measure of wine passes through all the water and is made equal to it, then either the whole will be four measures (for the wine has become equal to the water in quantity, so that [it is] two measures; for it will certainly not, when it has been made equal to two measures, still be one measure; for it is impossible for double to be equal to

15 half).[427] Or, conversely, the water will be equal to the wine and will be [one] measure; and in this way, conversely, the mixture will be two measures. For to say that the wine is extended and the water contracts and that thus [they] arrive at the mean, the water losing half a measure and the wine gaining this amount in addition, is an excessively absurd thing to ask. And the drop[428] mixed with the sea will

20 itself be equal in quantity to all the sea, or all the sea to the drop; for it is not otherwise possible for them to be made equal and mixed with one another according to their [theory].[429]

[425] Which is a claim that Alexander and other Peripatetics would themselves accept, while denying that soul can pass from one living creature to another. However, the Stoics allowed a limited survival of the soul after death: *SVF* 2.809-17, 821-2. – As an alternative to 'of a living creature' above Alan Lacey suggests 'than a living creature'.

[426] 'measure' = *kotulê*: approximately half a (UK) pint (one quarter of a litre).

[427] We might expect 'double to be equal to single' or 'the half to the whole'; but it is characteristic of Greek idiom to express the matter relatively, as here.

[428] In the similar statement attributed to Chrysippus in *SVF* 2.480 (Plutarch, *Comm. not.* 37 1078e) the drop is one of wine. At 141,22 below what is mixed with the sea is a drop of water; whether we are to suppose this already here is uncertain.

[429] Literally just 'according to them' (the upholders of the theory). Todd 1976, 87 n.251 compares the objections here with arguments at Plutarch, *Comm. not.* 37 1078ab and 1078ef (above, 124 n.416 and

{10} Further, how does the drop of water that is extended throughout the sea, being rarefied to such an extent, still remain water? For being dispersed and extended to such an extent it would sooner have become fire. For a dispersal much less than this produces air from water and fire from air.   25

{11} Further, as it is absurd to produce a magnitude from things without magnitude, so it is also absurd to produce no magnitude from [things with] magnitude; and this follows for those who make two bodies [be] in the same place. For [although] they are magnitudes they will not at all increase [the total magnitude].

[15]. How seeing comes about according to Aristotle.   141,29

This section begins with an account of colour as the effect of visible objects on the actually transparent; air or water must first be made actually, rather than potentially, transparent by illumination, and can then be affected by colour (cf. Alex., *DA* 42,19; Schroeder 1981, 217). Illumination and colouring, and the casting of shadows too, are not alterations but relations; illuminating and ceasing to be illuminated depend on the presence or absence of the light source just as being or not being on the right may depend on the movement of the person on the left (143,4ff., 144,29ff.). In other words, becoming illuminated is what we would now call a Cambridge change. This is Alexander's consistent doctrine (*In Sens.* 31,11-18, 42,26-43,1, 133,24, 134,11; *DA* 43.10)[430] connected, as here, with the instantaneous nature of illumination and vision. The doctrine also explains how the divine ether is not affected, though we see the stars through it, and how the moon is not affected through being illuminated by the sun (below 144,29ff.). For Alexander's general position on instantaneous change see further Sharples 1998b, 78-9 and references there: Heinaman 1998, especially 253.[431] For the intervening medium not

---

126 n.428), and also at Sextus, *PH* 3.60-61 and *M.* 9.261.

[430] Cf. Christensen De Groot 1983, 181; Schroeder 1981, 217; Accattino 1992, 54-56. I am grateful to Alan Towey for emphasising to me the importance of this point.

[431] The commentary of Abū l-Farağ on the *Physics*, based on a lost section of Philoponus, *In Phys.*, appears to attribute to Alexander the treatment of illumination as like the freezing of water part

becoming coloured cf. Alex. ap. Themistius, *In Cael.* 110.20ff., with the discussion of Rescigno 1999, 220-1.

The latter part of §15 is concerned with how sight judges various properties; convexity and concavity by shading, size by the angle subtended (so that a cone is involved, but not a physical cone of rays emitted from the eye). Alexander is aware that objects seem to move faster when we have a background to compare them with (147,10ff.), which is the reason, though he does not himself give the example, why we can see the setting sun moving, but not the sun high in the sky. His explanation of the apprehension of distance by habituation to the varying intensity with which things at different distances affect us (146.30ff., comparing the loudness of sounds) seems less satisfactory. Galen, *PHP* 7.7.4-5 objects that Aristotle's account of vision does not explain how we are aware of the position, size or distance of objects; De Lacy 1984, 681 notes that our present text discusses these issues, and there is presumably a connection between the two texts, whether or not we should think of our present text as responding directly to Galen.[432] The emphasis on the claim, essential for remedying the deficiencies in the Aristotelian theory, that illumination, coloration and vision take place in straight lines (145,19, 146,23,27, 147,23) – for we cannot in the Aristotelian theory say that light *travels* in straight lines – is noteworthy. See above, 96 n.317.

There is an Arabic translation of this section, no.13 in Dietrich 1964, edited with German translation by Gätje 1971, 140-174; cf. also 71 and id. 1966, 267-70, 272-3. Sorabji 1991, 249 translates 142,21-143,2. See also Accattino 1992, 55; Accattino and Donini 1996, 181; Rescigno 2000, 218-19.

141,30   Aristotle thinks that, just as the other senses come about when the sense-organs are affected, so seeing too comes

---

by part (682,1-7 Badawī 1964-65; Lettinck 1994, 460; Giannakis 1996, 168/177 no.15), but may not in fact intend the attribution to Alexander to extend to the case of illumination. Cf. Sharples 1998b, 79 n.198. (I am grateful to Elias Giannakis for correspondence on this point.)

[432] On Alexander's reactions to Galen cf. Sharples 1987, 1179, and references there: in addition, Accattino 1987, Todd 1995, 122-4, and Tieleman 1996.

about when the sight is affected, but not by its sending
something out and acting, unless someone were to call
being affected acting. And it is affected not by receiving
certain things which flow out from the objects of sight, but
when the transparent between the sight and the thing that
is seen is altered in a certain way by the object of sight[433] 35
and reports to the sight the form from the object of sight.
For everything that is transparent, whenever it is so in
actuality, that is when it is illuminated – for light is the 142,1
actuality of the transparent, qua transparent[434] – well, what
is transparent in actuality is in a way modified and affected
by colours in the same way in which the potentially transparent is modified, [when] it is illuminated, by the presence
of that which is of such a nature as to illuminate.[435]

What is of such a nature as to illuminate is the body of the 5
stars and fire and any such common nature there may be in
different bodies able to do this.[436] The presence of these in
the transparent is light,[437] and this is the transparent in
actuality. The transparent possesses its own perfection – I
mean the potentially transparent [does] – when it is illuminated, and it is what is illuminated that is transparent in the
proper sense.[438] So as the presence of things which are of 10
such a nature as to illuminate makes the potentially transparent actually transparent, so again the actually transparent takes on the colour of the things seen as a sort of
second light,[439] through their presence, receiving this as a
sort of second actuality. For colour is able to affect the

---

[433] Cf. Arius Didymus, *fr. phys.* 17 (Diels 1879, 456).

[434] Cf. Alex., *DA* 43,5-7, and for the sense of 'transparent' cf. 142
below.

[435] Cf. Alex., *In Sens.* 59,1-10; id., *DA* 42,19ff. Schroeder 1981,
217.

[436] Cf. Aristotle, *DA* 2.7 418b11-13, Alex., *DA* 43,9, 46,1-2, but
also 144,19-24 below.

[437] One might rather expect either 'the presence of these …
produces light' or 'the presence of the effect of these … is light'.

[438] Light is the actuality of the transparent: Aristotle, *DA* 2.7
418b9-10, Alex., *DA* 42,9-10, 43,4-8.

[439] Cf. Emilsson 1988, 54 and 159 n.47.

actually transparent as light[440] does the potentially [transpar-
15 ent], all that together which has the potentiality to be
modified by the presence of a particular sort of colour being
modified and coloured [by it] in a certain way.

The eye-jelly, too, is one of the things that are
transparent,[441] and it indeed along with the intervening air
which is illuminated, and itself no less than it, receives the
light, if it too is taken to be transparent, and through the
modification by the colours, by which it is modified in some
20 similar way to the external transparent, seeing and perceptive soul comes to be.[442] The colour does not appear as
being in the air,[443] but it is in the pupil,[444] because some

[440] Bruns queries the text here, arguing that one would expect
not 'light' but 'what is by nature such as to illuminate'. But Gätje
1966, 272 notes that the Arabic confirms 'light'. For colour as what
affects the actually transparent cf. Alex., *DA* 42,6-7.

[441] In Aristotle the Greek word *korê*, which normally means
the pupil of the eye, indicates the 'eye-jelly', the more or less
fluid contents of the eye; Sorabji 1974, 72 n.22, cf. Johansen
1998, 56 n.61. However, this is presumably because the eye-jelly
is visible through the pupil; and sometimes 'pupil' will be the
more natural translation. See above 94 n.309 and below 131
n.444, 140 n.473.)

[442] Bruns interprets the text thus, to avoid the implication that
the eye-jelly itself comes to be perceptive soul. (His worry, as his
reference to Alex., *In Sens.* 76.3 Thurot = 36.9 Wendland shows, is
not the implied materialism, but the location of sensation in the
eye-jelly.) But, even if the eye-jelly is not itself said to come to be
perceptive soul, it is striking that perceptive soul is said to be
produced as the result of a material process. Cf. above, 20 n.34.
Gätje 1966, 272 suggests *diaphanei <diakonos>*: 'by which it is
modified, acting as a messenger in a similar way to the external
transparent'.

[443] Moraux 2001, 354 n.162 suggests that a reference for this
point by Michael of Ephesus, *In GA* 88,7-9 (*CAG* vol. 14.3: falsely
attributed to Philoponus), to a 'second *logos* on the soul', apparently as his own work, is in fact a reference to this passage of the
Mantissa, together with 147,21 below. Luna 2001, 70 and n.158,
suggests that the reference in Michael is rather to Philoponus, *In
DA* 335,14ff.; this is supported by the fact that the term

transparent things are just transparent, while others, in addition to being transparent, are also reflective, through their smoothness and density being able to hold and collect together the reflection. So the things which are just trans- parent do not preserve in themselves what is seen in such a 25 way that it appears in them (and like this are as many of transparent things as are rare, [such] as air), but as many as share in a certain density and solidity, these display in themselves and preserve the image and shadow from what is seen. And like this among transparent things are mirrors and glass and transparent stones and, indeed, water; for it is more solid and dense than air and more able to hold and 30 collect together the images and shadows from the things that are seen. And it has been shown that the eye-jelly too is watery,[445] and the passage which penetrates from this to the primary [organ] of sense is like this and reports the form 143,1 and colour from the thing that is seen to the [organ] of sense.[446] This judges the colour that impinges by the impact from these; for this is the nature of sensation, to judge through the sense-organs the experiences that are reported through [them].

The modification [brought about] in the air and in the potentially transparent by fire and by colours is not like that 5 which we say comes about in things that are altered.[447] For

---

diaporthmeuein 'transmit' appears in both the Michael and the Philoponus passages, as she notes, but nowhere in the *Mantissa*.

[444] Referring to the reflected image seen by an observer in the pupil. Sorabji 1991, 230 and n.14 notes that the present text, unlike Aristotle in *De Sensu* 438a5-12 and Alexander in his commentary (*In Sens.* 24.26-7, 25.4-5; cf. also Alex., *DA* 62,1-5 with the comments of Sorabji 1991, 229-30), does not indicate that this image is simply a reflection and plays no part in the process of vision itself. Cf. Sharples (forthcoming, 2). For the contrast between water in the eye as able to retain the image and air as unable to do so cf. Alex., *DA* 43,18-44,13.

[445] Cf. Aristotle, *DA* 3.1 425a4-5; Alex., *DA* 44,6-7. Fotinis 1980, 59 n.1.

[446] Cf. Alex., *In Sens.* 59,11-14.

[447] 'modification' = *tropê*: cf. *trepetai* 'modified' at 142,2 above,

alteration is a change and comes about in time and with a
transition, but the transparent does not receive light and
colours in such a way as to be altered in these respects, but
the transparent is said to be affected in the same way as if
someone were to say that what comes to be on the right of
10   something has been affected without having been moved
itself or received any affection into itself. This is what the
modification of the transparent in accordance with light and
colours is like too; for it is by the presence of what illuminates or is coloured that the transparent comes to be like
this, as [it is] by relation to the [person] who stands alongside on the left that the [person] on the right [comes to be
situated on the right]. A sign that this is how it is that, as
the [person] on the right ceases to be on the right when the
15   one on the left changes his position, so light ceases when
the source of illumination changes its position, and similarly
when what is of such a nature as to be seen [does so,[448] the
transparent] ceases to be like this, not having received any
affection by a change in itself, but when the seeming alteration has happened to it in accordance with a relation.

    And light and colours seem to come to be in the
20   transparent as shadow does, in a way. For as shadow comes
about in the things that are shaded through the presence
alongside them of what is of such a nature as to cast a
shadow, so too light and colour. At any rate these too take a
hold all at once on as much of the air, and in such a way, as
they can take a hold from so great a distance, as also [does]
a shadow.

---

and for *tropê* as an equivalent for *metabolê* Accattino 1992, 55
n.48. Cf. Alex., *In Sens.* 134,11, with Accattino 1992, 53-6;
Accattino and Donini 1996, 181-3.

[448] Following Bruns' interpretation (143,16 n.). To supply '[the
transparent]' is difficult but required by the sense; when a blue
object, say, is removed the air between myself and it ceases to be
affected in such a way as to cause me to see blue in that position.
The Arabic translates as if the Greek had *pephukos* not *pephuko-
tos*: 'and similarly what is of such a nature as to be seen ceases to
be like this...'

[The following] is the greatest sign that what comes
about is neither an alteration nor a change of the transparent: everything that changes does so in time and proceeds   25
first and in a shorter time to what is closer, next and in a
greater [time] in this way to what is further. But light and
the forms of the things that are seen come to be altogether
and in a similar way in all the transparent over against them,
as also do shadow and darkness. Light departs from all the
transparent at the same time and comes to be in it all at the
same time. And on account of this Aristotle shows that   30
seeing comes about timelessly.[449] For a person sees [what
he sees] in however [small] a part of the time in which he
sees [it], and in just any part; and the things that do not
need time to be fulfilled and completed come to be
timelessly. For it is not being, but needing an interval of
time to be completed and become a whole ...[450] and in this
way being pleased, too, does not come about in time.

Of transparent things some are transparent in actuality,   35
some potentially. Always in actuality is the transparent in
the divine and eternal [beings];[451] for the eternal things do
not admit of potentiality. The potentially transparent is that   144,1
in things subject to coming-to-be. For this, like other things

---

[449] Bruns 1887, xvi notes that Alexander is here expressing his
own interpretation of what Aristotle says, rather than citing him
directly. Cf. Aristotle, *DA* 2.7 418b20-6, *De Sensu* 6 446b27-8.
Alex., *DA* 43,11 connects this point directly with light's not being
a body. For sensation being instantaneous see also Alexander
fr.16 in Giannakis 1996, 169 and 177; Lettinck 1994, 463.

[450] Bruns marks the text here as corrupt. The Arabic version
has 'Being in a time is not through coming about in a time; rather
what comes about in time is what needs an interval ...': that is, it is
not that something occurs or is in time that is the crucial factor,
but rather that it is a process *requiring* time.

[451] Cf. below 144,10-11, and (with Accattino 1992, 58) Alex., *In
Sens.* 45,26-46,3. As Accattino shows, Alexander, in regarding the
heavens as possessing in actuality the same transparency that
other bodies too can acquire, and as therefore being themselves
sources of light, is following Aristotle's reference to the heavens
in *DA* 2.7 418b12-13 rather than the doctrine of *Cael.* 2.7 289a19,
as Simplicius, *In Cael.* 442,4-12 notes. (Cf. Accattino 1992, 57-62.)

subject to coming-to-be, proceeds from potentiality to actuality, and air and as many things as are transparent in our
region are, before the presence of what is of such a nature
as to illuminate, matter for the transparent in actuality, that
5   is for light; the presence of what illuminates makes it[452]
transparent and colours it in a certain way. For light is as it
were the colour of the transparent.[453]

Air is not transparent *qua* air or water *qua* water. For
there are several bodies which differ from one another in
form but have the affection of transparency as something in
common.[454] For the eternal body and air and water, and
10   glass [objects] and certain stones share in this nature. The
eternal body is always transparent in actuality, as has been
said, the others sometimes potentially and sometimes in
actuality, and this sort of nature admits light. As many
things as do not share in such a nature cannot admit this.
This is why light does not pass through a wall or through
15   any other of the things that are not transparent; it is
because only the nature of the transparent is such as to be
affected in this way, in a certain way, as we said, receiving
light as its own proper colour.[455] These things are coloured
and illuminated not by the passing of some body through

[452] One might expect 'them'; the singular picks up the singular
'matter'.

[453] Light is *as it were* the colour of the transparent (above, §15
144,6, Aristotle, *DA* 2.7 418b11, Alex., *DA* 45,1, *Quaest.* 1.21 35,15;
cf. Alex., *In Sens.* 52,1.9), for only solid things have a colour of
their own (Alex., *In Sens.* 43,2-4, 46,21-47,8, *DA* 46,6-10, *Quaest.*
1.2 6,3, 6,17, 1.21 35,7-15. Cf. Accattino and Donini 1996, 180;
Sharples 1998a, 401-402.) The qualification 'as it were' is omitted,
and indeed light is said to be the most visible colour, at Alex., *In
Sens.* 43,13, 45,13, 47,1, *Mant.* §16 149,34; cf. also Alex., *DA* 44,13-
16, with Schroeder 1981, 218 n.16. Light is said to be received by
the transparent as its proper colour at 144,16 below and §16 150,2,
and contrasted with 'the other colours' at Alex., *DA* 46,3 (cf.
Accattino and Donini 1996, 191). Cf. Aristotle, *De Sensu* 3 439b2,
and below, 145 n.490, 148 n.504.

[454] Cf. Aristotle, *DA* 2.7 418b7-9.

[455] See above, n.453.

them; nor is it by being altered in themselves in a change in themselves that they admit light, but the presence in the transparent of fire or something like this is the cause of this. For it is not only the presence of fire that illuminates the transparent, but the etherial body, too, is like this, and certain other parts of sea-creatures and land-creatures and flying creatures and certain kinds of stones; it is not easy to include all these, in so far as they are like this, under a single name.[456] And this is why light should be said to be the presence in the transparent of fire *or something like this*.

Moreover if darkness, which is the privation of light, is the absence of these things or comes about through the absence of these things, it is reasonable to say that light is the presence of these things. Either this is what light and darkness are, or these are their causes. For not everything has such a nature as to be affected and disposed by every-thing, but different things are [such as] to be affected by different things, as the transparent is by those that have been mentioned already.

If light is the actuality of the transparent, it will be incor-poreal. More generally we also call what is illuminated light, and this is already a body. It has been shown that light is not an affection of the transparent, and neither is colour itself an affection, but the presence of these[457] in the trans-parent is by a certain relation. [Thus] the divine body is not subject to being affected, either, if the stars are seen through it. For the transparent is not affected by the objects

20

25

30

---

[456] See above, §9 128,6. The comparison between such objects on the one hand and fire and the heavens on the other is attrib-uted by Themistius, *In DA* 61,21-34, to book 3 of the treatise *On Vision* by Sosigenes, Alexander's teacher. Rose 1863, 373-4, comparing Alex., *In Sens.* 17,3-7 and Alex., *DA* 43,16-18 (above, 92) suggests that Themistius derived this information from Alexander's lost commentary on Aristotle's *DA.* Cf. Moraux 1984, 358-9; Accattino 1992, 58 n.52.

[457] Interpreted by Bruns ad loc. as 'the colours'. The Arabic has 'these bodies', which Gätje 1966, 273 refers to the sources of illumination, but this gives a less good sense. Rescigno 2000, 224 n.84 interprets as 'the light and the colour'.

35   of sight, as it is not by light either; for neither for us is to be
in the light to be affected, but it seems that to be illuminated
and to be coloured come about for transparent things in
much the same way as contemplation, where the inquirer
145,1   finds [the answer] and has understanding simultaneously,
as if the intellect came into contact and came to have understanding through the presence of the object of understanding. Just so the potentially transparent is illuminated
altogether by the presence of fire or something of that sort,
and what has been illuminated and is transparent in actuality is in turn given form in a way by the presence of colours,
5   colours coming to be in it in a similar way to light. In this
way neither would the moon be said to be affected, even
though it is illuminated by the sun. For as what is shadowed
is not affected, neither is what is illuminated.[458]

The fact that, when the things seen have moved away,
some of the colours still seem to be left behind in the eyes
of those who saw is not a sign of an alteration. For [the
10   eye][459] is affected in this way not as being transparent, but
as ensouled and able to form images.[460] For this is why it[461]

[458] On this passage cf. Rescigno 2000, 224-5.

[459] So the Arabic. The change from plural to singular is
awkward. See the next note.

[460] Bruns argues that this cannot refer to the eye because
phantasia does not take place in the eye (citing Alex., *DA* 68,5ff.,
where it is attributed to the primary sense-organ), and suggests
reading *empsukhou ... dunamenou*: 'as belonging to a being that
is ensouled ...'. A similar result could be achieved by taking the
awkward singular 'it is affected in this way' to refer not to the eye
(see the previous note) but more vaguely (hence the neuters) to
the person or the sensory faculty. Images in the sense-organs are
referred to at Aristotle, *Insomn.* 3 462a8-31; after-images, like
those referred to by our text, are treated as sensations at *Insomn.*
2 460b2-3, but attributed to *phantasia* at *DA* 3.3 428a15-16 referring back to 3.2 425b24-5. 145,7-9 here seems, as Anne Sheppard
notes, to be a verbal reminiscence of the latter, but with 'eyes'
substituted for 'sense-organs'. (I am grateful to Richard Sorabji
and Anne Sheppard for references in this note.)

[461] For the reasons indicated in the preceding note Bruns
suggests taking this either as referring to the person rather than

can still preserve for a time the movements that were produced in the sense-organs from external objects. And ensouled [creatures] are even at a subsequent time able to place before their eyes the images that they had. At any rate mirrors, even though they are smooth and bright, do not preserve in themselves anything of the colours that appeared in them when either the light or the [source] of illumination or the objects of sight have departed, because they are not affected and are not ensouled.

Sight and the eye-jelly, being transparent, are disposed in the [same] way by the light and by colours, which affect in a straight line what is transparent in actuality and illuminated, and this is how seeing comes about, not by something being sent out from the sight in the direction of the things* seen. A sign [of this] is the fact that certain very bright things sting[462] the eyes of those who see them, as loud noises [affect] hearing. To suppose that, because it is from a distance that we perceive what is seen, therefore the apprehension comes about there too, is [an] empty [argument]. For in the case of the other sensations too, although it is by an affection that they apprehend their own proper objects, nevertheless apprehension is of things at a distance.

Moreover certain colours appear also in the intervening transparent, since it itself receives the forms and acts as a messenger. At any rate certain things appear to be coloured by the colours of what is placed alongside them. What is [placed] on red or purple appears like this in colour,[463] if

---

the eye, or as impersonal (so the Arabic: I am grateful to Inna Kupreeva for this information): 'it is possible ...'.

[462] Literally 'bite'.

[463] Literally 'that which is placed on this colour appears red or purple', but in the Greek 'red or purple' precede 'this colour' and thus make the reference clear; the sentence cannot be reproduced literally in English. Cf. Alex., *DA* 42,16-19, and, with Moraux 1984, 757 n.290; Accattino and Donini 1996, 179-80 ad loc., Alex., *In Sens.* 50,10-11, Alex. ap. Averroes, *Comm. Magn. in DA* II.67,39-45 (pp.231-232 Crawford), Lucretius, 4.72-86, and Galen, *PHP* 7.7.2 (p.470.7-11 De Lacy). Galen argues that the

such colours are placed alongside, since the colours are
30   transmitted through the air, but are not seen there.

Moreover, duller colours affect the sight less, brighter
ones more and more strongly.

Moreover, as a result of different lighting and different
light, and positions in relation to those who see and to the
light, things that are seen appear different.[464] And the same
35   colour appearing close at hand and far away appears different; what is seen from far away [does] not [appear] white in
146,1 a similar way.[465] It is by such differences that sight apprehends the shapes that are seen. For it judges the external
outline of things that are seen by the difference in colour
from what surrounds; and that is why all those things
whose surrounding[s] are the same colour as them are hard
to see or not visible* separately. If the surface within the
5   external outline is of a single colour and flat [sight] also
sees [it] as such, being moved* in a uniform[466] way by the
colour which is the same and which is moved in a uniform
way through what is in between.[467] But if what is within [the
outline] is not flat, but uneven, even if it does not vary in
colour, [sight] judges [the shape] by the dissimilarity in the

---

phenomenon supports Aristotle's explanation of vision in terms of
the effect of colour on the air, immediately before going on to
object that Aristotle's theory cannot explain perception of size or
distance (above, 128).

[464] Ganson, forthcoming, compares [Aristotle], *De coloribus* 3
793b16-19, and argues that the similarities are sufficient to
suggest that the present section of the *Mant.* is drawing on that
passage.

[465] Cf. Aristotle, *Meteor.* 3.4 374b14. (I am grateful to Todd
Ganson for this reference.)

[466] Literally: '[all] in a similar way'.

[467] This interpretation involves taking *metaxu* at the beginning
of the sentence to refer to what is within the outline (as in the
next sentence; and cf. 146,31.32.34), but at the end of the sentence
to refer to what is between the thing seen and the eye (as at
141,34, 142,17, 147,17.19). The switch between two applications of
the same term seems awkward; but 'through' seems to require it.
The Arabic omits 'which is the same ... in between'.

apprehension of the colour. For the light does not fall in a similar way on all parts of what is uneven, because some of them are concave, some convex, some sideways on to the   10 [source] of illumination, some opposite to it. On account of these differences, even if what is seen is of a single colour, some [parts] of it seem dimmer,[468] others more conspicuous, and thus some will be seen as recessed and others as projecting. Painters imitate this when they want to show on the same plane what is uneven, and make some parts light while shading others.[469] Thus some [parts] of   15 [what they paint] appear projecting, others recessed, and as projecting those that are made more light, as recessed those that are shaded.[470]

[Sight] sees and judges size by the angle of the cone which is formed towards the sight. For it sees the things that it sees by a cone which has the pupil[471] as its vertex, and as its base the line which defines what [part] of the perceived body is seen and what not. But this cone comes   20 about not by the pouring forth of rays [from the eye], but from the thing that is seen. For colour is able to affect what is transparent in actuality, and the colouring, as it were, that comes about in this, coming about in straight lines in a similar way to light, attaches itself to everything situated opposite to it[472] but especially attaches itself to and

[468] The Arabic confirms Bruns' *achluôdestera* for *alloiôdestera*, though not using the comparative (Gätje 1966, 273).

[469] Cf., with Bruns, Alex., *DA* 50,26ff.

[470] Ganson, forthcoming, discusses this passage and 146,35ff. (below), and compares [Aristotle], *Probl.* 31.25 960a3ff.: he argues that in stressing variation in apprehension the present text is influenced by the sceptical arguments of Aenesidemus. I am grateful to Todd Ganson for discussion of details of the translation of this paragraph.

[471] See above, 130 n.441.

[472] Emilsson 1988, 160 n.51 comments on this passage: 'It is possible that Alexander had arrived at the idea that the affection produced by a large object is present as a whole at every point of the intermediate space'; cf. his comparison of Plotinus' and modern theories at op. cit. 54-5, and 140 n.474 below.

25   illuminates things that are smooth and bright (and the pupil[473] is like this); and [thus] certain cones are formed towards [the pupil] and from the thing seen, such as to receive the impression (*emphasis*) from it. For it is by a cone that the form of the visible thing becomes apparent (*emphainesthai*), in the case of each of the things seen directly.[474] It is by the angles of these cones that [sight] judges larger and smaller and equal things. For it sees [as] equal those things the sight of which involves equal angles, [as] larger those which involve larger ones.

30   Sight apprehends the distance from itself to what is seen, and the interval between the things that are seen, [in the following way. It apprehends] the interval by the angle of the cone, which is formed towards the pupil from what is between the things that are seen and itself. For it is by the size of this angle that it judges the interval between the things that are seen; things appear at a distance from one

35   another when there is something visible in the space between them. It perceives the distance from itself through

147,1 a certain habituation. For since of things that are seen those that are afar off affect us slightly, but those close at hand greatly, through habituation to such things [sight] supposes that the things that appear dimmer are afar off, but those which are more conspicuous and clearer [are] close at hand. The same thing occurs also in the case of voice and

5   hearing; and this is why those who are imitating people afar off emit their voice feebly.[475]

---

[473] i.e. the part of the eye-jelly that is in contact with the outside world.

[474] That observers at different points can each see the whole of the object naturally suggests an explanation in terms of visual cones, as can be seen from the accompanying diagram (not in the MSS).

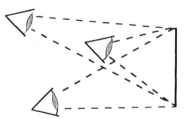

[475] Ganson, forthcoming, compares Alex., *DA* 50,24-51,4, which

[Sight] perceives movement by perceiving the interval and the distance. For whenever something appears not having the same interval in relation to some definite* thing, or not [having] the same distance in relation to sight itself, when the person seeing either is not in motion or does not realise that he is in motion, then [sight] sees what is seen as moving. In general [sight] perceives what is moving by judging it in relation to something that is stationary and definite. And this is why it apprehends as moving those things least that move in open spaces, those things most that move in narrow places and past other things. For they seem to pass alongside* each other more swiftly.

[Sight] perceives rest and number, rest by the denial of movement, number by the negation of continuity. For it says [that] things that are separated by an interval [composed of] bodies that are different in form [are] 'several'.

Since seeing comes about in this way, not by an affection and alteration of what [is] in between, but by a relation, the difficulty is also resolved which some people raise, how it is possible for those who see different or even opposite things, positioned diagonally to one another, to see [them]. For it will seem that the air in between, in that the colours collide with each other, that is in that <the cones from> those seeing things [positioned] diagonally intersect each other,*[476] receives opposite

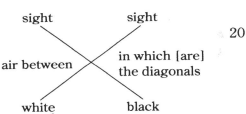

refers to optical illusions as at 145,32ff. above, and notes that our present passage, unlike Aristotle at *Meteor.* 3.4 374b14, is careful not to refer to 'distant things appearing darker', since from the point of view of the person seeing a similar visual effect may be interpreted (rightly or wrongly) *either* as the thing in question being darker than another, *or* as its being more distant than another.

[476] For the problem cf., with Bruns, Alex., *DA* 62,5ff. and *In*

colours at the same time. This is solved by the fact that the
air is not coloured, but through the relation to it of what is
seen the colour appears in it in a straight line with what is
seen. For nothing prevents the same thing from not
preserving the same relation to different things, just as
25   nothing prevents the same thing from being half of one
thing and twice another.[477]

147,26   [16]. That colour is the limit of the *diaphanes*.

The term *diaphanes* is often translated as 'transparent', but that is
incorrect, at least in this section and related texts. 'Transparent' is
here *dioptos*: the *diaphanes* is rather, for Aristotle in *De Sensu*
and for Alexander in his commentary thereon, the property which
makes bodies visible, which opaque bodies too possess (Aristotle,
De Sensu 3 439a24, 439b8; Alex., *In Sens.* 45,5-6.10, 49,28-50,3;
Quaest. 1.2 6,1-3. There is indeed a question whether it is
possessed by bodies which are completely black; see below, 148
n.496, 149 n.505). Cf. Schroeder 1981, 220-21, arguing that the
diaphanes is the illuminable. However, Aristotle in *DA* uses
diaphanes in a sense closer to our 'transparent';[478] that usage too
was influential, and indeed seems the more appropriate translation in other sections of the *Mantissa*. Since the tension between
the two uses is already present in Aristotle, and is explicitly recognised both in Alexander's *De sensu* commentary and in the
present text,[479] it would be hazardous to draw conclusions from it
about the authorship of different sections of the *Mantissa*.[480]

Sens. 30,12-18 (the latter in criticism of the theory of emitted visual
rays: cf. 98 n.325). The diagram translated here is found in the
margin of the primary MS V (drawn by the first hand) and in MS A.

[477] Sorabji 1991, 229 and n.9 points out that our text, unlike
Alex., *DA* loc. cit. and some later discussions, does not apply the
point to explaining why the faculty of sight can see different
colours simultaneously because it is not coloured itself.

[478] Aristotle, *DA* 2.7 418b6; cf. Ross 1955, 197.

[479] See below, 148,9 and 144 n.485; also 147 n.496.

[480] Alexander's discussion in his *DA* (42,4-46,19) begins by
restricting the *diaphanes* to bodies with no colour of their own
(42,7-8) but subsequently says that every coloured body shares in
diaphaneia (44,20-1).

There are close verbal parallels between parts of this text and Alex., *In Sens.* 43,17-47,30, noted by Bruns and by Wendland 1901 ad loc.: cf. also Thurot 383, Moraux 2001, 397 n.9. The topic is also discussed in Alex., *Quaestio* 1.2. Paradoxically, the *Quaestio* takes the form of an exposition of Aristotelian doctrine, while the present text, in spite of its title, is presented as a problem: 'Why ... if *diaphaneia* is present in all bodies, are not all *diaphanes?*' (148,9). The solution consists in a modification of the original claim: all bodies except totally black ones *are* in fact *diaphaneis*, but to varying degrees, those that are transparent most so of all. (There may be some implausibility in supposing that transparent bodies are the most clearly visible.) The connection between colour and surface indicated in the title of the present section is in fact discussed more fully in Alex., *DA* 46,6-19 and *Quaest.* 1.2.

See further Sharples 1992, 20-24; 1998a, 397-402.

Diaphaneia is a certain common nature which applies in   147,27
common to all bodies; some have a greater share in it, some
less, fire, air and water more, earth less, but it is present, at
any rate, in all bodies.[481] *Diaphaneia* is in a way the matter of   30
colour.[482] For as there is a certain matter of great and small,
and of light and heavy, and of the other oppositions
similarly, capable of receiving them in turn, so the
diaphanes is the matter of opposition in colour. So, since   148,1
every body is capable of receiving colour, every one is also
diaphanes. For this is what underlies colours, and the
nature of colours is clear in the limit of the definite
diaphanes.[483] For of bodies which are not transparent, and
which are definite and solid, only the limit is apparent, and   5
this is colour.[484] This is the clearest of *diaphanes* things,

[481] Cf. Alex., *In Sens.* 44,1-7, and below, 147 n.496. The claim being made is not just that the air and water present in all bodies, except in pure earth (and pure fire), are themselves *diaphanes.* Cf. Sharples 1998a, 397-8 n.77.

[482] Cf. Alex., *DA* 44,21-2, noted by Rovida, and 148,30 below, Alex., *In Sens.* 45,2-4, *Quaest.* 1.2 5,32; Accattino and Donini 1996, 187.

[483] Cf. 150,13ff. below; Aristotle, *De Sensu* 439b1-14, Alex., *In Sens.* 47,10, *Quaest.* 1.2 5,13ff.

[484] Aristotle, *De Sensu* 439b8-14; Alex., *Quaest.* 1.2 5,19ff.

being judged by its otherness than and dissimilarity to what surrounds it. The only bodies that are called *diaphanes* are the transparent ones; <other bodies too are apparent (*phainomena*) besides the transparent ones>,*[485] for their colour can be apprehended by sight. That through which this naturally appears, being able to receive its form, is called and is *diaphanes* in a special way.[486]

10   Why then, if *diaphaneia* is present in all bodies, are not all *diaphanes*? Or rather: bodies differ by possessing this nature more or less. For the more and the less come about through admixture of the opposite. What is opposite is what is least *diaphanes*, and this is earth. For what is opposite to what is most *diaphanes* is earth. This is clear from what

15   follows: we say that what is said [to be] potentially *diaphanes* becomes so in actuality through the presence of fire or something like that. So in proportion we take [as] close to fire, in nature and position, that which is most and

---

Schroeder 1981, 220-1.

[485]   A supplement seems required to avoid the implication that only transparent things are visible, and to enable 'this' in the following sentence to refer to the colour of solid things. Bruns' supplement in the text is based on Alex., *In Sens.* 45,11-15: '*diaphanes* in the proper sense, according to customary speech, are only those of bodies which are transparent, from <"to show" (*phainein*), because> "apparent" (*phainomenon*) is applied in its strict sense to what can be apprehended by sight because of light (*phaos*). ... So the things that have [light] as their colour are *diaphanes* in the proper sense'. (Translation from Sharples 1998a, 399, modified to incorporate Diels' supplement as given in Wendland 1901, ad loc.) Both in the commentary and in the present text the sequel shows that non-transparent things are *diaphaneis* to a lesser degree; and in both texts the claim is that transparent things are *diaphaneis* in the full or proper sense in fact, not just that they are so called in common usage. Bessarion in MS B added *dia* to the following clause: 'the only bodies that are called diaphanes are the transparent ones, for colour can be apprehended by sight *through* them'.

[486]   Cf. Alex., *In Sens.* 45,20-1.

most swiftly[487] filled with light (and this is what is most *diaphanes*), but [as] what is furthest [that which is] least [like this], and of the rest one more than another according to their remoteness from fire and everything which is by nature such as to give light.[488]

Well, of [bodies] subject to coming-to-be the closest body   20
to fire and what is by nature such as to give light is that beneath the moon, which we also call *hupekkauma*,[489] and after this air, third water, and furthest removed is earth. And for this reason the former, being most *diaphanes*,* are able to admit what is most visible, I mean light,[490] but earth not in a similar way. For this is opposite both to illumination and to what is most able to be illuminated, and this [latter]   25
we call matter. For all things which are of a nature to come to be in something else have something underlying them, which has a fitness to be given form in this respect, and this is their matter. For [such a matter] underlies heavy and light and great and small and hot and cold and the other things which are analogous to these. Just so colours and the opposition in them [have] a certain matter, and this is   30
diaphanes body.[491] For everything like this is able to admit colours in accordance with this capacity by which it is

---

[487] Mugler 1964, 100, notes that this introduces the un-Aristotelian idea that the speed of light varies according to the medium.

[488] With 148,12-22 cf. Alex., *In Sens.* 45,25-46,6.

[489] See above, 66 n.203.

[490] For light as what is most visible cf., with Accattino and Donini 1996, 186, 149,33-4 below and Alex., *DA* 44,13-14, *In Sens.* 43,13-14, 46,21-47,1, 47,13, *In Metaph.* 142,13-16; they note however that at Alex., *DA* 46,2-3, *In Sens.* 45,26-46,3 (and possibly *DA* 89,1; Accattino and Donini 1996, 288) what is most visible is rather the *source* of light. Moraux 1942, 89-90 (cf. Schroeder 1981, 218 n.16), notes, in the context of challenging Alexander's use of the light analogy at *DA* 89,1-2, that for Aristotle in DA 2.7 418a26-b3 it is colour, rather than light, that is visible; cf. above, 134 n.453.

[491] 148,25-30 are closely parallel to Alex., *In Sens.* 44,25-45,4. (However, for 'and this is *diaphanes* body' the commentary has rather 'this is the *diaphaneia* in bodies'.)

149,1   *diaphanes*. And this capacity is *diaphaneia*. This capacity is
present in all bodies, but in some more, in others less. To
the extent that each of them shares [in it], to that extent it
is able to admit colour.[492]

They possess opposite [attributes] not in accordance with
the capacities that are tangible. For in this way at least and
in respect of these water is more opposite to fire [than earth
5   is]. For it is hot and dry, water is cold and moist. But it is
not in this respect that fire [has the property of] giving light.
For other things too not like this in nature give light.[493] But
as earth is opposite to fire in its tendency [to move in a
certain direction] and in its proper and natural place and in
respect of rarity and density, that is fineness and thickness,
so earth is opposite to fire in respect of capacity for light,
10   and [in respect of] *diaphaneia* and light. Indeed air is akin to
fire, which is why it is swiftly burned up,[494] and water even
seems to be nourishment for fire. For in burning logs it is
the moisture in them that is burned; for smoke is like this.
But earth is furthest removed from [fire].[495]

And for this reason it is what is potentially fire that is
15   most able to admit light. This is the *hupekkauma*, and
second air and third water. Earth, being most removed from
fire, also shares least in the nature that is able to admit
light; and this is *diaphaneia*. For one of the opposites is the

[492]   Cf. Alex., *In Sens.* 45,5-11.
[493]   See above, 135 n.456 .
[494]   Aristotle refers to the dry exhalation being ignited at
Meteor. 1.4 342a36, and to air being ignited (*ekpimpranai*, the
same word as here) at id. 2.8 367a10; heat is said to burn up air in
some plants and so explain their redness at [Aristotle], *De plantis*
1.5 820b22. But what does not seem to occur in the Aristotelian
corpus is the view that fire requires air as nourishment; that
cutting off the supply of air extinguishes a fire was known, but is
explained by Aristotle (*Iuvent.* 5 470a9) through the need for
cooling air to temper the heat of the fire. Cf. also Theophrastus,
De igne 23, with the comments of Steinmetz 1964, 129; Vallance
1988, 38; Sharples 1998, 127 and n.359.
[495]   149.10-13 are closely parallel verbally to Alex., *In Sens.*
46,9-12.

privation.[496] What is opposite is what is most removed; and what is most removed is that after which there is no further transition to something else, and earth is like this, for it is the last of the things that subsist and the final [stage] in the 20 transition in this direction. So it is reasonable that it occupies the place of the privation of light; it does not itself receive light into itself, and when it is mixed with something else it obstructs and hinders it from being illuminated throughout. Air full of smoke shows [this], for it admits light less, because of the admixture of the earthy. And dust is like this. And for the same reason flame too is 25 not transparent, because the earthy is mixed with it, if flame is burning smoke. But glass and the *diaphanes*[497] things with which they close in houses are of [the nature of] water, as is clear from their origin; and this is why they are *diaphanes*. And horn and tortoise-shell consist mostly of water, which is why they become *diaphanes* when they are worked in a certain way; for that they are [mainly composed] of water they show*[498] by the fact that they can be softened.[499]

[496] The claim that the privation is one of the extremes in a scale of more and less (147,28-9 above) may be seen as an attempt to resolve the apparent inconsistency in saying that *diaphaneia* is present in all bodies to varying degrees, and also that it is not present at all in black ones; the least degree of presence is absence.

[497] Here *diaphanes* seems to be used more in the sense of 'transparent'.

[498] Reading *dêloi* for Bruns' *dêlon*: see Notes on the Text. (But *dêloi* could also be understood impersonally, giving the same sense as *dêlon*: 'is clear from the fact that'.)

[499] 149,20-9 are parallel, with close verbal correspondences at some points, to Alexander, *In Sens.* 46,13-21. Aristotle too argues that the reason that horn can be softened is that it contains some water; but he sees the fact that it cannot be melted as evidence that it contains relatively little (Aristotle, *Meteor.* 4.6 383a31, 4.9 385b11, 4.10 388b31, 389a11.).

30   That those *diaphanes* things that possess a greater
[proportion] of earth are less *diaphanes* is also shown by
wine-must. For it is earthier than the wine which has
settled. So for these reasons neither is earth *diaphanes*
itself, nor those things in which it is mixed.

So the things that are transparent and *diaphanes* possess
the greatest visibility and admit colour, that is light,[500] and in
35   addition provide the cause for other colours being seen. For
seeing is of what is *diaphanes* in actuality;[501] for colours
affect (*kinêtika*) this. But solid bodies with a definite
150,1   [shape], and those which are earthy or have a preponderance of earth are not transparent.[502] For they are not so
diaphanes, nor do they admit light as their proper colour.
But each of them has its own proper colour and is visible
according to this, in so far as it shares in the *diaphaneia* that
5   underlies colours. For it is by the admixture of an earthy
nature that they are deprived of being transparent (*diopta*).
For this applies primarily to [earth] among bodies.[503] But in
so far as it shares in *diaphaneia*, to this extent and in this
way it is coloured. For the things that are more *diaphanes*
have a colour like light, those near to these [have a] white
[colour],[504] and the things which have a more visible colour
must have more *diaphaneia* too. The things which are like
10   light and which are white are more visible, second those
which are adjacent to these in sequence, and least those

[500] Cf. above, 134 nn.453, 455.
[501] Cf. Alex., *In Sens.* 46,21-47,3.
[502] Cf. Alex., *In Sens.* 47,8-19; *DA* 45,9.
[503] Literally 'first of bodies it is affected thus'. Cf., with Bruns,
the use of *peponthen* at Alex.. *DA* 4.21. At *DA* 45,12-14, 17-18,
46,4-6 and *Quaest.* 1.2 7,4-7 Alexander speaks more explicitly of an
internal cause of *diaphaneia* in solid things, the amount of which
in relation to its opposite, earth (*DA* 45,9-11), is responsible for
differences in colour. Cf. Accattino and Donini 1996, 188-9, relating the theory to Aristotle, *De Sensu* 4 442a12.
[504] Accattino and Donini 1996, 190 and Towey 2000, 172 n.210
note that the colour resembling light is distinguished from white
here and at Alex., *In Sens.* 47,15-17, but identified with it at Alex.,
DA 45,15. See above, 134 n.453.

[that are] black. These too are indeed perceptible, but not visible in a primary way;[505] and this is proper to earth. But since everything that is *diaphanes* is visible, and everything that is visible is seen at its limit, everything that is *diaphanes* is visible at its limit. But colour exists insofar as it   15 is visible, so colour exists in that the *diaphanes* is visible; but it is visible, as we said, in respect of its individual limit. So colour is the limit of the *diaphanes*. For this alone is visible in actuality.[506]

[17]. From Aristotelian [tradition] concerning the first   150,19 appropriate thing.[507]

The Stoics saw virtue, which for them suffices for happiness (below, §20), as the culmination of a process of *oikeiôsis* or 'appropriation' which begins with the primary instinct for self-preservation (Diogenes Laertius 7.85 = *SVF* 3.178, and other texts in LS §57). Carneades objected that the Stoic account involved discarding and leaving behind what is natural (Striker 1996, 263: Cicero, *Fin.* 4.25); but his criticism leaves intact the assumption that 'the first appropriate thing' is the starting-point of ethical theory, and Striker 1996, 269 notes that our text shows that Antiochus of Ascalon's Peripatetic contemporaries in the first century B.C., like Antiochus himself, accepted the doctrine that 'the goal of life must be derived from the first object of desire' (which, she persuasively argues, was not the position of the Stoics themselves;

---

[505] That is, we 'see' complete blackness where we see nothing at all; blackness is the absence of illumination. Contrast the Stoic view in Aëtius 4.15.1-3, according to which darkness is seen by means of light from our eyes illuminating it. – After 'not visible in a primary way' the MSS add 'and it is by sharing more or less in these that bodies also [have] different colours', bracketed by Bruns as an intrusion into the text.

[506] With 149,36-150,12 cf. Alex., *In Sens.* 47,8-19.

[507] 'From Aristotelian tradition' renders *tôn para Aristotelous*. Alternatively, 'From the [teachings] of Aristotle'; but the translation in the text preserves the implication in the Greek that what follows is an interpretation of Aristotle rather than a verbatim report. Compare §22 and §23 below, and 110,4 above with Opsomer and Sharples 2000.

op. cit. 227-31, 263, 268-9, 288-93, 305). The present text is thus, as
Pohlenz 1967, vol.2 167 and n.158 and Moraux 1973, 209 note,
both an attempt to construct an Aristotelian position on a distinc-
tively Hellenistic issue (as are also, for example, Alexander's
treatises *On Fate* and *On Providence*) and also evidence for
earlier attempts to do the same. Cf. also Annas 1993, 39 and n.42;
Sharples 2001, 603-4. On *oikeiôsis* generally see Philippson 1932
(with discussion of our present text at 455 and 460-65); Pembroke
1971; Striker 1983 = Striker 1996, ch.13.

   I am grateful to Bob Todd for suggesting some of the wording
in the translation of this section, and to Inna Kupreeva for drawing
my attention to some nuances of the text.

150,20   Since there is something that is the object of appetition
and [something that is] appetitive, and there is also
something that is the ultimate object of appetition, namely
happiness,[508] and [since] what is ultimate is ultimate in
relation to something that is first, there will also be
something that is the first object of appetition. For in that in
which, being continuous, there is something that is ultimate,
there is necessarily also a starting-point, from which the
progression comes about, through the intermediates, to the
end and what is ultimate; so that, if there is some ultimate
25   object of appetition, there is some starting-point of this,
which they call the first appropriate thing.

   Well, there has been an enquiry by the philosophers as to
what this first appropriated thing is, and it did not seem the
same to all, but the difference concerning the first [appro-
priated thing], among those who speak about it, more or
less corresponds to that concerning the ultimate object of
appetition.[509] The Stoics then, but not all of them, say that

----

[508] Annas 1993, 35 and n.22 notes that the definition of the end
as the ultimate object of appetition or desire *(orekton)*, found also
at §20 162,34 below, does not occur in Aristotle himself, but does
occur at Arius Didymus ap. Stobaeus, *Ecl.* 2.7.6b 76,21-24
Wachsmuth (Stoic), id. 2.7.18 131,4 (Peripatetic) and at Sextus,
PH 1.25.

[509] This doxographical summary serves as an introduction to
the discussion of the specifically Aristotelian positions which
follow. But it is not taken up again in that discussion, even where

the living creature is the first thing appropriated to itself; for each living creature, as soon as it has come into 30 [existence],[510] is appropriated to itself, including also human beings.[511] But those of them who are thought to speak more subtly and to make more distinctions about this[512] say that it is to our own constitution and its preservation that we have been appropriated* as soon as we have come to be.[513] The followers of Epicurus, on the other hand, thought that pleasure is the first appropriate thing without qualification,[514] but they say as we progress this pleasure is subject to distinctions.[515] Others [thought it was] freedom from trouble, like the Megarians,[516] while for the Academics it 35

it could have been (see below, 158 n.537). *Mant.* §24, Alexander's *Fat.*, *Mixt.* and *Prov.* all begin with summaries of conflicting views, but in all these cases the subsequent discussion is linked to the summaries more explicitly than is the case in the present text. See Mansfeld 1988. I am grateful to Han Baltussen for raising this issue.

[510] Cf., with Magnaldi 1991, 6 and n.11, Cicero, *Fin.* 3.16, 5.24, and Plutarch, *De Stoic rep.* 1038b.

[511] Cf. Magnaldi 1991, 17 n.8.

[512] Philippson 1932, 455 suggests that this refers to Chrysippus, comparing Diogenes Laertius 7.85, and that the modification was intended to avoid the problem of a thing loving itself *simpliciter* raised by Aristotle, *EE* 7.6 1240a13-22 and [Aristotle], *MM* 2.11 1211a25ff.

[513] Richard Sorabji points out that Seneca, *Ep. Mor.* 121.14-17 resolves the problem that a creature's constitution changes during its life (see further below, 152,10ff., 35ff.) by arguing that it has *oikeiôsis* first of all to itself. Cf. Giusta 1964, vol.1 295 n.19. 150,25-33 = *SVF* 3.183.

[514] Cf. Cicero, *Fin.* 1.29-31 = LS 21A1-3.

[515] Giusta 1964, vol.1 262 notes that Cicero, *Fin.* 2.32 reports that for Epicurus animals and small children experience kinetic pleasure, but not the katastematic pleasure which consists in the absence of pain. For the distinction between the two types cf. LS 1 p.123; a sceptical account at Nikolsky 2001.

[516] 150,34-5 is fr. 196 in Döring 1972. Döring 154 questions the reliability of this report, along with that relating to the Academics (see the next note), but notes that Seneca, *Ep. Mor.* 9.1-3 (fr.195

151,1   was freedom from error.[517] For it is to this that they say we
are first in a state of appropriation[518], so as not to err in
anything. And in general each group, as we said, makes
suppositions about the starting-points in accordance with
the final objects of appetition.

[I] Some say that according to Aristotle we ourselves are
the first thing appropriate to ourselves. For if the object of
5   love is the object of appetition, and we love no-one in prefer-
ence to ourselves, and are not appropriated* to anything
else in this way (for* it is by reference back to ourselves
that we lay claim to other [people] and love someone),[519]
accordingly each person will be the first thing appropriate
to himself. This is the opinion of Xenarchus and Boethus,[520]

Döring) attributes to Stilpo the view that freedom from *pathos* is
the highest good (cf. Philippson 1932, 461). Living free from
disturbance was also the goal of life according to Hieronymus of
Rhodes (fr.13 Wehrli). See Modrze 1932, 312 n.62; White 2002,
80-1 and n.21.

[517] *aprosptôsia*, compared by Zeller 1903, 531 n.2 to Stoic
aproptôsia at Diogenes Laertius 7.46. Philippson 1932, 461,
suggests that the latter may have been the form in Alexander's
source here, but rejects Zeller's view that the reference is to
Academic suspension of judgement (*epokhê*), as that is hardly the
'first natural thing' in the Academic theory – we are all too prone
to jump to hasty conclusions. (Indeed Cicero, *Fin.* 3.31, explicitly
reports that for some members of the Academy resisting appearances was the ultimate end.) Rather, no-one wants to be wrong,
but it takes time to learn to suspend judgement and so avoid
being wrong.

[518] Or 'have an affinity'.

[519] Or, less probably (taking the ambiguous terms as neuter)
'we concern ourselves about other things and love certain things'?

[520] Literally, 'the associates of', but by a frequent usage indicating simply Xenarchus and Boethus (Peripatetics of the time of
Augustus) themselves. Cf. Moraux 1973, 178-9 and 208-10. The
same view is found in the report of Peripatetic views by Arius
Didymus ap. Stobaeus 2.7.13, p.118,12 Wachsmuth; cf. Philippson
1932, 465, and Moraux 1973, 209. Philippson argues that Xenarchus may have been Arius' source; Pohlenz 1940, 42 is doubtful.
Philippson 1932, 464 comments that Xenarchus' and Boethus'

on the basis of what is said about love in the eighth[521] book
of the *Nicomachean* [*Ethics*], where the beginning of the
passage is 'Perhaps it will become clear concerning these   10
things when the object of love has become known' up to 'it
will make no difference; for the object of love will be what
appears [to be good or pleasant]'.[522] And in the ninth book
he says similarly 'The facts disagree* with these arguments'
up to 'and so it is oneself that should be loved most'.[523]

---

formulations of the Peripatetic position show more direct Stoic
influence – mediated, he suggests, via Antiochus of Ascalon – than
those our text goes on to give.

[521] The reference to the eighth book is Bruns' emendation
(anticipated by Rovida); the MSS and the Aldine edition have
rather 'in the ninth book'. Kenny 1978, 37-8 n.4, suggests that this
and other anomalous references in our text (below, 154 n.523 and
159 n.541) indicate knowledge of an *Ethics* in eleven books; but
the explanation may be the simpler one that, as Bruns suggests,
Θ, which as a *letter* indicates the eighth book, was at some stage
in the transmission interpreted as the *numeral* for 9, and similarly
in the other cases. See Keaney 1968, 296 n.2.

[522] Aristotle, *EN* 8 1155b17-27. The whole passage runs as
follows: 'Perhaps it will become clear concerning these things
when we know what is loveable. For it seems that not everything
is loved, but what is loveable, and that this is good or pleasant or
useful. And it would seem that that is useful through which there
comes about something good, or pleasure, so that it will be the
good and the pleasant that are loveable as ends. So, do people
love what is good, or what is good for themselves? For sometimes
these are in disagreement; and similarly concerning what is pleasant. It seems that each person loves what is good for himself, and
that without qualification it is the good that is loveable, but for
each person what is [good] for that person. But each person loves
not what is good for himself but what appears to be. It will make
no difference; the object of love will be what appears [to be good
or pleasant] apparent.'

[523] *EN* 9 1168a35-b10: 'The facts disagree with these arguments,
not unreasonably. For people say one should love most the one
who is most dear, and the one who wishes goods is most dear to
the one for whom he wishes them, even if no-one is going to
know. And this is most the case for oneself in relation to oneself,

[Objection to I] But [this] opinion lacks distinctions. For we love ourselves either as being objects of appetition and as some thing separated from ourselves as one thing from another, for which we have appetition (for nothing has an appetition for itself, nor for what is present to itself, *qua* being present); or else, since it cannot be in that way – for we are not other than ourselves – we have appetition without qualification that we ourselves should exist. So [we have appetition that we should do so] also in a bad and painful condition.[524] For even when we are in these circumstances we still exist.[525]

[IIa] But there are those* who say that according to Aristotle the first appropriate thing is pleasure, they too themselves being prompted by what [Aristotle] says in the *Nicomachean Ethics*. For he says there are three objects of

---

and [so for] all the other things by which one who is dear is defined. For it has been said that all aspects of friendship start from oneself and extend to others. And all the proverbs are in agreement, like "a single soul" and "the goods of friends are shared" and "friendship is equality" and "the knee is closer than the shin". For all these things are most of all the case in relation to oneself. For one is most of all a friend to oneself. And so it is oneself that should be loved most.' Again, 'the ninth book' is Bruns' emendation, anticipated by Rovida, V and the Aldine referring to the tenth book. See the previous note. Giusta 1964, vol.1 285 n.17 compares also 1166a14-19. – Gottschalk 1987, 1117 comments that the passages cited do not actually support Boethus' and Xenarchus' view. The second passage seems more directly relevant than the first.

[524] Bruns suggests adding *ekhontes ouk alloi hêmeis hêmôn autôn*, 'so even when we are in a bad and painful condition we are not other than ourselves'. But this leaves the actual conclusion of the argument even less explicit than in the transmitted text.

[525] That is, if we simply say that we have an affinity to ourselves this will imply that we have a desire to go on existing in misery, whereas (Alexander presumably supposes) we in fact desire that happiness will replace the misery. As Alan Lacey points out to me, it is questionable whether this position does justice to the animal instinct for simple self-preservation. Cf. Gottschalk 1997, 112.

appetition, the noble, the advantageous and the pleasant.[526] An object of appetition is that to which we are appropriated. But we grasp the noble and advantageous when we advance in age; the pleasant, at once. If these are the only objects of appetition and things that are appropriate, and the first of these is the pleasant, then this will be the first thing that is appropriate to us. Moreover, if all appetition is for the good 25 or the apparent good, but the true good is the end, while the apparent good is not like this, and the apparent good is the pleasant, this will be the first object of appetition for us according to nature.

[Objection to IIa] This too is stated in a way that lacks make distinctions. For we have appetition either for the pleasant without qualification, or for [what is pleasant] in some way, [i.e.] that which is pleasant in some respect, having no unqualified appropriation to its coming about for us.

[IIb] Verginius Rufus and before him Sosicrates say that 30 each thing has appetition for perfection and being in actuality,[527] clearly [meaning by this] being active without

---

[526] *EN* 2 1104b30-31. These existence of these three objects of appetition is used to argue for freedom of human action from determinism in Alexander, *Fat.* 15 185,21-28, *Mant.* §23 174,17-24. See below, 163 n.549, 212 n.702.

[527] *energeiâi*, the same word that also indicates 'activity'. Similarly at 151,32 below. The form of the reference suggests that the interpretation is in fact Sosicrates', but Alexander knows it only through Verginius. Buecheler 1908, 190, suggests this may be L. Verginius Rufus (no.27 in RE), consul in 63 A.D. and guardian of the younger Pliny. For 'Sosicrates' the Aldine edition here gives 'Socrates', identified by Fabricius with the Socrates of Bithynia (no. 7 in *RE*) referred to as a Peripatetic by Diogenes Laertius 2.47 (see Lautner 1997, 304-5 n.42). But MS V has 'Sosicrates', and the reading in the Aldine is probably a simple error. Lautner suggests that Sosicrates may be the author of philosophical *Successions* recorded at Diogenes Laertius 2.84-85, 6.80, 7.163 (Lautner 1997, 305 nn.42 and 44; cf. Sosicrates [3] in *RE*) or the Sosicrates who was a pupil of Carneades (no.4 in *RE*; Philodemus, *Index Academicorum* XXIV.8 Dorandi). In either case it is striking that the interpretation offered is well-informed,

hindrance. And for this reason [Aristotle, they say,] says[528] that the object of appetition for us is being in actuality, that is being alive and the activities [deriving] from being alive, which are pleasant. For such activities in accordance with nature, as long as they are unhindered, are pleasant.[529]

152,1   But for each thing it is perfection that is good. The perfection of everything that is in potentiality is to become in actuality what it was in potentiality, and [being] a living creature does not consist in being active, but in having potentiality. For even [those who are] asleep are alive.[530] So, having appetition for being in actuality, [each person] will have appetition for his own proper perfection. This is good 5 for each, so we have appetition for this. It follows, for those who suppose that the first appropriate thing is being and living in activity, that they also say that pleasure is the first appropriate thing and the good.

In fact the end, too, is in harmony with this. For the end is being active in respect of intellect and being intelligent* in actuality, which depends on our having been appropriated to what is potential. For the human being when perfected has its being in being intelligent.[531]

10   [Objection to IIb] What is said needs distinction and definition; assuming that all activity from being alive is pleasant, do we have appetition for all of it as soon as we come into [existence], or not for all of it? Perhaps not for what is best, for this is final and ultimate. Or are they saying [that we have appetition] for that* [activity] which is in respect of what we are? At that time we have sensation, so [we have appetition for activity] in accordance with the [senses],[532] but subsequently we are rational. In the tenth 15 book of the *Nicomachean Ethics* [Aristotle] says 'for each

---

especially by comparison with that of Xenarchus and Boethus.
[528] Or just '... for this reason [Sosicrates] says'.
[529] Cf. Aristotle, *EN* 7 1153a14-15, 1153b9-12. Bruns conjectures 'and <to perform> the activities [deriving] from being alive'.
[530] Cf. Aristotle, *DA* 2.1 412a22ff.
[531] For the 'argument from perfection' cf. Striker 1996, 284.
[532] So Bruns, comparing 153,4 below.

[person] it is activity in accordance with its own proper condition that is most to be chosen.'[533]

[Solution I] These then are the opinions concerning the first appropriate thing according to those from the Peripatos. But the topic needs more careful distinction. Since the end is double, as Aristotle says,[534] on the one hand that which and the other for which, that *which* is happiness (for this is the ultimate and greatest of all good things and the goal), that *for which* is ourselves (for this is what is most the end for us, for happiness to come about for us); in relation to things it is happiness that is the end and the goal, but in relation to us it is ourselves being happy. So, since the end is double, there must be a certain double nature concerning the [first] principles too, each principle leading us, according to the continuity of the objects of appetition, to its proper end. So, as we say, the *first* object of appetition, too, is composite. For, [while] we are most appropriate to ourselves, we are not appropriated to ourselves without qualification, but to* good things coming about for ourselves. This then is the first thing appropriate to us, our [own] good, and it is for this that we have appetition.

But since it is impossible for us to have apprehension of the true good as soon as we come into [existence], we have appetition for the apparent good. And the apparent good is what is pleasant. So it is what is pleasant for us that is the first appropriate thing, that is, the apparent good. Even if it follows, because of the necessity of what follows from [their] arguments, for the others too who have spoken [of it] that they speak of [it as] the first appropriate thing, nevertheless they themselves did not make distinctions or differentiations, and some said [that the first appropriated thing] was us, others the external[535] thing which is pleasant,

[533] Aristotle, *EN* 10 1176b26-7. See below, 159 n.541.

[534] Bruns compares Aristotle, *Phys.* 2.2 194a35-6, *GA* 2.6 742a20; cf. *DA* 2.4 415b2, 20, *Metaph.* 12.7 1072b2.

[535] The suggestion is that view [I] refers to ourselves but not to pleasure, [IIb] to pleasure but not to ourselves, and that Alexander has improved on both by combining the two. But it hardly sees fair to interpret [IIb] as understanding the primary object of

35   but none of them has put it all together and completed the
       task. Accordingly both groups speak soundly, and at the
       same time both speak not soundly.

           [Solution II] Or rather: he who says that what is proper
       for each [person] is being in actuality, and being alive, and
153,1 activity* in accordance with his own being (for what is
       natural, in accordance with the being of each one, is pleas-
       ant and proper and the first object of appetition) does
       indeed speak in a way that involves distinction.[536] For the
       child, through not yet being rational, will not first be appro-
       priated to activity in this respect, but since it has sensation it
5   will be appropriated to the activities of the senses, and also
       to feeding itself.[537]

           In having appetition for unhindered activity in accordance
       with their being, [things] will have appetition for their own
       proper good and for pleasure, if pleasure is unhindered activ-
       ity of a natural state, and further for its coming about for
       themselves; for they have appetition for their own personal
       activity. For he who has appetition for his own proper
       activity, [i.e. for] that in accordance with how he is poten-
10   tially, clearly has appetition for unhindered [activity] (for
       what prevents and hinders activity must be avoided by the
       one who has appetition for it), and at the same time such
       [activity] is also pleasant. And the appetition is not for activ-
       ity without qualification, but for being active in it oneself;
       and, <having appetition> for [one's] own appropriated <activi-
       ty>,* one will have appetition for enjoying pleasure oneself,
       and all the more [so], since the pleasure accompanies the
       activity of a certain sort, towards which one is appropriated
       as a first [activity]. For one has not made pleasure the goal

---

appetition purely in terms of external things.

[536] In effect Alexander here takes over solution [IIb] and argues
that it already contains by implication the point concerning
chronological distinctions which he raised in his objection to that
view.

[537] Pohlenz 1967, vol.2 167 n.15 notes that the distinction drawn
here in the context of *oikeiôsis*, between the child which is not yet
rational and the person who has become so, is itself Stoic.

of one's appetition, but has this as accompanying the activity.[538] For everything which is in accordance with nature is pleasant. It is not the case that, having first enjoyed pleasure, one then on this basis has appetition for that through which he enjoyed pleasure. For nature does not require its own proper reasoning, but for things that come to be by nature the consequences of such a starting-point are in all cases the things [that come] after it and an end of a certain sort, if nothing hinders, not an object of forethought as in the case of the crafts, but constructed in such a way.[539]

And the end according to Aristotle is in harmony with such a starting-point,[540] being activity in accordance with virtue. In the tenth [book] of the *Nicomachean Ethics* Aristotle speaks as follows about this: 'One would think that all have appetition for pleasure, because all desire also to be alive. Life is a certain activity, and each is active concerning those things and in those things which he most likes. Pleasure perfects activities, and [perfects] living, for which they have appetition. Reasonably, then, they desire pleasure, too, since for each it perfects living, which is to be chosen.'[541]

[18]. That the virtues are implied by one another.   153,28

This section is one of the *Mantissa*'s characteristic 'batteries of arguments'. On the mutual implication of the virtues cf. Irwin

---

[538] Cf. Aristotle, *EN* 10 1174b14-1175a21, and, in connection with happiness, Ackrill 1974.

[539] That nature proceeds to its end if nothing impedes is Alexander's standard view; cf. *In Metaph.* 103,31ff., *Fat.* 4 168,3-7, *Prov.* 81,5-11 Ruland, and Alex. ap. Simplicius, *In Phys.* 311,1-19. For the contrast between art which calculates and nature which does not cf. *Fat.* loc. cit., *Prov.* 83,1-5. Sharples 1994b, 167 and n.15.

[540] For the need for the account given of the end to be in accord with that of the first appropriate thing see above, 151,3 and 152, 23.

[541] Aristotle, *EN* 10 1175a10-17. Here and at 152,14 above the MSS have κ', which as a numeral = 20. κ' may originally have been intended as the tenth letter of the alphabet rather than a numeral; or there may have been a copying error. (I am grateful to Bob Todd for discussion of this point.) See above, 153-4 nn.521-3.

1988, Gardiner 2001, and the other literature cited in the discussion of this section in Sharples 2000c. These arguments include those based on experience {1}, linguistic usage {2}, and ethical and psychological considerations {4}-{8}, including especially the role of practical wisdom {9}-{11}; but the distinction is not a rigid one (see below, 164 n.555).

The interrelation of the virtues is discussed elsewhere too in the texts attributed to Alexander. *Ethical Problems* 22 has the same title as the present section and is similar to 155,38-156,25 here; it seems to be an incomplete fragment (cf. Sharples 1990a, 56 nn.181, 183). *Ethical Problems* 8 and 28 consider whether virtue is a genus with particular virtues as species, or a whole of which particular virtues are parts; both of these texts, like arguments {8}-{11} here, assume that wisdom is essential for all the virtues.

On the present section see also Bruns 1884; Fortenbaugh 1984, 181-2; Annas 1993, 76 n.94; Sharples 2001, 610-11. Cf. also SVF 2.349, 3.295-304, with Duhot 1989, 223-4; Plotinus 1.2 [19] 7, with Merlan 1969, 121.

153,29   That the virtues are implied by one another might also be shown in the following way,[542] in that {1}[543] it is impossible to have some one of them in its entirety if one does not have the others too. For it is not possible to have justice in isola-

154,1   tion, if it belongs to the just person to act justly in all things that require virtue, but the licentious person will not act justly when something from the class of pleasant things leads him astray, nor the coward when something frightening is threatened against him if he does what is just, nor the lover of money where there is hope of gain; and in general every vice by the activity associated with it harms some

---

[542] As Pohlenz 1967, vol.2 169 points out, the term here used for 'be implied by one another' (*antakolouthein*) is Stoic: cf. Diogenes Laertius 7.125 = *SVF* 3.295, and Chrysippus ap. Plutarch, *De Stoic. rep.* 27 1046e = *SVF* 3.299.

[543] In this section the primary MS V marks paragraphs but without any marginal numbering. I have therefore reproduced the numbering of the secondary MS B in {braces}. I am grateful to Bob Todd for suggestions which have improved my translation of this section.

[aspect] of justice. Nor indeed can the licentious or unjust 5
person, or the one who has some other vice, be courageous;
for the licentious person will choose pleasure before the
activity of courage, and the unjust person will sometimes
choose advantage, neglecting action involving courage. It is
also possible to see traitors produced by these vices. And
how is it possible for the coward or the unjust person to act 10
with temperance and temperately? The unjust person will
give himself the advantage in pleasant things too, and the
coward will sometimes give in to certain shameful pleasures
on account of fear, when he is threatened by a tyrant, or
wanting to please himself right from the start he will
become accustomed to enjoy the same pleasures through
cowardice. And in general it is impossible for someone who
has any vice at all not to harm <the> activity of virtue by
[activity] involving this [vice];* so that he will not even have 15
[the virtue], which he thinks [he has], if he cannot employ
it on all occasions and in relation to all things to which activity involving this [virtue] relates.

{2} Moreover, those who are said to be good on account
of the presence of virtue differ from those who are said to
be good in respect of some craft or understanding, in that
[the latter] are said to be good with an addition – for we call
[someone] 'a good carpenter', 'a good cobbler', 'a good 20
geometrician', as a whole [in each case]; but the person
who has virtue is called 'good' without qualification and
without an addition, and it is impossible for the person to be
good without qualification who is not good in all respects.
So it is impossible a single virtue in isolation.

{3} Moreover, it is possible to show this same thing from
vice too. For one who has vice is bad without qualification,[544]
and* one who is bad without qualification cannot also be
good without qualification,[545] for he would have opposite 25

---

[544] The sequel shows that this must refer to the person who has
any vice. But in that case the claim appears to beg the question.

[545] In fact a person who is bad without qualification cannot just
'not be good *without qualification*'; he cannot be good in any way
at all.

[qualities] in the same respect at the same time concerning the same things. So it is impossible for one who has any vice to have virtue simultaneously.

{4} Moreover, if [i] the vices are not implied by one another – and how [could they be] when they are opposite to one another, given that some consist in excess and some in deficiency? – and if [ii] vice is sufficient for unhappiness, [iii] just a single vice will be sufficient for unhappiness.[546] But how is it possible to say that an unhappy person has any virtue?[547]

{5} Moreover, if virtue performs all its actions for the sake of the noble, *qua* noble – for virtue performs those among things that are done that are noble[548] – the person who has virtue will be a lover of what is noble. But the lover of what is noble loves what is noble in all things; and the person who loves what is noble in all things has all virtue. For if someone loved what is noble in courage, but not also what [is noble] in justice, he would not pursue what is noble in courage, either, *qua noble*. But if so, he would not be

___

[546] It is not immediately clear why the claim that (iii) a single vice is sufficient for unhappiness should be supported by *two* premisses, (i) that the vices do not imply each other and (ii) that vice is sufficient for unhappiness. The move from (ii) on its own to (iii) could indeed be blocked by the argument that 'vice' in (ii) means all vices rather than a single vice, and that could in turn be countered by the argument that a single vice implies all vices; but (i) is the contradictory of that. Perhaps the thought is rather that given (i) it is necessary to read (ii) in the sense of (iii). But the argument is hardly conclusive; that some vices are incompatible with others does not exclude the possibility that more than one vice is required for unhappiness. In any case it is being assumed that complete virtue is necessary for happiness.

[547] This argument assumes that the absence of wretchedness is necessary for virtue; which is equivalent by contraposition to the claim that virtue is sufficient for the absence of wretchedness, which can indeed be supported from Aristotle, *EN* 1 1101a6. See Annas 1993, 420, on the relation between that passage and the position of Antiochus of Ascalon.

[548] Cf., with Annas 1993, 123 and nn.249-52, Aristotle, *EN* 2 1105a31-2, 3 1115b11-13, 3 1116a11.

courageous, either. For everything that is noble is undifferentiated *qua* noble. For if [this person] does not know all   155,1
that is noble, he will not know this particular thing *as noble*;
for the knowledge of the noble, *qua* noble, is single. Or if he
knows it but does not choose it, he will not be a lover of
what is noble;[549] and so he will not even do *as being noble*
what he does do and choose. For as the lover of wine has an
affinity to every wine,[550] so the lover of what is noble   5
chooses and loves everything that is noble.

{6} Moreover, the virtues differ from one another not by
their goal but by the things with which they are concerned;
for they all have a single goal set before them, what is
noble, but they differ in that one is concerned with these
particular emotions, boldness and fear for example, another
with the pleasures through physical contact, another with
some other things. [So] the person who has a single virtue   10
also has the common goal of all virtue, what is noble. But
the person who has this as the goal of the things that he
does will do everything for the sake of this. And thus he will
have all the virtues, making what is noble his goal in all the
things that he does.

{7} Moreover, if every virtue of something is the culmination of the nature of that thing, the virtue of a human being,
too, will be the culmination of the nature and soul of a
human being. But the soul of a human being is rational,   15
though not simply but having several faculties, the one that
is rational in the proper sense and the other that is obedient
to reason;[551] and its virtue will be the culmination in each of

---

[549] Implying that one only loves what is noble if one always
gives it priority over all other considerations. (I am grateful to
Richard Sorabji for this point.) There is a tension between the
present argument and that from the possibility of alternative
motivations in *Fat.* 15 185,21-8 and *Mant.* §23 174,17-24 (see
above, 155 n.526 and below, 212 n.702); see also below, 164
n.555.

[550] Cf. Plato, *Republic* 5 475a; Simplicius, *In Cat.* 212,28. (I am
grateful to Inna Kupreeva for the latter reference.)

[551] Cf. Aristotle, *EN* 1 1098a4ff., 1103a2; Alex., *Probl. Eth.* 25
149,4-7.

the faculties of rational soul, so that a single one from among these would not, taken in itself, even be a virtue of a human being,. For it is not through being separated, i.e.

20 being able to subsist in themselves, that the virtues are all called by individual [names], but through belonging to different faculties[552] and being active concerned with different [subject-]matters. For complete virtue is a whole; its parts are courage, temperance, justice and each of the rest, which are not virtues without qualification, but concerned with specific things and accompanied by a [qualifying] addition;[553] for [virtue] without qualification is [virtue as] a whole. So, as in the case of other parts the parts considered

25 in the whole are parts [only] when they complete the whole,[554] but when they are separated-and come to be in themselves they are no longer parts, unless in name only; just so the virtues as parts [are]* virtues when they are in the whole [of virtue], <but no longer once they have been separated>,* except that we are in the habit of speaking of fitness [for various things] and good natural endowments as virtues, applying the name only. For as the person who has performed one action justly is not just if he is not similar in

30 all [his actions], just so one would not say[555] that the person who does certain things for the sake of something noble concerning a single [subject-] matter possesses virtue, if he did not pursue what is noble in a similar way everywhere and in every [case].

{8} Moreover, the virtue of the reasoning [part of the

---

[552] The relation between the different virtues and the different faculties is not made clear here, but cf. 155,31ff. below.

[553] So that, for example, courage would be 'the virtue concerning fear and boldness'. Cf. 154,19 above. (I am grateful to Inna Kupreeva for pointing out the parallel between the two passages).

[554] Inna Kupreeva points out to me that this terminology was used in Stoic discussions of virtue. See below, 184 n.619.

[555] This seems to be an analytic claim based on linguistic usage. (I am grateful to Alan Lacey for pointing this out.) This argument presupposes that it is possible to act for the sake of what is noble in some contexts but not in others, which is what arguments {5} and {6} denied.

soul] is understanding and knowledge of good things,[556] but of the emotional [part] the doing of good things. It is not possible to do good things if one is not acquainted with them and does not know them, nor is it possible to know that good things are good if one does not choose   35 them and have an inclination towards them;[557] a sign of this is that the one who chooses certain things also presupposes that these are good. [So] it is not possible to have the virtue of the reasoning [part] without [those of] the emotional, nor any of these without that and [without] each other.[558]

{9} Moreover, if knowing that good things are good has as a consequence choosing them also – for this is why we   156,1 say that the person who lacks self-control does not have knowledge in the proper sense and without qualification[559] – and knowing belongs to practical wisdom, choosing to the moral virtues, then the moral virtues will be a consequence of practical wisdom. But *it* [will] also [be a consequence of] *them*, if each of them is a virtue in acting in accordance with right reason,[560] that is, in accordance with practical wisdom.   5 And the moral [virtues will also be consequences of] one another, if the person who has one of these has both practical wisdom and the moral [virtues].[561]

---

[556] More strictly, this is the one among the virtues of the rational part that is relevant to ethics. Cf. Aristotle, *EN* 6 1139a3-17, 1143b14-17.

[557] This might seem to deny the possibility of lack of self-control. But see below, at n.559.

[558] 'emotional' = *pathêtikos*. Cf. Alexander, *In Top.* 145,23-32, 190,9-11; Arius Didymus ap. Stobaeus, *Ecl.* 2.7.1 (p.38.6 Wachsmuth) and 2.7.13 (p.117.9 Wachsmuth). Blumenthal 1996, 154-5; Sharples 2000c, §5 n.26.

[559] Cf. Aristotle, *EN* 7 1147b11-17.

[560] Cf. Aristotle, *EN* 6 1144b23.

[561] The structure of the argument, which is essentially Aristotle's at *EN* 6 1144b35-1145a2, is (i) practical wisdom is accompanied by (all) the moral virtues, (ii) any moral virtue is accompanied by practical wisdom, ∴ (iii) any moral virtue is accompanied by all the moral virtues.

{10} Moreover, if every action in accordance with virtue is a combination of having a goal of a certain sort and of being done in a certain way, and if to make the goal sound belongs to moral virtue, while to know what contributes to this belongs to practical wisdom,[562] how can [the one] be
10 separated [from the other]?

{11} Moreover, if it is impossible for someone to have practical wisdom if he does not have it concerning every-thing, someone who does have practical wisdom will be able to know all the things that are to be done. But in cases where it is not the appropriate goal that is set before us, it is impossible for the faculty which can know what contributes to [this goal] to be practical wisdom; for in these cases[563] the person with practical wisdom will not be able to judge and
15 know the things that must be done, but in all things it is the person with practical wisdom who is able to judge and know and do what must be done. So in all the things that are done he will have a goal set before him that is sound. And in this way he also has all virtue, if it belongs to the moral virtues to determine the best end and goal of things that are to be done, and the person with practical wisdom has the best goal determined in all things that are done. For it belongs to
20 the clever person to see what contributes to every goal, to the person with practical wisdom [to see] what [contributes] to the best [goal].[564] If then it is impossible to act in accordance with any of the moral virtues in the absence of practical wisdom, and practical wisdom is concerned with all the things that are done and combines all the moral virtues with itself (if it is a disposition which is able to act in accordance with reason concerning all the good things which belong to a human being qua human being – not some and not others, but all of them) [then]

---

[562] Cf. Aristotle, *EN* 6 1144a20-22, 1145a4-6; and on the discus-sion to which these claims have given rise, recently Smith 1996, who gives further references.

[563] I am grateful to Bob Todd for the suggestion that *ouketi* should be rendered by 'in these cases ... not' here.

[564] Cf. Aristotle, *EN* 6 1144a23ff.

practical wisdom will be accompanied by all the virtues. For   25
it is not easy, according to Theophrastus, to grasp the differences between the virtues in such a way that they do not
have something in common between them; but they are
given names according to what predominates [in each].[565]

[19]. That what is just [is so] by nature.   156,28

Aristotle deals with the question whether justice is natural in
EN 5 1134b18-1135a5, typically emphasising that there is truth
both in the claim that justice is conventional and in the claim
that it is natural. Aristotle however says little directly in that
chapter to demonstrate that natural justice exists. Christopher
Rowe has suggested that, as Aristotle is expressly concerned
with *political* justice, his reference to the best constitution
(1135a4-5) satisfies this requirement. However that may be, the
present discussion interprets the issue in wider terms and, as
Annas 1993, 144-5 notes, appeals to the claim that humans are
naturally social (for which see also Alexander, *Probl. Eth.* 24
147,24-148,4), and to the argument (used by Aristotle, below
168 n.567, but not explicitly connected by him with the thesis
that justice is natural) that human speech shows that human
beings are communal by nature. Cf. also Pohlenz 1967, vol. 2
169 and n. 17; Sharples 2001, 607-8, and (forthcoming, 3). I am
grateful to Bob Todd for suggestions that have improved my
translation of this section.

[1] That what is just [is so] by nature is shown by the fact   156,29
that <human beings> are communal by nature, but community cannot survive without justice. That [human beings]
are communal by nature is apparent from the clear facts; for
a human being is not such as to be able to live alone and by
himself. So, as we say that the other living creatures that
naturally gather in herds have this [characteristic] by
nature, so too human beings will have by nature the
[characteristic] of being communal, always spending life in   157,1
mutual community.

[565] 156,21-7 = Theophrastus, fr. L18 in Fortenbaugh 1984 =
Theophrastus, fr.460 FHS&G. The formulation could be seen as
anticipating Vlastos 1973, 234-46.

{2} Moreover, the living creatures that naturally gather in herds have this [characteristic] indeed by nature; for we say that that for which something has a natural impulse, not being led to it by teaching or habituation or necessity, belongs to it by nature, and it is in this way that the living creatures that gather in herds have being with one another in

5   accordance with a natural impulse. Nevertheless, although these things are so by nature, it is possible, I suppose, to separate one from being reared with the others and to rear it by itself, and some of those which naturally gather in herds with one another survive for a very long time when deprived of community with [the others]; but no human being would even survive if separated from other human beings.[566]

But the greatest sign that human beings are communal by

10 nature, and much more than all other living creatures, is that they alone are rational [*logikos*] and they alone can employ speech [*logos*], and that speech relates only to the indication of one's own thoughts and seeings to those who are with one.[567] At any rate when no-one is present with us, or when we do not want to indicate anything of our own* to any of those who are present or to learn anything from

15 them, we keep silence, being satisfied with thinking alone.[568] So, if there is something which is the only thing[569]

---

[566] Is this a claim about infants or about adults too? Whether or not one believes stories, ancient or modern, of children brought up by animals (like Romulus and Remus), hermits can survive in isolation. On the general issue of herds cf. Depew 1995. – The primary MS V marks paragraphs in this section but does not number the arguments: I have therefore reproduced the numbering of the secondary MS B in {braces}.

[567] Aristotle uses the fact that humans have speech by nature and that nature does nothing in vain to show that human beings are communal by nature, and in particular that human community is superior to that of other animals because it has a moral dimension (*Pol.* 1.2 1253a9-18. I am grateful to Richard Sorabji for this reference) but does not explicitly make this an argument for the natural rather than conventional nature of justice.

[568] Cf. the Stoic distinction between uttered speech (*logos prophorikos*) and internal speech or thought (*logos endiathetos*):

for which we employ the speech that has been given to us by nature, and nature produces and gives nothing in vain,[570] it will have given speech to us as being communal [beings].

{3} Moreover, one can employ the very statement, that what is just is [so] by stipulation, as evidence that human beings are communal by nature. For if all human beings need what is just and this agreement naturally – for [it is]   20 not that some do and some do not – and if they adopt this as something that preserves community, then [being] communal will belong to all human beings by nature.[571] And if community is by nature, then it is necessary for what is just, too, to belong to them by nature. For it is not possible to say that [they] need what is just, without also [saying] that what is just is by nature. For that, without which it is impossible   25 for some one of the things that belong to us[572] to be, must necessarily also [itself] be by nature. For example: it is impossible to see without eyes; and for this reason, since seeing is by nature, so too are the eyes by nature. Similarly ears are by nature, for it is not possible to hear without

---

SVF 2.135 = 223.

[569] Bruns conjectures *men* for *monon*: 'if there is on the one hand something for which we use ...'. But it is not unreasonable to argue that communication with others is the only thing for which we use speech, and the word-order of the Greek, though tortuous, is not impossible.

[570] Cf. Aristotle, *Cael.* 1.4 271a33, 2.11 291b14, *PA* 2.13 658a9, 3.1 661b24, *GA* 2.5 741b5, 2.6 744a36, *Pol.* 1.8 1256b20, and (with the qualification that this applies only to the primary products of nature) Alexander, *Fat.* 11 178,11, *Mant.* § 20 163,24, §25 183,25.

[571] With the argument that it is natural for human beings to make agreements as to what is just, even if the agreements themselves are conventional, one might compare the Epicurean claim that the development of language is natural even if some vocabulary is conventional (Epicurus, *Ad Hdt.* 75-6, Lucretius, 5.1028ff.; cf. also Alexander, *Quaest.* 3.11, and Todd 1976b, 140-6). Cf. Striker 1996, 266.

[572] Bruns says that the argument here requires the addition of '<by nature>'. It can perhaps be left to be understood from the context.

these, and hearing is by nature; and in general the sense-
organs [belong] to us by nature, since the activities
30   performed through them, too, belong to us by nature. If
then we are communal by nature, but community is impossible without justice, it is necessary for what is just, too, to
exist by nature.

{4} If, because different things are just among different
peoples, for this reason they[573] say that [what is just does]
not [exist] by nature, it is clear that they will say that that
which is the same among all [does exist] by nature.

{5} And if they will say that what is written down is based
on an agreement, and not by nature, for the reason that it is
written down, it is clear that it is necessary for these people
35   to say that what does not have its force depending on
writing is by nature and is not based on an agreement. But
there are many things like this, which* we are accustomed
to call, from the very [feature] that applies to them, 'unwritten laws',[574] which are common to all human beings, at any
158,1   rate those that are not incapacitated.[575] Respecting one's
elders and revering the divine and honouring one's parents
and betters are unwritten and common [elements of] justice
observed by nature among all human beings.[576] For they
neither make agreements with one another about these

---

[573] Probably hypothetical opponents introduced for the sake of
the discussion and not to be identified with any specific school. Or
is the reference to more recent Sceptic discussion? Cf. Sharples
(forthcoming, 3).

[574] Cf. Ostwald 1973.

[575] That natural justice is not found among those who are
'incapacitated' is not remarked by Aristotle in *EN* 5, but is
indicated, using rather the term *adiastrophos* 'uncorrupted', by
Anon., *In EN* 232,10, 233,15 and Michael of Ephesus, *In EN 5*
46,10, 47,6.13. Neither however refers to 'unwritten laws'.

[576] Aristotle in *EN* 5 gives no examples of universally accepted
justice. Anon., *In EN* 232,11-12 gives revering the gods, honouring
parents, and showing the way to those who are lost; Michael, *In
EN 5* 46,13-16 the same plus assisting the needy and helping up
someone who has slipped and fallen over. Cf. Sharples (forthcoming, 3).

things nor write them down, but taking these as agreed and
confirmed by nature as being so, they make laws about the   5
manner of the honour, some [that it should be] in this way,
some in that, and some thinking that they will do these
things through [actions] of this sort, others through those
of that sort, those in which each person is previously habitu-
ated; it is concerning these that, from this point on, justice
based on an agreement has its force. For it is justice and
legality based on an agreement that tells us to revere the
divine or honour our parents in this way or that. And for this   10
reason each of these things [is done] in different ways
among different peoples at different times; but honouring
[parents] and revering the divine is established in the
nature of human beings always and among all. And for this
reason [it does not apply] at one time but not at another, or
among some people but not among others.

[6] And in general one would not fail to hit the truth if one
said that those [elements of] justice exist by nature without
which it is impossible for community to exist. For it is not
the case that community[577] is by nature but the things   15
through which community is preserved are not;[578] but it is
necessary, since community is natural, that [the elements]
of justice through which community exists should exist by
nature.[579]

That it is justice that holds community together is clear
from those who are thought to be most unjust. These are
robbers, whose community with one another is preserved
by [their] justice towards one another. For it is on account   20
of [their] not taking advantage of one another and not
defrauding [one another], and [their] respecting what
seems to be superior[580] and preserving what has been

---

[577] Literally 'what is of community' (*to tês koinônias*). See
below, 228 n.757.

[578] The formulation is Stoic: 'not both (p and not q)' = 'if p then
q' (though the Stoics used the two different formulations to distinguish between different types of implication). Cf. Sharples 1983,
170.

[579] This section repeats the argument of 157,18ff.

[580] Or 'stronger'? But 'superior' has more point in the context

agreed, and assisting the weaker, that their community with
one another endures, [though] they do altogether the
opposite of these things to those whom they wrong. The
greatest sign that these things are just by nature is that, if
25   they agreed the opposite things to these with one another
as being just, their community could not endure, although it
would have followed [sc. if justice *were* purely a matter of
agreement] that everything that came about in [the context
of] an agreement would preserve community in a similar way.

But if certain things preserve community whether people
make an agreement or not, and the opposites of these
destroy it, then the things that preserve those who make an
agreement are by nature, even if they come about in accor-
30   dance with an agreement. For the agreement seems to be a
certain seeking for what is just by nature, and common
agreement on what has been found. But some of those who
seek also find what they are seeking for, and others miss it,
just as happens, indeed, in all the other things that are by
nature [such as] to be found by seeking.

{7} Moreover, those who decide to act unjustly and
engage in robbery do not examine the established laws and
35   engage in robbery and evil-doing through contravening
these, but, on the basis that the [actions] through which
robbing [takes place] are clearly injustices, they set about
[robbing].[581] But if certain things are unjust by nature, and
not [unjust merely] through contravening the things that
have been agreed on as just, it is necessary to say that the

(that robbers respect the law of the jungle, respecting the
stronger, also among themselves would hardly be surprising) and
also gives more point to 'seems', for among robbers who are
wicked nothing can actually *be* superior in the sense of being
better. – This argument combines Plato's observation that it is
justice between the members of a band of robbers that gives them
their strength (*Republic* 1 351c-352c) with the point that not just
any agreement has the nature of justice, which is reminiscent
rather of Epicurus (*Kuriai Doxai* 37-8). Cf. Striker 1996, 266.

[581] Literally: 'they go to it' (LSJ *agô* II.2). I am grateful to Inna
Kupreeva for discussion of this passage.

things opposite to these are just by nature. And that there
are* things that are unjust by nature is clear from the fact
that among all peoples, even those who have laws most   159,1
opposite [to each other's], there are certain things in
common which those who choose to act unjustly do to
those that they wrong. For almost all the things that
robbers do to those they wrong are the same among all
[peoples]. But if so, it is clear that the things opposite to
these which are unjust by nature, are just by nature. For
acting unjustly is nothing other than contravention of what   5
is just. So, if there is by nature something that is contravention of what is just, it is clear that much sooner will what is
just, contravention of which is unjust, be by nature. For
contravention of something is posterior to that of which it is
contravention. And[582] what is unjust by nature is nothing
other than contravention of and contrariety to what is just
by nature.

{8} Moreover, as it is in the case of the other virtues, so it
is reasonable that it should be also in the case of justice.[583]   10
In the case of each of the other [virtues] the things done by
them are of such a sort by nature. For the person who has
courage does things that are courageous by nature, and the
things that are done as a result of temperance are temperate
by nature, and similarly in the case of the others too. So
there are both actions that are just by nature and justice
[that is so by nature].

[20]. That virtue is not self-sufficient for happiness.   159,15

That virtue was sufficient for happiness was the claim of the
Stoics, in contrast to Aristotle's position (*EN* 1 1100a10-1101a21;
cf. Long 1968; Annas 1993, 364-84). The relation between virtue
and other goods had been a topic of controversy in the interpretation of Aristotle himself (cf. Annas 1993, 364-88, 412-25, and below
184 n.619). The present series of arguments shows signs of

---

[582] The Greek has 'For', but 'And' makes it clearer in English that
this is the second premiss in support of the conclusion at 159,6-7.

[583] This argument depends on justice being a virtue. But that
seems questionable. Cf. Williams 1980; Sharples (forthcoming, 3).

varying positions (182-3 n.615, 184 n.619, 185 n.624, 195 n.657) and is not always orthodox in its Aristotelianism (192 n.647). It also shows scant regard for the internal logic of Stoic positions, but is not alone in this among ancient polemics on this topic and on many others. An indication of the tradition of debate which lies behind this text may be given by Seneca, *Ep. Mor.* 85.31-8, which presents the question whether adverse circumstances hinder the perform-ance of an art or craft (below, 178 n.598, 192 n.646) as a debate between Peripatetics and Stoics, and which Striker 1996, 314 and n.22, following Donini, therefore suggests may reflect a continuing tradition of Peripatetic interest in the topic.

On the present text cf. Annas 1993, 397; Sharples, 2000b and 2001, 613-15. I am grateful to Inna Kupreeva and Bob Todd for corrections to my translation of this section at several points. The numbering of the arguments is that in the margin of V.

159,16   (1) If the person who has virtue is happy, and the person who is happy lives a happy [life] (for happiness is in a life), the person who has virtue has a happy life. The happy life is to be chosen, and <the life that is to be chosen is>* not [something] not to be wished for; so the happy life is not [something] not to be wished for. So the life that someone leaves voluntarily is not a happy life. But the person who 20   has virtue might sometimes voluntarily leave the life that is with virtue, on account of reasonable departure.[584] So the life that has virtue and that which is in accordance with virtue[585] is not happy. So virtue is not self-sufficient for

---

[584] Cf. *SVF* 3.757-759, 763, 765, 768. (159,19-21 here = *SVF* 3.767); and with the present argument cf., with Rovida, Alex., *In Top.* 166,33-167,2 = *SVF* 3.67, and also ibid. 173,11-14. But the argument fails to recognise the Stoic position; the Stoic sage will leave life by committing suicide when it is the proper thing to do (for example, in certain circumstances to save one's country or one's friends), and proper acts performed by the sage are virtuous acts. Consequently in committing suicide the sage is not selecting death *rather than* a virtuous life; he is selecting death in circum-stances where to remain alive would not be virtuous. See below, 177 n.596, and on Stoic attitudes to suicide generally cf. Rist 1969, 233-55.

[585] Bruns suggests adding *zôn*: 'and <the person who lives> in

happiness.

(2) Moreover, if the person who enquires whether virtue is self-sufficient for happiness is not conducting an absurd enquiry, but the person who enquires whether virtue is self-sufficient for *virtue* is conducting an absurd enquiry, each of these enquiries is not the same. But if these are not the   25 same, virtue and happiness are not the same thing. But the first: so the second.[586] If then virtue and happiness are different, it is clear that being happy does not [consist] in having virtue, just as playing the pipe does not [consist] in having [the art of] pipe-playing.[587] So happiness does not [consist] only in the disposition and possession of virtue.

(3) Moreover, if what is brought about by something is different from what produces it, and happiness according to   30 them is brought about by virtue, virtue is a different thing from happiness. But the first: so the second.

(4) Moreover, if happiness [consists] in life and is an activity, and virtue is a disposition, happiness and virtue are not the same thing.

(5) Moreover, if every craft produces something other than itself and not itself, but virtue according to them is a craft that produces happiness,[588] happiness, which is brought about by virtue, will be different from it.   160,1

(6) Moreover, if activity in accordance with virtue produces happiness, but virtue is not self-sufficient for activity in accordance with virtue, virtue is not self-sufficient for happiness. For either [virtue] is concerned with the selection of pleasant things, according to Epicurus,[589] or with the selection of things in accordance with nature, as the Stoics   5 think,[590] or with that of things which are appropriate in

---

accordance with virtue ...'

[586] Above, 73 n.231. Cf. Striker 1996, 299.

[587] The implication of the analogy is that happiness consists in the *exercise* of virtue. See arguments (4) and (6) below.

[588] Cf. Annas 1993, 169 n.36. 159,33-160,1 = *SVF* 3.66.

[589] This is not Epicurus' own formulation, but a rephrasing in terms taken from the Stoics. Cf. Sharples 2000b, 124.

[590] This formulation of the Stoic end (also at 163,32ff. below) is

whatever other way it may be; and all these must underlie its activities as matter, as for the craft of bronze-working [there underlie as matter] bronze, iron, fire, coals. It does not itself produce any of these, but uses them as things that underlie [it]. For activity in accordance with virtue does not produce the things that are in accordance with nature. If its activity is concerned with certain things that underlie,

10 which it does not itself produce, virtue is not self-sufficient for its own activities, since it also needs the things with which its activity is concerned, which are external to it. For these things do not, as *they* say,[591] have the role [merely] of *sine quibus non*,[592] but they set virtue in motion and are causes of its acting and being active. For it aims at them as craftsmen [aim] at their own proper material. At any rate,

15 they say that actions will be done away with for them if these things do not, by the differences among them, attract the virtues and set them in motion.[593] For neither would* pipes, if they contributed to our existence, for this reason not contribute to pipe-playing, but they would occupy the role of *sine quibus non*.[594] So it is not the case that, if the things that virtue uses belong to a human being necessarily

---

post-Chrysippean; cf. Diogenes of Babylon and Antipater of Tarsus as reported by Diogenes Laertius 7.87-9, Clement of Alexandria, *Strom.* 2.21 129.1-5, and Stobaeus, *Ecl.* 2.7.6a, p.76.9-13 Wachsmuth; Pohlenz 1967, vol.2 169 n.17; Long 1967, 75-86, especially 80 n.55 linking 160,3ff. here to Antipater.

[591] Striker 1996, 302 argues that this is the sense, rather than 'For, as they say, these things do not ...'

[592] I.e. things that make no active contribution; Bruns ad loc., citing 161.26ff. below.

[593] If some indifferents were not preferred to others, we would have no reason for choosing some rather than others, and hence no reason for acting at all. Cf. the criticism of Aristo at Cicero, *Fin.* 3.50. – 160,3-5 and 8-16 = *SVF* 3.64.

[594] Necessary conditions for our survival (such as health, or at least a minimum thereof) are not, by their status as necessary conditions, reduced to being *just* that; rather, by the Stoics' own argument, they play an active role by prompting proper actions.

and without them he does not exist, for that reason they do
not contribute to the activity of virtue, [even though they]   20
are different from it.

(7) Moreover, if for selection in accordance with nature
there is need of a healthy body and senses, which are external to virtue – for how would [a person] make the selection
of the things in accordance with nature in the [correct]
manner without these? But they are external to virtue –
virtue is not self-sufficient.

(8) And moreover, if the activity of virtue is concerned
with the selection of things that are in accordance with
nature and appropriate, and with the rejection and avoid-   25
ance of those that are opposite to these, clearly the things
must be present which [the person] is going to select.[595] For
these things are not indeed always present for a human
being. At any rate it is on account of lack of these that the
person who has virtue will sometimes make away with
himself. For the making away is not on account of inability
to select these things, which is the task of virtue, but on
account of their not being present, which does not depend
on [virtue].[596] If then the presence of these things does not
depend on [virtue], but its activity is concerned with the   30
selection of these things, virtue is not self-sufficient for its
own proper activity.

(9) Moreover activity in accordance with each craft is of

[595] Bruns does not begin a new sentence at the start of argument
(8), and it might be supposed that the number is inserted in the
margin of V as a mechanical response to 'and moreover'. But
argument (7) is concerned with the equipment, as it were, which
is needed for selection, (8) with the need for objects to select.

[596] 160,24-9 = *SVF* 3.766. That suicide for the Stoics is justified
by lack of external 'goods' is claimed at Cicero, *Fin.* 3.60-61 (*SVF*
3.763); Plutarch, *De Stoic. rep.* 14 1039de, 18 1042d (*SVF* 3.759),
Comm. Not. 11 1063de (part also = SVF 3.759), 22 1069d, 24 1070b,
and Stobaeus, *Ecl.* 2.7.11m (p.110,9 Wachsmuth = *SVF* 2.758). But
this is so in the sense that the appropriateness of suicide, as of
everything else, depends on the circumstances, not because virtue
is inadequate without indifferents. See above, 174 n.584, and cf.
Irwin 1998, 176; Kidd 1998, 293-4; Sharples 2000b, 131.

two kinds, one in conducive[597] [circumstances], as for the piper if he is healthy in body and has the sort of pipes he wants and nothing external troubles him, the other in [circumstances] that are not to be wished for and are opposite to the aforementioned ones. As for the other crafts the end is in activities that are concerned with what is wished for and which are in conducive [circumstances],* so also in the case of virtue, if indeed it too is a craft.[598]

(10) Moreover, if no craft is self-sufficient for its own proper activity because it needs things through which and on which to be active, and virtue too is a craft, nor will [virtue] itself[599] be self-sufficient for activity in accordance with it[self].

(11) Moreover, if virtue is concerned with the selection of the things in accordance with nature, but it is not possible to make a selection and judgement of certain things if one has not first got an impression concerning them, and this [impression] cannot be present for someone who does not

---

[597] For *prohêgoumena* 'conducive circumstances' (I owe the translation to Richard Janko), or 'favourable circumstances', in the context of virtuous activity and therefore of happiness, cf. Alex., *Probl. Eth.* 25 148,31-2, and Sharples 1990a, 64-5 n.220; Giusta 1961-2, 229-31; Grilli 1969, 439-44, 460-61; Huby 1983, 125-6.

[598] See 175 n.588 above. If the Stoics are to counter this argument, it must be by allowing a disanalogy between virtuosity in living and virtuosity in pipe-playing. Living may be like pipe-playing (or dancing) in that what matters is the performance rather than a separate end-product; but we do not normally say that a piper is playing well if he is doing the best he can with an inferior instrument, or a dancer if he does the best he can on a slippery floor. (Cf. however Seneca, *Ep. Mor.* 85.33, arguing that a storm does not hinder a navigator's work but it makes it more conspicuous, and (38) that the sage, even if poor, can help others by showing how poverty should be dealt with. Above, p.174). See Striker 1996, 319-20; Sharples 2000b, 128-130.

[599] Annas 1993, 397-400 notes that the Stoics could defend their position, implausibly indeed, by claiming that a skill need not be exercised – as the Stoic sage is both a king and a cobbler: Diogenes Laertius 7.122 = *SVF* 3.617, Horace, *Sat.* 1.3.124ff. See below, 181 n.612.

perceive [*aisthanesthai*] and perceive in a healthy way,
[then] perception that is healthy is needed for [virtue's]
activity concerning these things.[600] But [virtue] is not in
control of this, [so] it will not be in control of [its own] activ-   10
ity. For as it was not able to be active in the absence of the
things that underlie it,[601] which it did not itself control, just
so, if these things do underlie, but an impression has not
preceded, it is impossible for an impulse to occur,[602] and the
impression is from sensation [*aisthêsis*] in a certain
condition,[603] if the impressions do not deceive [the
person].[604] But if virtue is not self-sufficient either for the
existence of the things concerning which it is active, nor for
the impression and sensation without which it does not act,   15
it will not be self-sufficient for its own activity.

(12) Moreover, if it is possible for the person who has
virtue to suffer lethargy and melancholy[605] and clouding of

[600] Bob Todd draws my attention to Alex., *DA* 41,15-17, where
accurate perception of proper sensibles is said to require (i) a
healthy condition of the sense-organs, (ii) the thing perceived to
be in (an appropriate) position, (iii) a suitable distance between
the sense-organ and the object.

[601] 'Underlie' in the sense of being the objects with which it is
concerned; cf. Todd 1996, index p.224 s.vv. *hupokeimenon*,
hupokeisthai. I am grateful to Bob Todd for drawing my attention
to this. For 'which it did not itself control' cf., with Bruns, 160,6-8
above.

[602] For the full sequence, perception-impression-assent-impulse-
action, cf.. Alex., *DA* 72,16, drawn to my attention by Bob Todd;
also *Mant.* §23 173,29, *Fat.* 14 184,1.

[603] Retaining the MSS *phantasia de aistheseôs pôs ekhousês*.
Bruns in his apparatus conjectures *phantasiâi de <dei> aistheseôs
pôs ekhousês*, 'for impression there is need of perception in a
certain condition', but this seems unnecessary. (I am grateful to
Richard Janko for discussion of this passage.)

[604] Bessarion in MS B, and Bruns, conjecture *autên* for *auton*:
'do not deceive (the sensation)'. But sensation precedes impression rather than following it, and an anonymous referee points out
that *auton* can refer back to *aisthanomenôi* in 161,8.

[605] Chrysippus held that virtue can be *lost* because of *melancholia* (Diog. Laert. 7.127), but this section of *Mant.* seems

judgement and derangement, and it is impossible for a person in these [conditions] to be active in accordance with virtue, virtue [will not be] self-sufficient for its own proper activities. For how can those who are not [just] wanting to defend a position[606] say that the person who is deranged, and for this reason needs to be tied up and assisted by his friends, is acting wisely at that time?

(13) Moreover, if according to these people virtue rejects and avoids some indifferent things, but chooses and selects others, it will not be self-sufficient for happiness. For how can the person be happy who is in those [circumstances] that virtue rejects? For either it will not do well in rejecting these, or else it is not possible to be happy in the presence of those things that it is the task of virtue to reject.[607]

[13a] The senses themselves too, if they have the status of what is necessary for the existence of a human being, but do not also contribute towards the activities of virtue, will have the role of *sine quibus non*; but if, in addition to being necessary for the human being, they also contribute to actions, and virtue uses them for its own activities – for the impression is the foundation-stone of actions in accordance with virtue[608] – [then the senses] do not, in relation to

---

unaware of this (below, 191 n.644). Cf. argument (27) below. 161,16-24 = *SVF* 3.239.

[606] Cf. Alex., *Fat.* 12 180,4-5: 'this is what all those who are not defending some position accept'.

[607] For the Stoics, however, happiness lies in virtue, that is in attempting as far as possible to reject what is to be rejected; to fail in this, due to circumstances beyond one's control, does not diminish happiness.

[608] A point particularly apt against the Stoics, for whom knowledge, and hence virtue, was founded on 'apprehensive impressions', those that could not mislead. The present argument is reminiscent of the Academic Sceptics' objection that assent is impossible in the absence of such an impression (Sextus, *M.* 7.153-5 = LS 41C) and that the Stoics were wrong to claim that action was impossible in the absence of assent (Plutarch, *Adv. Colot.* 1122A-F = LS 69A), used here for the different purpose of demonstrating that virtue is not self-sufficient.

activities in accordance with [virtue], have the role of *sine quibus non*, as do heaven and earth and place and time.[609] For if we are going to act in accordance with virtue no matter what the condition of our sensations is,[610] [then] either we will assent to the false impressions from such sensations and perform the actions that follow on these – and how is that [characteristic] of a good person? – or, if we hold back and do not assent, we will do none* of the things that [follow] on [these impressions], so that we will not be active in any respect at all. If [virtuous people] do some other things,[611] but hold back concerning these, the person who has virtue will not according to this act in accordance with virtue in respect of everything in his life, so that [virtue will not be] self-sufficient for its own proper activities, [seeing that] on account of the absence of certain things [viz. the reliable impressions] it does not even perform [the activities]. To say that people are active even when they are asleep,[612] on the grounds that they remember certain things – for when they wake up they have the memory and have

35

40

162,1

---

[609] Argument [13a] is marked as a new paragraph in V, but not there numbered as a new section. 161,26-37 = *SVF* 3.63. Cf. above, argument (6); also Cicero, *Topica* 59 and Clement of Alexandria, *Stromateis* 8.9.25 = *SVF* 2.345, with Hankinson 1998, 249-50, 336-7.

[610] The start of the present paragraph might lead one to expect the point to be that receiving reliable impressions depends on the condition of one's sense faculties; but this connection does not seem to be made, and the argument seems rather to relate to the content of sensations, which may reflect external conditions as much as internal ones. Compare argument (11) above.

[611] The suggestion is not that they will *per impossibile* do things other than those that are virtuous; rather that they will act virtuously on other occasions but will refrain from action when they do not have a reliable impression, and so will not act virtuously in these last cases. To this it could be objected that it is, precisely, virtuous to refrain from action when you cannot be sure of how things are.

[612] Alexander imagines his opponents replying to the preceding argument, that accurate sense-impressions are necessary for virtuous action, by contending that action is not to be understood in the ordinary sense of the term.

not lost it – is just like saying that people who are asleep see, since when they wake from sleep they see and have not lost the power of seeing.

(14) Moreover, if it is not the happiness of a soul that is being sought, but that of a human being, and it is agreed
5 that a human being is composed of soul and body, each of which [have] their own proper goods and evils which are different from one another, just as they too themselves are different from one another, how does it not follow that the end and good of that which is composed of both needs the good of both of these things of which it is composed?[613] But if so, the good of the soul is not self-sufficient for the end of the human being, but it also needs the [goods] of the body;
10 and the goods of the body are health, which is concerned with the good blending of the primary bodies in which [the body] has its being; strength, which consists in the good tension of the secondary bodies and those composed of these; beauty, which consists in the good shape and proportion of the tertiary and anhomoiomerous bodies which we call the proximate parts of the body.[614] For as in the case of
15 the soul there is need for all the virtues of every faculty for the end of the human being, so it is also in the case of the body.[615]

---

[613] Cf., with Madvig 1876, 519, Cicero, *Fin.* 4.26; also below, 163,12ff.

[614] Cf. Chrysippus in *SVF* 3.471 = Galen, *PHP* 5.2.33, where however strength is the proportion and good tension in the *sinews*; also Aristotle, *Top.* 3.1 116b18-22 with Alexander, *In Top.* 236,10-16 ad loc., Arist. *Phys.* 7.3 246b4-8, *Eudemus* fr. 45 Rose³ = Philoponus, *In DA* 145,4-5; Jaeger 1948, 44 n.1. (I am grateful to Inna Kupreeva for these references.) Cf. also Galen, *PHP* 5.3.17 (beauty and health only).

[615] Compare Carneades' criticism of the Stoic position (above, 149). Striker 1996, 288 argues that this objection only has force against an attempt to derive the end from the primary natural things, which is, she argues, not an accurate account of the original Stoic position, but a distortion originating from Carneades and passed on by Antiochus to Cicero (Striker 1996, 227-31, 263, 268-9, 288-93). See also below, on 163,12-18. The present passage

(15) Moreover, virtue wants the things for which human beings have a natural affinity[616] to be in a good condition, and does not wish to have them not in a good condition; and [a human being] has a natural affinity not only to himself and his parts and faculties and perfections, but also to those around him, parents, friends, relatives, fellow-citizens; for [a human being] is a communal and political creature. [So] it is clear that if these things are in good condition and are preserved they make some contribution to his own proper good and end and to all the things that he needs to be able to preserve both himself and each [member] of those [groups] for whom he has a natural affinity. So he also needs the beneficial goods,[617] which can either produce the things that are to be chosen on their own account for a human being – these are those for which he has a natural affinity – or preserve them or ward off their opposites.

(16) Moreover, if happiness is completeness of good things and each of the things for which we have a natural affinity is some good, how is there not need of all of these for completeness of good things? For to say that we have an affinity for a plurality of things, but that it makes no difference to us how they are, is to say things that are inconsistent.[618] If we need them, how could anyone be said to be happy in the absence of these things that he needs, if happiness is something without lack and complete?*[619]

---

suggests that bodily goods are not good purely as instruments for virtue; cf. below, 184 n.619.

[616] *oikeiousthai*: see §17 above.

[617] For Arius Didymus(?) ap. Stobaeus, *Ecl.* 2.7.19, p.134,20-135,1 Wachsmuth, 'beneficial' goods are those that produce and preserve goods of three other types, those that are honourable (god, the ruler, one's father) or praiseworthy (justice, wisdom) or potencies (wealth, rule, power). Cf. Alexander, *In Top.* 242,7 = Aristotle fr.113 Rose³, and Aspasius, *In EN* 32,16: also [Aristotle], *MM* 1.2 1183b35ff., though the actual term 'beneficial' is not there used. Cf. Sharples 1983b, 142, 144; 2000b, 136.

[618] 162,29-30 = *SVF* 3.185.

[619] Or 'perfect' (*teleios*). The Stoics would simply reject the claim that these things are goods in the proper sense of the term

(17) Moreover the common notions concerning happiness suppose that it is self-sufficiency of life – for they conceive[620] the happy person as without lack – and suppose

35 that happiness is the ultimate object of desire;[621] but they also say that living in accordance with nature and life in accordance with nature are happiness, and in addition to these [points] they say that living well and having a good life and a good living are happiness[622]. If happiness is conceived of as like this, but virtue is self-sufficient for none

163,1 of these, neither will it be self-sufficient for happiness. Is the person who has virtue in [a state of] self-sufficiency and not

---

or necessary for happiness. For happiness as a 'fullness' or completion (*sumplêrôma*) made up from goods of the soul, goods of the body and external goods cf. Aristotle as reported by Diogenes Laertius 5.30, and Critolaus reported by Arius Didymus(?) ap. Stobaeus, *Ecl.* 2.7.3b p.46,10-20 Wachsmuth; also, with Giusta 1964, vol.1 326 n.2, [Plato], *Definitiones* 412d, and Cicero, *Tusc. Disp.* 5.29. Stobaeus' source itself argues rather that bodily and external goods are *used* by virtuous activity; so too Aspasius, *In EN* 24,3ff. Cf. Annas 1993, 413-14; Sharples 1999b, 86-7. The claims (i) that external goods are part of the end along with virtue and (ii) that external goods have instrumental value for virtue, though not incompatible, are independent; and the arguments collected in §20 vary as to which view they follow. See below, arguments (20) and (35). The terminology of fullness or completion was used by the Stoics, as Inna Kupreeva points out to me in connection with §18 155,25 above, but for the Stoics it is the *virtues*, and *just* the virtues, which 'complete' happiness; cf. *SVF* 3.73, 106, 107, and below, 195 n.657. See White 2002, 87-8.

[620] *proeilêphasin*, etymologically connected with *prolêpsis*, the Stoic term for those common notions that arise naturally. 'Common notions' too was originally a Stoic term, but adopted by others too to refer to general consensus. Cf. Sandbach 1930; Todd 1973; Scott 1988 and 1995, 179-186, 201-210; Obbink 1992. I am grateful to Bob Todd for discussion of this point and for some of the above references. 162,32-163,1 = *SVF* 3.65.

[621] See above, 150 n.508.

[622] Magnaldi 1991, 65-6 n.3 compares this passage with Arius Didymus(?) ap. Stobaeus, *Ecl.* 2.7.6e pp.77,16-19, 78,1-6 Wachsmuth, and also with Michael, *In EN* 598,30 = *SVF* 3.17.

in need of anything in his life? Rather, there are many things which the person who has virtue needs: health, strength, prosperity, and many other things; and this is so also according to those according to whom virtue is supposed to be self-sufficient for happiness.

For they say that there are some things which are preferred by the wise person and have value, and certain 5 things which are proper and exercise attraction; but also that, if virtue together with these and virtue alone were alternatives, the wise person would never choose [virtue] in isolation, if he were able to take [virtue] accompanied by the other things.[623] But if this is so, it is clear that the wise person will have need[624] of them; for it would be ridiculous of him to select them but not relate the selection of them to any [end]. How then will virtue still be the ultimate object of 10 desire, and that achieving which we would no longer desire anything else? And how will it be sufficient in itself for living? And if not for these, neither for happiness. For it is established that happiness is like this.[625]

[623] Similarly Cicero, *Fin.* 4.59 (Antiochus against the Stoics) and Alex., *In Top.* 211,9-14 = *SVF* 3.62 (cf. Irwin 1998, 173). In fact it is not clear that a choice between virtue without wealth and virtue plus wealth on one single occasion could ever actually arise; either the proper thing to do in the circumstances is to select wealth, in which case rejecting it would not be virtuous, or else it is proper to reject it, and to select it would not be virtuous. (Cf. Sharples 1996, 110; 2000b, 131-134.) 163,4-8 = *SVF* 3.192.

[624] Greek *khreia* is ambiguous between 'need' and 'use'. Even if we pass over the difficulty in the previous note, the argument in fact establishes only that the wise person has a *use* for preferred things, not that he actually *needs* them for happiness. But we have been told at 163,2 that 'there are many things which the person who has virtue needs (*deitai*)'; so *khreia* is nevertheless being understood as 'need'. Cf. Rist 1969, 9, suggesting that the Stoics' use of the term *khreia* was misinterpreted by their opponents; Kidd 1955, 160; Edelstein and. Kidd 1989, 640; Sharples 2000b, 132. (Arguments 18 and 20 below do however emphasise the *use* of other things for virtuous action.)

[625] I.e., as Inna Kupreeva points out to me, satisfying all three of the definitions just stated ('the ultimate object … sufficient in

If it is established that the life according to nature is
happy, how is virtue self-sufficient for this? For nature,
15   which gave us the soul, also gave us the body, and gave us
an affinity to the perfections and sort of arrangements that
are needed for each of them, so that the person who is
deprived of the natural perfection of either of these will not
live in accordance with nature, 'in accordance with nature'
being understood as 'in accordance with the will of
nature';[626] and if not this, neither happily.[627]

(18) Moreover, the body, which is an instrument, has
been given to us by nature for actions in accordance with
20   nature, and in everything which needs an instrument the
excellence of the instrument contributes to that for the sake
of which the instrument is; [so] the excellence of the body
will contribute to actions in accordance with nature and life
in accordance with nature. So it is not possible to live in
accordance with nature without the excellences of the body;
and if so, not to be happy either.

(19) Moreover, nature does nothing in vain; for neither
25   does any other craft do any of the things brought about by it
in vain, but each of the things brought about by a craft
contributes to the proper end of [the craft]; and nature is a
sort of divine craft, so that the things brought about by it,
too, will contribute to the proper end of that in which they
come about.*[628] And both bodily and external goods will

---

itself for living'). For 'and if not for these' one might rather expect
'and if not for this'; but Alexander writes as if all three definitions,
rather than just the last, had made explicit reference to
sufficiency.

[626] Cf. 162,17 ('virtue ... does not wish') and below, 164.1-2
('nature would not will them').

[627] The argument of this paragraph recalls argument (14)
above. 163,14-18 = *SVF* 3.180.

[628] For the claim that nature does nothing in vain see above,
169 n.570. The present passage (in which I have simplified the
sentence-structure of the Greek) is noteworthy for the way in
which it bases the claim concerning nature on an analogy
between nature and craft. Stoic nature is 'craftsmanlike'
(*tekhnikos*) according to Galen (*SVF* 2.411), and god is 'crafts-

give us an affinity for this,[629] and so these too contribute to
the end that is natural for us, and our affinity to them is not   30
in vain. So virtue is not self-sufficient for the end for a
human being in accordance with nature, if it is self-sufficient
neither for the acquisition nor for the preservation of the
things for which we have a natural affinity.

(20) Moreover, if these things fall to virtue to select
according to them,[630] and nature introduces virtue for the
sake of the selection of these things which are proper for
us, and of the rejection of their opposites,[631] should we   35
select bodily and external goods, but not also care about
them? Why this, and not also obtain them? Why obtain
them, but not also direct the use of them towards
something? To what then, if not towards the end? For   164,1
nature would not wish them, or virtue command them, or
the wise person select them, if it made no difference
whether [we] have them or not.[632] For neither does any
other craft select anything for the sake of selecting itself
alone, but the selection of everything relates to the end. The   5
end is in the use of the things that are selected, not in the
selection of the things subject [to selection]. And in general
how is it not absurd to say that virtue applies to this alone,

---

manlike fire' at *SVF* 2.1027). Cf. also Plato, *Leg.* 10 892b. (I am
grateful to Julius Tomin for drawing my attention to the Plato
passage.)

[629] That is, bodily and external goods (preferred indifferents)
play a part in our moral development by means of *oikeiôsis*. But
this does not in itself show that they are still necessary once virtue
has been achieved.

[630] Or 'fall under virtue's selection'. *têi aretêi* here depends
grammatically on *piptei*; I am grateful to Julius Tomin for pointing
this out. 163,32-6 = *SVF* 3.194.

[631] Virtuous action *is* the selection; but a distinction is drawn
between virtue and virtuous action. At 160,5 virtue was described
as 'concerned with' the selection.

[632] Cf. Striker 1996, 313, suggesting that this argument may go
back to Carneades. The rhetorical series of questions is noteworthy, and may preserve something of the style of an earlier source.
(Cf. however also arguments 13, 17, 35.)

to the selecting? For if the possession of the things that are
selected is indifferent and does not contribute to the end,
the selection will be empty and in vain.[633]

But if happiness consists in living well, virtue is not self-
10   sufficient for this either. For the person who is said to live
well is the one who employs virtue and lives in accordance
with virtue and performs some action. For living well for a
human being consists in action of a certain sort, and of
actions some involve acquisition, others make use of the
things acquired.[634] The end will not be in those that involve
acquisition, for these are for the sake of something else, but
in those that make use. For neither for craftsmen is the end
15   in the acquiring of the things* they use, but in the use of
these things in accordance with the craft. And for virtue,
which is itself a craft, the final point and the end are not in
the selection and acquisition of certain things, but in the use
of the things that have been acquired. But if happiness and
living well are located in the activities and actions that
involve use, and these [can]not [take place] without bodily
and external goods and the things which are proper and
20   natural, which virtue selects, virtue will not be self-sufficient
for living well and for happiness.

(21) Moreover, if the body has been given by nature to
human beings as an instrument for actions, its goods too
will contribute to the good in actions of a human being and
to the end, as also in the case of the crafts. For the good of
25   the pipes [contributes] to playing them well. But if so, virtue
is not self-sufficient for happiness. For if these things
contributed nothing to activity in life and happiness and the
end, the body would have been given to us by nature in

---

[633] Cf. Cicero, *Fin.* 4.46; Plutarch, *Comm. Not.* 1071a-e, 1072d-f.
The present argument differs from these in that, while similarly
insisting that selection among indifferents must be for the sake of
some end, it is prepared to concede that that end may be the *use*
of the selected indifferents as the materials of virtue. 164,7-9 =
SVF 3.193.

[634] Compare Plato, *Euthydemus* 280b-281b; also [Aristotle],
Oeconomica 1344b23. I am grateful to Inna Kupreeva for drawing
my attention to these passages.

vain. For it is not the case that those things, which help when present, do not, when absent, diminish the work which they help.[635]

(22) Moreover, if the things that are for the sake of medicine are also for the sake of the health that is brought about by it,[636] and as many things as [are for the sake] of the   30
art of navigation [are] also for the sake of the successful voyaging which it brings about, [then] also as many things as are for the sake of virtue will also be for the sake of happiness, if happiness is a product of this. And they themselves say that bodily and external [goods] are for the sake of virtue, so that it can select and acquire them;[637] so that these things are useful also for the end. But if so, virtue is not self-sufficient for the end.[638]

(23) Moreover, as many things as are for the sake of the   35
doctor *qua* doctor are also [for the sake] of health, which is the end and goal of the doctor; and as many things as are for the sake of the navigator, *qua* navigator, are also [for the sake] of successful voyaging, which is the end of the navigator. And so as many things as are for the sake of the human being *qua* human being are also for the sake of his end, that is for the sake of happiness. But bodily and external [goods]   165,1
are for the sake of the human being and *qua* human being, so that [they are also for the sake of] happiness. So virtue is not self-sufficient for the end.

(24) Moreover, if we say that someone acts as he is

---

[635] Cf. arguments (18), (19) above.

[636] Aristotle, *Metaph.* 12.10 1075b10 says that medicine is in a way health, being the form in the mind of the agent; but for the contrast between health and the doctor cf. *EN* 10 1174b25-6.

[637] 164,32-3 = *SVF* 3.194.

[638] To the argument of this and the following section one might object that it shows, not that virtue is not sufficient for happiness, but that external goods are necessary for virtue and hence for happiness as well. But a distinction is again to be drawn between virtue and virtuous action, as between the art of navigation and the voyaging; the claim that virtuous *action* is necessary for happiness is regarded as entailing that virtue without action is insufficient.

minded, not because he acts in whatever way [he does]
having a mind, but because [he acts] as his mind wishes,
5   and according to his soul not because [he acts] having a
soul, but because [he acts] as his soul wishes, just so the
person who acts in accordance with virtue will act in accordance with virtue not because he has virtue, but because
[he acts] as virtue wishes, in the [circumstances] and
through the [instruments that virtue wishes]. Being happy
consists in acting in accordance with virtue. So being happy
consists in [acting] in accordance with the will of virtue. But
it is in accordance with the will of virtue to be accompanied
10   by the things selected for it and proper [to it] and
constructed for the sake of it. So these things also
contribute[639] to activity in accordance with virtue, that is to
happiness. But if so, virtue is not self-sufficient.[640]

(25) Moreover, for the piper playing well consists in
playing, and playing is not indifferent for the piper with a
view to playing well and his own proper end*; and similarly
15   in the case of the other crafts. Just so, if for the person who
is happy being happy consists in living well, living will not
for him be [a matter of] indifference with regard to living
well, but will contribute to living well. But if so, virtue is not
self-sufficient for the end, if according to this we gain not
living, but only <living> well.*[641]

(26) Moreover, if the person who has virtue very much
wants[642] both bodily and external goods to be present to

---

[639] *phora* is from the adjective *phoros*, as in 167,28 below; I am
grateful to Inna Kupreeva for pointing this out. She compares also
tôi phoron einai ('being a contribution') in 167,15 below. Julius
Tomin has suggested to me that we may here have deliberate
word-play ('things the Stoics call *adiaphora* are in fact *phora*').

[640] Cf. arguments (13) and (22). Characteristically, this ignores
the Stoic view that one can display virtue by making good use of
unpreferred indifferents.

[641] I.e., to achieve happiness you need not only to live well, but
to be alive. Cf. Striker 1996, 302 n.8. But being alive is already
presupposed in having virtue (cf. below, argument (28)).

[642] The Stoics would not accept that bodily and external 'goods'
are proper objects of 'wanting' (*boulêsis*).

himself, and preserves them when they are present and 20
selects and obtains them when they are not present, and
prays to the gods for them, it is clear that he will want these
things as being worsted with regard to the [end] set before
them if they are not present. But if he is worsted, when the
opposites of these things are present to him, how is he
happy?[643]

(27) Moreover, if it is possible for the person who has
virtue to be mad or ill, and no-one would say that the mad
person is happy when he is mad, or the person who is ill or 25
the one who is asleep, being happy will not consist in having
virtue.[644]

(28) Moreover, if in general virtue needs certain things in
order to exist and to be active in any way at all, and a
person's being happy consists in activity in accordance with
it, how could it be self-sufficient for happiness, when it
needs certain things from outside for its being active, in
which being happy consists?

(29) Moreover, if the things in accordance with nature are
objects of appetition for the wise person, and the wise 30
person has appetition for nothing in vain, these things, for
which he has appetition, will be referred to his own proper
end and will contribute something to his happiness.[645]

[643] This essentially repeats the point of argument (17) above.

[644] Cf. argument (12). A contrast is again drawn between
simply having virtue and acting in accordance with it; cf. above,
arguments (3), (4), (6), and for the incompatibility of happiness
with being asleep Aristotle, *EN* 1 1099a1, 10 1176a34. The Stoics
recognised the onset of madness as a reason for the sage to
commit a proper suicide, but it is not clear that they would accept
that a person who had become mad was still virtuous or happy.
They would certainly accept that a person could be ill while being
virtuous; but they would simply reject the idea that such a
person's happiness was in any way diminished by the illness,
even if his scope for activity as ordinarily understood was
lessened.

[645] Cf. arguments (20) + (19). In the present argument 'doing
nothing in vain' is applied not to nature, as in (19), but to the sage
(who indeed lives in accordance with nature).

(30) Moreover, either virtue achieves the end by using certain things in addition, or entirely by itself. If by using things in addition, it is not self-sufficient for the end; if by

35 itself, virtue and happiness will be the same thing. But we see in the case of the crafts that such a thing is impossible. For in the case of each three things are needed for the end, the end, the one who achieves the end, and that which introduces the end. The one who achieves is the doctor or navigator, the end is successful voyaging or health, and

166,1 what introduces these is medicine or the art of navigation. And in the case of happiness the one who achieves it is the wise person, the end is happiness, and what introduces it is virtue. So, just as medicine is not health, but produces health, and the art of navigation, which produces successful voyaging, is not successful voyaging,[646] just so neither will

5 virtue, which produces happiness, be happiness.[647] For none of the things that produces anything produces itself. So virtue is not self-sufficient for the happiness that is brought about by it.

(31) Moreover, if each of the craftsmen has the things, which he selects in accordance with his craft, as contributing to the end of the craft, [then] the person who has virtue, too, will select the things, which he selects in accordance with virtue, as contributing to the end for himself. But he

10 selects bodily and external [goods], if indeed virtue came in altogether for the sake of the selection of these things. For it is not the case that, being virtue, it selects certain things

---

[646] The Stoics however claimed that wisdom (the art of living well) is analogous to acting or dancing, which have their end in the performance itself, rather than to navigation or medicine: Cicero, *Fin.* 5.24 = *SVF* 3.11; Seneca, *Ep. Mor.* 85.32 (above, 178 n.598); LS vol.1 p.410. The Stoic sage is, precisely, a virtuoso in living: Becker 1998, 106ff.

[647] This is a development of argument (3) above. Julius Tomin points out that the analogies of medicine and navigation involve an un-Aristotelian view of the relation between virtue and happiness; happiness is not an end-product of virtue as health is of medicine or success in voyaging (assuming that means reaching the destination, or at least reaching dry land) is of navigation.

in vain.[648] So it is not self-sufficient.

But if, because all the other crafts too select both bodily and external goods, they say that these are not instruments of virtue, first it must be said that there is nothing strange in the same things being useful for several crafts. Next, none 15 of those [practitioners of the crafts] selects them as being a craftsman of some particular craft, except incidentally. For it is not qua being a piper or a navigator that someone selects wealth or fame, but qua human being. As for health, even if it is an instrument for those [crafts] too, it is primarily by virtue that these things[649] are selected; for this is its task. For it selects and judges these, so that they will be its 20 instruments and contribute to the end that is brought about by it.[650]

(32) Moreover, we see well by the excellence of that with which we see, and hear well through the excellence of that with which we hear, and for that reason we also live well through the excellence of that with which we live, so that happiness will be by the excellence of the soul;* for it is with the soul that we live.[651] But it is not the case that for this reason we will need nothing else from outside besides the excellence of the soul for living well. For in the case of 25 the eye too it is with the eye that we see and with its excellence that we see well; but nevertheless to see well we need

[648] Cf. arguments (19), (20), (29). The formulation fails to bring out that for the Stoics the external goods are the means and selection the end, not the other way around.

[649] sc. wealth, fame and health.

[650] If the Stoics really argued that what is an instrument of one craft cannot be the instrument of another, their argument seems weak. It seems right to object that virtue, being a general craft (cf. §18 154,17ff.), has a particular relation to preferred indifferents of general relevance, such as health and wealth.

[651] 166,21-4 = *SVF* 3.57. Von Arnim comments 'this argument (*conclusio*) seems to be Chrysippus' own'. (The text in fact presents the whole argument as the first part of a conditional: 'Moreover, it is not the case that, if we see well ... it is with the soul that we live, for this reason we will need nothing from outside...'. As elsewhere, I have simplified the syntax.)

light and certain other things. For [we need] nothing
casting a shadow, and a proportionate distance, and a
certain magnitude, and the colour that is going to be seen.
Just so, we live well by excellence of soul, but we need
30   certain other things that contribute to this and are instruments [for it]. For indeed we also do things in the crafts
well in accordance with the crafts and through excellence in
them, but nevertheless for the ends of the crafts we also
need certain other things, which are different from the
crafts. Virtue then too, as a craft, will be productive of happiness, but not for that reason without matter and its own
proper instruments.[652]

35   (33) Moreover, if virtue is said to be self-sufficient for
happiness in the way in which each of the crafts is [self-
sufficient] for its proper task, because they do not need
some other craft in addition in order to produce their
[product], [this is] sound* (for virtue does not need some
other faculty and craft in addition in order to produce happiness along with it);* nevertheless, according to this
[argument] it will, similarly to the [other] crafts, need in
167,1 addition certain other things in order to fulfil its own proper
task. If however someone says that the virtues are self-
sufficient for happiness in this way,[653] that they do not need
anything in addition from outside at all, he will not speak
soundly. For virtue, like the crafts, needs many things from
outside in order to achieve its end, as has been shown. To
5   say that, just as it is the art of pipe-playing that can make
right use of every tune that is given to it, so it is virtue that
makes use of every thing, is indeed sound;[654] but an
additional distinction needs to be made. Just as the art of
pipe-playing is not able to do this without its own proper
instruments, neither can virtue; this is the task of it alone,
but not without the things that contribute to it.
     (34) Moreover it is not the case that, since [virtue] uses

---

[652] See argument (10) above.

[653] For 'in this way' (*houtôs*) Bruns suggests 'without qualification' (*haplôs*).

[654] 167,4-6 = *SVF* 3.204.

all things in a fine way, for that reason [its] employment of   10
every thing creates happiness,[655] but rather a certain sort of
employment of the things that are wished for [does so]. For
there are certain things which are not wished for that befall
the good person; he makes good use of [these] too
themselves, but his activity concerning them* and his
making use of these things in such a way does not produce
happiness.

(35) Moreover, with a view to what on earth do the things
which are proper and* preferred, and capable of good use,
and having value, have these names, if they contribute
nothing to happiness? For everything that is preferred is   15
preferred with a view to something, and it is through
contributing to the [end] set before [us], more than
something else [does], that it is said for this reason also to
be preferred with a view to the end, and it is clear that its
preferring contributes to happiness. If it does not contribute
to this, but to life in accordance with nature, it is worth
asking them about life in accordance with nature, whether it
is a good, or not good but itself proper and preferred, or   20
alien[656] and unpreferred, or altogether indifferent. For apart
from these there is no other answer that can be given. For
they will not say that it is an evil.* Well, if it is a good, how
will the things that complete and produce it not also be
good themselves, so that the preferred things will be
goods?[657] And then, not only what is noble will be good; for
the life according to nature [will be too], if it is going to be a   25
good   and   contribute   to   happiness,   if   happiness   is

---

[655] 167,9-10 = *SVF* 3.205.

[656] I.e. not something to which we have appropriation
(*oikeiôsis*); cf. argument (17) above.

[657] The Stoic answer would be that life according to nature is
indeed a good, but that this does not mean that preferred indifferents, as opposed to correct selection in the circumstances
whatever they may be, are necessary for it. 'Complete and
produce' echoes Critolaus' view; cf. 184 n.619 above. 'Complete
and produce' (*sumplêrôtika kai poiêtika*) is also the Stoic
description of the relation of the *virtues* to happiness (*SVF*
3.106-7).

completeness of good things; so virtue will not be self-sufficient for happiness.[658] If [life in accordance with nature] is alien and unpreferred or indifferent, how is it not ridiculous to say that the things that produce it are preferred? For why should the things that contribute to this be preferred rather than those [that contribute] to its opposite? But if it

30 itself is preferred and has value similarly to those things, and it is on account of it that the things that produce it, too, are like this, we will ask them with a view to what it is preferred and has value, just as [we will] also concerning the things that produce this. For everything that is preferred is preferred with a view to something. Well, if they say 'with a view to happiness', then the life in accordance with nature will contribute to happiness, and so too

35 will the things that produce this, and virtue will not be self-sufficient for it. But if they say with a view to something

168,1 else, the same argument* [will] also [arise] concerning that, and so to infinity.

(36) In general, if virtue is self-sufficient for making our life happy in the extreme and blessed, how is making away with oneself reasonable for the person who has virtue [and so] is in a blessed [condition of] life? Just as it is absurd to say that Zeus wants to die, so it is absurd to say that the

5 person who lives with equal blessedness [to him] reasonably makes away with himself from this life, seeing that bodily and external things are indifferent and neither produce nor remove happiness, and virtue, which alone establishes the blessed life and preserves it securely by its presence, never leaves the wise person.[659] For to want to

---

[658] To distinguish between virtue and 'life according to nature' involves interpreting the latter in an un-Stoic sense (or building on arguments like (14) and (16)). Punctuating after *agathon* in 167,25 with MS B and the Aldine would give 'for the life according to nature, if it is going to be a good, will also contribute to happiness, if happiness is completeness of good things'. But the context requires that the goodness of the life according to nature should be inferred from its contributing to happiness, not vice versa.

[659] Chrysippus, though not Cleanthes, did allow that the wise person could lose his virtue: Diogenes Laertius 7.127 = *SVF* 3.237.

leave life and virtue itself,[660] when no evil is present or expected and the extreme of happiness is present for [the wise person], is amazing and inconsistent with what is reasonable. For how is it reasonable for some* virtue to suggest this to the wise person?[661] For it is not reasonable, as in the case of some other thing, to say also in the case of happiness, that he has enough of it. For there is no satiety of happiness and virtue. Appetition of the ends extends to infinity, and they are not referred to anything else.[662] To suppose that making away with oneself is reasonable is [the mark] of those who agree that it is impossible for life to be happy without bodily and external [goods].

(37) Moreover, if making away with oneself is reasonable, but we are prevented by something from making away with ourselves, how is life not wretched in [circumstances] of the sort on account of which it is reasonable to make away with oneself?[663] And if life is wretched, it is clear that it is no

10

15

See above, 179 n.605, 191 n.644.

[660] Or perhaps, as Inna Kupreeva suggests to me, 'for virtue itself to want to leave life'. This would involve an even more blatant disregard of the Stoic position, which is precisely that suicide can sometimes be the virtuous course of action. See the next note.

[661] 168,1-8.11-12 = *SVF* 3.764. This ignores the point that in circumstances where suicide is the proper course of action the sage who commits suicide is preserving his virtue rather than abandoning it; above, 174 n.584, 177 n.596.

[662] If one becomes dissatisfied with something, one is judging it by reference to something else. But the ultimate good cannot be judged by reference to anything further. To avoid the implication that an infinite desire can never be satisfied, happiness must be complete at every instant; cf. (of pleasure) Aristotle, *EN* 10 1174b5. I am grateful to Alan Lacey and Richard Sorabji for discussion of this point.

[663] This seems like a final flourish, at least to argument (36) if not (originally) to §20 as a whole: the virtuous person will not be happy if prevented from a proper suicide. But happiness for the Stoics does not depend on success in what is beyond one's power. On 168,1-20 cf. Irwin 1998, 176.

20   longer happy. So that according to this argument at least,
      happiness will not be something that cannot be lost, either.

168,21   **[21]. That female and male are not different in species.**

         The starting-point of this text is, as Bruns notes, Aristotle's discus-
         sion at *Metaph.* 10.9 1058a29-b25. Aristotle's solution to the
         question why male and female are not different species is that the
         difference is due to the matter, and that the same seed can produce
         both; and this is made the occasion for a general discussion of the
         distinction between differences in species or form on the one hand
         and those due to matter on the other. Our text is essentially an
         expansion of Aristotle's explanation, with the addition of a discus-
         sion of the relation of the differentia to the genus (169,7-23; below,
         200 n.668). The question naturally arises of the relation between
         this text and Alexander's lost commentary on *Metaphysics* 10; but
         the omission of 10.7-9 from the commentary of pseudo-Alexander
         removes even that possible source of evidence. Cf. also, with de
         Haas 1997 171 n.24 and 202 n.119, Alex., *In Top.* 51.5-6.
             Bostock 1994, 139-40 argues that Aristotle is not entirely consis-
         tent on this issue even within the *Metaphysics*, for at 7.9 1034b2-3
         he seems to suggest that the production of woman from man is an
         exception to the principle of generation of like by like. But, while
         Bostock is right to point out that Aristotle in the *GA* sees the
         production of female children as a failure of male form to master
         female matter (below, 199 n.666), the passage in 7.9 itself can be
         read as suggesting that the exception is purely verbal.
             Rovida compares Proclus, *In Platonis Rempublicam* I 237,5ff.,
         252,22ff. Diehl, which reports the Peripatetics as saying that male
         and female are the same in species though their virtues are differ-
         ent, while the Stoics maintain the reverse.
             On this section see further Sharples 1986.

168,22   Aristotle says that female and male are not differences in
         living creature that produce [different] species, because in
         general these are the differences that divide genera into
         species, [namely] those* that involve opposition and
         contrast in respect of the account [*logos*], while material
25   differences and affections of what underlies do not make
         [things that possess them] different in species. For this
         reason white and black, though opposite, do not produce a

specific division and difference of body. For these are affections of what underlies, not a division of the common form[664]
and account of body.

Well, since female and male too have their difference in
respect of a material affection, they do not make living
creatures different in species. For these differ by concoction   30
and lack of concoction and heat and coldness of the underlying matter. And[665] these affections are not proper to living
creature in respect of its substance and account, but are in
respect of what underlies and the matter and the body. And
for this reason the same seed can become both female and
male,[666] but not rational or irrational, or a winged [creature]
or a land [creature].

And for the same reason particular human beings, though   35
they differ from one another, are not different in species.
For they differ from one another by material affections, not
in respect of their account and of difference in this; for [they   169,1
differ] by quality of flesh, and quantity, and the like. So the
bronze circle and the wooden one are different, but not
different in species, because their difference is in respect of
what underlies, not of the account.[667] And so it is also in the
case of individual human beings. For opposition in the

---

[664] *eidos*, which can also be translated by 'species'; it is the
characteristics of the species that are due to the form. Cf.
Sharples (forthcoming, 4).

[665] Literally 'for', explaining why this clause too contributes to
the foregoing argument. But 'and' seems more natural here in
English.

[666] So Aristotle, *Metaph.* 10.9 1058b23; but he simply states that
the sperm 'has been affected in some way', without specifying the
details. For Aristotle the sex of the offspring depends on whether
the male principle in the semen does or does not prevail over the
female principle in the menstrual blood, and this will be affected
by the condition of both: *GA* 4.1 776b15ff., 4.3 768b25ff. So the
same seed may produce a male or female depending on the condition of the menstrual blood, but it is also true that from the same
menstrual blood a male or a female may be produced, depending
on the condition of the seed from the male.

[667] The same example at Aristotle, *Metaph.* 10.9 1058b12.

5   account produces species that differ, but affections in
respect of what is material do not. So male and female are
not different in species, since they do not differ in respect of
their account, but in respect of a material affection.

That male and female are not differences that divide [the
genus] and produce species is clear also from these
[points]. For they are differences either of human being, or
of some other species, in which one [part] is male, the other
10   female, or of living creature, the genus of these. But they
are not a difference that divides human being. For the
proper differences that divide something do not extend
beyond that which they divide; for example, none of the
differences that divide living creature occurs outside living
creature or belongs to anything which is not a living
creature. For the differences that properly dissect
something must be contained within what is dissected by
15   them. For if any seem to extend beyond the things which
are dissected by them, it is because they do not [belong]
properly to these, but to the genera above them, that they
seem to exceed the former, not occurring outside the latter.
For example, if someone dissects 'living creature with feet'
by 'two-footed', the difference <in respect of> 'two-footed'*
seems to be also in every living creature. For it is present
also in winged [living creature]; for it is 'living creature' that
20   it properly divides, and it can no longer be spoken of
extending beyond this. For there is not anything that is
two-footed and is not a living creature. So female and male
will not be differences dissecting 'human being',[668] since
they are [present] also in other living creatures, and not in
human beings alone.

---

[668] As part of his statement of the problem Aristotle notes that
'male' and 'female' are proper differentiae of 'living creature' in a
way that 'white' and 'black' are not (*Metaph.* 10.9 1058a32-4), but
not that they are not proper to 'human being'.

So for this reason they will not be differences of any of the other species of living creature; and neither is it possible to say that they dissect living creature and produce species. 25 For differences that are divided in opposition to each other cannot be present together in the same species. For neither can rational and irrational be in the same species, nor footed and winged and aquatic, nor two-footed and footless, but female and male exist in the same species. For they are in human being, which is the same in species,[669] and in horse and dog and similarly in the others which are generated 30 from pairing. So female and male are not differences which dissect; and so neither are male and female different in species, and consequently neither are woman and man.

[22]. [From] Aristotelian [tradition] concerning what 169,33 depends on us.[670]

The assertion in this section that uncaused motion exists is in direct contradiction to Alex., *Fat.* ch. 24, and the connection of what depends on us with weakness and falling short (rather than with acting rightly when there is the possibility of falling short) combines a readiness to pursue the implications of a philosophical problem with a scant regard for the plausibility of the conclusion thereby reached. It is difficult to believe that this text is a statement by Alexander himself of a position which he endorses (as opposed to a record of a view with which he does not himself agree).[671] The originator of the position however deserves credit for seeing the need to relate a non-deterministic account of responsibility to an account of indeterminism in the world as a whole, an issue which Alexander himself in *Fat.* does not adequately pursue: cf. Sharples 1983, 21-2, and Magris 1996, 25, 41.

Schroeder 1997, 103-106, taking up the comparison with certain aspects of the thought of Plotinus noted at Sharples 1975b, 52, has

---

[669] This assumes what the argument is setting out to prove.

[670] See above, 149 n.507.

[671] For the latter view cf. Bruns 1892, xiii. He compares §2 110,4ff. above (he might better have compared 112,5ff); the difference however is that in the latter case the statement of the unacceptable view is followed by a rebuttal (113,12ff.), which is not the case here. See also below, 205 n.683.

suggested that this section may itself be post-Plotinian; but Accattino has challenged Schroeder's similar claim regarding §2 (above, 37 n.87), and here too the influence may be in the other direction.

This text is translated into English by Sharples 1975b, reprinted in a revised version in Sharples 1983a, 94-97, and reprinted with further revision here. Cf. also Merlan 1969, 85-8; Donini 1974, 165-8, Sorabji 1980, 65-6, 86; Corrigan 1996, 186; Schroeder 1997, 107-109; Bobzien 1998a, 409, 1998b, 157 n.39, 169; Hankinson 1998, 360-2; Salles 1998, 71-3; Opsomer and Steel 1999, 253-4; Sharples 2001, 578-80.

169,34   About what depends on us an opinion like the following was also stated.[672] If the nature of all [people] is not alike, but differs (for by nature some are well-endowed and others ill-endowed),* and nature has the greatest influence towards [people's] coming to be of one sort or another, and after nature habits, choice too coming to be of a certain sort as a result of both of these, one might be altogether at a loss as to how choice will still depend on us. For indeed, even if one were to regard teaching too as a cause[673] [of our

170,1   choices], not even learning depends on us. (I mean that sort of 'depending on us' of which the opposite too is both possible and depends on us,[674] which is the sort of thing we maintain what depends on us to be.)* And this would be an even greater difficulty, if nothing were to come to be

---

[672] It is unclear whether this relates only to the statement of the problem (down to 170,7) or to the whole of this section including the solution; if the latter, we would have a clear indication that the solution proposed is not necessarily one that the author of the piece himself endorses.

[673] Or, perhaps, 'as the cause': Donini 1974, 166.

[674] For 'what depends on us' as involving possibility for opposites cf. Sharples 2001, 548 and references there to recent discussions. The present section however adopts a 'one-sided' interpretation of what depends on us, identifying it with the actions that result from weakness (cf. Sharples 1975b, 49-52), and apparently for that reason Bruns, citing 171,23, questions the authenticity of 'and depends on us' and deletes 'which ... to be'.

without a cause; and this too is what all thought.*[675] For the cause of the things which are brought about by us at the present must exist beforehand, and it is impossible that the same cause should be [the cause] of opposites; but if this [is   5 so], all things that come to be come to be of necessity, for their causes have been laid down beforehand. That this then should be so is necessary, unless some uncaused motion is discovered.

But it is discovered and it does exist; and when this is shown both what depends on us will be preserved, and the fortuitous and the things that depend on luck. Aristotle too thinks that there is some uncaused motion, as is stated in   10 the fifth book of the *Metaphysics*.[676] The existence of uncaused motion is established, if it should be shown that there is not-being[677] in the things that are, diffused somehow among them and accompanying them. For if there is somehow not-being in the things that are (and there is, for there is *per accidens* being in the things that are;* for what is not, if it attaches as an accident to anything,* is spoken of as being something *per accidens*) there would be some uncaused motion, and if this existed   15 the point set before us would have been shown. And that not-being is somehow in the things that are in actuality one could easily learn from considering them.

For if some of the things that are are eternal, and others perish, the difference between these would not be present in them as a result of any other cause than their sharing in not-being. For it is as a result of the mixture and blending and presence of this that slackness and weakness come to   20 be in the things that are not eternal and prevent them from always existing and always being in a similar state. For if   171,1 there were not any not-being in the things that are, nothing

---

[675] The reference is apparently to a school-discussion: cf. Donini 1974, 167 n.70; Sharples 1975b, 41 and nn.; 1990, 109.

[676] Aristotle, *Metaph*. 6.2 1026b13ff. Cf. Sharples 1975b, 48 and n.111. Eudemus said that the accidental seems not to exist: fr.55 Wehrli.

[677] Literally 'what is not'.

good would come to be either.[678] But if it is as a result of the
mixture of not-being that perishable things are such [as
they are], and in addition to them things that are false, and
if there are some things among the things that are that are
perishable and perish and are false, [then] there is some
5   not-being in them. And this is sound when taken
conversely, too; if there is not not-being in the things that
are, it will not be the case that certain of the things that are
are perishable. So there is not-being.

    If then not-being is diffused among and mixed with the
things that are subject to coming-to-be, and things that
come to be are preceded[679] by certain causes which are not
themselves eternal either, there is some not-being in causes
10   too, and this is what we call a cause *per accidens*. For what
is *per accidens*, when it is present in the same things *qua*
causes, would be a cause *per accidens*. For when anything
follows on a certain cause, the cause not existing for the
sake of this thing's coming about, then what precedes is
called the cause *per accidens* of this thing that followed on
it, that is, not a cause. So what* followed on this cause came
about without a cause, for [it did] not [do so] on account of
15   a proper cause of its own. This, when it occurs in external
causes, produces luck and the fortuitous;[680] when in the
[causes] in us, what depends on us.

    For nature and habit seem to be cause[s] in us of choice;
but, to the extent that there is not-being in these, to such an
extent [there is not-being] also in choice. And for this
reason we sometimes choose those things of which the
cause has not been laid down in us beforehand, on account

---

[678] Because the existence of one opposite logically requires that
of the other; goodness cannot exist if imperfection does not. For
egigneto of the MSS in 171,2 Bruns conjectured *ephieto*, '[they]
would not desire the good': but this (adopted in Sharples 1983)
seems speculative and leaves the argument still elliptical.
[679] *prohêgeitai*, cf. *prohêgoumenon* in 171.13 below. Cf.
Sharples 1975b, 49; 1983, 132-3; Hankinson 1998, 246-7.
[680] For the claim that the fortuitous is what is uncaused cf.
Proclus' criticism of 'the Aristotelians' at *In Tim.* I 262,9 Diehl. (This
was brought to my attention in a seminar given by Carlos Steel).

of the weakness and slackness of mortal nature; for   20
[otherwise][681] we would always be moved in a similar way in
the same situations.[682] But the nature of not-being, as I
said,[683] removes eternity and activity always in the same
manner from those things in which it is [present].* So it is
those things that we choose without a cause and with no
cause existing beforehand that are said to depend on us;[684]
and the opposites of these, too, are possible, as that cause
has not been laid down beforehand that, if it *had* existed
beforehand, would certainly have made it necessary that   25
this should come to be. For this reason it often happens that
some who are similar in nature and have been brought up in
the same habits come to differ from one another, as a result
of the uncaused choices.[685]

Not-being is neither mixed with many of the things that
are, nor is there much of it in those things in which it is
present, but [it is] in few of the things which are and in a
small amount. For it is in those of the things that are in   30
which there is non-eternity; that is, the [region] around the
earth. And this region is very small in relation to all the
world. For if the earth has the ratio of a point to all the
heaven, according to the astronomers,[686] and not-being is

[681] Similarly supplied by Caninius 1546 and by Nourrisson 1870, 64.

[682] For 'in the same situations' here, and for 'in the same manner' in the next sentence, Nourrisson has 'for the same ends': but this seems less to the point in the present context. (Cf. however Alex. *Fat.* 15 185,21ff., *Mant.* §23 174,13ff., and below 212 n.702). On 'weakness' (*astheneia*) of matter in the Aristotelian tradition cf. Guldentops 2001, 191 n.8.

[683] This may, but perhaps need not, suggest that the author is presenting the argument as his own rather than just reporting it (see the introductory note to this section).

[684] Cf. Salles 1998, 72 and n.25, arguing rightly that the causes in question here are efficient rather than final. (They may indeed be our desires, existing before we act, to achieve certain ends.)

[685] The connection here of the question of choice specifically with *character-forming* choices is noteworthy. Cf. Alex., *Fat.* 27 197,3-8, 28 199,9; Sharples 2001, 565 and n.360.

[686] Cf. Geminus, *Eisagoge* 17.16, 186,11-13 Manitius. Taub

concerned with this and the things in it, it would be
concerned with a very small [part].—And it is in even these
things in an obscure sort of way and not for the most part.*
35   For in the things which are subject to coming-to-be there is
on the one hand that which is for the most part, of which
172,1 nature is the cause, but as much as is released from nature
and its power for [making] the things that come to be
according to it come to be of necessity – that is, what is for
the least part, in which is situated that which can also be
otherwise – it is with this that the weakness that results
from not-being, too, is concerned. So not-being is not in the
things that are of necessity (and for this reason neither is
5   the contingent),[687] nor is it in those things* in which there is
being-for-the-most-part, to the extent that they are like this,
but in the things that are opposed to these, that is, in those
that are for the least part; and it is in these that things due
to luck and fortuitous things are [located], and those which
are said to depend on us in the proper sense.

For those choices of which nature or training and habit
are the cause are said to depend on us in the sense that
they come about through us; but those which <come about>
without a cause and* in accordance with not-being, these*
10   in this way preserve what is said to depend on us in the
proper sense, coming about through weakness of nature;
and what depends on us is this, of which the opposite too
could have been chosen by the one who chose this. So what
depends on us involves[688] that which through the existence
of not-being has weakened the continuity of the causes in
us; and it has this position, becoming a cause in cases

1993, 84.

[687] 'the contingent' = *to endekhomenon*, picking up 'that which
can also be otherwise' (*to endekhomenon kai allôs ekhein*) in
172.2-3.

[688] Literally 'occupies' (*katekhei*), taking *to eph' hêmin* as
subject both of *katekhei* and of *tautên tên khôran ekhei* (= 'it
occupies this position' in the next clause). (This corrects the
position taken at Sharples 1975b, 40 n.25 and 63 n.168; 1983a,
174.)

where the necessary cause has failed on account of the
mixture and interweaving of not- being in what is.   15

[23]. [From] Aristotelian [tradition] concerning what 172,16
depends on us.[689]

This discussion is not marked by the radical divergence from
Alexander, *Fat.* that occurs in §22, and may for the most part be
seen as a development and bringing together of points from *Fat.*,
especially chs. 11, 15, 27 and 29. The concluding discussion of the
extent to which natural endowment does and does not affect
capacity for virtue can be seen as mediating between the positions
of *Fat.* 6 and 27, in a discussion that is developed further in *Probl.
Eth.* 9 and 29; cf. Sharples 2001, 564-5, 588-92.

   This section is translated into English in Sharples 1983a; the
present translation is a revision of that version. There is an Arabic
version (no. 25 in Dietrich 1964) edited by Badawī 1971, no.12,
and also, with German translation, by Ruland 1976. Cf. also
Gercke 1885, no.73; Donini 1974, 168-170; Sharples 2001, 580.

Of the things that are brought about and put together by 172,17
the divine power that comes to be in the body that is subject
to coming to be, as a result of its proximity to the divine[690] –
and this [power] we also call 'nature' – the most honourable

---

[689] See above, 150 n.511 and 204 n.679.

[690] i.e. to the divine body, the heavens; cf. Alex., *Fat.* 25 195,11.
'Proximity' = *geitniasis*: the noun is applied to the part of the
sublunary that is closest to the heavens at Alex., *Quaest.* 2.3 49,16,
and the participle *geitniôn* at Aristotle, *Meteor.* 1.1 338b21,
followed by Alexander, *In Meteor.* 7,10-14 (to which the present
text is a close verbal parallel) and *Prov.* 75,1-4 Ruland. Cf. Fazzo
and Zonta 1998, 48 n.62. For the divine power cf. Alex., *In Metaph.*
104,8, *Quaest.* 2.3 47,30, 49,28-30, *Princ.* §§128-9, 132 in
Genequand 2001; and for the general doctrine of the influence of
the heavens on the sublunary, Alex., *In Meteor.* 6,15, *Quaest.* 1.25
41,15-19, 2.19 63,25 and Alex. ap. Philoponus, *In GC* 291,18; also
above, §2 113,8-9. See Genequand 1984, 114; id. 2001, 2, 18-19;
Sharples 1987, 1188, 1216-17; Fazzo and Zonta 1998, 41, 63-8;
Fazzo 2002a, 190-91.

20   is the human being.[691] For this alone of things here [on
      earth] has a share in the most perfect of the powers of soul,
      and this is mind, and he alone has rational soul, in respect
      of which he is able to deliberate and enquire about the
      things he should do, and is not like the other living
      creatures. These, in virtue of their not sharing in such a
      power, we call irrational, following and assenting to the
      appearances that impinge on them and doing without
25   examination each of the things that they do. For the human
      being alone* of the other living creatures is able, after an
      appearance has impinged on him that something should be
      done, to enquire about it and deliberate, whether he should
      assent to what appeared or not. And when he has deliber-
      ated and decided, accordingly he sets out[692] either to do or
      not to do either [alternative]; and he goes for* whichever
30   [alternative] he preferred as a result of the deliberation.
      And on account of this [the human being] alone of all living
      creatures has his acting depending on himself, because he
      has the power also of not doing this same thing. For the
      choice of the things that should be done depends on
173,1 himself, if deliberating and deciding depend on himself. For
      [having these things] depending on himself is the same as
      being a starting-point and productive cause of those things
      which we say depend on himself.

      What depends on us is located in those things with which
      deliberation, too, is concerned. And we deliberate neither
      about things that have come to be [already] nor about those
      which are already, but about those which are in the future
5   and are able also not to come to be,* and of which the cause
      is intelligence.[693] For these things can both be done by us
      and not. So it is in these that what depends on us, too, is
      located, and a human being is a starting-point and cause of
      the things that are done through him, having this as a

      [691] Similarly Alexander, *Prov.* 77.6-11 Ruland, and *Quaest.* 2.3
      48,19-22; Fazzo 2002a, 190 and nn.427-8.
      [692] *horman,* cognate with *hormê* 'impulse'.
      [693] Cf. Alex., *Fat.* 11 178.28-179.3, *Probl. Eth.* 29 160,5-16;
      Aristotle, *EN* 3 1112a21ff.

special [gift] from nature as compared with all the other things that are brought about by her, because he alone is also a thing [that is] rational by nature and has the power of deliberation. For it is in this that what is rational has its 10 being.

But if the cause is the starting-point of those things of which it is the cause, and the human being is the starting-point of the things that are done by him[self], he will also be the cause of these things.[694] If then it is absurd to enquire after and speak of the starting-point of a starting-point(for that thing of which there is some other starting-point is not a starting-point without qualification), there will not, either, be some productive cause [of the actions] laid down before-hand, other than choice and will and decision of a certain 15 sort and [in short] the human being [himself][695] (for [other-wise] he would no longer remain a starting-point); but the cause of the things that are done by himself is himself and [his] decision and choice and the productive cause of these,[696]

---

[694] Cf. Alex., *Fat.* 15 185,7-21. Here as there the position advocated is similar to that of Carneades in Cicero, *Fat.* 23-5, and to Richard Taylor's 'agent causation', and like these it may from a determinist perspective seem to evade rather than to solve the dilemma of determinism or uncaused motion. The ultimate source is Aristotle; *EN* 3 1113a6, 1113b18, 21, 6 1139b5, *EE* 2.6 1222b15ff. See Sharples 1983a, 146-8; 2001, 556-61; and below, 174,3-12.

[695] So Bruns, comparing 173,16 and 174,9f. The argument is slightly awkward, because in what precedes and follows the question is, if B causes C, whether there is a further cause of *B*, whereas here the question is rather whether *C* has any cause other than B. One might translate, with Sharples 1983a, 98, 'there will not, either, be some other productive cause laid down before-hand of choice and will and decision of a certain sort and [in short] of the human being [himself]'; but, even as rhetorical exaggeration, the claim that there is no productive cause of a human being himself is, simply, false.

[696] 'The productive cause of these' is perhaps best taken as referring to deliberation (cf. 174,9); but the expression is very obscure. (It would be less so if we followed the Arabic in reading *bouleuseôs* 'deliberation' rather than *boulêseôs* 'will' in 173,14; but

but of these things themselves there is no longer anything else [that is the cause]. For if these things are a starting-point, and there is no starting-point and cause of what is called a starting-point[*arkhê*] in the proper sense (there is a principle [*arkhê*] of the man's being and coming to be, but not of his choosing these things or those; for this [is what] being [is] for him, that is,* [it is] to have such a power in himself),* <man's power and capacity of action depend on himself>.[697]

For how would deliberating even be useful any longer, if we had causes of what we do laid down beforehand? And how would the human being any longer be more honourable than the other living creatures, if deliberating were shown to be useless? And [it would be] useless if preferring something as a result of deliberation and choosing that which we preferred did not depend on us. To say that the 'appearance' is the cause of [our] deliberating about what appeared is not at all absurd;[698] but to regard not the deliberation but the appearance as the cause also of [our] doing this particular thing is to do away with deliberation, and [so] with [the appearance's being a] cause, as we hold it to be; [for we hold it to be] the cause of something that exists.[699] So, if what appeared is the cause of the deliberating, the deliberation of the decision, the decision of the impulse, and the impulse of what is done, nothing among these will be

---

Alexander's usual word for 'deliberation' is *boulê*, and the sandwiching of 'deliberation' between 'choice' and 'decision' would be odd.)

[697] Bruns postulates a lacuna here: I have translated Ruland's conjectural supplement, based on 172,30f. above. In MS B the grammatical difficulty has been solved rather by the addition (as a note above the line) of 'there would not be any other cause of them' after 'of what is called a beginning in the proper sense' in 173,19.

[698] This should probably not be taken as indicating that the 'appearance' *necessitates* our deliberating (let alone *how* we deliberate and what decision we reach). Cf. Alex., *Quaest.* 3.13 107,25-37.

[699] I.e., if deliberation does not exist, 'appearance' cannot be its cause (so Bruns ad loc.).

without a cause.

And just as deliberating shows that something depends on us, so does repenting of certain things that have been done and blaming ourselves and our own choice; for such blame is evidence that we are responsible for having then done what has been done. But to look for some other cause of [our] having preferred this particular [course of action] 35 as a result of the deliberation is to do away with deliberation. For the essence of deliberating is in being able 174,1 to decide and choose what appears best as a result of the deliberation. The person who takes this away from deliberation leaves only the name of deliberation.

For to say that, when all the external circumstances are similar, either [i] someone will choose, or even do, the same things or [ii] something will be without a cause, and that of these [ii], that something should come to be without 5 a cause, is impossible, while [i], that [someone] chooses the same things when the circumstances are the same, shows that the external causes have control over the things that we do – this is not sound. For neither is it necessary for a human being always to choose the same things when all the circumstances are the same, nor is the action without a cause, if it does not come about in the same way. For the deliberation and the choice and the decision and the human 10 being are the cause of action of this sort, [and the human being], having in himself the power of deliberating about the circumstances, has also the ability not to make the same choice from the same things.[700]

And this is not asserted unreasonably, nor is what is said special pleading. For if [the agent] had one goal to which he referred his decision, it would be reasonable that he should always choose the same thing from among the same things, 15 if at least he always had and preserved the same [position in] relation to the goal set before him, towards which he looked in making his decision between them. But since there are several ends, looking towards which he makes his decision and choice of the things that should be done (for

---

[700] See above, 202 n.674.

he has both the pleasant and the advantageous and the noble before his eyes), and these are different from one
20   another, and not all the things surrounding [him] have the same relation to each of these, making his decision between them and choice from among them at one time with regard to the pleasant, at another with regard to the noble, at another with regard to the advantageous, he* will not always do the same things or always choose the same things when all the circumstances are the same, but on each occasion those things which seem to him most condu-cive to the goal on which he has decided. And by means of
25   this one might resolve the argument which attributes responsibility for[701] the actions to the 'appearance' on the grounds that no-one would ever do anything contrary to what appears better to him. For there are several goals with reference to which the decision about the 'appearance' is made.[702]

Moreover,* even if someone chooses the same things when the circumstances are the same, it does not at once follow that he chooses these things[703] necessarily and that
30   the external things are the causes of the decision. For in the case of each choice it is possible to show that before doing and preferring something he was also able to choose the opposite; for he does not choose these things because he is

---

[701] Or: 'the cause of'.

[702] With the argument of this paragraph cf. Alex., *Fat.* 15 185,18-186,3. The three ends described here are Aristotelian (*EN* 2 1104b30ff.), but for Aristotle they are either the ends of different groups of people (*EN* 1 1095b14; cf. §17 151,18-27 above) or, for the good person, they coincide (*EN* 2 1105a1). Moreover, if they are regarded as ends between which a person chooses on a specific occasion, as the present argument requires, the dilemma arises: are they then judged in terms of some further end, or is the choice between them arbitrary? Cf. Sharples 2001, 569-70.

[703] Sharples 1983a follows the Arabic here, emending the trans-mitted Greek text to give 'the same things'. But this is redundant when a reference to 'the same things' has just preceded, and 'these things', the reading of the Greek MSS, gives a better flow to the sentence.

not able to choose their opposites, but because they seem more reasonable to him. At any rate it is possible for him, wanting on some occasion to show that his choice is not necessitated, and being contentious about this, to choose also what does not seem reasonable.[704]

Moreover, if the disposition in accordance with which we deliberate is not always similar,[705] we will not always choose the same things from the things that surround us, [even though they] are similar. But if, in the same circumstances, people who are not similar do not choose the same things, it is clear that the cause even of the choice of similar things is not the circumstances being similar but the person whom they surround being in a similar [condition].[706]

And in general, to try to show by argument that there is something depending on us, when it is so evident, is [the action] of those who do not know how to judge what is clear and what is not. For this is apparent, as we said, from many things: from deliberating, from repenting, from giving advice, from condemning certain people, from exhorting, from praising, from blaming, from honouring, from punishing, from teaching, from commanding, from seeking prophecies, from praying, from habituating, from legislating. For in general all human life, making use of these [activities] and those of this sort, bears witness that nothing is so peculiar to the human being, as compared with the other living creatures, as what depends on us.

And that the beginning of our coming to be of a certain sort in character – on account of which we make choices [of] different [sorts] – rests with ourselves,[707] [this] is clear

35

175,1

5

10

---

[704] Cf. Alex., *Fat.* 29 200,2-7; Donini 1974, 182ff.; id. 1987, 1253; Frede 1984, 290 n.20; Bobzien 1998b, 170; Salles 1998, 73-4; Sharples 2001, 568-9.

[705] Literally, 'if we are not always alike with respect to the disposition ...'

[706] This argument is, as Bobzien 1998a, 410 points out, in itself entirely compatible with a determinist position.

[707] Literally, 'we ourselves possess the beginning'. For the general claim cf. Aristotle, *EN* 3 1114a4-31, *Alex.*, Fat. 27, *Probl. Eth.* 9; Bondeson 1974.

from the fact that it is through habit that we come to be of a certain sort, and that most of our habits depend on us. For even if someone developed bad habits at first when he was still a child, yet by nature all people, when they are fully developed, are capable of perceiving the things that are noble. At any rate no one who is in a natural state lacks the conception of which things are just and which unjust, which noble and which base.[708] And neither do they fail to realise that it is from developing habits of a certain sort that they become capable of choosing and of doing either the things that are noble or those that are base.[709] At any rate those who want to practise and learn something turn to advancing themselves to the [goal] set before them through habituation, since they are not ignorant of the strength of habit for achieving the [goal] set before one. For to whom is it not clear, that it is through doing things that are temperate that temperance comes about? But if neither the things that are noble <nor those that are base>* are* unknown to those who are still in a natural state and not yet incapacitated[710] by wickedness, and* the route to them depends on us and is clear, it will depend on us both to come to be of a certain sort in character and to acquire the dispositions as a result of which we will choose and do these things or those.

Good or bad natural endowments for certain things, as long as they preserve a person in his own proper nature,[711] contribute only to the easier or more difficult acquisition of the things for which [people] are well or badly endowed by nature. For it is possible for all people who are in a natural

---

[708] Cf. Alex., *Probl. Eth.* 9 129,3-19; 18 139,9; 29 160,34. Sharples 1990, 36 n.100.

[709] Cf. Aristotle, *EN* 3 1114a9-10.

[710] Cf. Alex., *Probl. Eth.* 29 160,34; Aristotle, *EN* 1 1099b19; Donini 1989a, 111, and 1989b; Sharples 2001, 588-92. Donini points out that the reference is to the effect of behaviour during one's life, not to an innate incapacity.

[711] Or, with Bruns' conjecture *mê pêrôsi* for *têrôsi*, 'as long as they do not destroy man in his own proper (i.e., human) nature'. Cf. Aristotle, *EN* 7 1148b15-1149a20.

state and not perverted*[712] in their judgement and choice to acquire virtue, and possible [to do so] through one's own [agency]. And for this reason some people who are rather poorly endowed by nature often become better than many who are well endowed by nature for virtue, remedying the deficiencies of their nature by the power that comes from themselves.   30

[24]. On luck.   176,1

This section is for the most part a straightforward and orthodox presentation of the Aristotelian doctrine of luck and chance as set out in *Physics* 2.5-6. (I use 'luck' as the translation of *tukhê* in the specific sense relating to human activity, 'fortuitous' for *to automaton*, its counterpart in natural coming-to-be, and 'chance' for the genus covering both of these.) Cf. Alex., *Fat.* chs. 8 and 24; also Alex. ap. Simpl., *In Phys.* 343,14-20; Sharples 2001, 540 and n.197.

The present section does however make two distinctive contributions. One is the way in which it develops, in the context of *bad* luck (178,18-22) the connection between purpose and regularity, chance and infrequency indicated by Aristotle at *Phys.* 2.5 196b36, 197a4 and *Metaph.* 5.30 1025a18-19. (Cf. below 221 n.727, and, on the general issue, Judson 1991, 82-95; Sharples 2001, 538-9. Significantly, Simplicius, *In Phys.* 348,6-14, cites Alexander as emphasising this point, presumably in the lost *Physics* commentary. Secondly, whereas *Fat.* 8 rejects the definition of luck as 'a cause obscure to human reasoning' by saying that the causes of chance events are obvious, the last section of the present discussion (179,6-23) argues that the definition reduces chance to a purely epistemic status.

The present discussion starts with a classification of causes; this was clearly a standard school-procedure (cf. *Fat.* chs. 3-6), particularly appropriate here given the way in which Aristotle's

---

[712] For *adiastrophois* (an emendation: see Notes on the Text) cf. Diogenes Laertius 7.89 (*SVF* 3.228); Sextus Empiricus, *PH* 3.194; Anon., *In EN* (*CAG* 20) 232,10, 233,15; Eustratius, *In EN* (*CAG* 20) 259,3, 403,11; Michael of Ephesus, *In EN* (*CAG* 22.3) 46,10, 47,6.13; and cf. *diestrammenoi* in Alexander, *Probl. Eth.* 9 129,11. Rovida here refers to the *Eudemian Ethics*: *adiastrophos* does not occur there, but *diastrophos* does at 2.10 1227a21, 30, 31. Cf. Sharples 2001, 588 n.524, 590 n.535; above, 170 n.575.

discussion of chance in *Phys.* 2.4-6 follows that of the four causes in 2.3. The question arises of the relation of the present text to Alexander's lost *Physics* commentary: it does not make the mistake, for which Alexander is criticised by Simpl., *In Phys.* 338,36-339,2, of defining the result of luck rather than luck itself. (Cf., however, 219 n.721 below.) See also below, 218 n.720, 220 n.723.

This section is translated into English and discussed in Sharples 1983b, of which the present version is a revision. Cf. also Sharples 1975b 46-9; Opsomer and Steel 1999, 254.

176,2   Sufficient evidence that luck and the fortuitous are among the things that are is provided by people's common conception; but what each of them is and with which of the things that are it is concerned, [these are questions where] the majority are no longer the masters of teaching the opinions
5   that have been established. For they do not agree either with themselves or with one another about these things, though they agree in the opinion that each of them exists. It is worth while, then, considering what their nature is and with which of the things that are their coming-to-be is concerned.[713]

Well, these too seem to be numbered among causes; for luck seems to be the cause of the things that come to be
10   from luck, and the fortuitous of things of that sort.[714] Since then there are four causes, about which it is our custom often to speak, the material [cause] and that in respect of the form and the productive [cause] and the end, it is necessary that each of these things too should be among these, if indeed they are causes.

Well, no one would give luck and the fortuitous as the causes as *matter* of the things that come to be as a result of them; for luck is not something which underlies and is
15   shaped and given form by something as matter. For [matter] persists when it receives the form, and is a cause

[713] With this paragraph cf. §25 [A] below, and Alex., *Fat.* ch.2. (Aristotle starts his discussion of chance by saying that some even doubt its existence: *Phys.* 2.4 195b36. See below, §25 179.26-29.)

[714] i.e. 'of such as come to be fortuitously'.

of the things that come to be by being present in the things
that have come to be from it; but luck and the fortuitous are
not present in the things that come to be on account of
them. For the thing that comes to be in accordance with
luck does not itself have luck in itself.* But on account of
this it is not as form and essence that these things are
causes of the things that are on account of them, either; for   20
the form is present in that of which it is the cause, coming
to be in the matter and remaining, but neither of these [is
present in this way]. But neither are luck and the fortuitous
cause[s] as the end and 'that for the sake of which'; for luck
is not the goal of any of the things that come to be, as the
goal of each of the things that come to be for the sake of
something is definite, but each of these [luck and the fortui-
tous] is indefinite.

But if luck is not among any of these three causes, either   25
it is not the cause of anything, or it will be among the
productive [causes]. Now, it is for the sake of something
that the productive causes bring about the things that are
brought about by them, and they have some definite end set
before them, as [with] nature and skill and choice, but
neither the fortuitous nor luck is the same as any of these.
For each of [luck and the fortuitous] seems to be something
other besides these; and these on the one hand are definite   30
and lead to something definite, but what is [a matter] of
luck[715] is unstable and indefinite.   177,1

If then luck and the fortuitous seem to be causes of
certain things, but are not the same as any of the [types of]
cause, there is a risk that they do not exist at all, or else
some other manner of cause must be sought. Well, to say
that they do not exist at all is absurd, when they are things
believed to have such great power among the things that
are; but what other manner of cause could there be besides   5
those that have been mentioned already? – Perhaps then,
since of causes some are [causes] in themselves and others

---

[715] See below, 228 n.757; here the periphrasis has slightly more
point, but 'luck is unstable and indefinite' would have made the
point well enough.

accidental – for there *are* some causes that are accidental;
for that which attaches as an accident to what is a cause in
itself and in the proper sense is [itself] a cause accidentally,
and that very thing itself to which this attached was a cause
in the primary sense.* The doctor is in himself the cause of
10   health, the pale person accidentally, if this [sc. being pale]
should be an accidental attribute of the doctor; for what
attaches as an accident to what produces is [itself] a productive cause accidentally.[716] Moreover, the doctor is the
productive cause accidentally of, for example, thinness if
this should attach as an accident to the person who is being
cured.[717] – Since then of causes some are [causes] in
themselves and others accidental,[718] and luck cannot be
15   placed among causes [that are causes] in themselves, it will
be among [causes that are] accidental. For the things that
are definite would not be accidental, but those that are
accidental are indefinite and unstable, just as that which is
[a matter] of luck[719] is accustomed to be; for the things
which can attach as accidents to what is a cause in itself and
in the proper sense are indefinite [in their variety], and all
these themselves become causes accidentally.[720]

But if luck is a cause accidentally, it must attach as an
20   accident to some one of what we speak of as causes in the
proper sense. Since then luck seems to produce something
(for we say that the things that are in accordance with luck
come to be and have come to be 'from luck'), [luck and the

---

[716] Aristotle's example is the piper who is the accidental cause
of a house, because the builder also happens to be a piper (*Phys.*
2.5 197a14-15).

[717] Orelli compares Arist. *Phys.* 2.3 194b36. However, thinness
is there cited as an example of a means to the end health, rather
than as an accident.

[718] Aristotle, *Phys.* 2.3 195a32. Alexander is cited for this point
by Simplicius, *In Phys.* 337,10-11, as is noted here by Rovida.

[719] Above, 217 n.715.

[720] Cf. Aristotle, *Phys.* 2.5 197a8 and 14-17. Simplicius, *In Phys.*
340,30-341,9 criticises Alexander for interpreting the latter
passage as relating to final rather than productive causes; the
present passage avoids this implication.

fortuitous] must necessarily attach to some one of the productive causes, if they are to keep their place among the causes. But the productive causes in the proper sense are nature and skill and choice. All those things, which produce [something] in the proper sense and definitely, produce the   25
things which are brought about by them for the sake of some end, and we see that all the things that come about for the sake of something are brought about by some one of these; so luck attaches as an accident to some one of these.

But since it seems that the things that are in accordance with luck are among the things that are [matters] of choice (for the things that we say come to be from luck are those for the sake of which we would also have chosen to do something, in order to obtain those of them in the case of which we speak of 'good luck', and in order not to obtain   30
those to which we apply 'bad luck'), luck will be [something that] accompanies the things that come to be in accordance with choice, and among these it will be a cause accidentally. For when we do something in accordance with choice, but there happens to us not the end that was intended in accordance with the choice, but something else comes about accidentally, the action that came about in accordance with choice is the cause of what happened but was not intended;   35
and we say that this has come about from luck. If, to the person who digs in accordance with choice for the sake of   178,1
planting, there happens as a result of the digging the finding of some treasure, we say that the finding of the treasure has come about from luck; but [it would] not [have done so] from luck if he had dug for the sake of this. For then the digging would have been the cause of the finding not accidentally, just as neither [is] the planting   5
[accidental][721]; but as it is [it is the cause of the finding] accidentally, for it was not for the sake of this that it came about.[722] – So luck is that which comes about in accordance

---

[721] One would have expected 'neither [is it the cause] of the planting [accidentally]', which requires the addition of one letter (*tou* for *to*); but the MSS are unanimous. See above, 216.

[722] For the example cf. Aristotle, *Metaph.* 5.30 1025a16-19, *EN* 3

with choice, when it becomes the cause of something accidentally; and what comes about for the sake of something will always come to be an indefinite cause in this way, and luck will be a cause accidentally – not without qualification, however, but among the productive [causes] that come to be for the sake of something, and of these among those in accordance with choice.[723] For we do not speak of what is from luck in the case of the things that come to be in accordance with nature, when something else comes to be contrary to the goal of nature,[724] as with monstrosities. Of these too what comes to be by nature is the cause accidentally, but this is not [a matter] of luck. [So too] those things of which the things that come to be in accordance with skill become causes accidentally, for example in the case* of things that are misshapen;[725] luck is not responsible in the case of these things either. So [luck] is [to be found] among the things that are in accordance with choice, as we said.

When, therefore, that which comes to be in accordance with choice becomes the cause accidentally of some success, as digging of the finding of treasure, we call this 'good luck'; when of something bad, 'bad luck[726] – for

---

1112a27; Alex. *Fat.* 8 172,25-30, 24 194,17-19.

[723] Cf. Aristotle, *Phys.* 2.6 197b1-8; Alex., *In Phys.* fr. 2 Giannakis 1996, which as Giannakis notes is the probable source of Simplicius, *In Phys.* 340,1-7; also Lettinck 1994, 136.

[724] Alexander, *In Phys.* fr.2 Giannakis 1996 explicitly identifies the 'goal of nature' with form.

[725] Bruns, rightly rejecting Orelli's claim that this refers to tightrope-walkers (!) and acrobats, takes it rather as a reference to the artificial production of misshapen monsters, comparing [Longinus], *De sublim.* 44.5; but what is wanted is a case where skill leads to a result which is *not* intended. Probably there is a quite general reference to cases where products of skill or craft turn out misshapen though the maker did not intend this.

[726] Aristotle, *Phys.* 2.5 197a25-27 reserves the terms used here, *eutukhia* and *dustukhia*, for *great* good fortune and great misfortune, speaking of *agathê* and *phaulê tukhê* in cases of lesser magnitude.

example, if someone digging were bitten by some serpent which he found in the very [act of] digging, when the place was not otherwise suited to serpents of that sort; for if there 20 was a multitude of serpents [there] and this person dug without care, it was not luck that was the cause of his being bitten, but a certain lack of consideration and foresight of his own.[727]

What is [a matter] of luck is like this and is a cause in this way;[728] 'the fortuitous' is customarily applied also to the things that come to be from luck, but nevertheless to a greater extent in the case of the things that are by nature. For when that which comes to be by nature is followed by 25 something else, and not that for the sake of which it came to be, we say that this has come to be 'fortuitously', as with monstrosities. For when that end, for the sake of which something comes to be by nature,[729] does not [itself] come to be, we say that [that which comes to be by nature] has itself come to be 'in vain', and we say that what followed upon it has come to be 'fortuitously', because what has come to be in vain is a cause accidentally.[730] And, in a word, everything that follows on what comes to be in accordance 30 with nature, [but] is not that for the sake of which it came to be, is said to have come to be fortuitously. Thus the stone 179,1 which was carried downwards and fell in such a way that it

---

[727] This is to be contrasted with Alex., *Fat.* 8 172,25-30, which considers only the good luck of finding treasure and mentions only purpose, not likelihood. The discussion of bad luck as well has clearly played a part in prompting the explicit reference to likelihood; for, while it might make sense to say that finding treasure was not 'luck' if one was looking for it, however small the chance of finding it (so Frede 1982, 283; 1984, 282-3; cf. Sharples 2001, 538-9) it would be less plausible to say that being bitten by serpents only ceases to be (bad) luck if one dug with the express *purpose* of being bitten.

[728] Above, 217 n.715.

[729] Literally: 'for the sake of which that, which comes to be by nature, comes to be'.

[730] An attempt to derive *automatôs* 'fortuitously' from *auto* 'itself' and *matên* 'in vain'; cf. Aristotle, *Phys.* 2.6 197b22-32.

is possible to sit on it acquired this position fortuitously, [the position] following on the natural downwards motion of the stone on account of its weight.[731] In a similar way, too, the horse which went to a particular place on account of
5   food, but was on account of this saved from the enemy; for [the horse] too the natural appetite for food was the cause of its being saved, [though] it did not go for the sake of being saved.[732]

To say that luck is 'a cause obscure to human reasoning'[733] is not [the assertion] of those who are laying down some [real] nature [that] luck [has], but of those who are saying that luck consists in people's being in a certain state in relation to the causes;[734] in this way the same thing will be from luck for one person but not for another, when
10 one knows its cause and the other does not.

Moreover, since there are several causes of the same thing, if there are [causes] of four types, and it is possible that some people should know some of these but not others, the same thing will at the same time be from luck and not from luck for the same person, if he knows some of its causes but does not know the others; for the distinction has not been made, from ignorance concerning which of the

---

[731] This conflates two examples in Aristotle: the tripod which falls in such a way that one can sit on it (*Phys.* 2.6 197b16-18, where the sense must be that the tripod was originally positioned so as to form a seat, and happened to fall in such a way that it did so once again. Cf. Themistius, *In Phys.* 55,2, Simplicius, *In Phys.* 347,8, 352,9.20, Philoponus, *In Phys.* 288,6) and the stone that falls and accidentally strikes someone (*Phys.* 2.6 197b30-32). Similarly Simplicius, *In Phys.* 336,35.

[732] Aristotle, *Phys.* 2.6 197b15-16; Alex., *Fat.* 8 173,8-10.

[733] The Stoic position (*SVF* 2.965, 966, 971; but not originating with them, cf. Aristotle, *Phys.* 2.4 196b6), criticised also in Alex., *Fat.* 8 174,1ff.. For the complaint, made here but not there, that it makes chance a subjective matter, cf. Boethius, *In Ciceronis Topica* 372,16 Orelli and Baiter. This definition of chance is also reported in Alex., *In Phys.* fr.1 Giannakis 1996; cf. Lettinck 1964, 136.

[734] 179,6-9 = *SVF* 2.967.

causes luck [arises].

If they say that luck is not the cause which is obscure to   15
some people, but that which is in general [obscure] to all
people, they would not even allow that luck exists at all,
[since] they grant that the art of prophecy exists and assert
that it brings knowledge of the things which seem to others
to be obscure.[735] And if wanting to make this distinction[736]
they should say that luck is the cause which is obscure to
those lacking knowledge, according to this argument the
things that come to be in accordance with knowledge and   20
skill will, for those who lack knowledge and skill, be from
luck; for neither does the person who is not a carpenter
know the cause[737] of the things that are [matters] of carpen-
try, nor the person who is not a musician that of things
musical, nor any other person who lacks a skill the things
that are [matters] of that skill;[738] for it is in knowing the
causes (explanations) of the things that come to be in accordance with skill that skill [consists].

[25]. On fate.   179,24

This text is apparently an attempt to cast material from both the
constructive (chs. 2-6) and the critical (chs. 7-38) sections of
Alexander's *De fato* into the form of an (at any rate superficially)
more structured and positive account of Alexander's doctrine of
fate.[739] I say 'superficially', because there are internal tensions
within the account; see below, 228 n.754. For a full discussion see
Sharples 1980. This section is translated into English in Sharples
1983a, of which the present translation is a revised version. A
medieval Latin version is published in Thillet 1963, who attributes
it to William of Moerbeke. See also Freudenthal (1884) 14-16;

[735] 179,14-18 = *SVF* 2.967.
[736] i.e. that ruled out at the beginning of the previous sentence,
'not ... *some* people, but ... all people'.
[737] Or: explanation.
[738] Here, by contrast with 217 n.715 above, the periphrasis (in
the plural) is to the point and not redundant.
[739] So already Orelli 1824, 327 n.1; cf. Freudenthal 1884, 14-16.
Cf. below, 225 n.745, 233 n.766; but also 234 n.769.

Gercke 1885, nos. 108, 124; Donini 1977, 182 n.16; Sharples 1980, and 2001 581-2; Thillet 1987, 107; Fazzo 1988, and 2002a, 22 n.17; Mansfeld 1988, 182 n.4.

[A - Statement of the Problem]

179,25   Concerning fate it is worth considering what it is and in which of the things that are [it is located]. That fate is something is sufficiently established by the common conception of human beings (for nature is not in vain and does not aim wide [sc. of the truth]. Anaxagoras is not deserving of credence when he testifies against the common opinion; for he says that fate is not anything at all,

30   but that this name is an empty one.)[740] But as to what it is and in what [it is located], the conception of human beings is no longer sufficient to indicate this.[741] For they cannot agree either with one another or with themselves about

180,1   this. For they change their opinion concerning fate with the times and the circumstances. At one time they posit fate as something inevitable and inescapable, and subordinate to it all the things that are and come to be; at another it is possible to hear them often speaking of what is contrary to fate and of what is contrary to destiny. And for the most part

5   those for whom those things that are matters of luck do not go well, and those that are matters of judgement and of their own choice are not any more healthy either, flee to fate as to some refuge,[742] transferring from themselves to it responsibility for[743] the things that have not been done, or are not being done, by themselves as they should be. And at these times these people say that all things come to be in

---

[740] Similarly Alex., *Fat.* 2 165,19-23. See Sharples 1983a, 125-6. Fazzo 2002a, 22 n.17 well compares the similar discussion at Alex., *Prov.* 1,9 Ruland.

[741] Cf. Alex., *Fat.* 2 165,23-5, and above §24 176,3-5.

[742] The word for 'refuge' here, *krêsphugeton*, used several times by Herodotus (5.124, 8.52, 9.15, 9.96), is rare enough to suggest a deliberate literary flourish; the source may be Chrysippus' similar remark about the *wicked* (*SVF* 2.1000).

[743] Or: 'the cause of' (*aitia*).

accordance with fate; but when their luck changes for the
better, they no longer abide by the same opinion. But those   10
for whom the things that are a matter of their own judgement [go] successfully, and all those that come from luck
are in harmony, [these] attach responsibility for[744] the
things that come to be to themselves rather than to fate.
Others again hold either themselves or the divine responsible for all things that go successfully, but in the case of what
[goes] less well call upon [the name of] fate.[745]

And there are certain religious charlatans, who observe   15
the weakness of the majority [of people] in judgement
concerning fate and the things that come to be in accordance with it, and their readiness, on account of their love
of self and their being conscious that they themselves have
[achieved] nothing successful, to believe that fate is responsible for all the things in which they go wrong. [So the
charlatans] declare that everything that comes to be does
so in accordance with fate, and profess some art of this sort
according to which they say they are able to foreknow and   20
to declare beforehand all the things that will be in any way
at all, since none of them comes to be without a certain
necessity, which they call fate. And taking as their supporters those who are responsible for their having this art,[746]
they persuade the majority of people, assailing them in difficult circumstances[747] and misfortunes when they are all but
praying that it should be shown [to them] that this is how
this matter is. In accordance with a sort of experience and   25
understanding of such matters, and observation of the
sequence in them, they foretell with a sure aim certain of
the things that will ensue for those in such a condition; and,

[744] Cf. the preceding note.

[745] With the argument of this paragraph cf. *Fat.* 2, where
however the divergent views on fate are presented as those of
different groups of people and not only as the responses of the
same people to different circumstances.

[746] i.e. the determinists whose doctrine of fate justifies the divin-
ers' claims; Bruns 1893, 17.

[747] For *peristaseis* referring specifically to adverse circumstances cf. LSJ s.v., II(b).

saying that they are able to [do] this as a result of their art concerning fate, they collect no small rewards for such malpractice, those who put them to the test gladly giving to
30   them as being supporters and defenders [of themselves] concerning their own errors. And these [people] have persuaded the majority of humankind – who have on account of idleness neglected to consider how these matters [really] are, and what is the position of fate in the things that are – to say that all the things that come to be do so in accordance with fate.[748]

But since not even those who call upon [the name of] fate to a considerable extent appear to entrust everything to it in
181,1   the conduct of life (for the truth is sufficient to show that those who can be trusted to speak falsely are inconsistent with themselves),[749] it is worth our while to begin from [the point made] above and see, what is the nature of fate and in what things [it is located] and how far the power it has extends.

[B -Where Fate is located]

181,4   And first let us consider with which of the things that are it is reasonable to say [fate] is concerned; for when this becomes clear it will be useful also with respect to our other enquiries concerning it.[750] Well, to place it over all the

---

[748] The argument of this paragraph is not directly parallelled in *Fat.*

[749] More fully and hence more clearly in *Fat.* 16 186,20-23: 'it is not even possible to persuade any of [those who say that all things come to be in accordance with fate] not to do those things which they do in the manner of those who have the power both to do them and not to do them ...; such great strength, and clear evidence from the things that come to be, does the truth have.'

[750] While *Fat.* 3-6 similarly establishes the nature of fate by an argument from elimination, it – like §24 above – takes as its starting-point the four Aristotelian causes rather than, as here, the sphere in which fate operates. The approach of the present text is arguably better suited to a doctrine which emphasises the limitations of fate. The following argument shows a similarity to that

things that are and to say that all the things that are are in accordance with fate, in a similar way both those that are eternal and those that are not, is not reasonable, especially when it is not agreed [even] by those who most of all sing the praises of fate as the cause of all the things that come to be. For it is not reasonable to say that the eternal things are 10 in accordance with a fate of this sort; it is ridiculous to say that the diagonal is incommensurable with the side[751] in accordance with fate, or that it is on account of this that the triangle has its internal angles equal to two right [angles],[752] and in general it is in no way reasonable to say that those things which are always the same and in the same state are so in accordance with fate.

But neither [is it reasonable to say that] all the things that come to be [do so in accordance with fate]. For as many of these too as have a coming-to-be and movement which is 15 orderly and definite, these too fall outside fate. For it is not in accordance with fate that the sun comes to be at the winter or the summer solstice, nor yet does each of the heavenly bodies[753] have fate as the cause of its own proper motion, but just as it is free in respect of its being and essence from a cause of this sort, so it is in respect of its own proper activities. And for this reason fate is not the 20 cause of any of the things that are eternal or that come to be always the same and in the same way, but the activity of fate seems to be in the things that are subject to coming-to-be and passing away. For it is in the things that are fitted for opposites as far as their natural endowment is concerned that the power of fate seems to be located, holding them in one of the opposite [states] and keeping them in it

---

applied to *deliberation* in Aristotle, *EN* 3 1112a21ff., and, following this, Alex., *Probl. Eth.* 29 160,5ff.; cf. above, 208 n.693.

[751] For the example cf. Aristotle, *Metaph.* 5.12 1019b24, 9.4 1047b6, *EN* 3 1112a22-3, and many other examples at Bonitz 1870, 185a7-16; Alex. *Fat.* 30 200,21.

[752] A frequent example in Aristotle: Bonitz 1870, 770b17-30.

[753] Especially the planets, as the following reference to proper, peculiar motions shows.

25   according to a certain ordered sequence. For it is those
things that would not be as they are without fate that seem
to be kept in their present order by fate; and such are none
other of the things that are than those subject to coming-
to-be and passing away, so it is somewhere here that what is
[a matter] of fate too [is located].[754]

But since of these things also some come to be in accordance with skill and with some reasoning of the type
involved in skill, others in accordance with choice, others in
30   accordance with nature, we must consider in which of these
what is [a matter] of fate [is located], if it cannot be in them
all. Well, to say that the things that come to be in accordance with skill are and come to be in accordance with fate
is in no way in harmony with [people's] opinions concerning
fate. For it is ridiculous to say that a bed or a bench has
come to be in accordance with fate, or that a lyre has been
tuned in accordance with fate; for in this way we shall call
35   every skill fate.[755] But neither will the things of which choice
is the cause be in accordance with fate; for the starting-point
182,1 of these things is in us and not outside, but fate is not in us.
Even if fate is concerned with the same things with which
what depends on us is concerned, it is [something] other
than what depends on us. So we must remove from fate
those of the things subject to coming-to-be, too, that come
to be in accordance with skill and choice.[756] And when these
are removed there are left remaining those things for which
5   nature is the cause of [their] coming-to-be; and it is in these
things, too, that what is [a matter] of fate[757] is thought to
have power. For if someone wished to consider and
examine the opinions that have been laid down concerning

[754] This passage is difficult to reconcile with the treatments of
exceptions to fate, and of contingency, in *Fat.* 6, 9, and below
184,13-27, 185,15ff.; cf. Sharples 1975a, 271-4; 2001, 582.
[755] Cf., with Orelli 1824, 328 n.14, Alex. *Fat.* 5 169,10-12.
[756] With this argument by elimination cf. *Fat.* 5 169,3-6, 169,19.
[757] The periphrasis 'what is of fate', which might have seemed
appropriate at 181,28 and 30 above where the reference was to the
effects of fate, here seems a purely stylistic variant; the simple
'fate' would have been equally suitable.

fate, he will not find that they place fate concerning any
other things or in any things other than those that come to
be by nature, and of these most of all in the [nature][758] of
living creatures and of those things that result from combinations of the things subject to coming-to-be. For it is not
very usual to say that the changing of the elements into one   10
another comes about in accordance with fate.

[C - Does Fate admit of exceptions ?]

What is in accordance with fate, then, being located in the   182,11
things we have previously stated, and this having become
clear, it [naturally] follows after this to enquire whether
[what is in accordance with fate] is such as to be necessary
and inevitable [*aparabatos*], in accordance with the poet
who says[759]

> I say that no man has escaped his destiny,   15
> Whether base or noble, when he has once been born.

or whether it is such that one can go against it [*parabain-
esthai*] and that it does not in every way have necessity in
itself.

Well, from the common judgement of people concerning
this we have neither of these [positions] firmly laid down;
for at one time they sing the praises of what is [a matter] of   20
fate as [being] necessary, at another they do not believe
that it* preserves its continuity in every way. For even those
who exercise themselves greatly in their arguments on its
behalf as being necessary, and attribute everything to it, do
not seem to believe in it in the conduct of life; for they often
call on [the name of] luck, admitting that this is some cause
other than fate, and they do not cease from praying to the   25
gods, on the assumption that something can be brought
about by [the gods] on account of the prayers even contrary

[758] Understanding 'nature' is suggested as a possibility here by
Donini 1977,182 n.16; the expression is as he says tortuous, but
does not seem impossibly so. Cf. Sharples 1980, 81 and n.65.
[759] Homer, *Iliad* 6.488.

to fate; moreover they also deliberate about the things they
should do, although they say that these too are in accordance with fate, and they call in advisers and do not hesitate
to make use of prophecies, on the assumption that it is
possible for them to guard against some one of the things
that are fated if they learn [of it] in advance. But since these
people turn out to be in obvious disagreement with
themselves in this way concerning the most important
matters (for their ingenious arguments to show that these
things are consistent are certainly most unpersuasive), and
since it is thought that in the things that are subject to
coming-to-be and passing away there is also the contingent,
which is the cause of nothing coming to be necessarily in
the things in which it is, it is worth considering whether
[the contingent] exists or not. For if this naturally [existing
thing] is defined it [will] very greatly contribute towards our
finding the essence of fate.

(1) Well, common usage is sufficient to establish [the
existence of] the nature [of the] contingent.[760] For none
even of those who say that all things come to be from necessity does not bear witness in living and in the activities of
life to [the fact] that both some of the things that come to
be can not come to be and [some] of the things that do not
come to be [can] come to be.

(2) Moreover, this is also easy to show by argument. For
many of the things that come to be are believed to come to
be, some from luck, some from the fortuitous; and that
there is also something that depends on us is so clear that
not even those who try to give the things that are [matters]
of fate such force that they are altogether necessary can
resist this belief. But if there is something that depends on
us, and this is concerned with the same things that it turned
out fate is concerned with, it is excluded that fate should be
inevitable and unable to be impeded and necessary; for it is
impossible to say that those things, the choice or not of

---

[760] Literally: 'the nature that is contingent.' The numbering of
this paragraph and the next reflects marginal numbering in MS V.

which begins with us,[761] are necessitated.

But it is necessary for those who say that fate exists to say that it is concerned with the same things with which what depends on us, too, [is] concerned. For whether they were to say [i] that it is the ends [of action] alone that come to be in accordance with fate, or whether [ii] they say that [it is]   15
the actions too, which the ends turn out to follow,[762] either way it follows that they say that fate is concerned with the same things with which what depends on us [is] also concerned. If [ii] someone were to say that the actions too are in accordance with fate, what was posited is at once clear, for it is in these that what depends on us, too, is [located]. But if [i] [he were to say] that the ends alone, for the sake of which the actions [are performed], [are in accordance with fate], and ends of a certain sort follow on actions of a certain sort (for it is not indeed the case that the same   20
end follows on what has been done in whatever way at all), it is necessary to say that the actions too, which ends of this sort follow, are fated. For the end that is in accordance with fate will not follow if the actions that lead to it have not preceded. And it is with these that what depends on us is concerned.

That there is something that depends on us will also be clear from the following points – if indeed one must use demonstrative arguments concerning things that are clear: 25
namely, [1][763] none of the things that are brought about by nature as its primary [ends] comes about in vain, and deliberating, which is in human beings by nature and is a primary work of nature (if indeed it is by this most of all that [the] human being is thought to differ from the other living creatures) comes about in vain, having come to be for nothing* if he who deliberates is not in control of choosing

---

[761] Literally: 'of which we are the beginnings to choose them or not.'

[762] Aristotle draws a similar distinction with regard to our responsibility for the way the goals of action appear to us at *EN* 3 1114b16-21.

[763] Supplied: V numbers argument (2) at 184,4 below.

30 anything as a result of the deliberation.[764] But it is as having
     power over this that we deliberate by ourselves concerning
     the things we should do, and do not yield to irrational
     appearances and follow them in a similar way to the other
     living creatures;[765] and that we call in as advisers whoever
184,1 we see are more able than ourselves, to assist in the judge-
     ment and choice of the courses that are set before us. And
     when [we are] concerned with greater and more difficult
     [matters], at this point we do not hesitate to call in the gods
     too as advisers, asking that we should learn from them,
     either through oracles or through counsels* or through
     certain dreams, which we should rather choose of the
     things about which we enquire.

5   (2) Sufficient to establish [that there is something that
     depends on us] are the codes of law, too, in which it is
     ordered that certain things should be taught* and the
     things that should be done are commanded, and those who
     obey these are honoured, those who do not are punished.

     (3) But indeed if there is something that depends on us
     the contingent [*endekhomenon*] too exists, if at least it
     depends on us both to do something and not to. And if this
     exists it is impossible that what is [a matter] of fate should
     be necessary, being in those things in which what depends
10   on us too has a place.

     (4) Prayers to the gods, too, are sufficient to establish that
     there are certain things which are contingent, some people
     asking them to avert certain things, others [asking them] to
     give good things, on the assumption that there are some
     things which can [*endekhomenôn*] both be brought about
     by the gods and not [be brought about by them] on account
     of our request.

     (5) And moreover it is possible to learn this also from the
     natural constitution of each of the things that are. For

---

[764] Cf. Alex., *Fat.* ch. 11, and above, 169 n.570, 208 n.693.

[765] Cf. Alex., *Fat.* 11 178,17-24, 14 184,1-8. The translation
follows Caninius in interpreting *tois alogois tôn allôn zôiôn* as
pleonastic for 'the other, irrational animals' and depending on
paraplêsios. This corrects Sharples 1983, 176 and 277.

nature itself has given to those things which are and come   15
to be of necessity no fitness for the opposite, but unfitness
for the [states] that are impossible; for they would have
fitness for change into these in vain, [since] they cannot be
otherwise [than they are]. For we see that neither does fire
have in itself the capacity for coldness, nor snow that for
blackness, nor the things that are heavy that for lightness,
at least while they remain what they are, nor [does] any of   20
the eternal things [have the capacity] for being destroyed.
But those things for which it is not necessary that they
should be and remain determinately in one of the opposite
[states], these have from nature readiness also for change
to the opposite [state]. Such are most of the things subject
to coming-to-be and passing away, with which one of the
opposites is not cognate; for each of them is able both to
undergo the opposites and not, that is,* it can [*endekhetai*]   25
both undergo [them] and not. But what can change into the
opposite [state] is not of necessity in that one of [the
opposite states] in which it is already.[766]

That not all things that come to be do so of necessity is
established both by what depends on us, as we said, and by
luck, which is capable of interrupting the continuity of the
things that are thought to come to be in a certain order. But
if it is no less clear than [that] fate [exists] that there is   30
something that depends on us, and that many things come
to be both from luck and from the fortuitous, and altogether
that in the things that are subject to coming- to-be, in which
fate too is located, there is also the nature of the contingent,
and this excludes what is necessary, it is impossible that
fate should be something which is necessary and which one
cannot go against.*

[D - Fate as individual nature]

But it is agreed that all the things that come to be in   185,1

---

[766] For the existence of the contingent as an argument against
the universality of fate cf. Alex., *Fat.* ch.9. The appeal at 184,16-18
to nature doing nothing in vain does not occur in that chapter.

accordance with fate come to be in accordance with a
certain order and sequence and have a certain succession in
themselves. For it is not indeed the case that the things that
are [matters] of fate are like the things that [result] from
luck; for the latter are unstable and come to be infrequently
and are almost without a cause,[767] but that which is in accor-
5   dance with fate is entirely the opposite; for they say that
[fate] is a chain of causes.[768] But neither does fate seem to
be the same as what is in accordance with choice; for the
continuity of [fate] is often interrupted by us and our
choice.

However, we see that there are the following causes in
the things that come to be and pass away besides the nature
which puts them together and fashions them: choice and
10   the fortuitous and luck (for that which is in accordance with
skill is not [present] in these). But that which is [a matter]
of fate does not seem to be the same as any of these. We are
left, then, with fate being nothing other than the proper
nature of each thing. For that which is [a matter] of fate is
not in what is universal and common, for example simply
[in] living creature or human being,* but in the individuals,
Socrates and Callias. And in these the nature that is peculiar
to them is, [through] being of a certain sort, the beginning
15   and cause of the ordered pattern that comes to be in accordance with it.*[769] For it is from this, in general, that
[people's] lives and their endings result, when it is not
impeded by certain things.

At any rate we see that the body too, through being like
this or like that as a result of nature, is affected both in
disease and in death following its natural constitution.* But
not of necessity; for treatments and changes of climate and
20   doctors' orders* and advice from the gods are sufficient to

[767] Or 'without an explanation' (*anaitia*).

[768] 185,1-3 and 5 = *SVF* 2.920.

[769] 185,14-33 are a closely parallel, but compressed, version of
Alex., *Fat.* 6 170,9-171,7. That passage may itself reflect earlier
Peripatetic discussions not entirely assimilated to their place in
Fat., and the present section of *Mant.* can be seen as smoothing
over the difficulties. See Sharples 1980, 81; 2001, 532.

break this pattern. And in the same way in the case of the soul too one could find actions and choices and lives becoming different from, [and] contrary to, the natural constitution. For 'people's character is their guardian spirit' according to Heraclitus,[770] that is, their nature.

For people's actions and lives and the endings of their lives turn out for the most part to follow their natural   25
constitutions and dispositions. The person* who is eager for battle and loves danger by nature [meets] some violent death for the most part, for this is his* fate and nature; and the person who is licentious and spends his life in pleasures [for the most part meets death] in intemperate behaviour, he who is of an enduring [nature] that through excess of labours and persistence in troubles, the person who is   30
illiberal that from eagerness over what is indifferent,[771] on account of which they act unjustly and neglect themselves and labour beyond their power. It is on this account, at any rate, that it is customary to reproach such people, [saying that] the person himself became the cause of his own death.

If what is in accordance with fate is like this, we shall not say any longer that prophecy is useless, either, [as] it foresees what will result in accordance with nature and assists [us] through advising and ordering us to resist the   35
natural sequence [when it inclines to] the worse.[772] Neither will the nature of luck be done away with, but it will be   186,1
responsible for certain things, coinciding with the things that come to be in accordance with choice.[773] And still more

[770] Heraclitus, 22B119 DK.
[771] 'What is indifferent'; i.e. external, material goods. Our text – unlike *Fat.* at this point – uses the Stoic technical term.
[772] The passage in a corresponding position at *Fat.* 6 171,7-11 rather makes the point, more explicitly relevant to the foregoing argument, that nature's admitting of exceptions explains why prophecies are not always fulfilled. Cf. 186,8-9 below.
[773] cf. *Mant.* §24 178,15, and for *ekhein aitian* = 'be responsible for', Alex., *Fat.* 16 187,24. One might expect the nominative *sumpiptousa*; the Latin version indeed has the nominative, but this is not good evidence unless one also regards its *causa* and

will the divine and the assistance that comes from it, and prayers and entreaties from us, keep their proper place, when that which is [a matter] of fate is like this.[774] And in agreement with these things, too, will be the saying that
5 many things come to be contrary to destiny and contrary to fate, as the poet somewhere shows saying

> Lest you come to the house of Hades even before it is destined.[775]

And this opinion might also be established by the [fact]* that the prophets do not hit the mark in everything that they foretell.
10 It is in no way remarkable that people do not turn out to hold this opinion concerning fate. For the majority do not aim badly concerning things in their outline, but [when it comes to] the particular [details] and defining [them] and making [them] exact they make many errors. For the former is the work of nature, the latter of understanding.

Aristotle already mentions the name of fate in the first
15 book of the *Meteorology* as follows: 'but the cause of all these things must be supposed to be that at fated times there comes about, just as winter does in the seasons of the year, a Great Winter in some great cycle.'[776] And it seems that in these words he is saying that fate is nature (for the fated times, the winter and [that] of the other things, are those which have a reciprocal succession which is natural,
20 but not inevitable and necessitated).[777] And in the fifth book

---

erit as directly reflecting the Greek.

[774] Cf. Alex., *Fat.* ch. 17.

[775] Homer, *Iliad* 20.336. Also cited in the context of the identity of fate and nature and the question whether fate admits of exceptions at Gellius, *Noctes Atticae* 13.1.2.

[776] Aristotle, *Meteorologica* 1.14 352a28. Fazzo 2002a, 22 n.17 compares the appeal to Aristotelian texts in Alex., *Prov.* 91,5ff. Ruland (= 156.16ff. Fazzo and Zonta).

[777] That is, winter or spring may come earlier or later; it is not being suggested that, for example, winter might be followed by

of the *Physics*, too, he again mentions fate as follows: 'are there then comings-to-be which are forcible and not fated, to which those that are in accordance with nature are opposite?';*[778] through which it is again clear that he uses the name of fate in connection with the things that come to be in accordance with nature. For if he says that what is in accordance with nature is opposite to what is not fated,* and what is contrary to fate is opposite to what is in accordance with fate, what is in accordance with fate will be the same as what is in accordance with nature. For it is not possible to say that several things are opposite to what is not in accordance with fate, [if] this last is one thing;[779] [firstly] what is in accordance with fate, which clearly is opposite to it, and [secondly] what is in accordance with nature, [this] being other than what is in accordance with fate. And Theophrastus very clearly shows in his *Callisthenes* that what is in accordance with fate is the same as what is in accordance with nature,[780] [as does] also Polyzelus[781] in the book that is entitled *Concerning Fate*.

25

30

---

summer without spring intervening at all. Cf. Alex., *Quaest.* 3.5 89,13-18 and Sharples 1994a, 133 n.255.

[778] Aristotle, *Phys.* 5.6 230a32.

[779] For the principle that one thing can have only one opposite (Plato, *Protagoras* 332ce) cf. the discussion of whether, if one opposite is ambiguous, the other must also be, in Alex., *Probl. Eth.* 11, *In Top.* 99,2-20, 100,31-101,14, 183-7, with the discussion in Sharples 1985; also Fazzo 2002b, 181.

[780] Theophrastus, fr.504 FHS&G. Cf. Fortenbaugh 1979; 1984, 44, 230-32.

[781] Polyzelus (6) in *RE* 21.2 (1952) col.1865; otherwise unknown.

Notes on the Text

Greek MSS (containing all of *Mant.* unless otherwise indicated):
A = Milan, Ambros. gr. H43 sup (431) [15th].
a = editio Aldina, Victor Trincavellus, Venice 1534.[783]
B = Venice, Marc. gr. 261 (725) [<1468]. B^2 = corrections by Bessarion.[784]
C = Madrid, cod. reg. 109 [1464]. (§§22-5).
D = Berlin, DSB, Phillipps 1558 (gr. 260) [16th]. (§22, part).
F = Milan, Ambros. gr. F88 sup (V416/348) [1462] (§§22-5).
H = Copenhagen, KB, Fabricius 88 [15th] (§§24-5).
K = Vienna, NB, philos. gr. 110 [16th]. (excerpts from §§1-17 and §25).
L = Leiden, Univ., Scaliger gr. 51 [15th]. (§§22-4).
M = Munich, Bayerische Staatsbibl., MS gr. 417 [15th]. (§2).
N = London, BL, Harleian 5597 [?]. (§2, part).
P = Paris, BN, ancien gr. 1739 [15th]. (§§22-4).
Q = Paris, BN, ancien gr. 1996 [16th]. (§§22-4).
R = Paris, BN, ancien gr. 2544 [16th]. (§§22-4).
V = Venice, Marcianus gr. 258 [9th]. V^2 = contemporary corrections;
       V^3 = corrections by Bessarion.[785]

Arabic[786] =
(§2)   Finnegan 1956 + Badawi 1971, no.5.
(§9)   Badawi 1971, no.3.
(§15) Gätje 1971, 140-163: cf. id. 1966, 272-273.
(§23) Ruland 1976, 193-210.

Latin =
(§2)   Théry 1926, 69-83 (from the Arabic, by Gerard of Cremona).
(§25) Thillet 1963, 109-116 (from the Greek, by William of Moerbeke)

Rovida = notes by Cesare Rovida in copy of Aldine ed. in Ambrosiana Library, Milan (S. Q1. VIII.30: cf. Fazzo 1999, 69).

[783] In the following notes 'MSS' includes the Aldine edition.
[784] Mioni 1981, 377. Cf. Thillet 1982, 31 n.3.; Fazzo 2002, 39 n.54.
[785] Mioni 1976, 286 and n.6; Thillet 1982, 28 and n.2.
[786] I am grateful to Inna Kupreeva and Fritz Zimmermann for assistance in using the evidence of these texts.

102,10. Translating Bruns' conjectural supplement <*ou gar phtheiro*>*menês tês psukhês* at the end of the lacuna.

102,27. Add <*psukhê*> as suggested by Bruns.

104,8. Add *merê*, conjectured by Rovida. Bruns suggested adding *organa* after *dunamesin*, but Rovida's suggestion seems preferable both stylistically and palaeographically.

107,8 Read *ouden* for *oude* with MN and the first corrector of B.

109,21 Retain the MSS *eisin*: Bruns corrects to *estin* because of the neuter plural subject, but cf. Bruns 1887, 211; 1892, 261, s.v. 'Neutrum'. That *nous* here is singular makes the plural verb more difficult but not impossible, especially as *nous* is a collection of thoughts.

110,13 Add *onta auta* after *energeian* with Accattino 2001, 22.

113,7 Read *anô phoran* for *anaphoran* with Accattino 2001, 25 and 59. He notes that with *anaphoran* the genitive *tôn theiôn* is anomalous, the expected Greek being rather *tên pros ta theia anaphoran* or (as in 113,15 below) *tên epi ta theia anaphoran*. The difference between a relation to the heavenly bodies and action with the heavenly bodies is hardly clear, though it may indicate the absence or presence of a causal role for the heavens; however, against Moraux' proposal (1942, 154) to delete *pros tên tôn theiôn anaphoran* 'in respect of the relation to the heavenly bodies', as a gloss intended to explain 'on its own' (a proposal which he withdrew in his 1984, 420 n.71) is the fact that it would make Alexander at 113,15-16 below attribute to his opponents without qualification a view which would then only be present in option [2] here and not in option [1].

114,5. Retain *ekeinê*, the reading of the later MSS, against Bruns' emendation *ekeinou*. *ekeinei* in the primary MS V is corrupt but is closer in medieval pronunciation to *ekeinê* than to *ekeinou*, and the former gives an intelligible, if more roughly expressed, sense.

114,17. Retain *tôn sômatôn*, deleted by Bruns.

115,12. Read *hôs hê hulê sôma aneideon*, suggested by Accattino and Donini (1996) 135.

115,23. Read *hêmeteron* <*sôma*>, conjectured by Bruns, and delete *hê*.

115,26-27. Read *oute gar hai kata aisthêsin ... ou*<*te hai*> *topikai*. With *oude gar hai kata aisthêsin ... ou topikai* of the MSS the sense would be 'For neither are the [movements] in sensation or imagination or being affected, which are in respect of alteration, spatial movements of the soul in itself, but [rather] of the combination [of soul and body]'; but the double negative *oude ... ou* is awkward, and whether the psychological movements are spatial or not is left, as Pamela Huby points out to me, as an unwanted ambiguity which is in any case irrelevant to the point of the passage. I owe the emendation, and the interpretation of this passage to Inna Kupreeva.

116,5. Read <en> *tôi sômati* with the first corrector of B.

116,7. Read *sunephtharmenôn kai sunêlloiômenôn* (genitive), as conjectured by Bruns.

116,8. Omit *ti* after *ouketi*. It is not (as Bruns claims) present in V or in any other MS; and in the parallels cited by Bruns *tis follows men*.

117,31. Delete *empnoi, têi de psukhêi*, as suggested by Bruns; the transmitted text would give the sense 'that we respire in virtue of that by which we respire, and that we are ensouled in virtue of the soul', but this does not give an argument for identifying soul with breath. The required sense would be given by 'that we have soul in virtue of that by which we respire, and that we respire in virtue of breath' (*hôi anapneomen toutôi esmen empsukhoi, tôi de pneumati empnoi*).

119,16. Read *prakta*, which is in fact the reading of V and the other MSS, for Bruns' *praktika*.

119,23. Omit Bruns' *tôi*. It is not in fact present in any MS.

120,1. Either read *to*, the apparent reading of MS B after correction and conjectured by Rovida, for *tou*, or omit *tou* altogether. Ellis 1994, 76 n.16 retains *tou* and understands *tou en hôi* as a further quotation of Aristotle, *Cat.* 1a25: 'nothing... is said to be a this-something and 'that in which' without form', explaining the genitive *tou*, which does not fit the grammatical context in Alexander himself, as part of the quotation. Usener's emendation of *eidous* to *eidos* would give, as Bruns in his apparatus indicates, 'and nothing, with reference to being a this-something in actuality, is a form apart from that in which it is said to be'; but the sequel at 120,2ff. shows that what is wanted is a denial that the subject can exist independently, not that the predicate can. One would however expect *ouden de pros to einai* in 119,35-120,1 to go together in the sense of 'it is completely irrelevant to...'; a marginal comment may have been incorporated into the text, perhaps complaining about the irrelevance to the argument of the latter part of 119,34 (above, 65 n.197. I am grateful to Richard Sorabji for this suggestion).

120,7. Read *hôi* for *hôs* (so, conjecturally, Rovida, and Bruns in his apparatus)

120,31 Read *puri* with Bruns for *nun*, 'in that in which it has its being now'. The latter is the original reading of V, but the contemporary corrector wrote *p...r* above the line; this was a case in which the archetype was hard to read. Cf. Bruns 1887, viii.

121,4-5. Punctuate, following MSS V (where the full stop is not very obvious, but there is a marginal paragraphos) and B, with a comma after *hupokeimenôi* in 4 and a full stop after *psukhên* in 5; *ê* 'or rather', introducing a solution, normally begins a sentence, and cf. *men* ...

de in 4.

121,16. Read *phusikôn ousiai* for *phusikôn ousiôn*. The MSS text cannot stand, because *pantôn* is masculine, *ousiôn* feminine. If we read rather *phusikôn <genesis ex> ousiôn* (so, conjecturally, Bruns in his apparatus) the sense would be 'all natural things which are substances in a proper sense <come to be from> substances'. This would in context tend to suggest that natural substances are formed of material parts which are themselves substances composed of matter and form. But, as the sequel shows, the substances which make up natural substances are here not their material parts, but their own form and matter.

123,20. Do not add *<ei>* with Bruns.

124,19. Read *<diêk>onta*, suggested by Bruns in his apparatus.

124,25. Read *hoi* with the MSS for Bruns' *hai* (a misprint?).

126,3-5. Transpose this paragraph to follow 126,5-10, as suggested by Bruns. In its transmitted position it obscures the reference back of 'such things' in 126,5, which must be to the pure bodies of 126,1-3.

126,18. Omit *de* and remove the full stop after *phusin*; cf. Bruns' discussion in his apparatus.

129,28. Read *opsontai*, conjectured by Bruns. The MSS *ophthêsontai*, 'how will several people be seen?', could suggest, wrongly, that for *one* person alone to see several people through the same window involves several rays passing through the same pores.

131,23. Read *pôs, dêlon hôs*, suggested by Bruns, for *hopôs dêloun*.

131,33. Read *kekhalasthai tôi mê dunasthai*, suggested by Inna Kupreeva, for *tôi kekhalasthai mê dunasthai* (*tôi <mê> kekhalasthai mê dunasthai* Bruns, rejected by von Arnim, *SVF* 2.868).

132,5. Read *ton* for *ta* as suggested by Bruns in his apparatus.

133,31. Read *khroan* with all the MSS for Bruns' *khroas* 'colours'.

135,26. Read *katoptrôn <ê> hudatôn <tôn> emphainomenôn* with Avotins 1980, 438 n.38: *katoptrôn <ê> hudatôn emphainomena* conjectured by Bruns.

137,16. Read *epi* for *hupo*, following Bruns' conjecture.

137,24. Read *ê <to> apo*, conjectured by Bruns.

138,33. Read *<tôi> autôi*, conjectured by Bruns.

139,35. Omit *hautou* after *dexamenon* with V³ and the later MSS. V originally had (*h*)*autou* with no breathing. If *hautou* is interpreted as 'a body other than itself' it adds little to the sense; if it goes with the following *meston*, 'full of itself', as comparison with Alex., *DA* 20,10 (noted by Inna Kupreeva) would suggest, the word order is tortuous. And (*h*)*autou* could easily have arisen from *hautou sôma* in the previous line, as Inna Kupreeva points out to me.

140,36. Punctuate after *mallon*, with the MSS, rather than before it with

Bruns.

145,19. Read *pros ta horômena*, conjectured by Bruns in his apparatus and confirmed by the Arabic (Gätje 1966, 273).

146,3. Read *<mê> horata*, conjectured by Bruns in his apparatus and confirmed by the Arabic (Gätje, loc. cit.).

146,6. Read *kinoumenê*, conjectured by Bruns in his apparatus and confirmed by the Arabic (Gätje, loc. cit.).

146,12. Read *akhluôdestera* for *alloiôdestera*, conjectured by Bruns and confirmed by the Arabic, though it does not itself use the comparative (Gätje, loc. cit.).

147,7. Delete *êi*. It may represent *ê*, originally inserted through a mistaken contrast with *mê ... diastasin,* and then changed to *êi* because of *hotan.* Bruns conjectured *êremoun* or *kai menon* in place of *êi,* comparing 147,10.

147,13. Read *antiparallattein,* conjectured by Usener, for *hautê parallattein* ("[the sight] seems to pass [these] most quickly") of the MSS. and the Arabic version (Gätje 1966, 273); Bruns conjectured *tauta parallattein,* "these seem to pass each other most quickly".

147,20. Read *temnousin allelous <hoi kônoi hoi apo> tôn ta diagônia ...,* suggested by Bruns. As an alternative Bruns suggests *temnei* for *temnousin,* with the colours as subject. The plural verb could be retained with the neuter plural subject (see above on 109,21); but the genitive absolute with *autôn* is awkward. The Arabic suggests 'the rays from the people seeing intersect each other' (*temnousin allela<s hai aktines hai> apo tôn ta diagônia horôntôn,* Gätje 1966, 273); but a reference to rays from the people seeing seems out of place after the rejection of such a theory in §9 and here at 146,20-1.

148,7. Accept Bruns' conjectural supplement *phainomena gar kai ta alla sômata para ta diopta.* See 144 n.485 above.

148,23. Punctuate before *malista* with the MSS, not after with Bruns.

149,29. Read *dêloi* with the MSS rather than *dêlon* with Bruns. Bruns based his emendation on the parallel passage in Alex., *In sens.* 46,20 Wendland 1901: but whereas Thurot 1875, whose edition Bruns was using, has *dêlon,* basing this on the medieval Latin version of the commentary, the Greek MSS of *In sens.,* followed by Wendland, read *dêloi.*

150,32. Read *oikeiôsthai,* which, rather than *ôikeiôsthai,* is, contrary to Bruns' claim, the reading of the primary MS V. Similarly at 151,5 below. This section is therefore consistent in using the spelling in *oi-* for the perfect tense: similarly at 151,21, 152,8, 152,26, 153,3, 153,5. Similarly throughout §20 below the unaugmented form of the perfect is used: *oikeiôtai* at 162,16.18.23.25, *oikeiômetha* at 162,27.32 and *oikeiôsthai* at 162,29. Cf. Bruns 1887, 212.

151.4-5. Begin the parenthesis at *kai gar*, not at *philoumen* with Bruns.

151,12. Read *diaphônei* with the text of Aristotle, rather than *diaphanei*, 'By these arguments the facts will be clear', with V and Bruns.

151,18. Read *hoi* without an accent, as in V. Bruns in his apparatus suggests adding the accent, and for the relative introducing a participial phrase compares 168,24 where he has it in his text; but in fact there all the MSS have the article without an accent. In the present passage Bruns was anticipated by MS B: nevertheless, the change seems unnecessary.

152,8. Read, with Rovida, *noêtikon* for *noêton* of V and Bruns, as the sense surely requires.

152,13. Read *tês* for *têi* (Bruns conjectures *tên*).

152,26. Read *tôi*, suggested by Todd, for *tou* (*to* conjectured by Bruns in his apparatus).

153,1. Read *energeian* for *en sunekheiâi*, following Bruns' suggestion in his apparatus but omitting his *kata phusin* before *energeian*. I am grateful to Bob Todd for the suggestion that *en sunekheiâi* originated in a hard-to-read *energeian*.

153,12-13. Insert *<oregomenos energeias>* after *oikeias* at the end of 153,12, and remove Bruns' square brackets. (This is a development of a suggestion by Inna Kupreeva, modified by Bob Todd.)

154,14-15. Read *têi kat' ekeino lumainesthai <tên> tês*, suggested by Bruns in his apparatus.

154,25. The parenthesis should start with *hama gar* in 154,25, not in 154,24 with Bruns.

155,27. Omit *eisin*, absent from V and added by A and B[2]: and after *aretai* insert *<ouketi de khôristheisai>*, conjectured by Bruns.

157,14. Bruns adds *noêmatôn*, 'any of our own thoughts', but this seems unnecessary and makes the reference too specific.

157,36. Accept Bruns' conjecture *polla <ha>*.

158,38. Read *hoti d' estin* with an accent on the first syllable of *esti*, with V against the later MSS and Bruns.

159,18. Read, with Bruns' conjectural supplement, *bios hairetos, <ho de bios hairetos> ouk aboulêtos*.

160,17. Read *êsan <an>*, conjectured by Bruns.

160,33. Delete comma after *aulous*, as suggested by Richard Janko.

161,2. Read *prohêgoumenois* for the MSS *prohêgoumenais* with Giusta 1961-2, 254 and Huby 1983, 126.

161,36. Read *oude* for *ouden de* of the MSS with von Arnim (*SVF* 3.63).

162,32. V has the question-mark after *teleion* which Bruns omits.

163,28. Close parenthesis after *telos*, not in 163,30 with Bruns; I owe this suggestion to Richard Janko.

164,14. read *tauta* for *ta*, as suggested by Richard Janko.

165,14. Delete *to aulein* as a gloss, as suggested by Richard Janko.

165,18: Read *eu <zên>*, suggested by Richard Janko.

166,23. Von Arnim (*SVF* 3.57) proposes *<hê> tês psukhês aretê eudaimonia* ('it is the excellence of the soul that will be happiness'). Bruns' *<têi> tês psukhês aretêi eudaimonia*, followed in the translation above, involves more emendation (V has the nominative *aretê*). Since however our author goes on to say that the excellence of the soul is not sufficient for living well, it seems awkward to identify the excellence of the soul with happiness; for that would then imply that happiness is not sufficient for living well.

166,37. Insert a comma after *poiein* with MS B; also independently suggested to me by Inna Kupreeva.

166,39. Close parenthesis after *poiein*, not in 167,1 with Bruns.

167,12 Adding *hê* before *peri*; it has been added above the line in MS B, and was independently suggested to me by Kupreeva.

167,13. Read *oikeia <kai> proêgmena* with von Arnim (*SVF* 3.145).

167,22. Insert a full stop after *auton*, as Richard Janko points out to me.

168,1. Accept Bruns' conjecture *peri ekeinou <logos>*.

168,11. Read *tina* for Bruns' *tên*. The reading of the primary MS V here is unclear, but the surviving traces suggest *tina*, in the contemptuous sense of 'some', rather than *tên*, though it must be admitted that V does not have the second accent on *eulogon* that *tina* would require.

168,24 Read *hai* (no accent) with V, rather than *hai* (grave accent) with Bruns; cf. 151,18 above.

169,18 Read *he <kata to> dipoun diaphora*, conjectured by Bruns.

169,35 End the parenthesis with *aphueis* (so Gercke 1885, 111), not with *ginetai* (37) as Bruns.

170,2. Retain *hopoion – axioumen*. Bruns brackets this clause as an interpolation. But it has some point, as showing that the difficulty is one raised in the context of Alexander's own doctrine. See 202 n.674.

170,3. Read *<ho> kai*, conjectured by Bruns and approved by Donini 1974, 167 n.70.

170,13 Read *en tois ousin (<esti de, epei en tois ousin> esti ... ti on)*, suggested by Bruns in his apparatus.

170.13. Read *<ei tini> sumbebêken, esti legomenon* (*ei* coni. Bruns: *tini* added by the contemporary corrector of V in the margin).

171,13. Read *aition. <to> ara*, conjectured by Bruns: so already Caninius 1555.

171,21. Punctuate before *tauta*, with the MSS, rather than after it with Bruns. For the double accusative cf. LSJ, s.v. *aphairein* II.1.

171,34. Read *ouk epi* for *ouketi*, as suggested by Caninius 1555.

172,4-5. Read *oute en hois to*, conjectured by Bruns, for *oude to en tois* of the MSS.

172,9. Read *hai <d>e <gignontai> anaitiôs kai*, with Bruns, for *hai **e anaitioi has* of V.

172,9. Read *de* with Bruns and MSS FLPQR for *dei* of Va (marked as an error in V; *d'ei* B, *dê* AC)

172,25. Read *monos*, the true reading of VAB, for *monon* CFLPa Bruns.

172,30. Read *erkhetai <epi touto>*, conjectured by Bruns

173,5. Omit the first *genesthai*: it is added to V by a hand apparently different both from the contemporary corrector and from Bessarion's, and is otherwise present only in one Greek MS, A, and in the Arabic version which however omits *kai mê genesthai*. Cf. Alex., *Fat.* 166,12-13, 169,7.14, 190,25, 205,19, 212,15.

173,20. Read *autôi, toutesti* for *toutestin autôi* of the MSS with Sharples 1983.

173,21. Read *hautôi* with the Arabic version for *autôi* of the Greek MSS.

174,22. Delete *kai* with Sharples 1983 (also omitted by MSS QR).

174,27. Read *eti* with the Arabic version for *hoti* of the Greek MSS. Hans-Joachim Ruland informs me that the literal translation of the Arabic would be *oud' eti* (or *kai*) *ei*; he compares its rendering at 174,35.

175,21. Read *mête ta kala <mête ta aiskhra>*, suggested by the Arabic version.

175,22. Read *[ouk] agnoeitai hê te hodos* for *ouk agnoeitai hê ge* (*te* MS B) *hodos* with Sharples 1983.

175,28. Read *adiastrophois* for V's *astrophois* with Rovida and with Sharples 1983.

176,18. Read *enhuparkhonta; ou gar auto to*, conjectured by Bruns, for *enhuparkhon; to gar auto touto* of the MSS.

177,8. Read *auto touto* with MS H and Bruns. All the other MSS, including both V and A, the copy of V from which H in turn derives, have *auto toutou*: 'that thing itself to which this attached was a cause of this in the primary sense'. This however gives the wrong sense. The reading of H appears to be a conjectural emendation.

178,14. Delete *têi* with Bruns in his apparatus.

182,20. Read *autên*, with V, the majority of later MSS and the medieval Latin version, for Bruns' *autês*, which is taken from, and occurs only in, the later MS C.

183,29-30. Retain *gegonotos kenôs*, deleted on grounds of redundancy by Orelli following Bloch and by Bruns. The words are in all the MSS and are reflected in the medieval Latin translation; prolixity and literary affectation are not alien to the style of this section of *Mant.*, and the variation in tense means that the phrase is not altogether redundant.

184,3. Read *sumboulôn* (accented on the last syllable) with Bruns 1893, 15 n.2 (cf. Alex., *Fat.* 31 202,7) for *sumboulon* (accented on the middle syllable, meaning 'advisers') of the MSS.

184,5. Read *didaskaliai*, conjectured by Bruns (and anticipated, but with the nominative singular, in Caninius 1555) for *didaskaliais* of the MSS.

184,25. Read *tout<esti>*, conjectured by Caspar Orelli in Orelli 1824 and by Bruns in his apparatus, for *tout'* of the MSS.

184,33-185,1. Read *parabathênai*, as the sense requires, with the later MSS, rather than *parabasthênai* with V and Bruns.

185,13. Read *zôiôi, anthrôpôi*, conjectured by Bruns and accepted by Donini 1974, 163 n.65, for *zôiôn, anthrôpôn* of the MSS.

185,15. Read *kata tautên* with Donini 1974, 163 n.65 for *kata tauta* of MS H, the medieval Latin version and Bruns (V has *kata tauta* with no accent on *tauta*, and BFa and Caninius interpret it as *kata ta auta* 'in the same way'.)

185,18. Omit Bruns' comma after *phthorais*, with V and the majority of the MSS. Cf. Alex., *Fat.* 6 170,13.

185,20. Do not punctuate after *iatrôn*.

185,26. Read *tôi ... hapsimakhôi kai philokindunôi* with Bloch cited by Orelli 1824, rather than the genitive plurals of all the MSS, Orelli and Bruns, because this allows retention of the reading of the majority of MSS in 185,28 below. Orelli argues (329-30) that a change from the plural to singular between line 26 and line 28 is not unlikely: but while the writings attributed to Alexander are often careless in their use of pronouns (cf. Sharples 1994a, 112 n.35), the corruption in 185,26 would be easy. The corresponding passage in Alex., *Fat.* (6 170,21-22) has the singular throughout.

185,28. Read *autou* with the majority of the Greek MSS and the medieval Latin version, against H's *autôn*, adopted by Bruns. See the previous note.

186,8. Before *tous* add *tou*, inserted by a later hand in B and conjectured by Bruns.

186,22. Punctuate with a question-mark after *phusin*.

186,24. Read *tôi mê*, inserted as a correction in B and suggested by the marginal note *vel "ei quod non fatatum"* in MS O of the medieval Latin version, for *mê tôi* of the Greek MSS.

Abbreviations and Bibliography

DK   H. Diels, ed. W. Kranz, *Die Fragmente der Vorsokratiker*, 10th ed., Berlin 1952.

FHS&G   W.W. Fortenbaugh, P.M. Huby, R.W. Sharples and D. Gutas, *Theophrastus of Eresus: Sources for his Life, Writings, Thought and Influence*, Leiden 1992.

KRS   G.S. Kirk, J.E. Raven and M. Schofield, *The Presocratic Philosophers*, Cambridge 1983.

LS   A.A. Long and D.N. Sedley, *The Hellenistic Philosophers*, Cambridge 1987.

LSJ   H.G. Liddell and R. Scott, rev. by H.S. Jones and R. McKenzie, *A Greek-English Lexicon*, 9th ed., Oxford 1940.

RE   A.F. von Pauly and G. Wissowa, *Real-Encyclopädie der classischen Altertumswissenschaft*, Stuttgart 1894-1978.

SVF   H. von Arnim, *Stoicorum Veterum Fragmenta*, Leipzig, 1903-1924.

P. Accattino, 'Ematopoiesi, malattia cardiaca e disturbi mentali in Galeno e in Alessandro di Afrodisia', *Hermes* 115 (1987) 454-73.

—'Alessandro di Afrodisia e la transmissione della forma nella riproduzione animale', *Atti dell' Accademia delle Scienze di Torino* 122 (1988) 79-94.

—'Alessandro di Afrodisia e gli astri: l'anima e la luce', *Atti dell'Accademia delle Scienze di Torino* 126 (1992) 39-62.

—'Generazione dell'anima in Alessandro di Afrodisia, *de anima* 2.10-11.13?', *Phronesis* 40 (1995) 192-201.

—*Alessandro di Afrodisia: De Intellectu*, Turin 2001.

—and P.L. Donini, *Alessandro di Afrodisia: L'anima*, Rome and Bari 1996.

J.L. Ackrill, 'Aristotle's Definitions of *psuche*', *Proc. Arist. Soc.* 73 (1972-3) 110-33.

—'Aristotle on Eudaimonia', *Proc. Brit. Acad.* 60 (1974) 339-59 = A.O. Rorty, ed., *Essays on Aristotle's Ethics*, Berkeley 1980, ch.2.

F. Alesse, *Panezio di Rodi e la tradizione stoica*, Naples 1994.

K. Algra, *Concepts of Space in Greek Thought*, Leiden 1995.

J.E. Annas, *Hellenistic Philosophy of Mind*, Berkeley 1992.

—*The Morality of Happiness*, New York 1993.

G.E.M. Anscombe and P.T. Geach, *Three Philosophers: Aristotle, Aquinas, Frege*, Oxford: Blackwell, 1961.

H. von Arnim, *Hierokles: Ethische Elementarlehre*, Berlin 1906 [Berliner

Klassikertexte, 4].

E. Asmis, *Epicurus' Scientific Method*, Ithaca 1984.

—'Epicurean Epistemology', in K. Algra, J. Barnes, J. Mansfeld and M. Schofield, eds., *Cambridge History of Hellenistic Philosophy*, Cambridge 1999, 260-94.

I. Avotins, 'Alexander of Aphrodisias on Vision in the Atomists', *Classical Quarterly* 30 (1980) 429-54.

A. Badawī, *Arisṭūṭālīs, aṭ-Ṭabīa*, Cairo 1964-5.

—*Commentaires sur Aristote perdus en grec et autres épitres*, Beirut 1971.

—*Histoire de la philosophie en Islam*, Paris 1972 (Études de philosophie médiévale, 60).

R.W. Baldes, 'Democritus on Visual Perception: Two Theories or One?', *Phronesis* 20 (1975) 93-105.

H. Baltussen, 'Theophrastean echoes? The *De sensibus* in the Platonic and Aristotelian tradition', in W.W. Fortenbaugh and G. Wöhrle, eds., *On the Opuscula of Theophrastus*, Stuttgart 2002 (Philosophie der Antike, 14) 39-58.

B.C. Bazán, 'L'authenticité du "de intellectu" attribué à Alexandre d'Aphrodise', *Revue philosophique de Louvain* 71 (1973) 468-87.

L.C. Becker, *A New Stoicism*, Princeton 1998.

S. Berryman, 'Euclid and the Sceptic: A Paper on Vision, Doubt, Geometry, Light and Drunkenness', *Phronesis* 43 (1998) 176-96.

H.J. Blumenthal, *Aristotle and Neoplatonism in Late Antiquity*, London 1996.

—and H. Robinson, eds., *Aristotle and the later tradition*, Oxford 1991 (*Oxford Studies in Ancient Philosophy*, supplementary volume).

S. Bobzien, 1998a. *Determinism and Freedom in Stoic Philosophy*, Oxford 1998.

—1998b. 'The inadvertent conception and late birth of the free-will problem', *Phronesis* 43 (1998) 133-75.

W. Bondeson, 'Aristotle on responsibility for one's character and the possibility of character change', *Phronesis* 19 (1974) 59-65.

D. Bostock, *Aristotle: Metaphysics Books Z and H*, Oxford 1994.

H. Bonitz, *Alexandri Aphrodisiensis commentarius in libros Metaphysicos Aristotelis*, Berlin 1847.

—*Index Aristotelicus*, Berlin 1870.

I. Bruns, 'Un chapitre d'Alexandre d'Aphrodise sur l'âme', in *Mélanges Graux*, Paris 1884, 567-72.

—*Supplementum Aristotelicum* 2.1, Berlin 1887.

—*Supplementum Aristotelicum* 2.2, Berlin 1892.

—*Interpretationes variae*, Kiel 1893.

F. Buecheler, 'Prospographica', *Rheinisches Museum* 63 (1908) 190.

W. Burkert, 'Air-imprints or *Eidola*: Democritus' aetiology of vision',

Illinois Classical Studies 2 (1977) 97-109.

M.F. Burnyeat, '*De Anima* II.5', *Phronesis* 47 (2002) 28-90.

R.G. Bury, ed., *Sextus Empiricus, The Outlines of Pyrrhonism*, London and New York 1933.

A. Caninius Anglarensis, *Alexandri Aphrodisiensis ... de anima liber secundus*, Venice 1555.

B. Carrière et al., *Le Peri Nou attribué à Alexandre d'Aphrodise, introduction, traduction et notes*, Diss. Montreal, 1961. [I have not myself seen this publication.]

V. Caston, 'Epiphenomenalisms: Ancient and Modern', *Philosophical Review* 106 (1997) 309-363.

J. Christensen de Groot, 'Philoponus on De Anima 2.5, Physics 3.3, and the Propagation of Light', *Phronesis* 28 (1983) 177-196.

K. Císař, 'Epicurean Epistemology in Lucretius' *De rerum natura* IV 1-822', *Listy filologické* 124 (2001) 1-54.

S. Marc Cohen, 'Hylomorphism and Functionalism', in Nussbaum and Rorty 1992, 57-73.

K. Corrigan, *Plotinus' theory of matter-evil and the question of substance: Plato, Aristotle, and Alexander of Aphrodisias*, Leuven 1996.

A.C. Crombie, *Styles of Scientific Thinking in the European Tradition*, London 1994.

P. De Lacy, *Galen on the Doctrines of Hippocrates and Plato* [Corpus Medicorum Graecorum 5.4.1.2], Berlin, part 1 (books 1-5) 1978, part 2 (books 6-10) 1980, part 3 (Commentary and Indices) 1984.

D.J. Depew, 'Humans and other political animals in Aristotle's History of Animals', *Phronesis* 40 (1995) 156-181.

H. Diels, *Doxographi Graeci*, Berlin 1879.

A. Dietrich, 'Die arabische Version einer unbekannten Schrift des Alexander von Aphrodisias über die Differentia specifica', *Nachr. Göttingen*, 1964, phil.-hist. Kl., 85-148.

J. Dillon, *Alcinous, The Handbook of Platonism*, Oxford 1993.

K. Döring, *Die Megariker, Kommentierte Sammlung der Testimonien*, Amsterdam 1972.

P.L. Donini, 'L'anima e gli elementi nel De Anima di Alessandro di Afrodisia', *Atti dell' Accademia delle Scienze di Torino*, classe di scienze morali, storiche e filologiche, 105 (1971) 61-107.

—*Tre studi sull'aristotelismo nel secondo secolo d.C*, Turin 1974.

—'Stoici e Megarici nel de fato di Alessandro di Afrodisia', in G. Giannantoni, ed., *Scuole socratiche minori e filosofia ellenistica*, Bologna 1977.

— 'Il "De fato" di Alessandro di Afrodisia: questioni di coerenza', *Aufstieg und Niedergang der römischen Welt* II.36.2 (1987) 1244-59.

—1989a. *Ethos: Aristotele e il determinismo*, Alessandria 1989.

—1989b. 'Volontarietà di vizio e virtù (Aristotele *Ethica Nicomachea* III.1-7)', in E. Berti e L.M. Napolitano Valditara, eds., *Etica, Politica, Retorica: Studi su Aristotele e la sua presenza nell' età moderna*, L'Aquila 1989, 3-21.

—'Alessandro di Afrodisia e i metodi dell' esegesi filosofica', in C. Moreschini, ed., *Esegesi, parafrasi e compilazione in età tardoantica: Atti del Terzo Congresso dell' Associazione di studi tardoantichi*, a cura di. Naples, 1995, 107-29.

—and B. Inwood, 'Stoic Ethics', in K. Algra, J. Barnes, J. Mansfeld and M. Schofield, eds., *Cambridge History of Hellenistic Philosophy*, Cambridge 1999, 675-738.

H.J. Drossaart Lulofs, *Nicolaus Damascenus On the Philosophy of Aristotle*, Leiden 1965.

J.J. Duhot, *La conception stoïcienne de la causalité*, Paris 1989.

L. Edelstein and I.G. Kidd, eds., *Posidonius, Vol.2 Commentary, ii. Fragments 150-293*, Cambridge 1989.

J. Ellis, 'The Trouble with Fragrance', *Phronesis* 35 (1990) 290-302.

—'Alexander's Defense of Aristotle's Categories', *Phronesis* 39 (1994) 69-89.

G. Endress, 'Alexander Arabus on the First Cause', in C. D'Ancona and G. Serra, eds., *Aristotele e Alessandro di Afrodisia nella tradizione Araba*, Padova: Il Poligrafo, 2002, 19-74.

J. van Ess, 'Über einige neue Fragmente des Alexander von Aphrodisias und des Proklos in arabischer Übersetzung', *Der Islam* 42 (1966) 148-68.

S. Everson, *Aristotle on Perception*, Oxford 1997.

A. Falcon, *Corpi e movimenti: Il De caelo di Aristotele e la sua fortuna nel mondo antico*, Naples 2001.

S. Fazzo, 'Alessandro di Afrodisia e Tolomeo: Aristotelismo e astrologia fra il II e il III secolo d.C.', *Rivista di storia di filosofia* 4 (1988) 627-649

—'Philology and philosophy in the margins of early printed editions of the ancient Greek commentators on Aristotle, with special reference to copies held in the Biblioteca Nazionale Braidense, Milan', in C. Blackwell and S. Kusukawa, eds., *Philosophy in the sixteenth and seventeenth centuries: conversations with Aristotle*, Aldershot 1999, 48-75.

—*Aporia e sistema: La materia, la forma, il divino nelle Quaestiones di Alessandro di Afrodisia*, Pisa 2002 (Pubbl. della facoltà di lettere e filosofia dell'Università di Pavia, 97).

—(2002b) 'Alessandro di Afrodisia sulle "contrarietà tangibili" (*De Gen. Corr.* 2.2): fonti greche et arabe a confronto', in C. D'Ancona and G. Serra, eds., *Aristotele e Alessandro di Afrodisia nella tradizione Araba*, Padova: Il Poligrafo, 2002, 151-89.

—and M. Zonta, *Alessandro di Afrodisia: La Provvidenza, Questioni sulla Provvidenza*, Milan 1998.

J. Finnegan, 'Texte arabe du *Peri Nou* d'Alexandre d'Aphrodise', *Mélanges de l'Université Saint Joseph* (Beirut) 33 (1956) 157-202.

W.W. Fortenbaugh, 'Theophrastus on Fate and Character', in G.W. Bowersock et al., eds., *Arktouros: Hellenic Studies presented to Bernard W.M. Knox*, Berlin 1979, 372-5.

—, ed., *On Stoic and Peripatetic Ethics: the work of Arius Didymus* (Rutgers University Studies in Classical Humanities 1, 1983).

—*Quellen zur Ethik Theophrasts*, Amsterdam 1984.

—'Theophrastus on Emotion', in Fortenbaugh, Huby and Long 1985, 209-29.

—, P.M. Huby and A.A. Long, eds., *Theophrastus of Eresus: On his Life and Work*, New Brunswick 1985 (Rutgers University Studies in Classical Humanities, 2).

A.P. Fotinis, *The De Anima of Alexander of Aphrodisias*, Washington, D.C. 1980.

D. Frede, 'The dramatisation of determinism: Alexander of Aphrodisias' *De fato*', *Phronesis* 27 (1982) 276-98.

—'Could Paris (son of Priam) have chosen otherwise? , *Oxford Studies in Ancient Philosophy* 2 (1984) 279-92.

J. Freudenthal, 'Die durch Averroes erhaltenen Fragmente Alexanders zur Metaphysik des Aristoteles untersucht und übersetzt', *Abh. Berlin* 1884, phil.-hist. Kl., no.1.

H. Gätje, 'Zur arabischen Uberlieferung des Alexander von Aphrodisias', *Zeitschrift der deutschen morgenländischen Gesellschaft* 116 (1966) 255-78.

—*Studien zur Überlieferung der aristotelischen Psychologie im Islam*, Heidelberg 1971 (Annales Universitatis Saraviensis, Reihe: Philos. Fakultät, no.11).

E. Gannagé, 'Matière et éléments dans le commentaire d'Alexandre d'Aphrodise *In De Generatione et Corruptione*', in C. D'Ancona and G. Serra, eds., *Aristotele e Alessandro di Afrodisia nella tradizione Araba*, Padova: Il Poligrafo, 2002, 133-49.

T. Ganson, 'Inference from Appearances in Alexander of Aphrodisias' Theory of Vision', forthcoming.

S.M. Gardiner, 'Aristotle's Basic and Non-Basic Virtues', *Oxford Studies in Ancient Philosophy* 20 (2001) 261-95.

C. Genequand, 'Quelques aspects de l'idée de la nature, d'Aristote à al-Ghazālī, *Revue de Théologie et de Philosophie* 116 (1984) 105-29.

—*Alexander of Aphrodisias On the Cosmos*, Leiden 2001.

M. Geoffroy, 'La tradition arabe du *Peri nou* d'Alexandre d'Aphrodise et les origines de la théorie farabienne des quatre degrés de l'intellect', in C. D'Ancona and G. Serra, eds., *Aristotele e Alessandro di Afrodisia nella tradizione Araba*, Padova: Il Poligrafo, 2002, 191-231.

A. Gercke, 'Chrysippea', *Jahrb. f. Klass. Phil.* Supplbd. 14 (1885) 689-781.

E. Giannakis, 'Fragments from Alexander's Lost Commentary on Aristotle's Physics', *Zeitschrift für Geschichte der Arabisch-Islamischen Wissenchaften* 10 (1996) 157-87.

E. Gilson, 'Les sources gréco-arabes de l'augustinisme avicennisant', *Archives d'histoire doctrinale et littéraire du moyen-âge* 4 (1929) 5-150.

M. Giusta, 'Sul significato filosofico del termine *proēgoumenos*', *Atti dell'Accademia delle Scienze di Torino* 96 (1961-2) 229-71.

—*I dossografi di etica*, Turin 1964.

—*L'opusculo pseudogalenico hoti hai poiotêtes asômatoi*, *Memorie dell' Accademia delle Scienze di Torino*, cl. di scienze morali, etc., 4 ser. 34, 1976.

—'Due capitoli sui dossografi di fisica', in G. Cambiano, ed., *Storiografia e dossografia nella filosofia antica*, Turin 1986, 149-201.

T. Göransson, *Albinus, Alcinous, Arius Didymus*. Göteborg 1995. (Studia Graeca et Latina Gothoburgensia, 61).

H. Gottschalk, 'Aristotelian Philosophy in the Roman world', *Aufstieg und Niedergang der römischen Welt*, II.36.1 (Berlin 1987) 1079-1174.

—'Continuity and change in Aristotelianism', in R. Sorabji, ed., *Aristotle and After*, London 1997 (*Bulletin of the Institute of Classical Studies*, suppl. vol. 68) 109-15.

E. Gowers, revised B. Fraser, *The Complete Plain Words*, 2nd ed., Harmondsworth 1973.

A. Grilli, 'Contributo alla storia di *proēgoumenos*', in *Studi linguistici in onore di V. Pisani*, Brescia 1969, 409-500.

G. Guldentops, 'Themistius on Evil', *Phronesis* 46 (2001) 189-208.

F.A.J. de Haas, *John Philoponus' New Definition of Prime Matter*, Leiden 1997.

—'Mixture in Philoponus: an encounter with a third kind of potentiality', in J.M.M.J. Thijssen and H.A.G. Braakhuis, eds., *The Commentary Tradition on Aristotle's De Generatione et Corruptione*, Turnhout 1999, 21-46.

—'Did Plotinus and Porphyry disagree on Aristotle's *Categories*?', *Phronesis* 46 (2001) 492-526.

I. Hadot, 'La tradition manuscrite du commentaire de Simplicius sur le Manuel d'Épictète', *Revue d'Histoire des Textes* 8 (1978) 1-108.

R.J. Hankinson, *Cause and Explanation in Ancient Greek Thought*, Oxford 1998.

A. Hass, 'Antike Lichttheorien', *Archiv für Geschichte der Philosophie* 20 (1907) 345-86.

M. Hayduck, ed., *Alexandri Aphrodisiensis in Aristotelis Metaphysica commentaria*, Berlin 1891 (CAG 1).

R. Heinaman, 'Alteration and Aristotle's activity-change distinctions', *Oxford Studies in Ancient Philosophy* 16 (1998) 227-57.

P.M. Huby, 'Peripatetic definitions of happiness', in Fortenbaugh 1983, 121-34.

B. Inwood, *Ethics and Human Action in Early Stoicism*, Oxford 1985.

T.H. Irwin, 'Disunity in the Aristotelian virtues', with a comment by Richard Kraut and a reply by Irwin, in J. Annas and R.H. Grimm, eds., *Oxford Studies in Ancient Philosophy* suppl. vol. 1, 1988, 61-88.

—'Socratic paradox and Stoic theory' in S. Everson, ed., *Ethics*, Cambridge 1998 (Companions to Ancient Thought, 4), 151-92.

W. Jaeger, Aristotle: *Fundamentals of the History of his Development*, tr. R. Robinson, Oxford, 2nd ed. 1948 (First German edition: Berlin, 1923).

T.K. Johansen, *Aristotle on the Sense-Organs*, Cambridge 1998.

A. Jones, 'Peripatetic and Euclidean theories of the visual ray', *Physis* 31 (1994) 47-76.

L. Judson, 'Chance and "Always or for the most part" in Aristotle', in L. Judson, ed., *Aristotle's Physics: a collection of essays*, Oxford 1991, 73-99.

J.J. Keaney, 'The early text tradition of Theophrastus' *Historia plantarum*', *Hermes* 96 (1968) 293ff.

A. Kenny, *The Aristotelian Ethics*, Oxford: Clarendon Press, 1978.

I.G. Kidd, 'Stoic Intermediates and the End for Man', *Classical Quarterly* 5 (1955) 181-94 = Long 1971, 150-72. [References to the reprinted version].

—'Plutarch and his Stoic contradictions', in W. Burkert et al., eds., *Fragmentsammlungen philosophische Texte der Antike*, Göttingen 1998, 288-302.

G.S. Kirk, J.E. Raven and M. Schofield, *The Presocratic Philosophers*, 2nd ed., Cambridge 1983.

I.V. Kupreeva, *Alexander of Aphrodisias on Soul as Form* (de anima *1-26* Br.), diss. Toronto, 1999.

L. Labowsky, 'William of Moerbeke's manuscript of Alexander of Aphrodisias (Bessarion Studies III)', *Medieval and Renaissance Studies* 5 (1961) 155-62.

H. Lackenbacher, 'Zur Disposition und Quellenfrage von Lukrez 4.1-521', *Wiener Studien* 32 (1910) 213-38.

P. Lautner, '*legei* oder *lêgei?* Amelios und Sosikrates(?) bei *Timaios* 37a6-7 (bei Proklos, *In Tim.* II.300.23-301.5 Diehl)', *Hermes* 125 (1997) 294-308.

J.G. Lennox, 'Kinds, forms of kinds, and the more and less in Aristotle's biology', in A. Gotthelf and J.G. Lennox, eds., *Philosophical Issues in Aristotle's Biology*, Cambridge 1987, 339-59.

P. Lettinck, *Aristotle's Physics and its Reception in the Arabic World*, Leiden 1994.

F.A. Lewis, 'Aristotle on the relation between a thing and its matter', in T. Scaltsas, D. Charles and M.L. Gill, eds., *Unity, Identity and Explanation in Aristotle's Metaphysics*, Oxford: Clarendon Press, 1994, 247-77.

D.C. Lindberg, *Theories of Vision from Al-Kindi to Kepler*, Chicago 1976.

A.C. Lloyd, 'The principle that the cause is greater than its effect', *Phronesis* 21 (1976) 146-56.

—*Form and Universal in Aristotle*, Liverpool 1981 (ARCA, Classical and Medieval Texts, Papers and Monographs, 4).

A.A. Long, 'Carneades and the Stoic *telos*', *Phronesis* 12 (1967) 59-90.

—'Aristotle's Legacy to Stoic Ethics', *Bulletin of the Institute of Classical Studies* (London) 15 (1968) 72-6.

—ed., *Problems in Stoicism*, London 1971

J. Longrigg, 'Elementary Physics in the Lyceum and Stoa', *Isis* 66 (1975) 211-29.

C. Luna, *Trois Études sur la tradition des commentaires anciens à la Métaphysique d'Aristote*, Leiden 2001.

A. Madigan, 'Alexander on Species and Genera', in L.P. Schrenk, ed., *Aristotle in Late Antiquity*, Washington, DC 1994, 74-91.

I.N. Madvig, *Cicero: De finibus bonorum et malorum libri quinque*, 3rd ed., Copenhagen 1876.

J.M. Magee, 'Sense organs and the activity of sensation in Aristotle', *Phronesis* 45 (2000) 306-330.

G. Magnaldi, *L'oikeiosis peripatetica in Ario Didimo e nel De finibus di Cicerone*, Florence 1991.

A. Magris, *Alessandro di Afrodisia, Sul Destino*, Florence 1996.

J. Mansfeld, '*Diaphonia* in the argument of Alexander, *De fato* chs. 1-2', *Phronesis* 33 (1988) 181-207.

—'Doxography and Dialectic. The Sitz im Leben of the "Placita"', *Aufstieg und Niedergang der römischen Welt* II.36.4 (1990) 3056-3229.

C.C. Meinwald, 'Prometheus' Bounds: *Peras* and *Apeiron* in Plato's *Philebus*', in J. Gentzler, ed., *Method in Ancient Philosophy*, Oxford 1998, 165-80.

P. Merlan, 'Zwei Untersuchungen zu Alexander von Aphrodisias', *Philologus* 113 (1969) 85-91.

E. Mioni, 'Bessarione scriba e alcuni suoi collaboratori', in *Miscellanea Marciana di Studi Bessarionei*, Padua 1976, 263-318.

—*Bibliotecae Divi Marci Venetiarum Codices Graeci Manuscripti*, vol.1, Rome 1981.

C.V. Mirus, 'Homonymy and the matter of a living body', *Ancient Philosophy* 21 (2001) 357- 73.

A. Modrze, 'Zur Ethik und Psychologie des Poseidonios', *Philologus* 87 (1932) 300-31.

P. Moraux, *Alexandre d'Aphrodise: Exégète de la noétique d'Aristote*,

Liège and Paris 1942.

—'Aristoteles, der Lehrer Alexanders von Aphrodisias', *Archiv für Geschichte der Philosophie* 49 (1967) 169-82.

—*Der Aristotelismus bei den Griechen von Andronikos bis Alexander von Aphrodisias, Bd. I: Die Renaissance des Aristotelismus im 1. Jh. v. Chr.*, Berlin 1973.

—'Le *De Anima* dans la tradition grecque. Quelques aspects de l'interpretation du traité, de Theophraste à Themistius', in G.E.R. Lloyd and G.E.L. Owen, eds., *Aristotle on Mind and the Senses*, Cambridge 1978, 281-324.

—*Der Aristotelismus bei den Griechen von Andronikos bis Alexander von Aphrodisias, Bd. II: Der Aristotelismus im I. und II. Jh. n. Chr.*, Berlin 1984.

P. Moraux† (ed. J.Wiesner), *Der Aristotelismus bei den Griechen von Andronikos bis Alexander von Aphrodisias, Bd. III: Alexander von Aphrodisias*, Berlin 2001.

G. Movia, *Alessandro di Afrodisia tra naturalismo e misticismo*, Padua 1970.

C. Mugler, *Dictionnaire Historique de la Terminologie optique des grecs*, Paris 1964.

B. Nikolsky, 'Epicurus on Pleasure', *Phronesis* 46 (2001) 440-65.

J.F. Nourrisson, *De la liberté et du hasard: essai sur Alexandre d Aphrodise suivi du Traité du Destin*, etc., Paris 1870.

M.C. Nussbaum and A.O. Rorty, eds., *Essays on Aristotle's De Anima*, Oxford 1992.

D. Obbink, '"What all men believe must be true": common conceptions and *consensus omnium* in Hellenistic philosophy', *Oxford Studies in Ancient Philosophy* 10 (1992) 193-231.

J. Opsomer and R.W. Sharples, 'Alexander of Aphrodisias, *De intellectu* 110.4: 'I heard this from Aristotle'. A modest proposal', *Classical Quarterly* 50 (2000) 252-6.

—and C. Steel, 'Evil without a cause: Proclus' doctrine on the origins of evil, and its antecedents in Hellenistic philosophy', in T. Fuhrer and M. Erler, eds., *Zur Rezeption der hellenistischen Philosophie in der Spätantike*, Stuttgart 1999, 229-60.

J. Orelli, ed., *Alexandri Aphrodisiensis De fato quae supersunt*, Zurich 1824.

E. Orth, 'Les oeuvres d'Albinos le platonicien', *L'Antiquité Classique* 16 (1947) 113-14.

M. Ostwald, 'Was there a concept *agraphos nomos* in Classical Greece?', in E.N. Lee, A.P.D. Mourelatos and R.M. Rorty, eds., *Exegesis and Argument: Studies in Greek Philosophy presented to Gregory Vlastos*, Assen 1973 (Phronesis suppl. vol. 1), 70-104.

D. Papadis, *Die Seelenlehre der Alexander von Aphrodisias*, Bern 1991.

S. Pembroke, 'Oikeiosis', in Long 1971, 114-49.

R. Philippson, 'Das "Erste Naturgemäße"', *Philologus* 87 (1932) 447-66.

S. Pines, '*Omne quod movetur necesse est ab aliquo moveri*: a refutation of Galen by Alexander of Aphrodisias and the theory of motion', *Isis* 52 (1961) 21-54 = *Studies in Arabic versions of Greek texts and in medieval science* (*The collected works of S. Pines*, vol.2), Jerusalem and Leiden, 1986, 218-51.

M. Pohlenz, *Grundfragen der Stoischen Philosophie*, Abh.Göttingen, phil.-hist. Kl. 3.26, 1940.

—*La Stoa: storia di un movimento spirituale*, rev. V.E. Alfieri et al., Florence 1967.

A. Preus, '*On Dreams* 2 459b24-460a33 and Aristotle's *opsis*', *Phronesis* 13 (1968) 175-82.

—'Animal and human souls in the Peripatetic school', ΣΚΕΨΙΣ 1 (1990) 67-99.

M. Rashed, 'A "new" text of Alexander on the soul's motion', in R. Sorabji, ed., *Aristotle and After*, London 1997 (*Bulletin of the Institute of Classical Studies*, suppl vol. 68) 181-95.

A. Rescigno, 'Alessandro di Afrodisia in Arist. *De caelo* 279b17-280a27: qualche considerazione', in G. Abbamonte, A. Rescigno, A. and R. Rossi, eds., *Satura, collectanea philologica Italo Gallo ab amicis discipulisque dicata*, Naples 1999, 207-43.

O. Rieth, *Grundbegriffe der Stoischen Ethik*, Berlin 1933.

J.M. Rist, *Stoic Philosophy*, Cambridge 1969.

H. Robinson, 'Form and the immateriality of the intellect from Aristotle to Aquinas', in Blumenthal and Robinson 1991, 207-26.

V. Rose, *Aristoteles Pseudepigraphus*, Leipzig 1863.

T. G. Rosenmeyer, 'One strike will do: a Lucretian puzzle', *Scripta Classica Israelica* 18 (1999) 25-44.

W.D. Ross, *Aristotle: Parva naturalia*, Oxford 1955.

—*Aristotle: De Anima*, Oxford 1961.

Rovida: see p.238.

H.-J. Ruland, *Die arabischen Fassungen zweier Schriften des Alexander von Aphrodisias: Über die Vorsehung und über das liberum arbitrium*, diss. Saarbrücken 1976. [Ruland's pagination is also indicated in Fazzo and Zonta 1998, above.]

R. Salles, 'Categorical Possibility and Incompatibilism in Alexander of Aphrodisias' Theory of Responsibility', *Méthexis* 11 (1998) 65-83.

F.H. Sandbach, '*Ennoia* and *Prolepsis* in the Stoic theory of knowledge', *Classical Quarterly* 24 (1930) 45-51 = Long 1971, 22-37.

F.M. Schroeder, 'The analogy of the active intellect to light in the *De anima* of Alexander of Aphrodisias', *Hermes* 109 (1981) 215-25.

—'The potential or material intellect and the authorship of the *De intellectu*: a reply to B.C. Bazán', *Symbolae Osloenses* 57 (1982) 115-125.

—'The Provenance of the *De Intellectu* attributed to Alexander of Aphrodisias', *Documenti e studi sulla tradizione filosofica medievale* 8 (1997) 105-120.

F.M. Schroeder and R.B. Todd, *Two Aristotelian Greek Commentators on the Intellect: The* De Intellectu *attributed to Alexander of Aphrodisias and Themistius' Paraphrase of Aristotle* De Anima *3.4-8,* Toronto 1990 (Medieval Sources in Translation, 33)

D. Scott, 'Innatism and the Stoa', *Proceedings of the Cambridge Philological Society* 39 (1988) 123-153.

—*Recollection and Experience,* Cambridge 1995.

D.N. Sedley, 'Three notes on Theophrastus' treatment of taste and smells', in Fortenbaugh, Huby and Long 1985, 205-7.

—*Lucretius and the Transformation of Greek Wisdom,* Cambridge 1998.

R.W. Sharples, 1975a. 'Aristotelian and Stoic conceptions of necessity in the *De fato* of Alexander of Aphrodisias', *Phronesis* 20 (1975) 247-68.

—1975b. 'Responsibility, chance and not-being (Alexander of Aphrodisias *mantissa* 169-172)', *Bulletin of the Institute of Classical Studies* 22 (1975) 37-64.

—'Alexander of Aphrodisias' second treatment of fate? *De anima libri mantissa,* pp.179-186 Bruns', *Bulletin of the Institute of Classical Studies* 27 (1980) 76-94.

—1983a. *Alexander of Aphrodisias: On Fate,* London 1983.

—1983b. 'The Peripatetic classification of goods', in Fortenbaugh 1983, 139-59.

—'Ambiguity and opposition; Alexander of Aphrodisias, *Ethical Problem* 11', *Bulletin of the Institute of Classical Studies* 32 (1985) 109-16.

—'Species, Form and Inheritance: Aristotle and After', in A. Gotthelf, ed., *Aristotle on Nature and living things: philosophical studies presented to David M. Balme,* Pittsburgh 1986, 117-28.

—'Alexander of Aphrodisias: Scholasticism and Innovation', *Aufstieg und Niedergang der römischen Welt* II.36.1 (1987) 1176-1243.

—1990a. *Alexander of Aphrodisias: Ethical Problems,* London 1990.

—1990b. 'The School of Alexander', in R. Sorabji, ed., *Aristotle Transformed: The Ancient Commentators and their influence,* London 1990, 83-111.

—*Alexander of Aphrodisias Quaestiones 1.1-2.15,* London 1992.

—Review of Blumenthal and Robinson 1991, in *Classical Review* 43 (1993) 87-9.

—1994a. *Alexander of Aphrodisias Quaestiones 2.15-3.16,* London 1994.

—1994b. 'On Body, Soul and Generation in Alexander of Aphrodisias', *Apeiron* 27 (1994) 163-70.

—*Stoics, Epicureans and Sceptics,* London 1996.

—1998a. 'Alexander and pseudo-Alexanders of Aphrodisias: Scripta minima. *Questions* and *Problems, makeweights* and prospects', in

Wolfgang Kullmann, Jochen Althoff and Markus Asper, eds., *Gattungen wissenschaftlicher Literatur in der Antike*, Tübingen 1998 (Scriptoralia, 95) 383-403.

—1998b. *Theophrastus of Eresus: Sources for his Life, Writings, Thought and Influence, Commentary volume 3.1, Sources on Physics*, Leiden 1998.

—1999a. 'On being a *tode ti* in Aristotle and Alexander', *Méthexis* 12 (1999) 77-87.

—1999b. 'Aspasius on *Eudaimonia*', in A. Alberti and R.W. Sharples, eds., *Aspasius: the earliest extant commentary on Aristotle's* Ethics, Berlin 1999 (Peripatoi, 17) 85-95.

—2000a. 'Alexander of Aphrodisias *Quaestio* 2.21: a question of authenticity', *Elenchos* 21 (2000) 361-79.

—2000b. 'The sufficiency of virtue for happiness: not so easily overturned?', *Proceedings of the Cambridge Philological Society* 46 (2000) 121-139.

—2000c. 'The unity of the virtues in Aristotle, in Alexander of Aphrodisias, and in the Byzantine commentators', *Etica e Politica* 2.2 (2000): www.univ.trieste.it/~dipfilo/etica_e_politica/2000_2/

—'Schriften und Problemkomplexe zur Ethik', in Moraux 2001, 513-616.

—2002a. 'Eudemus' Physics: Change, Place and Time', in W.W. Fortenbaugh and I. Bodnár, *Eudemus of Rhodes*, New Brunswick 2002 (Rutgers University Studies in Classical Humanities, 11), 107-126.

—2003. 'Theophrastus, On Dizziness', in W.W. Fortenbaugh, R.W. Sharples and M. Sollenberger, *Theophrastus on Sweat, Dizziness and Fatigue*, Leiden 2003.

—2002b. 'Some problems in Lucretius' account of vision', in *Leeds International Classical Studies* 2002 (http://www.leeds.ac.uk/classics/lics/2002/200202.pdf)

—(forthcoming, 1) 'Alexander of Aphrodisias on the nature and location of vision', in R. Salles, ed., *Metaphysics, Soul, and Ethics: Themes from the work of Richard Sorabji*, Oxford.

—(forthcoming, 2) 'Alexander of Aphrodisias: what is a *mantissa*?', in P. Adamson et al., eds., *Philosophy, Science and Exegesis*, London.

—(forthcoming, 3) 'An Aristotelian Commentator on the Naturalness of Justice', in C.J. Gill, ed., *Ancient and Modern Approaches to Ethical Objectivity*, Oxford.

—(forthcoming, 4) 'Aristotelian Form in *Metaphysics Z* 8'. Forthcoming in a special issue of *Science in Context* edited by S. Cuomo and R. Netz.

C. Shields, 'The Homonymy of the Body in Aristotle', *Archiv für Geschichte der Philosophie* 75 (1993) 1-30.

G. Simon, *Le regard, l'être et l'apparence dans l'optique de l'antiquité,*

Paris 1988.

A.D. Smith, 'Character and Intellect in Aristotle's Ethics', *Phronesis* 41 (1996) 56-74.

M.F. Smith, *Diogenes of Oenoanda: The Epicurean Inscription*, Naples 1993.

R. Sorabji, 'Body and Soul in Aristotle', *Philosophy* 49 (1974) 63-89, reprinted at J. Barnes, M. Schofield and R. Sorabji, eds., *Articles on Aristotle*, vol.4, London 1974, 42-64.

—*Necessity, Cause and Blame*, London 1980.

—'From Aristotle to Brentano; the development of the concept of intentionality', in Blumenthal and Robinson 1991, 227-59.

C. Steel, 'Neoplatonic versus Stoic Causality', in C. Esposito and P. Porro, eds., *La causalità* (Quaestio 2.2), Turnhout and Bari 2003, 77-93.

P. Steinmetz, *Die Physik des Theophrast*, Bad Homburg 1964 (Palingenesia, 1).

G. Striker, 'The role of *oikeiosis* in Stoic ethics', *Oxford Studies in Ancient Philosophy* 1 (1983) 145-68.

—*Essays on Hellenistic Epistemology and Ethics*, Cambridge 1996.

L.C. Taub, *Ptolemy's Universe*, Chicago 1993.

G. Théry, *Autour du decret de 1210: II, Alexandre d'Aphrodise* (Bibliothèque Thomiste 7), Le Saulchoir Kain 1926.

P. Thillet, *Alexandre d Aphrodise, De Fato ad imperatores, version de Guillaume de Moerbeke*, Paris 1963 (Études de philosophie médiévale, 51).

—'Matérialisme et théorie de l'âme et de l'intellect chez Alexandre d'Aphrodise', *Revue philosophique de France et de l'Étranger* 106 (1981) 5-24.

—'Elementes pour l'histoire du texte du *De fato* d'Alexandre d'Aphrodise', *Revue d'histoire des textes* 12 (1982) 13-56.

—*Alexandre d'Aphrodise: Traité du Destin*, Paris 1984.

—'Alexandre d'Aphrodise et la poésie', in J. Wiesner, ed., *Aristoteles, Werk und Wirkung; Paul Moraux gewidmet*, vol. 2, Berlin 1987, 107-19.

C. Thurot, Alexandre d'Aphrodisias, *Commentaire sur le traité d'Aristote De Sensu et Sensibili, edité avec la vieille translation latine*, Notices et extraits des MSS de la Bibliothèque Nationale 25 (1875) no.2.

T. Tieleman, 'The Hunt for Galen's Shadow: Alexander of Aphrodisias, *De anima* 94.7-100.17 Bruns Reconsidered', in K.A. Algra, P.W. Van Der Horst and D.T. Runia (eds.), *Polyhistor: Studies in the History and Historiography of Ancient Philosophy presented to Jaap Mansfeld*, Leiden 1996, 265-83.

R.B. Todd, 'The Stoic common notions: a re-examination and re-interpretation', *Symbolae Osloenses* 48 (1973) 43-76.

—'ΣΥΝΕΝΤΑΣΙΣ and the Stoic theory of perception', *Grätzer Beiträge* 2 (1974) 251-61.

—1976a. *Alexander of Aphrodisias on Stoic Physics*, Leiden 1976.

—1976b. 'Alexander of Aphrodisias on *De interpretatione* 16a26-9', *Hermes* 104 (1976) 140-6.

—'Peripatetic Epistemology before Alexander of Aphrodisias: The Case of Alexander of Damascus', *Eranos* 93 (1995) 122-8.

—*Themistius: On Aristotle* On the Soul, London 1996.

A. Towey, *Alexander of Aphrodisias On Aristotle* On Sense Perception, London 2000.

F. Trabucco, 'Il problema del "De philosophia" di Aristocle de Messene e la sua dottrina', *Acme* 11 (1958) 97-150.

M.M. Tweedale, 'Alexander of Aphrodisias' views on universals', *Phronesis* 29 (1984) 279-303.

J. Vallance, 'Theophrastus and the Study of the Intractable: Scientific Method in *De lapidibus* and *De igne*', in W.W. Fortenbaugh and R.W. Sharples, eds., *Theophrastean Studies*, New Brunswick 1988 (*Rutgers University Studies in Classical Humanities*, 3) 25-40.

G. Vlastos, 'The Unity of the Virtues in the *Protagoras*', in G. Vlastos, *Platonic Studies*, Princeton 1973, 221-69.

W.E. Wehrle, 'The definition of soul in Aristotle's *de anima* ii.1 is not analogous to the definition of snub', *Ancient Philosophy* 14 (1994) 297-317.

F. Wehrli, *Die Schule des Aristoteles*: 8, *Eudemus von Rhodos*, 2nd ed., Basel 1969.

P. Wendland, ed., *Alexandri in Aristotelis librum De Sensu commentarium*, Berlin 1901 (*CAG* 3.1).

J. Westenberger, *Galeni qui fertur de qualitatibus incorporeis libellus*, diss. Marburg 1906.

S. White, 'Happiness in the Hellenistic Lyceum', in L.J. Jost and R.A. Shiner, eds., *Eudaimonia and Well-being: ancient and modern conceptions*, Kelowna BC 2002 (*Apeiron* vol.35 no.4), 69-93.

J. Whiting, 'Living Bodies', in Nussbaum and Rorty 1992, 75-91.

B.A.O. Williams, 'Justice as a Virtue', in A.O. Rorty, ed., *Essays on Aristotle's Ethics*, Berkeley 1980, 189-99.

—'Hylomorphism', *Oxford Studies in Ancient Philosophy* 4 (1986) 189-99.

F. Wimmer, *Theophrasti Eresii opera*, Paris 1866.

M.J. Woods, 'Particular forms revisited', *Phronesis* 36 (1991) 75-87.

K. Wurm, *Substanz und Qualität: ein Beitrag zur Interpretation der Plotinischen Traktate VI.1-3*, Berlin 1973 (Quellen und Studien zur Philosophie, 5).

J. Zahlfleisch, 'Die Polemik Alexanders von Aphrodisias gegen die verschiedenen Theorien des Sehens', *Archiv für Geschichte der Philosophie* 8 (1895) 373-86, 498-509; 9 (1896) 149-62.

E. Zeller, *Die Philosophie der Griechen in ihrer geschichtlichen Entwicklung*, 3.1, 4th ed. E. Wellmann, Leipzig 1903.

English-Greek Glossary

above, be: *epanabainein*

absence, absent: *apeinai, apoleipesthai,
apousia, ouk einai*

abstract: *aphairein*; abstraction:
aphairesis

Academics: *Akadêmaïkoi*

accident, be accidental attribute of:
sumbainein; accidental(ly): *kata
sumbebêkos*

accompany: *hepesthai, sunodeuein*

accord(ance): *akolouthos, sunâidein*

account: *logos*

accurately: *exakribôs*

accustomed, be: *eiôthenai, philein*;
become accustomed: *ethizesthai*

achieve: *peripoiein, tunkhanein*

acquainted with, be: *gnôrizein*

acquire: *analambanein, ekhein,
ktasthai, peripoiein, proslambanein*;
acquire already: *prolambanein*;
acquire in addition: *proslambanein*;
acquire portion, acquire share in:
metalambanein

acquisition: *analêpsis, ktêsis, peripoiêsis*;
involving acquisition: *ktêtikos*

act, acting, action: *energein, poiein,
praxis, prassein/prattein*; able to act:
praktikos; concerned with/produc-
tive of action: *praktikos*

active, activity: *energeia, energein,
ergon*

actual, actuality, actually: *energeia,
energein, entelekheia*

add: *proskrinein, prostithenai*; be
added: *prosginesthai*; add in
exchange: *antiproskrinein*

addition *proskrisis, prosthêkê*;
acquire/gain in addition: *proslambanein*; make additional distinction:
prosdiastellein

adjacent, be: *geitnian, parakeisthai*

admit: *dekhesthai, prosdekhesthai*; (=
concede): *homologein*; able to admit:
dektikos; cannot admit, do not
admit: *anepidektos*

admixture: *mixis*

adopt: *paralambanein*

advance: *proagein, proienai*

advantage, take advantage: *pleonektein,
pleon ekhein*; advantageous:
sumpheron

advice: *sumboulia*; give advice, advise:
sumbouleuein, sumbouleuesthai;
adviser: *sumboulos*

afar off: *porrô, porrôthen*

affect: *kinein*; be affected: *gi(g)nesthai,
paskhein, pathêtikos, pathêtos*; affection, being affected: *pathos*; be
affected along with: *sumpaskhein*;
able to affect: *kinêtikos*; easily
affected: *eupathes*

affinity: *oikeios, oikeiôsis, oikeioun*

against, go: *parabainein*

age: *hêlikia*

agree, be in agreement: *homologein,
exhomologein, sumphônein*; be
agreed on: *sunkeisthai*; agreement:
homologia, sunthêkê; make agreement: *suntithesthai*

aim, aim at: *stokhazesthai*; aiming wide:
astokhos; with a sure aim: *eustokhôs*

air: *aêr*

akin: *oikeios*

alien: *allotrios*

alive, be: *zên*

all at once, all of a sudden: *athroôs*

allow: *sunkhôrein*

alter: *alloioun*

alteration: *alloiôsis*

altogether: *athroôs, holos*

amazing: *thaumasios*

ambiguous: *homônumos*

analogous: *analagon*; analogously:
analogôs; analogy: *analogia*

angle: *gônia*

angry, become/grow: *orgizesthai,
thumousthai*

anhomoeomerous: *anhomoiomerês*

animal: *zôion*; wild animal: *thêrion*

apparent: *dêlos, phaneros, phainesthai*,

emphainesthai

appear: *phainesthai*; appear in: *emphainesthai*; appear incidentally: *paremphainesthai*

appearance: *phantasia*

appetite, appetition: *orexis, oregesthai*; object of appetition: *orektos*; appetitive: *orektikos*

apple: *mêlon*

application: *prosbolê*

apprehend, apprehension, apprehensive: *antilambanesthai, antilêpsis, antilêptikos, lambanein*; able to apprehend: *lêptikos*; can be apprehended: *lêptos*

appropriate, appropriation: *oikeios, oikeioun, oikeiousthai, prosoikeioun*; be appropriate: *prosêkein*

aquatic: *enhudros*

argument: *logos*; (demonstrative): *apodeixis*; (ingenious): *heurêsilogia*

arrangement: *kataskeuê, taxis*

art: *tekhnê*

asleep, be: *koimasthai*

assent: *sunkatathesis, sunkatatithesthai*

assert: *tithenai*

assist: *boêtheia, boêthein, sunairesthai, sunergos*; assistance: *boêtheia*

astronomer: *astrologos*

attach: *anaptein, sumbainein*; attach to: *huparkhein*; attach self to: *proshizein*; attach as accident: *sumbainein*

attract: *epispasthai*; exercising attraction: *epispastikos*

attribute: *anatithenai*; be attribute, be accidental attribute of: *sumbainein*

attunement: *harmonia*

avoid: *ekklinein, pheugein*; to be avoided: *pheuktos*; avoidance: *ekklisis*

awake: *diêgeirein*

awareness: *sunaisthêsis*

away: make away with: *exagein*; making away with self: *exagôgê*

axe: *pelekus*

bad: *kakos, phaulos*; in bad condition: *mokhthêros*; bad luck: *dustukhia*; bad natural endowment: *aphuïa*

bark: *phloion, phloiôdês*

barley: *krithê*

base: *aiskhros, kakos, phaulos*; (base of cone): *basis*

basis: *aphormê*

beauty: *kallos*

become: *gi(g)nesthai*

bed: *klinê*

begin, beginning: *arkhê, arkhesthai*

being: *einai, ousia*; not-being: *mê on*

belief, believe: *dogma, pisteuein, pistis*

belly: *koilia*

belong: *huparkhein*

bench: *bathron*

bend, bending: *klasis, anaklasis, klazein*

beneficial: *ôphelimos*; benefit: *ophelos*

between: *metaxu*; in between: *mesos*

bind hair: *diadeisthai*

bite: *daknein*; being bitten: *plêgê*

bitterness: *pikrotês*

black: *melas*; *melainein, melania*

blame: *aitia, aitiasthai, psegein*

blend: *kerannunai, krama*

blending: *krasis*; good blending, satisfactory blending: *eukrasia*

blessed, blessedness: *makarios*

block in advance, block the way: *epiprosthein*

blood: *haima*; with blood: *enhaimos*

blow: *pnein*

body, bodily: *sôma, sômatikos*; heavenly body: *astron*; without body: *asômatos*

bold: *thrasus*; boldness: *tharros*

bonds: *desmos*

bone: *ostoun*

book: *sungramma*

born, be: *gi(g)nesthai*

break: *ekkrouein*; break up: *dialuein*; easily broken: *euthraustos*

breath: *pneuma*; breathe: *anapnein*; breathing: *anapnoê*

bright: *diaugês, lampros*

bring about: *poiein*

bronze: *khalkos*; art of bronze-working: *khalkeutikê*

brought about, be: *gi(g)nesthai*

build up: *oikodomein*

building: *oikos*

bulk: *onkos*

burn: *kaiein*; burn up: *ekpimprênai*; burning: *kaustikos*

burst: *rhêgnunai*

bury deep within: *katabussoun*

call in: *parakalein*; call on [name of]:
epiboasthai

capacity: *dunamis*

care, without: *aperiskeptôs*; care about:
epimeleisthai; careful: *epimelês*

carpenter, -ry: *tektôn, tektonikos*

cast shadow: *episkotein*

category: *genos, katêgoria*

cause: *aitia, aition, aitios, parekhein*;
regard/give as cause: *aitiasthai*;
cause movement/change: *kinein,
kinêsis*; cause to grow: *auxanein*;
without a cause: *anaitios*

certain state, be in: *pôs ekhein*; certain
thing, a: *tode ti*

chain: *heirmos*

change, changing: *allattein, ameibein,
hupallagê, hupallattesthai, kinein,
kinêsis, metaballein, metabolê,
metapiptein*; cause change: *kinein*;
change direction: *metakineisthai*;
change place: *metabainein*; change
position: *methistasthai*; change with:
summetaballein

character: *êthos*; characterise:
kharaktêrizein

charcoal: *anthrax*

charlatan, religious: *goês anthrôpos*

child: *paidion, pais*

choice: *hairesis, prohairesis*; make
choice: *prohaireisthai*; [matter] of
choice: *prohairetikos*

choose: *haireisthai, hairesis, prohaireisthai*; capable of choosing: *prohairetikos*; to be chosen: *hairetos*

circle: *kuklos*

circumference: *perix*

circumscribe: *perigraphein*

circumstance, difficult circumstance:
peristasis, perihistasthai

claim: lay claim to: *antipoieisthai*

clear, clearly: *dêlos, enargês, gnôrimos,
katadêlos, phainesthai, phaneros,
prodelôs*; clear facts: *enargeia*; not
clear: *adêlos*

climate: *aêr*

close eyes: *epimuein*

close in: *phrattein*

clouding of judgement: *skotôsis*

coal: *anthrax*

coalesce: *sumphuesthai, sunistasthai,*
sunkrinesthai

cobbler: *skuteus*

code of law: *nomothesia*

cognate: *sumphutos*

coincide: *sumpiptein*

cold, coldness: *psukhros, psukhrotês*

collect, collect together: *athroizein,
eklegein*

collide: *sumballein*

colour: *epikhrônnunai, khrôma,
khrômatizein, khrônnunai, khro(i)a*;
of a single colour, the same colour:
homoiokhrous, homokhrous;
varying in colour: *anhomoiokhrous*;
without colour, colourless: *akhrous*

colouring: *khrôsis*

combination: *sumplokê, sunamphoteros,
sunkeisthai, sunkrisis*

combine: *sunkrinein*

come about, come to be: *genêtos,
gi(g)nesthai, periginesthai*; come in
to take place of: *anteisienai*; come to
be (present) in: *engi(g)nesthai*

coming to be: *genesis, genêtos*

command *keleuein, prostassein*

common: *koinos*; have in common:
koinônein; communal: *koinônikos*;
community: *koinônia*

complete: *exergazesthai, sumplêrôtikos,
sumpleroun, teleios, teleioun*; completely: *athroôs*; completeness: *sumplêrôsis*;
completing: *sumplêrôtikos*

composed, composite: *sunkeisthai,
sunthesis, sunthetos*; composed of:
ek; composition: *sunthesis, sustasis*

compound: *sunamphoteros, sunkrima,
sunthetos*

comprehend: *katalambanein*

compress: *sustellein*; undergo compression: *sunkrinesthai*

concave: *koilos*; concavity: *eisokhê,
koilotês*

concede: *sunkhôrein*

conceive: *prolambanein*; concept:
epinoia; conception: *prolêpsis*;
lacking conception: *anennoêtos*; be
conceptually prior: *proepinoeisthai*

concoction: *pepsis*; (lack of): *apepsia*

condemn: *katagignôskein*

condition; *hexis*: in bad condition:
mokhthêros

conducive, be: *prohêgeisthai, sunteinein*
conduct: *praxis*
cone: *kônos*
confirm: *kuroun, pistoun*
conflict: *diamakhê*
confuse: *sunkhein*
connate: *sumphutos*
conscious, be: *suneidenai*
consequence, be: *hepesthai*
consideration: *theôria*; lack of
   consideration: *aboulia*
consist in: (*einai*) *en*
consistency, consistent: *sumphônia*
conspicuous: *eusêmos*
constitution: *hexis, kataskeuê, sustasis*
construct: *kataskeuazein*
consume: *analiskein, katanaliskein*
contact: *haphê*; be in contact:
   haptesthai, sunaptein; come into
   contact: *thinganein*
contain within: *periekhein*
contemplation/-ive: *theôrein, theôrêtikos*
contentious, be: *philoneikein*
contingent: *endekhomenos*
continually, continuity, continuous(ly):
   adialeiptos, sunekheia, sunekhês/ -ôs
continue: *diamenein*
contract: *sunagesthai, sustellesthai*
contradiction: *antiphasis*
contrariety: *enantiôsis*
contrast: *antithesis*
contravene: *parabainein*; contravention:
   parabasis
contribute, make contribution: *sumball-
   esthai, sunergein, sunergos,
   sunteinein, suntelein*; contributing,
   contribute: *phoros, sunergos*
control: in control, have control: *kurios*;
   self-controlled: *enkratês*; lacking
   self-control: *akratês*
convert: *methistanai*
convex: *kurtos*; convexity: *exokhê,
   kurtotês*
copper: *khalkos*
correspond, corresponding: *sumbolon,
   ginesthai kata*
counsel: *sumboulê*
couple: *suzeugnunai*
courage: *andreia*; courageous: *andreios*
coward: *deilos*; cowardice: *deilia*
craft *tekhnê, tekhnêtos, tekhnikos*;

craftsman: *dêmiourgos, tekhnitês*
create: *poiein*; create in: *empoiein*
creature, living creature: *zôion*
credence, deserving of: *axiopistos*
crush: *thlan, thlibein*
cubit: *pêkhus*
culmination: *akrotês*
cure: *hugiazein*
custom. customary: *ethos, eiôthenai*
cut: *temnein*; cut off: *apolambanein,
   apotemnein*
cycle: *periodos*

danger: loving danger: *philokindunos*
dark, darkened, darkness: *skoteinos,
   skotos, zopheros*; darken:
   episkotein, zophoun
day: *hêmera*
death: *phthora, thanatos*
deceive: *diapseudesthai*
decide: *diagignôskein, krinein*;
   decision: *krisis*
declare beforehand: *promênuein*
deep, deep down: *bathus*; bury deep
   within: *katabussoun*
defeat, defeated: *hêtta*
defend: *phulassein*; defender: *sunêgoros*
deficiency: *endeia*
define: *horizein, dihorizein*; definite:
   hôrismenos; definition: *dihorismos,
   horismos, horos*
defraud: *pseudesthai*
deliberate, deliberation: *boulê,
   bouleuesthai, bouleutikos*
demonstrating, demonstration, demonstrative argument: *apodeixis*
denial: *apophasis*
dense, density: *pakhumeres, pakhus,
   puknos, puknotês*; become denser:
   pakhunesthai; making denser:
   pakhuntikos; less dense: *leptoteros*;
   make less dense: *leptunein*
deny: *apophasis*
departure: *ekkrisis, exagôgê*
depend(ing) on: *artasthai, epi* + dat.
depositing: *katabolê*
deprive: *sterein*
depth: *bathos, buthos*
derangement: *parakopê, parakoptein*
derive, deriving from: *apo/para*
deserving of credence: *axiopistos*

desire, desirable: *ephetos, ephiesthai, epithumein, oregesthai, orektos*

destiny, destined: *moira*

destroy: *phtheirein*; easily destroyed: *euphthartos*; destruction: *phthora*

determinate: *aphôrismenos*; determine: *horizein*

develop: *auxanein*; be fully developed: *teleiousthai*

diagonal: *diametros*; diagonally: *diagônios*

die: *apothnêiskein*

differ, be different, difference: *diapherein, diaphora, diaphoran ekhein, heterotês, parallattesthai*; different: *allos kai allos, diaphoros, heteros*

differentia, differentiate, differentiated: *diaphora, diaphoros*; make differentiations: *diastellesthai*

difficult: *khalepos*; (circumstance): *peristasis*; difficulty: *aporia*; raise/be difficulty: *aporein, prosaporein, aporeisthai*

diffuse: *khein, paraspeirein*

dig: *oruttein, skaptein*

digestion: *pepsis*

diluted honey: *melikraton*

dim: *akhluôdês*

diminish: *elattoun, meioun*

direct: *sunteinein*

directly: *ep' eutheias*

disagree: *diaphônein*; be in disagreement: *diaphônian ekhein*

discerning, discernment: *kritikos*

discover: *heuriskein, katamanthanein*

discus-thrower: *diskeuôn*

disease: *nosos*

dispersal: *diakrisis*; disperse: *diakrinein, diakritikos*

display: *diadeiknunai*

dispose: *diatithenai*; disposition: *diathesis, hexis*

dissect, dissecting: *temnein, tmêtikos*

dissimilar(ity): *anhomoios, anhomoiotês*

distance *apostasis, apostêma, diastêma*; be at a distance: *aphistasthai*; distance travelled forth: *prohodos*

distant: *porrô, porrôthen*

distinction, distinguish: *diarthrôsis, diarthroun, dihairein, dihorizein*; involving distinction: *diêrthrômenôs*; lacking distinctions: *adiarthrôtos*; make

additional distinction: *prosdiastellein*

divide, dividing: *dihairein, dihairetikos*; divide in opposition: *antidihairein*

divine: *theios*

division: *dihairein, dihairesis*

do: *energein, poiein, prassein/prattein*; doing: *praxis*; should be done, should do, to be done: *poiêteos, prakteos*; that is done, to be done: *praktos*; able to do, capable of doing: *praktikos*

doctor: *iatros*

dog: *kuôn*

double: *diplasios, diplous, dittos*; double nature: *diphuïa*

downwards, carry: *katapherein*; downwards motion: *kataphora*

downwind: *kata ton anemon*

drag: *helkein*

dream: *oneiros*

drop: *stalagmos*

dry, dryness: *xêros, xêrotês*

due to luck: *tukhêros*

dull: *amudros*

dust: *koniortos*

eager for battle: *hapsimakhos*

eagerness: *spoudê*

ear: *ous*

earth: *gê*; earthy: *gêïnos, geôdês*

easy, easily *rhâidios, eukolos*; easily affected: *eupathês*; easily broken: *euthraustos*; easily destroyed: *euphthartos*; easily moved: *eukinêtos*

eclipse: *ekleipsis*

ejection: *proptôsis*

elders: *presbuteroi*

element: *stoikheion*

emit: *aphienai*; emit light: *lampein*

emotion: *pathos*; emotional: *pathêtikos*

employ: *khrêsthai*

empty: *kenos*

end: *peras, telikos, telos*; end, at this or that: *enteuthen ... enteuthen*

ending: *katastrophê*

endowed: be endowed by nature: *phuein*; well-endowed: *euphuês*; endowment: *paraskeuê*; bad/good natural endowment: *aphuïa, euphuïa*

endure: *summenein*; enduring: *karterikos*

enemy: *polemios*

enmattered: *enhulos*

enquire, enquiry: *zêtein, zêtêma*
ensouled: *empsukhos*
ensue: *akolouthôs einai*
enter: *eisienai, eiskrinesthai, emptôsis, epienai*; enter before, enter first: *proempiptein*; enter in: *empiptein*; enter in beforehand: *proeisienai*
entering: *emptôsis*; entering in: *embadon*
entirety, in: *holoklêros*
entitle (book): *epigraphein*
entreaty: *deêsis*
entrust: *pisteuein*
entry: *emptôsis*
equal, equally: *episês, isos*; extend equally: *parekteinein*; make equal, become equal: *isoun, exisoun, parisoun*
equivalent: *isos*; be equivalent: *dunasthai tauton*
err, error: *dihamartanein, hamartêma, prosptaiein*: freedom from error: *aprosptôsia*
escape: *ekpiptein, pheugein*
essence: *einai, ousia, ti ên einai*
established, be: *keisthai*
eternal, eternity: *aïdios, aïdiotes*
etherial: *aitherios*
even: *homalês*
evidence: *marturion, marturesthai, marturein*
evident: *enargês*
evil: *kakos*; engage in evil-doing: *kakourgein*
exact, make: *exakriboun*
examination, without: *anexetastôs*
exceed: *huperballein*
excellence: *aretê*
excess: *huperbolê*
exchange, add in: *antiproskrinein*; be transferred by exchange: *antimethistasthai*
exercise self: *diateinesthai*
exhort: *protrepein*
exist: *einai, huphistashai*; exist before-hand: *prohuparkhein*; naturally exist-ing thing: *phusis*; existence: *einai, huparxis, hupostasis*
exit: *exhodos*
expand: *diakrinein*
expect: *prosdokan*
experience: *pathos, tribê*
explain: *poiein* ; explanation: *logos*

extend: *apoteinesthai, dierkhesthai, dihêkein, ekteinein, epiteinein*; extend equally, extend throughout: *parekteinein*; extending beyond: *epi pleion*; extended: *diastatos*
external, externally: *ektos, exô, exôthen*
extreme *akros, eskhatos*
eye: *omma, ophthalmos*; close eyes: *epimuein*; eye-jelly: *korê*

fact: *ergon*; clear facts: *enargeia*
faculty: *dunamis*
fail: *epileipein*; fail to hit: *hamartanein*; fail to realise: *lanthanein*
fairy-tale, like a: *muthôdês*
fall: *piptein*; fall under: *hupoptôtos*
false, falsely: *pseudês, pseudos*
fame: *doxa*
fashion: *dêmiourgein, diaplattein*
fate: *heimarmenê*; be fated: *katheimarthai*; fated: *heimarmenos*
fear: *phobos*
feature: *pathos*
feeble, feebly: *adranês*
feed: *trephein, trephesthai*
fellow-citizen: *politês*
female: *thêlus*
fill, filled: *anapimplanai, plêrês, plêroun*
final: *eskhatos, teleutaios, telikos*
find: *heuriskein, lambanein*; finding: *heuresis*
fine, fineness (opp. to density): *leptomerês, leptos*; in a fine (= noble) way: *kalôs*
fire: *pur*
firmly *bebaios, -ôs*
fish: *ikhthus*
fit: *prosoikeioun*; fitness: *epitêdeiotês*; fitted: *epitêdeios*
flame: *phlox*
flat: *epipedos, homalês*
flee: *katapheugein*
flesh: *sarx*
float on: *epipolazein*
flow: *rhein, rheuma*; flow out: *aporrhein*
fluid: *hugros, hugron*; fluidity: *hugrotês*
flying: *ptênos*
follow, follow on, following: *akolouthein, akolouthos, epakolouthein, epi, hepesthai*; followers: *hoi peri*; what follows: *akolouthia*

food: *trophê*

footed, with feet: *pezos*; footless: *apous*

force: *iskhus*; forced, forcible: *biaios*; give force to: *kratunein*

foreknow: *progignôskein*

foresee: *prohorasthai*; lack of foresight: *apronoêsia*

foretell: *prolegein*

forethought: *pronoein*

forge: *elaunein*

form (noun): *eidos*; similar in form: *homoiomorphos*; without form: *aneideos*; give form (to): *eidopoiein*

form (verb): *sunhistanai*; form images: *phantasiousthai*

fortuitous(ly): *automatos, -ôs*

foundation-stone: *krêpis*

fragrance: *euôdia*

free: *eleutheros*; be free from: *kathareuein*; freedom from trouble: *aokhlêsia*; freedom from error: *aprosptôsia*

freeze: *pêgnusthai*

friend: *philos*

frightening: *phoberos*

from (tradition): *para*

frost: *pagos*

fulfil: *apodidonai, sumplêroun*

full: *anapleôs, mestos, plêrês*; be fully developed: *teleiousthai*

function: *ergon*

gain: *lêma, periginesthai*; gain in addition: *proslambanein*

gather in herds: *sunagelazesthai*

general: *koinos*; in general: *epi to pan, haplôs, holôs, holon, katholou*

generated: *genêtos, gi(g)nesthai*

genus: *genos*

geometrician: *geômetrês*

get: *lambanein*; get hold of: *epilambanein*

give: *didonai, apodidonai, dosis, nemein*; be given off: *aperkhesthai*; give in: *endidonai*

gladly: *asmenôs*

glass: *hualos, huelos*

glow-worm: *lampuris, pugolampis*

glue: *kolla, kollan*

goal: *skopos*

god: *theos*

gold: *khrusos*

good: *agathos, eu, spoudaios*

grasp: *lambanein, antilambanesthai*; grasping: *lêpsis*

grow, growth: *auxanein, auxein, auxêsis*; of/concerned with growth: *auxêtikos*

guard against: *phulattesthai*

guardian spirit: *daimôn*

gut: *entera*

habit, habituate, habituation: *ethos, ethizein, proethizein, sunêtheia*

Hades: *Aïdês*

half: *hêmisus*

hand: *kheir*

happen: *apantan, ginesthai, sumbainein*; happen to, have something happen to: *paskhein*

happiness: *eudaimonia*; producing happiness: *eudaimonikos*; happy: *eudaimôn*; be happy: *eudaimonein*

hard: *sklêros*; hardness: *sklêrotês*

harm: *lumainesthai*

harmony, in: *sunâidein, sunôdos*

hate: *misein*

have to: *khrênai*

head: *kephalê*

health: *hugieia*; be healthy: *hugiainein, hugiazesthai, rhônnusthai*; in a healthy way: *hugiôs*

heap: *sôros*

hear: *akouein*; hearing: *akoê*

heat, give heat: *thermos, thermotês, thermainein*

heaven: *ouranos*; heavenly body: *astron*; heavenly: *ouranios*

heaviness: *barutês*; heavy: *barus*

help: *ôphelein*

herds, gather in: *sunagelazesthai*

here (= in the sublunary region): *entautha, enthade, têide*

hinder: *empodistikos, empodizein, kôluein*; hindrance: *empodion*; without hindrance: *anempodistos*

hit the mark: *epitunkhanein*; fail to hit: *hamartanein*

hold: *ekhein, katekhein, stegein*; hold back: *epekhein*; hold together: *sunekhein*; get hold of, take a hold, *epilambanein, -esthai, lambanein*

homeomery: *homoiomereia*

homogeneous: *homoeidês*

honey, diluted: *melikraton*; mixture of

honey and wine: *oinomeli*
honour: *timan, timê*; honourable: *timios*
hope: *elpis*
horn: *keras*
horse: *hippos*
hot: *thermos*
house: *domos, oikia, oikos*
human, human being, humankind: *anthrôpos, anthrôpinos*

ice: *krustallos*
idea: *epinoia*
idleness: *argia*
ignorance: *agnoia*; be ignorant: *agnoein*
ill, be: *nosein*
illiberal: *aneleutheros*
illogical: *alogos*
illuminate, give/be source of illumination: *phôtizein, proslampein*; illuminated: *diaugês, phôs ekhein*, (by sun): *hêliousthai*
ill-endowed: *aphuês*
image: *eidôlon, eikôn, phantasma*; form images: *phantasiousthai*
imagination: *phantasia*; imagine: *phantasiousthai*
imitate: *mimeisthai*
immaterial: *ahulos*
immortal: *athanatos*
impact: *prosballein, prosbolê*
impede: *empodizein*; unable to be impeded: *akôlutos*
imperceptible: *anaisthêtos, anepaisthetos*
imperishable: *aphthartos*
impinge: *prospiptein*
implant: *entithenai*
implied by one another: *antakolouthein*
impression: *emphasis, phantasia*; receive impression: *apomattesthai*
imprint: *anamassein*; imprinting: *anamaxis*
impulse *hormê, rhopê*; of impulse, impulsive: *hormêtikos*; have/exercise impulse: *horman*
inability: *adunatein*
inactive: *argos*
incapacitate: *pêroun*
incidentally: *kata sumbebêkos*; appear incidentally: *paremphainesthai*
inclination: *prosklisis*

include: *perilambanein, emperilambanein*
incommensurable: *asummetros*
inconsistent, be: *makhesthai*
incorporeal: *asômatos*
increase: *auxanein, sunauxanein*
indefinite: *ahoristos, apeiros*
indication: *mênusis*
indifferent, indifference: *adiaphoros, arrhepês*
indisputable: *anamphilektos*
individual, individually: *atomos, idios, idiâi, kath' hekasta, kat' idian*
induction: *epagôgê*
ineffective, make: *ekluein*
inescapable: *anapadrastos*
inevitable: *aparabatos*
infinite, infinity: *apeiros*; ad infinitum: *eis/ep' apeiron*
inflate: *phusan*
influence: *iskhus*
information, inform: *mênusis*
ingenious argument: *heuresilogia*
injustice: *adikêma*
inquirer: *zêtein*
instrument, instrumental: *organon, organikos*
intangible: *anhaphês*
intellect: *nous*; of intellection, intelligent: *noêtikos*; intelligence: *dianoia*; intelligible: *noêtos*
intemperate behaviour: *akrasia*
intermediate: *metaxu*
internal: *entos*
interrupt: *diakoptein*; interruption: *dialeipsis*; have interruptions: *dialeipein*
intersect: *temnein*
interval: *diastasis, diastêma*
intervening: *metaxu*
interweaving: *sumplokê*
invisible: *ahoratos*
iron: *sidêros*
irrational: *alogos*
isolation, in: *kekhôrismenos*

jar: *kados*
jelly of eye: *korê*
judge: *dokimastikos, krinein*; judging, (able to) judge: *kritikos*; judge in relation: *sunkrinein*; judgement, judging: *gnômê, krisis*; clouding of judgement: *skotôsis*

just, justice: *dikaios, dikaiosunê*
juxtaposition: *parathesis, sunthesis*

keep: *phulassein/phulattein*
kind: *eidos, genos*
know: *eidenai, gi(g)nôskein, gnôrizein*;
    able to know: *gnôristikos*; knowable:
    epistêtos, gnôstos; do not know:
    agnoein; well-known: *gnôrimos*
knowledge: *epistêmê, gnôsis*; bringing
    knowledge: *gnôstikos*; have knowl-
    edge: *eidenai*; lacking knowledge:
    anepistêmôn

labour: *ponein, ponos*
lack: *endeia*; without lack: *anendeês,
    anepideês*
lamp: *lukhnos*
land-: *khersaios*
last: *eskhatos*
law: *nomimon, nomos*: code of law:
    nomothesia; make laws: *nomothetein*
lay down: *tithenai*; lay down
    beforehand: *prokataballein*
lead (metal): *molibdos*
learn *manthanein, katamanthanein*;
    learn in advance: *promanthanein*
least *elakhistos, hêkista*; for the least
    part: *ep' elatton*
left: *aristeros*
legality: *nomimon*
legislate: *nomothetein*
lethargy: *lêthargos*
licentious: *akolastos*
life: *bios, zôê*; have life: *bioun*; spend
    life: *zên, katazên*
light (opp. heavy): *kouphos*; lightness:
    kouphotês
light (illumination) *phôs, lampein*; like
    light: *phôtoeidês*; to light (lamp):
    haptein; give/be source of/make
    light: *phôtizein*
lighting: *augê*
like (= take pleasure in): *agapan*
limit: *peras*
line: *grammê*; straight line: *eutheia*
liquefy: *khein*
liquid: *hugros*; liquid measure: *kuathos*;
    liquidity: *hugrotês*
live, living; *bioun, zên*; living well, good
    living: *euzôïa*; living creature: *zôion*

log: *xulon*
look, look at: *blepein, horan*; look for:
    zêtein; look into: *apoblepein*; look
    up: *anablepein*
lose: *apoballein*; be at a loss: *aporein*;
    cannot be lost: *anapoblêtos*
love: *aspazesthai, philein, philia*; object
    of love: *philêtos*; should be loved:
    philêteos; loving danger: *philokindu-
    nos*; lover of money: *philokhrêmatos*;
    love of self: *philautia*; lover of what is
    noble: *philokalos*; lover of wine:
    philoinos
luck: *tukhê*; bad luck: *dustukhia*; due to
    luck: *tukhêros*; good luck: *eutukhia*
lung: *pneumôn*
lyre: *lura*

mad, be: *mainesthai*
made, be: *gi(g)nesthai*
magnitude: *megethos*; without
    magnitude: *amegethês*
maimed: *pêros*
maintain: *axioun*
make: *parekhein, poiein, tithenai*; make
    away with: *exagein, exagôgê*
male: *arrên*
malpractice: *kakotekhnia*
man: *anêr*
mark on, mark upon: *ensêmainein*; hit
    the mark: *epitunkhanein*
master of: *kurios*
matter, material: *hulê, hulikos*; be a
    matter of: *(einai) en*
may possibly: *endekhesthai*
mean (middle): *mesos*
measure: *kotulê, kuathos, metrein,
    anametrein*: one measure: *kotuliaios*;
    three measures: *trikotulaios*
medicine: *iatrikê*
meet: *apantan*
melancholy: *melancholia*
membrane, like: *humenôdês*
memory: *mnêmê*
mention: *mnêmoneuein*
messenger, act as: *diakoneisthai*
mid-day, of: *methêmerinos*
migrate: *metabainein*
mind: *nous*; as one is minded: *kata noun*
mirror: *katoptron*
misfortune: *sumphora*

miss: *dihamartanein*

misshapen: *diastrophos*

mix *kirnan, enkerranunai, mignunai, summignunai*; mixed: *miktos*; mixing, mixture: *migma, mixis*

modify, modification: *trepein, tropê*

moist, moistness, moisture: *hugros, hugrotês*

money, lover of: *philokhrêmatos*

monstrosity: *teras*

moon: *selênê*

moral: *êthikos*

mortal: *thnêtos*

most: for the most part: *epi polu, hôs epi to pleiston*

motion *kinêsis, phora*; be in motion, set in motion: *kinein, kinêtikos*; downwards motion: *kataphora*

mould round: *periplattein*

mouth: *stoma*

move: *kinein, kinêsis, metakomizein, metapherein*; (around): *peripherein*; (away): *apienai*; (backwards): *anakhôrein, hupokhôrein*; (with): *sunkinein*; hard to move: *duskinêtos*; easily moved: *eukinêtos*; movement: *kinêsis, phora*; cause movement: *kinein*

mud: *pêlos*

music, art of music: *mousikê*

musical, musician: *mousikos*

mutual: *pros allêlous*; mutual replacement: *antiperistasis*

name: *onoma, onomasia, prosêgoria*; in name only: *homônumôs*

narrow: *stenos, stenoun*; make narrow: *eis stenon sunagein*; narrow place: *stenôpos*

natural, naturally: *phusikos, -ôs, phusis, kata phusin, phuein*; bad natural endowment: *aphuïa*; naturally existing thing: *phusis*; good natural endowment: *euphuïa*

nature: *phusis, kata phusin*; be by/in nature, be endowed by nature, be natural, be of a nature to: *phuein*; double nature: *diphuïa*

navigation, art of: *kubernêtikê*

navigator: *kubernêtês*

necessary, necessarily, necessity,

necessitate: *anankaios, -ôs, anankê, katanankazein, katênankasmenôs*

need: *dein, deisthai, epideisthai, khreia, khrênai*; need in addition: *prosdeisthai*

negation: *apophasis*

neglect: *amelein, aphiesthai, oligôrein*

night: *nux*; at night: *nuktôr*

noble: *esthlos, kalos*: lover of what is noble: *philokalos*

noise: *psophos*

nothing, for: *kenon*

notion: *ennoia*

not-being: *mê on*

nourish, nutrition: *trephein*; nourishment: *trophê*; of nourishment, nutritive: *threptikos*

number: *arithmos, katarithmein*; numerically: *arithmôi*

obey: *peithesthai*; be obedient: *hupakouein*

obscure: *adêlos, agnôstos, amudros*

observation: *theôria*; concerned with observation: *theôrêtikos*; observe: *horan, katanoein, têrein, theôrein*

obstruct: *antiphrattein*

obtain: *ktasthai, tunkhanein*

occasion: *kairos*

occur: *gi(g)nesthai, piptein*; occur outside: *ekpiptein*

odour: *osmê*; possess odour: *ozein*; transmitting odour: *diosmos*; odourless: *aosmos*

oil: *elaion*

open space: *akhanês, eurukhôria*

opening: *opê*

operate: *energein*

opine: *doxazein*; opinion: *doxa*

opposite: *enantios, hupenantios, katantikru*; be opposed/opposite: *antikeisthai*; opposition: *enantiôsis, enantiotês*; divide in opposition: *antidihairein*

oracle: *khrêsmos*

order: *keleuein*; order, ordered, ordering: *taxis, prostaxis*; orderly: *eutaktos*

organ, organic: *organon, organikos*

organise: *dioikein*

origin: *genesis*

otherness: *heterotês*

outline: *perigraphê, tupos*

outside: *exô, exôthen, thurathen*
ox: *bous*

pain: *algêdôn*; feel pain: *algoun*; be
  pained: *lupeisthai*; in painful condition: *lupêrôs*
painter: *zôigraphos*
painting: *graphê*
pairing: *sunduasmos, suzugia*
pale: *leukos*
paradoxical: *paralogos*
parent: *goneus*
part: *meros, morion*; for the least part:
  ep' elatton; for the most part: *epi
  polu, hôs epi to pleiston*
particular: *epi merous, hode (tis), kath'
  hekasta*; this particular: *tode ti*; in a
  particular way: *idios, idiâi, kat' idian*
pass, pass through: *diekpiptein, dierkhesthai, dihêkein, ienai, khôrein*;
  pass alongside: *antiparallattein*
passage (text): *lexis*; (opening): *poros*
passing away: *phthora*; that passes
  away: *phthartos*
pattern: *taxis*
peculiar: *idios, idiâi, kat' idian*
penetrate: *dihêkein*
per accidens: *kata sumbebêkos*
perceive, perception: *aisthaneshai,
  aisthêsis*; perceived, perceptible,
  perceptibility: *aisthêtos*; capable of
  perceiving: *dihoratikos*; perceptive:
  aisthêtikos
perfect: *teleios, teleioun*; perfection:
  akrotês, teleiotês
perform, performing: *energein, poiein,
  prassein/prattein, praktikos*
perish: *phtheiresthai*; perishable:
  phthartos
persist: *menein, hupomenein*; persistence in troubles: *kakopatheia*
person: *anthrôpos*
perverted, not: *adiastrophos*
philosopher: *philosophos*
pierce: *nuttein*
pipe: *aulos*; play pipes: *aulein*; art of
  pipe-playing: *aulêtikê*; piper: *aulêtês*
pith: *enteriônê*
place (= location): *khôra, topos*; in
  place: *topikos, -ôs*; narrow place:
  stenôpos; change place: *metabainein*;

come in to take place of: *anteisienai*
place (= put): *histanai, tithenai*; be
  placed alongside: *parakeisthai*; place
  over: *epitassein*
plane: *epipedos*
plant: *phuteuein, phuton*; plant-like:
  phutikos
plausible: *pithanos*
pleading, special: *aitêma*
pleasant: *hêdus*
please: *areskein*; be pleased: *hêdesthai*
pleasure: *hêdonê, hêdesthai*
poet: *poiêtês*
point: *sêmeion*; point at issue: *pro-
  keimenon*; final point: *eskhatos*;
  highest point: *akrotês*
political: *politikos*
poor: *phaulos*
pore: *poros*
portion: acquire portion: *metalambanein*; possess portion:
  koinônein
posited, be: *keisthai*
position: *khôra, taxis, thesis*; be positioned:
  keisthai; change position: *methistasthai*
possession: *ktêsis*
potential, potentially, potentiality: *dunamis*
pottery: *keramos*
pour forth, pour out: *ekkhein, ekkhusis,
  prokhein*
power: *dunamis, exousia, iskhus*; have
  power: *dunasteuein*
practical wisdom: *phronêsis, phronimos*
practise: *askein*
praise: *epainein, humnein*
pray, prayer: *eukhesthai, eukhê*
precede: *prohêgeisthai*
precious stone: *lithos*
predicate: *katêgorein*
predominate: *pleonazein*
prefer: *proagein, prokrinein*; preferred:
  proêgmenos; preferring: *proagôgê*
prepare: *paraskeuazein*
presence: *pareinai, parousia*
present, *huparkhein, enhuparkhein,
  sunhuparkhein, engi(g)nesthai,
  paraginesthai, pareinai*
preservation: *têrêsis*; preserve:
  *diasôzein, phulaktikos, phulassein/
  phulattein, sôzein, têrein*; preserving,
  that preserves: *phulaktikos, sôstikos*

press (against/forwards/upon): *eperei-dein*; pressing, pressure: *antereisis, epereisis*; exert pressure: *antereidein*
prevail: *kratein, epikratein*
prevent: *kôluein, kôlutikos*
primary, primarily: *prôtos, prohêgoumenos*; in a primary way, in the primary sense: *prohêgoumenôs*
principle: *arkhê*; random principle: *apoklêrôsis*; rational principle: *logos*; ruling principle: *hêgemonikon*
prior, be conceptually: *proepinoeisthai*
privation: *stêrêsis*
problematic: *aporos*
proceed: *aperkhesthai, proienai, prokhôrein*
produce: *gennan, poiein, poiêtikos*; be produced: *gi(g)nesthai*; thing produced: *poiêma*; produce in: *empoiein*; producer: *poiêtês*; product: *ergon*; productive: *poiêtikos*
profess: *hupokrinesthai*
progress: *proienai*; progression: *prohodos*
project: *exekhein*; projection: *exokhê, probolê*
prompt: *kinein*
proper, properly: *idios, idiâi, kat' idian, oikeios*; properly, in a proper way, in the proper sense: *kuriôs*
property: *idion*
prophecy, art of prophecy: *mantikê, manteia*; seek prophecies: *manteuesthai*; prophet: *mantis*
proportion *analogia, summetria*; in proportion: *kata logon*; proportionate: *summetros*; proportionately: *kat' analogian*
prosperity: *euporia*
provide: *parekhein*
providence: *pronoia*
proximate: *prosekhês*; proximity: *geitniasis*
punish: *kolazein*
pupil: *korê*
puppet-strings, pulling: *neurospastikos*
pure: *eilikrinês*
purple: *halourgos*
pursue: *diôkein, metadiôkein*
push: *ôthein, proôthein*
put together: *sunhistanai, suntithenai*: be put together: *sunkeisthai*

qualify: *poioun*
qualification, without: *haplôs*
quality: *poiotês*; without quality: *apoios*
quantity: *posos, posotês*
quench: *aposbennunai*

radiance: *augê*
random principle: *apoklêrôsis*
rare, rarity: *araios, leptomerês, leptos, manos*; rarefy: *leptunein, leptuntikos*
ratio: *logos*
rational: *logikos*; rational principle: *logos*
ray: *aktis*
readiness, ready: *paraskeuê, prokheiros, rhâidios*
real existence: *hupostasis*
rear: *anatrephein, anatrophê*
reason, reasoning: *aitia, logos, logismos, logistikos*; reasonable, reasonably: *eikotôs, eulogos, kata logon*
receive: *dekhesthai, anadekhesthai, lambanein, paradekhesthai*; capable of receiving: *dektikos*; receive impression: *apomattesthai*
recessed, be: *eisekhein*
reciprocal succession: *antapodosis*; be related reciprocally: *allêlôn einai*
recognise: *gi(g)nôskein, gnôrizein*
red: *phoinikous*
reference, refer: *anaphora*
reflection: *anaklasis, emphasis*; reflective: *emphanês*
refuge: *krêsphugeton*
refute: *elenkhein*
region: *topos*; in our region: *par' hemin*
reject: *diôthein*; rejection: *apoikonomia*
rejoice: *khairein*
relate: *anapherein, anaphoran ekhein, einai pros*; be related reciprocally: *allêlôn einai*; relation: *anaphora*; relation, (relative) state: *skhesis*; judge in relation: *sunkrinein*
relative (family): *oikeios*
release: *paraluein*
religious charlatan: *goês anthrôpos*
remarkable: *thaumasios*
remedy: *iasthai*
remember: *mnêmoneuein*
remoteness, according to their: *hôs ekhôsin apostaseôs*
remove: *anhairein, aphairein,*

parapherein; be removed: aphistasthai, methistasthai
repent: metaginôskein, metanoein
replacement, mutual: antiperistasis
report: anangellein, diangellein
reproach: epilegein
reproduce, reproduction, reproductive:
gennan, gennêtikos
request: aiteisthai, aitêsis
require: deisthai, khrêzein
resist: antiblepein, enhistasthai; resistance: antibasis, antitupia; hav(ing)
resistance: antitupein, antitupês
resolve: luein
respect: aideisthai, timan
respire, respiring: empnous
responsibility: aitia; responsible: aitios;
be responsible (for): aitian ekhein;
hold/make responsible: aitiasthai
rest (opp. movement): stasis
result: apo-/sum-bainein, gi(g)nesthai
retreat before: hupokhôrein
return, undergo in: antipaskhein
revere, reverence: sebein
reverse: empalin, hupenantios
reward: misthos
re-shape: metaskhêmatizein
ridiculous: geloios
right: dexios, orthos
risk: kinduneuein
rob: lêisteuein; robber: lêistês
role: logos
room (space): khôra; (part of building):
oikêma, oikidion, oikos
root: rhiza
rotate: dinein
roughness: trakhutês
route: hodos
rub: tribein
ruling principle: hêgemonikon
run away: kheisthai

sake: for the sake of: heneka/-en, kharin
satiety: koros
satisfy: arkein
save: sôzein; being saved: sôtêria
scatter: skedannunai, skidnanai
science: epistêmê
sculpture: andriantopoiïkê
sea: pelagos, thalatta, thalattios
season: hôra

second: deuteros
secure, securely: bebaios, -ôs
see: horan, opsis, sunhoran, theasthai;
hard to see: dushoratos; seeing:
horan, opsis, theama; (of) seeing:
horatikos; thing seen: horatos
seed: sperma
seek,seeking: zêtein, zêtêsis
select, selection: eklegesthai, eklektikos, eklogê; selected: eklektos
self-controlled: enkratês; self-sufficient,
self-sufficiency: autarkês, autarkeia;
lacking self-control: akratês; love of
self: philautia; making away with
self: exagôgê
send before, send forth: propempein;
send out, sending out: ekpempein,
ekptôsis; be sent out: (di)ekpiptein
sensation: aisthêsis; object of sensation:
aisthêtos; of/having (power of)
sensation: aisthêtikos
sense (perception): aisthaneshai,
aisthêsis; of sense-perception,
[organ] of sense: aisthêtikos; sense-
organ: aisthêtêrion
sense (meaning): sêmainomenon; in
the primary sense: prohêgoumenôs;
in the proper sense: kuriôs; in the
sense that: houtôs ... hôs
sensible: aisthêtos; sensing: aisthêsis;
sensitive: aisthêtikos
separable, can be separated: khôristos
separate, separate off: apokrinein,
diakrinein, diaspan, dihorizein,
khôrizein, khôristos; be separated,
khôris ginesthai; khôristos;
separately: idios, idiâi, kat' idian,
kath' hauto(n); separation: ekkrisis
sequence: akolouthia; in sequence:
akolouthos
serpent: herpeton
serve, serving: diakoneisthai,
diakonikos, hupêretein, hupêretikos
set in motion: kinein, kinêtikos; set out:
horman
settle (of wine): kathistasthai
shade: episkiazein, episkotein
shadow: skia; cast shadow: episkotein;
shady: suskios
shameful: aiskhros
shape: morphê, skhêma, skhêmatizein;

good shape: *euskhêmosunê*; similar in shape: *homoioskhêmôn*

share: *koinos*; share in: *koinônein*; acquire share in: *metalambanein*; have share: *metekhein*; sharing in: *metousia*

sharp: *oxus*

ship: *naus*

should: as should be: *deontôs*

showing: *deixis, deiktikos*

shut in: *sunkleiein*

side: *pleura*; on each side: *hekaterôthen*; sideways on: *ek plagiou*

sieve: *koskinon*

sight: *horan, opsis*; object of sight: *horatos*

sign: *sêmeion*

silence: *hêsukhia*

silver: *arguros*

simple: *haplous*; simply: *haplôs*

sine quibus non: *hôn ouk aneu*

sing praises of: *humnein*

sit: *kathezesthai*

situated, be: *keisthai, proskathêsthai*

size: *megethos*

skill: *tekhnê*; lacking skill: *atekhnos*; of type involved in skill: *tekhnikos*

sky: *ouranos*

slacken: *khalan*; slackness: *atonia*

sleep: *koimasthai*; wake from sleep: *exhupnizesthai*

slip round: *periolisthanein*

small: *brakhus, mikros, oligos*; very small: *elakhistos*; smallness: (s) *mikrotês*

smell: *osmê*; smell (sense of): *osphrêsis*; without smell: *aosmos*

smoke: *kapnos*

smooth: *leios*; smoothness: *leiotês*

snow: *khiôn*

soft: *malakos*; can be softened: *malaktos*; softness: *malakotês*

solid: *stereos*; solidity: *stereotês, sterrotês*

solstice: *tropê*

solve: *luein*

soul: *psukhê*; of, belonging to soul: *psukhikos*; having soul: *empsukhos*; without soul: *apsukhos*

sound (= valid): *hugiês*; (= noise): *psophos*

so-called: *legein*

space: open space: *akhanês, eurukhôria*; spatial: *topikos*

special: *exhairetos, idios*; special

pleading: *aitêma*

species: *eidos*; producing species: *eidopoios*; specific: *eidikos*

speech: *logos*; of speech: *phônêtikos*

speed: *takhos*

spend life: *zên, katazên*

spirit: guardian spirit: *daimôn*

split: *skhizein*

spread out: *platunein*

spring: *krounos*

squeeze out: *ekpurênizein*

stamp: *tupoun, ektupoun*; stamping: *tupos, tupôsis*

star: *astêr, astron*

start, starting-point: *arkhê*

state (condition) *hexis, skhesis*; be in a certain state: *pôs ekhein*; relative state: *skhesis*

stationary, be: *êremein, menein*

statue: *agalma, andrias*

status: *khôra*

stick: *baktêria, rhabdos*

stimulate: *muôpizein*

sting: *daknein*

stone: *lithos*

stop, come to: *histasthai*

straight: *euthus*; straight line: *eutheia*

stream off, streaming off: *aporrhein, aporrhoe, aporrhoia*

strictly: *kuriôs*

strike, strike upon: *prospiptein*; striking: *plêktikos*

strong: *iskhuros*

struggle: *biazesthai*

subject, be subject: *hupokeisthai, hupokeimenon*; be subject to: *piptein*

subordinate: *hupotassein/ hupotattein*

subsist: *huphistashai*

substance: *ousia*; of substance: *ousiôdês*

subtle: *kharieis*

success(ful): *dexios*; (voyaging): *euploia*

succession: *ephexês*; reciprocal succession: *antapodosis*

sufficient, sufficient in self: *autarkês, hikanos*; be sufficient: *arkein*; self-sufficiency: *autarkeia*

suitable, suited: *epitêdeios*

summer: *therinos*

sun: *hêlios*; sunny: *aleeinos*; be illuminated by sun: *hêliousthai*

superfluous: *periergos*

superior: *kreittôn*
supervene: *ginesthai ... epi*
supply: *khorêgia*
support: *okhein*; supporter: *boêthos*
suppose: *hêgeisthai, hupolambanein, prolambanein, tithenai*; make supposition: *hupotithesthai*
sure: with a sure aim: *eustokhôs*
surface: *epipedon, epiphaneia*
surround: *periekhein, perihistasthai*; surrounding: *perix*
survive: *diamenein, diarkein, menein*
sweep aside: *parasurein*
sweetness: *glukutês*
swift: *takhus, takheôs, thatton*
take, take hold of, take on: *lambanein*; ; be taken to be: *ekkeisthai*; take a hold: *epilambanein, -esthai*; take advantage: *pleonektein*; take away: *aphairein*; take up: *analambanein*; come in to take place of: *anteisienai*
tangible: *haptos*
task: *ergon*
teach: *didaskein*; teaching, taught: *didaskalia*
temperance: *sôphronein, sôphrosunê*; temperate (ly): *sôphronikos, sôphronôs*
tendency: *rhopê*
tension: *entasis, enteinein, sunentasis, sunenteinein, tasis, tonos, tonikos*; good tension: *eutonia*
terminate: *apolêgein*
testify against: *antimarturein*
theory: *doxa*
thickness: *pakhus*
thing: *pragma*; (naturally existing): *phusis*
think: *dianoeisthai, dokein, hêgeisthai, noein, oiesthai*; thinking: *noêsis*; think of: *ennoein*; able to think, thinking, of thinking: *noêtikos*
thinness: *iskhnotês*
this-something: *tode ti*
thought: *epinoia, noein, noêma*
threaten: *apeilein*
three measures: *trikotulaios*
throat: *pharunx*
through, extend: *dihêkein*; go through: *khôrein, dia... khôrein*; pass through: *dierkhesthai, dihêkein, khôrein*; pass right through: *diekpiptein*; throughout: *di' holou/ holês/ holôn*; extend

throughout: *parekteinein*
throw: *rhiptein*
tied up, being: *desmos*
time: *kairos, khronos*; of time: *khronikos*; timelessly: *akhronôs*
tin: *kattiteros*
tiny: *brakhus*
together: *athroôs, hama*
topic: *topos*
torch: *daïs*
tortoise-shell: *khelônion*
touch: *haphê, haptesthai, psauein*; that can be touched: *haptos*
tradition: *para*
training: *agôgê*
traitor: *prodotês*
transfer: *metapherein*; be transferred by exchange: *antimethistasthai*
transformation: *metabolê*
transition: *metabasis, metabolê*
transmit: *diapempein*; transmitting odour: *diosmos*
transparency, transparent: *diaphaneia, diaphanês, dioptos*; (not): *adioptos*
transport along with: *summetapherein*
trap: *apolambanein*
travel, travel out: *apienai, pheresthai*
treasure: *thêsauros*
treatment: *epimeleia*
trial of, make: *peirasthai*
triangle: *trigônos*
trouble: *enokhlein*; freedom from trouble: *aokhlêsia*; persistence in troubles: *kakopatheia*
true, truth: *alêthês, alêtheia*
try: *peirasthai*
tune: *harmozein, melos*
turn: *trepesthai*; turn out: *peripiptein, sumbainein*; in turn: *palin, para meros*
twice: *diplasios*
two-footed: *dipous*; of two [kinds]: *dittos*
type, of similar: *homogenês*
tyrant: *turannos*

ultimate: *eskhatos*
umpersuasive: *apithanos*
unable, be: *adunatein*
uncaused: *anaitios*
undergo: *paskhein, antipaskhein*
underlie: *hupokeisthai, hupokeimenon*
understand: *epistasthai*; understand as:

akouein; understanding: *epistêmê, epistêmôn, epistêtos, sunesis*
undo: *ekluein*
uneven: *anisos, anômalos*
unfitness: *anepitêdeiotês*
unfold: *exhaploun*
unhappy: *kakodaimôn*; unhappiness: *kakodaimonia*
unhindered: *anempodistos*
unilluminated: *aphôtistos*
unite: *henoun, sunagein*
universal: *katholou*
unjust: *adikos*; act unjustly: *adikein*
unknown, be *agnoeisthai*
unmixed: *amigês, amiktos*
unmoved: *akinêtos*
unpreferred: *apoproêgmenos*
unreasonably: *alogós*
unstable: *astatos*
unwritten: *agraphos*
unwrought: *argos*
use, usage: *khreia, khrêsis, sunkhrêsis*; use, make use (of): *khreian ekhein, khrêsthai*; use, use in addition: *proskhrêsthai*; use up: *analiskein*; involving use, making use of: *khrêstikos*; useful: *khresimos, pro ergou*; useless: *akhrêstos*
usual: *sunêthês*

vain: in vain: *kenon, matên*
value: *axia*
vegetative: *phutikos*
vertex: *koruphê*
vessel: *angeion*
vice, vicious state: *kakia*
victory, victorious: *nikê*
violent: *biaios*
virtue: *aretê*
visible, visibility: *horatos*; be visible: *phainesthai*; object of vision: *horatos*
voice: *phônê*
void: *kenon*
voluntarily: *hekôn*
voyaging, successful: *euploia*

waggon: *hamaxa*
wake: *diegeiresthai, exhupnizesthai*
walk, walking: *badizein, peripatêtikos*
wall: *toikhos*
want: *boulesthai, ethelein, thelein*

ward off: *alexêtikos*
warmth: *alea*
water: *hudôr*; water-(creatures): *enhudros*; watery: *hudatôdês*
wax: *kêros*
weak: *asthenês*; weaken: *exasthenein, marainein*; weakness: *astheneia*
wealth: *ploutos*
weight: *barutês*
well (advb.) *eu, kalôs*; less well: *kheiron*; well-endowed: *euphuês*; well-known: *gnôrimos*; living well: *euzôïa*
well (water): *phrear*
wheat: *puros*
white: *leukos*; whiteness: *leukotês*
whole, as a whole: *holos, pas, sunholos*
wickedness: *kakia*
wide, aiming: *astokhos*
wild animal: *thêrion*
will: *boulêma, boulêsis*
wind: *anemos*
windpipe: *artêria*
wine: *oinos*; (lover of): *philoinos*; (mixture of honey and): *oinomeli*; wineskin: *askos*; wine-must: *gleukos*
winged: *ptênos*
winter: *kheimerinos, kheimôn*
wisdom: *see* practical wisdom
wise: *sophos*; wisely: *phronimôs*
wish: *boulesthai*; wished for: *boulêtos*; not (to be) wished for: *aboulêtos*; wishing: *boulêsis*
withdraw: *antiperihistasthai, khôrein*; withdrawal: *aphodos*
within: *metaxu*
without, from: *thurathen*
witness: bear witness: *marturein*
woman: *gunê*
wood: *hulê, xulon, xulinos*
work: *ergazesthai, ergon*
world: *kosmos*
worsted, be: *elattousthai*
wrestle: *palaiein*
wretched: *athlios*
write down: *graphein*; writing: *grammata*; written down: *engraphos*
wrong, do wrong: *adikein*; go wrong: *hamartanein*

year: *eniautos*
yield: *eikein*

Greek-English Index

This index is selective both in the words included and in respect of the entries for the more common words. * indicates an emendation to Bruns' text, [ ] a word deleted from the text, < > a word supplied in the text. References are to the page and line numbers of Bruns' text, which appear in the margin of this translation.

aboulêtos, not (to be) wished for, 159.18; 160.34; 162.17; 167.11

aboulia, lack of consideration, 178,21

adêlos, obscure, not clear, 175,20; 179,7.15.17.18

adialeiptos, continuous, 135,2

adiaphoros, indifferent, indifference, without difference, 101,24; 116,21-5; 154,36-155,1; 161,22; 164,7; 165,13. 16; 168,6; 185,30

adiarthrôtos, lacking distinctions, 151,13.27-8

adiastrophos, not perverted, 175,28*

adikein, act unjustly, (do) wrong, 158,23.33; 159,1-5; 185,31

adikêma, injustice, 158,35

adikos, unjust, 154,5-11; 158,18.36.38; 159,4.7-8; 175,15

adioptos, not transparent, 148,4

adranês, feeble, feebly, 147,5

adunatein, be unable, inability, 160,28

aêr, air, 102,8; 103,34; 107,1; 115,16-19; 120,13.20.27.29; 123-149 passim; climate, 185,20

agalma, statue, 103,28

agapan, like, 153,25

agathos, good, 106,9.12; 151-156 passim; 162-167 passim; 184,11

agnoein, be ignorant, do not know, be unknown, 175,19.22; 179,10.13

agnoia, ignorance, 179,14

agnôstos, obscure, 101,7

agôgê, training, 172,8

agraphos, unwritten, 157,37; 158,2

ahoratos, invisible, 126,7.9

ahoristos, indefinite, 176,24; 176,30-177,1; 177,16.17; 178,7

ahulos, immaterial, 108,2.17.25;

109,30; 115,13

aideisthai, respect, 158,1

Aïdês, Hades, 186,7

aïdios, eternal, eternity, 143,36; 144,1.9. 11; 170,17.20; 171,8.30; 181,7.10.20; 184,20

aïdiotes, eternity, 171,21-2

aiskhros, base, shameful, 154,12; 175,15.16.<21>

aisthaneshai, sense, perceive (by sense), perception, 105,27; 107,3; 109,11; 113,20; 114,3; 118,17-38; 119,18-19; 128,23.24; 145,22; 146,35; 147,6.10.14; 161,8

aisthêsis, sensation, sense, sensing, perception, 103-111 passim; 113,31; 115,26; 118,38; 119,7-14; 125,11; 126,1. 19; 130,17; 131,33; 137,2; 141,30; 143,3; 145,24; 153,4; 160,21; 161,8-34

aisthêtêrion, sense-organ, 110,9.10; 113,20; 141,31; 143,3; 145,12; 157,28-9

aisthêtikos, sensitive, of sense/ sensation/perception, perceptive, 103,19-20; 105,13.-27; 118,30; 119,3-12; 128,22; 142,20.32; 143,1; 152,13; 153,4

aisthêtos, sensible, object of sensation, perceived/perceptible, perceptibility, 101,19; 107-110 passim; 111,1; 113,19-20.29-35; 114,1-4; 119,14; 125,11; 126,18-23; 133,13; 145,24-5; 146,20; 150,11

aitein, *aiteisthai*, ask (for), request, 136,28; 141,19; 184,11

aitêma, special pleading, 174,13

aitêsis, request, 184,12

aitherios, etherial, 144,20

aitia, cause, reason, 104,28; 106,7.14.17;

109,24; 140,31; 144,19; 149,25.35;
168,34; 170-79 passim; 181,9.18-19.35;
182,2.5; 185,1; blame, responsibility,
173,33; 174,25; 180,7.12; *aitian ekhein*,
be responsible, 173,34; 178,15; 186,1
aitiasthai, regard/give as cause, blame,
hold/make responsible, 140,8;
169,39; 173,27.33; 176,13; 180,13.18
aition, cause, 102,4; 107,31; 108,20; 133,3;
140,9; 144,27; 160,13; 170,4. 6; 171-9
passim; 181,21; 182,33; 185,5.8; 186,15
aitios, cause, responsible, 111,34; 173,11.
16; 174,10; 177,9; 180,22; 185,33
Akademaïkoi, Academics, 150,35
akhanês, open space, 147,11
akhluôdês, dim, 146,12; 147,2-3
akhrêstos, useless, 173,23-4; 185,34
akhronôs, timelessly, 143,30-3
akhrous, colourless, without colour,
106,31-2; 114,11.14; 136,24
akinêtos, unmoved, 106,6
akoê, hearing, 145,21; 147,4
akolastos, licentious, 154,2.5-6; 185,28
akolouthein, follow, 140,37-8; 152,5;
162,6; 183,16-22; 185,26
akolouthia, sequence, what follows,
152,32; 180,26; 181,25; 185,2.36
akolouthos, follow, following, in
accordance with, in sequence, what
comes next, 103,21; 150,10; 151,2;
152,31; 158,26; 161,35; 182,12; 185,18;
akolouthôs einai, ensue, 180,27
akôlutos, unable to be impeded, 183,11
akouein, hear, 110,4; 157,28; 166,22;
180,3; understand as, 163,18
akrasia, intemperate behaviour, 185,29
akratês, lacking self control, 118,9; 156,1
akros, extreme, 168,2.9
akrotês, culmination, perfection,
155,13-14.18; 162,19
aktis, ray, 127,27-30; 128,20-1.31;
129,15-25; 130,3.11; 130,19; 146,21
alea, warmth, 132,36
aleeinos, sunny, 132,13
alêtheia, truth, 158,14
alêthês, true, truth, 117,11.28.30;
151,25; 152,28; 181,1
alexêtikos, ward off, 162,26
algêdôn, pain, 104,25
algoun, feel pain, 117,17
allattein, change, 112,7; 113,18-19

allêlous: *pros allêlous*, mutual, 156,34;
allêlôn einai, be related reciprocally,
104,32
alloiôsis, alteration, 115,27; 137,27;
143,6.24; 145,9; 147,17
alloioun, alter, 138,38; 141,34-5;
143,5-6.8; 144,18
allotrios, alien, 167,20.27
alogos, illogical, irrational, 114,21;
131,4; 168,34; 169,26; 172,23; 183,31;
alogôs, unreasonably, 174,12
amegethês, without magnitude, 141,26
ameibein, change, 113,22
amelein, neglect, 154,8
amigês, unmixed, 109,30
amiktos, unmixed, 126,6-8.22
amudros, dull, obscure, 145,31; 171,34
anablepein, look up, 130,2; 135,6;
137,20.36; 138,2
anadekhesthai, receive, 143,10.17;
147,21
anaisthêtos, imperceptible, 113,35
anaitios, uncaused, without a cause,
170,3-15; 171,14.22.27; 172,9; 173,31;
174,4-9; 185,4
anakhôrein, move backwards, 130,24
anaklasis, reflection, bending, 134,18.24
analagon, analogous, 102,26
analambanein, acquire, take up, 107,25;
123,23; 137,1
analêpsis, acquisition, 175,26
analiskein, consume, use up, 111,20;
134,31; 137,7; 138,22
analogia, analogy, proportion, 110,6;
137,11; *kat' analogian*, proportionately, 104,3-4
analogon, analogous, 107,22.30; 148,29;
analogôs, analogously, 101,28
anamassein, imprint, 137,1
anamaxis, imprinting, 137,25-6
anametrein, measure, 135,5
anamphilektos, indisputable, 101,9
anangellein, report, 137,2
anankaios, -ôs, necessary, necessarily,
necessity, 105,17-18; 131,9-10;
160,18; 161,26.28; 170,7; 172,14;
182,13-21.33; 183,8.11; 184,9.21.33
anankê, necessity, necessary, necessarily, 112,6; 131,12; 140,18; 141,6;
150,22; 152,32; 157,3.23-34;
158,16.37; 170,5; 171,25; 172,1-4;

174,7; 176,12; 177,22; 180,21;
183,2.13.20; 184,15.26-7; 185,19
anapadrastos, inescapable, 180,1
anapherein, relate, 163,9
anaphora, reference, be referred,
relation, 108,20-1; 113,[7].15; 151,6-7;
168,15; *anaphoran ekhein*, be
referred, relate, 157,13; 164,4-5;
165,30-1; *anaphoran poieisthai*, refer,
174,14
anapimplanai, fill, 123,26-9; 148,17
anapleôs, full, 149,23
anapnein, breathe, 117,31; 129,4
anapnoê, breathing, 129,3-4
anapoblêtos, that cannot be lost, 168,20
anatakolouthein, be implied by each
other, 119,6
anatithenai, attribute, 174,25; 182,22
anatrephein, rear, 157,6
anatrophê, rearing, being reared, 157,6
Anaxagoras, Anaxagoras, 179,28
andreia, courage, 154,6-8; 154,34-5;
155,22; 159,12
andreios, courageous, 154,5.36;
159,11-12
andriantopoiïkê, sculpture, 102,2
andrias, statue, 102,19; 103,28
aneideos, without form, 104,19;
115,12-13
aneleutheros, illiberal, 185,30
anemos, wind, 129,22; 135,33; 136,22-3;
139,26; *kata ton anemon*, downwind,
136,5
anempodistos, unhindered, without
hindrance, 151,31-4; 153,6-10
anendeês, without lack, 162,32
anennoêtos, lacking conception, 175,14
anepaisthêtos, imperceptible, 135,4
anepideês, without lack, 162,33
anepidektos, cannot admit, do not
admit, 143,36; 144,13
anepistêmôn, lacking knowledge,
179,18-20
anepitêdeiotês, unfitness, 184,16
anêr, man, 169,32; 182,15
aneu: *hôn ouk aneu*, sine quibus non,
160,12.17; 161,28.31
anexetastôs, without examination,
172,24-5
angeion, vessel, 115,32
anhaphês, intangible, 126,9

anhaptein, attach, 180,12
anhomoiokhrous, varying in colour,
146,8
anhomoiotês, dissimilarity, 146,8; 148,6
anisos, uneven, 146,14
anômalos, uneven 146,7.9
anhomoiomerês, anhomoeomerous,
162,13
anhomoios, dissimilar, 174,37
antakolouthein, be implied by one
another, 153,28-9; 154,27
antapodosis, reciprocal succession,
186,19
anteisienai, come in to take place of,
123,20
antereidein, exert pressure, 133,14
antereisis, pressure, 133,13
anthrax, coal, charcoal, 120,18-32;
140,38; 160,7
anthrôpinos, human, 179,7
anthrôpos, human, human being,
humankind, person, people, 104,37;
106,4; 107,20; 110,32; 137,18; 150,30;
152,9; 155,14-19; 156,23-34; 157,8-22.
38; 158,3-12; 160,18.26; 161,26-
162,31; 164,11-165,2; 166,17; 168,35;
169,4-10.21-9; 172,19-175,28; 176,3;
179,8-16.26-30; 180,23.30-1; 182,18;
183,26.28; 185,13. 23; 186,10;
(contemptuous) *goês anthrôpos*,
religious charlatan, 180,14
antibasis, resistance, 130,24
antiblepein, resist, 183,8
antidihairein, divide in opposition,
114,10; 169,25
antikeisthai, be opposed, be opposite,
121,30; 148,12; 156,25; 158,28; 159,4;
163,35; 167,29; 170,1.5; 171,24; 172,5.
11; 174,31-2; 181,23-4; 184,16-26
antilambanesthai, apprehend, grasp,
106,27.30; 107,12.15; 109,14.16; 136,25;
145,24; 146,2.31; 147,12; 151,22
antilêpsis, apprehension, apprehending,
apprehend, 106,29.32; 107,7-14;
110,10; 111,4-5; 128,21; 131,2.25.28;
133,37; 135,3.7; 136,12-13.32; 137,6.
32; 145,23-5; 146,8; 152,28
antileptikos, apprehensive, apprehend,
106,31; 107,2-14; 137,33
antimarturein, testify against, 179,28
antimethistasthai, be transferred by

exchange, 129,3.5-7
antiparallattein, pass alongside, 147,13
antipaskhein, undergo in return, 114,32
antiperihistasthai, withdraw, 138,32.34
antiperistasis, mutual replacement, 129,1
antiphasis, contradiction, 114,9
antiphrattein, obstruct, 149,22
antipiptein, be objection, 113,12
antipoieisthai, lay claim to, 151,6
antiproskrinein, add in exchange, 134,32
antithesis, contrast, 168,24
antitupein, have resistance, 125,21.26
antitupês, (having) resistance, 125,9.12.25
antitupia, resistance, 125,15-26; 136,1
aokhlêsia, freedom from trouble, 150,34-5
aosmos, odourless, without smell, 107,1; 114,15
apantan, be encountered, happen, happen to, meet, 130,3-4; 137,5; 177,32-4; 178,1
aparabatos, inevitable, 180,1; 182,13; 183,10-11; 186,19
apeilein, threaten, 154,3.12
apeiros, indefinite, infinite, infinity, 104,20; 123,7.12; 124,3; 125,37; 126,9; 168,1.14; *eis/ep' apeiron*, ad infinitum, 114,6.29; 121,15
apepsia, lack of concoction, 168,30
aperiskeptôs, without care, 178,21
aperkhesthai, depart, be given off, proceed, 123,15-19; 124,11.13
aphairein, abstract, remove, take away, 110,19; 125,37-126,1; 171,21; 174,2; 182,2-4
aphairesis, abstraction, 111,16
aphienai, emit, 147,5
aphiesthai, neglect, 180,31
aphikneisthai, reach, 137,14-15.25
aphistasthai, be at a distance, be removed, 145,22.25; 146,34; 149,13-18; *pleon aphistasthai*, be further away, 139,21-2
aphodos, withdrawal, 113,10
aphorismenos, determinate, 129,1.26; 184,21
aphormê, basis, 151,8
aphôtistos, unilluminated, 131,33-8;

132,2.4
aphthartos, imperishable, 108,29; 113,3
aphuês, ill-endowed, 169,35
aphuïa, bad natural endowment, 175,25
apienai, depart, go/move away, travel, travel out, 134,7; 135,30; 137,10; 138,1.18; 143,29; 145,7.15
apithanos, umpersuasive, 182,31
apobainein, result, 185,34-5
apoballein, cast away, lose, 113,1; 120,15; 123,21; 141,17-18; 162,1-3
apoblepein, look into, 133,8
apodeixis, demonstrating, demonstration, demonstrative argument, 116,1; 118,27; 183,25
apodidonai, give, fulfil, 125,14; 167,1
apoginesthai, depart, 116,2
apoikonomia, rejection, 160,25; 163,35
apoios, without quality, 104,19; 113,33; 114,17; 124,7.8
apoklêrôsis, random principle, 123,10
apokrinein, separate off, 135,1
apolambanein, cut off, trap, 133,3; 139,18
apolêgein, terminate, 128,31
apomattesthai, receive impression, 133,29
apophasis, denial, deny, negation, 114,10.12; 147,14
apoproêgmenos, unpreferred, 167,20.27
aporein, be at a loss, raise difficulty, be difficulty, 123,16; 147,17-18; 169,38; 170,2
aporia, difficulty, 112,6; 131,5; 147,17
aporos, problematic, 134,24
aporrhein, stream off, flow out, 134,31-4; 135,28; 136,20; 137,10-14.27; 138,17.18; 141,33
aporrhoê, streaming off, 135,29; 138,4.14.16.21
aporrhoia, streaming off, stream off, 128,15; 130,12; 134,37; 136,29-33; 137,5.9; 138,17
aposbennunai, quench, 128,16
apostasis, distance, 147,8; *hôs ekhôsin apostaseôs*, according to their remoteness, 148,19
apostêma, distance, 146,30.35; 147,6
apoteinesthai, extend, extend forth, 128,1-2.22
apotemnein, cut off, 129,12
apothnêiskein, die, 168,4

apotropê, avert, 184,11
apous, footless, 169,28
apousia, absence, 123,14; 144,24-25;
  161,40
apronoêsia, lack of foresight, 178,22
aprosptosia, freedom from error, 150,36
apsukhos, without soul, 102,29; 114,4-9.
  23; 115,14; 120,15
araios, rare, 136,23
areskein, please, hold view, 139,34;
  154,12-13
aretê, virtue, excellence, 113,30; 114,35;
  116,13; 121,27; 123,22; 153,21-156,25;
  159,9-168,14; 175,29-30
argia, idleness, 180,31
argos, unwrought or inactive, 115,8
arguros, silver, 101,25
aristeros, left, 143,13-15
aristos, best, 152,12; 156,18-20; 174,2
Aristotelês, Aristotle, 103,4; 106,19;
  107,30-1; 108,30-109,1; 110,4(?). 5;
  112,20; 113,3; 113,27; 119,22; 120,33;
  141,29-30; 143,30; 150,19; 151,3.19;
  152,17-18; 153.20-2; 168,22; 169,33;
  170,9; 172,16; 186,14
arithmos, number, 102,13; 147,13. 14;
  arithmôi, numerically, 125,4
arkein, be sufficient, satisfy, 140,24;
  157,15
arkhê, beginning, principle, start, starting-
  point, 101,12; 103,30; 105,10.17; 150,23-
  153,20; 173,1-19; 175,10; 181,36;
  183,11; 185,14
arkhesthai, begin, 101,13; 121,2; 129,13;
  181,2
arrên, male, 168,21-22.29.33; 169,5-9.21.
  28.31
arrhepês, indifferent, 167,21.27
artasthai, depend on, 152,8
artêria, windpipe, 115,18
askein, practise, 175,17
askos, wineskin, 115,19; 124,20; 125,21
asmenôs, gladly, 180,29
asômatos, incorporeal, without body,
  102,13-14; 104,18; 112,7; 113,25-8;
  115,4-117,27; 121,11-15.28; 138,29-31;
  144,30
aspazesthai, love, 154,33-5; 155,5-6
astatos, unstable, 176,30; 177,17; 185,4
astêr, star, 130,10
astheneia, weakness, 170,20; 171,19;

172,3.10; 180,15
asthenês, weak, 128,2.7; 158,22
astokhos, aiming wide, 179,27
astrologos, astronomer, 171,32
astron, star, heavenly body, 128,1;
  129,33; 132,10-17.29; 138,35; 142,5;
  144,34; 181,17
asummetros, incommensurable, 181,11
atekhnos, lacking skill, 179,20.22
athanatos, immortal, 108,30; 111,31;
  112,5; 114,20
athlios, wretched, 168,18.19
athroizein, collect, collect together,
  142,23.30
athroôs, together, altogether, all at
  once, all of a sudden, completely,
  139,18; 142,15; 143,21.27; 145,3
atomos, individual, 119,26; 169,4
atonia, slackness, 170,20; 171,19
augê, lighting, radiance, 138,4; 145,32
aulein, play pipes, 159,28; 160,17;
  164,24; 165,13.14
aulêtês, piper, 160,33; 165,12-13; 166,16
aulêtikê, art of pipe-playing, 159,28;
  167,5.7
aulos, pipe, 160,16,33; 164,24
autarkeia, self-sufficiency, 162,33; 163,1
autarkês, sufficient, self-sufficient, sufficient in self, 128,10; 137,15; 154,28-9;
  159,15-168,2
automatos, -ôs, fortuitous(ly), 170,8-9;
  171,15-16; 172,7; 176,2-28;
  178,23-179,2; 183,6; 184,31; 185,10
auxanein, auxein, grow, growth, cause
  to grow, increase, develop, 103,37;
  105,11.26; 110,31; 112,2; 116,2.15;
  118,16-17; 123,14.23; 124,13-20;
  126,9; 139,35
auxêsis, growth, 104,1; 118,21
auxêtikos, of/concerned with growth,
  105,7; 118,13
axia, value, 163,5; 167,13.30-1
axiopistos, deserving of credence,
  179,28
axioun, ask, maintain, 170,2; 184,2-3

badizein, walk, walking, 104,36; 105,25;
  117,18; 119,2
baktêria, stick, 130,17; 131,25; 133,6.32-6
barus, heavy, 126,28; 147,31; 148,27;
  184,19

28; 139,16; 141,34-145,26; 146,22; 147,26-150,17

diapherein, differ, (be) different, make difference, 102,27-28; 103,38; 115,12; 116,19-31; 118,29; 119,5; 124,7.25-31; 125,19; 126,21; 127,5-12; 131,14.38; 137,6-7; 142,6; 147,18; 148,11; 151,11; 154,17; 155,7; 162,6.29; 164,2-3; 168,35-6; 169,5-7; 171,27; 174,19; 183,28

diaphônein, disagree, 151,12

diaphônian ekhein, be in disagreement, 182,30

diaphora, difference, differentia, differ, differentiate, 101,28; 102,4; 103,32; 104,29.33; 114,13; 116,30; 118,28.37; 124,24.33; 127,5-8; 128,23; 146,1-3.11; 150,27; 155,8; 156,26; 160,15-16; 168,22-169,30; 170,18; *diaphoran ekhein*, differ, 118,36; 169,35

diaphoros, different, differentiate, 101,25; 104,31; 115,37; 116,30; 118,31; 145,32.35; 150,[12]; 168,30; 169,2; 175,10; 185,22

diaplattein, fashion, 104,30

diapseudesthai, deceive, 161,13

diarkein, survive, 157,7.8

diarthrôsis, distinction, 152,10.16

diarthroun, distinguish, distinction, 150,31.34; 153,2

diasôzein, preserve, 110,4

diaspan, separate, 135,13

diastasis, interval, 147,7

diastatos, extended, 125,16

diastellesthai, make differentiations, 152,33

diastêma, distance, interval, 130,9; 135,3.5; 136,13; 139,21.23; 143,22-3.33; 146,30-3; 147,6.15; 166,28

diastrophos, misshapen, 178,14

diateinesthai, exercise self, 182,21-2

diathesis, disposition, 104,24-5; 117,9; 185,25

diatithenai, dispose, 122,28-9; 144,27-8; 145,17

diaugês, bright, illuminated, 127,34; 145,14

didaskalia, teaching, taught, 157,2; 169,39; 176,5; 184,5

didaskein, teach, 175,5

diegeirein, awake, 136,10-11; *diegeiresthai*, wake up, 162,1

diekpiptein, be sent out, 129,10; pass right through, 135,34; 136,2

dierkhesthai, pass, pass through, extend, 123,27; 128,34; 129,25-9; 130,5; 131,21-2; 138,26; 139,3; 140,26.31

dihairein, divide, division, make distinction, 101,15; 105,26; 114,8-11; 127,31-2; 129,10-16; 152,32; 169,12

dihairesis, division, 101,13; 114,7; 168,27-8

dihairetikos, dividing, divide, 168,23; 169,7.11.20

dihamartanein, miss, make error, 158,32; 186,12

dihêkein, extend, extend through, pass through, penetrate, 115,7.36; 115,37-116,1; 116,5; 123,25.29; 124,14.19*; 131,11.17; 133,22-3; 139,29-33; 142,32

dihoratikos, capable of perceiving, 175,13

dihorizein, define, make distinction, separate, 147,15; 179,13.18; 186,12

dihorismos, definition, 152,10

dikaios, just, justice, 153,31; 154,1-5; 155,29; 156,28-159,13; 175,14

dikaiosunê, justice, 153,31; 154,35; 155,22; 156,30; 157,31; 158,19; 159,10.14

dinein, rotate, 123,2

dioikein, organise, 113,7.12

diôkein, pursue, 155,31

dioptos, transparent, transparency, 148,7; 149,25.32; 150,1.5

diosmos, transmitting odour, 123,22

diôthein, reject, 161,21-5

diphuïa, double nature, 152,23

diplasios, double, twice, 130,8; 141,14; 147,25

diplous, double, 133,12

dipous, two-footed, 169,18.21.27

diskeuôn, discus-thrower, 102,5

dittos, double, of two [kinds], 103,17; 117,23; 152,17.22; 160,31

dogma, belief, 183,8-9

dokimastikos, judge, 166,19-20

domos, house, 186,7

dosis, give, 184,11

doxa, opinion, theory, 131,6; 151,8.13; 152,16; 169,34; 176,6; 179,28; 180,1.10; 181,32; 182,6-9; fame, 166,17

doxazein, opine, 106,5

dunamis, dunamei, potential,

potentially, potentiality, capacity,
faculty, power, 101,23; 103,4-9;
104,11-115,11; 118 passim; 119,20;
120,24.28; 123,8; 140,24; 142,3-145,2;
148,14.31-149,14; 152,1-2.9; 153,9;
155,16-21; 162,3.15. 19; 166,38;
172,1.17-23; 173,21; 184,18; 185,31
dunasteuein, have power, 182,5
dunasthai tauton, be equivalent, 114,12
dushoratos, hard to see, 146,3
duskinêtos, hard to move, 132,4
dustukhia, bad luck, 177,30; 178,18

eidenai, know, have knowledge,
155,34.38; 156,2; 175,2; 179,11.21.23
eidikos, specific, 168,27
eidôlon, image, 130,12; 134,28-34; 135
passim; 136,1-25; 137,30
eidopoiein, give form (to), 127,4. 14-17;
145,4; 148,27; 176,15
eidopoios, producing species, 168,22;
169,8
eidos, form, kind, species, 101,23-
104,20; 106,1.21.-109,14; 111,7-19;
113,20.27; 115,9-13; 116,16-17.30;
117,21.28; 119,26-122,14; 125,18.28;
127,5-12; 137,1-2.26; 138,5; 141,35;
143,1.27; 144,8; 145,26; 146,?7; 147,16;
148,9; 168,21-36; 169,3-31; 176,11-20
eikein, yield, 183,31
eikôn, image, 142,28.31
eikotôs, reasonable, reasonably,
103,4-8; 108,26.30; 109,3; 140,13;
149,20
eilikrinês, pure, 125,36; 126,2.22
einai + dat., being, essence, 124,38;
126,12.20; 174,1; *ti ên einai*, essence,
176,19; *einai ek*, (be) composed of,
116,18; 117,16; 124,5-6; 162,4-8; *einai
en*, see *en*; *einai pros*, relate,
154,16-17; and see *mê on*
eiôthenai, be accustomed, customary,
customarily, 104,12; 155,28; 157,36;
178,23; 185,32
eisaphikneisthai, come to, 186,7
eisekhein, be recessed, 134,12.17;
146,13-17
eisienai, come in, enter, 110,24; 137,37;
139,18
eiskrinesthai, enter, 112,31
eisokhê, concavity, 135,24.26

ek plagiou, sideways on, 146,10
ekkeisthai, be taken to be, 142,19
ekhein apo/para, derive, 122,15; 151,33
ekkhein, pour out, 140,22
ekkhusis, pouring forth, 127,28; 146,21
ekklinein, avoid, 161,22
ekklisis, avoidance, 160,25
ekkrinesthai, depart, 112,31
ekkrisis, departure, separation, 112,32;
125,35
ekkrouein, break, 185,19
eklegein, collect, 180,29; *eklegesthai*,
select, 160,26.28; 161,22; 163,9.35;
164,2-8,33; 165,20; 166,7-17
ekleipsis, eclipse, 132,16
eklektikos, select, 164,20; 166,19
eklektos, selected, 165,10
eklogê, selection, select, 160 passim;
161,6; 163,9.32-4; 164,4-16; 166,10-19
ekluein, undo, make ineffective, 132,3-5;
133,8
ekpempein, send(ing) out, 128,7-26;
129,1-6.22.33; 136,32; 137 passim;
141,32; 145,19-20
ekpimprênai, burn up, 149,11
ekpiptein, escape, 126,1; be sent out,
127,31-7; occur outside, 169,17
ekptôsis, sending out, 127,35
ekpurênizein, squeeze out, 132,29
ekteinein, extend, 141,16
ektos, external(ly), 106,29; 124,15;
142,20; 152,33; 163,28-36; 164,19.32;
165,1.20; 166,10.13; 168,6.16; 171,15;
174,3.6.29
ektupoun, stamp, 133,30
elaion, oil, 140,6
elakhistos, very small, least, 136,26;
148,13; 149,17; 171,31
elattôn: ep' elatton, for the least part,
172,2.6
elattoun, diminish, 164,28; *elattousthai*,
be worsted, 165,21-2
elaunein, forge, 140,35
elenkhein, refute, 134,16
eleutheros, free, 181,19
elpis, hope, 154,4
embadon, entering in, 135,21
emperilambanein, include, 104,9
emphainesthai, appear in, become
apparent, 134,20-3; 135,26; 142,21.25;
145,14-15.25; 146,27-8; 147,23

emphanês, reflective, 142,23
emphasis, reflection, impression, 133,9; 142,23-4; 146,26
empiptein, enter in, 136,5-6.17-18
empnous, respiring, respire, [117,31]
empodion, hindrance, 106,29
empodistikos, hinder, 153,10
empodizein, hinder, impede, 135,2; 153,19; 185,17
empoiein, create in, produce in, 107,33; 120,7
empsukhos, ensouled, having soul, 102,24.28; 104,22; 106,10.15; 114,4-9. 23; 115,7.18.22.30-6; 117,31; 145,10-16
emptôsis, entering, entry, enter, 134,28; 135,8.23; 136,17
en, einai en, consist in, be a matter of, (have being) in, be located in, 105,20; 106,22; 116,35 (see note); 119,17-19; 138,11; 159,27-32; 162,11-12; 164,11; 165,7.13.15. 26-9; 173,10; 179,8
enantios, opposite, 119,27-8; 121,25-6; 122,28-31; 125,4.31; 126,14.21-2; 130,3; 131,10.35; 134,20; 138,31.37; 139,13-14; 147,18.21; 148,12-13.24; 149,3-18; 154,25-8; 158,23.38; 160,25-6.34; 162,26; 165,23; 168,26; 185,5; 186,22-8
enantiôsis, opposition, contrariety, 107,5; 125,28; 148,30; 159,9; 168,24; 169,4
enantiotês, opposition, 147,31.32
enargeia, clear facts, 156,31
enargês, clear, evident, [124,24]; 139,24; 147,3; 148,5; 175,1; 183,7.24; 184,30
endeia, deficiency, lack, 154,28; 160,27; 175,31
endekhesthai, be able, be possible, may possibly, can, 134,19-20; 165,24; 172,2.11; 173,4-5; 179,11; 184,12.25-6; *endekhomenos*, contingent, 172,4; 182,32; 183,1; 184,7.13.32
endidonai, give in, 154,11
energeia, activity, active, actuality, actually, 101,19; 103,13; 104,16.35; 105,21.25; 106,25-113,2.18.32; 114,1; 118,28-33; 119,1; 120,1.9.23-8; 122,3; 123,8; 124,4-8; 126,19; 133,7; 137,8; 139,10.34; 141,36-154,17; 157,29; 159,32; 160-1 passim; 164,18.26; 165,11. 27-8; 167,12; 170,16; 171,22; 181,20; 183,3
energein, act, be active, activity, action,

do, perform (activities), operate, 103,16-19; 104,5; 109,5; 110,24; 112 passim; 113,2; 118,31-5; 119,2; 151,31; 152,2.7; 153,12.24; 154,1-10; 155,21; 156,21-2; 160,13; 161 passim; 165,27. 29; actual, 107,26
engi(g)nesthai, (come to) be (present) in, 106,3; 133,30-1; 134,6; 170,20; 172,18
engraphos, written down, 157,33-4
enguthen, (from) close at hand, 134,27; 145,34
enhaimos, with blood, 118,3
enhidruein, establish, 158,12
enhistasthai, resist, 114,6-7; 185,35
enhudros, aquatic, water (creatures), 129,4; 132,27-8; 169,27
enhulos, enmattered, 108,3.21
enhuparkhein, be present in, 105,16-17; 106,7; 113,17; 115,21; 125,31; 176,16-20
eniautos, year, 186,16
enkerranunai, mix with, 171,28
enkratês, self-controlled, 118,8-9
ennoein, think of, 112,25
ennoia, notion, 162,33
enokhlein, trouble, 160,34
ensêmainein, mark on, mark upon, 133,27.30
entasis, tensioning, 130,20; 134,24
entautha, here (in the sublunary region), 113,14-15
enteinein, tension, 131,38; 132,12-17
entelekheia, actual, actuality, 103-4 passim; 107,18; 117,21; 121,16-21; 144,12.29
entera, gut, 104,2
enteriônê, pith, 104,3
enteuthen ... enteuthen, at this end or that, 131,38-132,1
enthade, here (in the sublunary region), 113,7.9.10
entithenai, implant, 111,31
entos, internal, 181,12
epagôgê, induction, 122,21
epainein, praise, 175,4-5
epakolouthein, follow, follow on, 104,31; 171,11-14; 178,25-30; 179,2-3
epanabainein, (be) above, 169,16
epekhein, have, 171,32; hold back, 161,35.37; occupy, 160,18
epereidein, press (against/forwards/

134,1-6; 139,2; 149,22

homalês, even, flat, 134,16-17; 139,14

homoeidês, homogeneous, 131,6

homogenês, of similar type, 115,12

homoiokhrous, of a single colour, 146,11

homoiomereia, homeomery, 125,34

homoiomorphos, similar in form, 134,34

homoioskhêmôn, similar in shape, 134,34.36

homokhrous, of a single colour, the same colour, 146,4.5

homologein, admit, agree, be in agreement, 138,8; 158,4; 162,4; 181,9; 182,24; 185,1; 186,4

homologia, agreement, 158,30

homônumos, ambiguous, 116,25; 125,18-19; *homônumôs*, in name only, 155,26-7

hôra, season, 186,16

horan, see, seeing, sight, look (at), observe, 101,10; 111,33; 117,18; 119,14; 125,3; 126,3-5; 127,27-138,13 passim; 141,29-147,23 passim; 149,34-5; 150,14; 154,9; 157,26; 162,2-3; 165,35; 166,21.26-8; 174,16; 177,25-6; 181,2; 183,33; 184,18; 185,8.17

horatikos, (of) seeing, 142,20; 162,3

horatos, visible, visibility, object of sight/vision, thing seen, 107,32; 119,15; 125,10.12; 126,4.6; 128,10; 130,17; 131,30; 134,9.11; 136,9; 137,35. 37; 141,33.35; 144,34-5; 145,16; 146,3. 27.34; 148,23; 149,33; 150,3-18

hôrismenos, definite, 147,7-11; 148,3-4; 149,36; 176,23-30; 177,16-25; 181,15

horismos, definition, [124,25]

horizein, define, determine, 105,12-13; 110,20; 111,9.14.17; 124,32; 137,11. 28; 146,19; 156,18-19; 182,34-5

horman, set out, have/exercise impulse, 119,17; 157,2; 172,28

hormê, impulse, 105,17.30; 119,8; 157,5; 161,12; 173,30

hormêtikos, impulsive, of impulse, 105,15-34; 106,16; 119,5.8

horos, definition, 104,8

houtôs ... hôs, in the sense that, 172,8

hualos, huelos, glass, 133,18; 138,28; 142,28; 144,10; 149,26

hudatôdês, watery, 142,31

hudôr, water, 102,8.19; 103,34-5; 115,16. 20; 120,13.20.27-9; 122,19-20; 127,2-26; 128,17.29; 129,2-4.23-4; 132,20-38; 133,9.11.27; 134,10; 135,26; 138,10; 139,25-6; 140,1-5.30; 141,9-25; 142,29; 144,7.9; 147,29; 148,22; 149,4-15.27-9

hugiainein, be healthy, 102,32; 103,1; 160,21.33; 161,8-9

hugiazein, cure, 177,13; *hugiazesthai*, be healthy, 102,34

hugieia, health, 102,33-4; 103,1; 114,35; 162,10; 163,2; 164,29.35; 165,38; 166,2-3.18; 177,10

hugiês, sound, 114,8; 117,1.21; 156,8.16; 166,37; 167,6; 171,5; 174,7; *hugiôs*, in a healthy way, 161,8; soundly, 152,35; 167,3

hugros, hugron, moist, moistness, liquid, fluid, 126,30; 127,2-26; 132,20; 133,26.28; 149,5

hugrotês, fluidity, liquidity, moistness, moisture, 118,3-4; 131,24; 133,27; 149,12

hulê, matter, 101,23.27; 102,13; 104,20; 106,20.22; 108,4.14-29; 109,14; 111,19; 112,10.17.27; 113,23.34; <115,12>; 117,28; 119,26-122,7; 123,8.37-8; 124,1-8; 125,27; 126,10; 144,4; 147,30-1; 148,1.25-30; 155,21.30; 160,6.14; 166,34; 168,31.33; 176,13.15.21; wood, 132,18

hulikos, material, concerned with matter, involving matter, 106,19-113,2; 115,5; 168,24.29.36; 169,5.6; 176,11

humenôdês, like membrane, 136,3-4

humnein, sing praises of, 181,8; 182,20

hupakouein, be obedient, 155,17

hupallagê, change, 122,1; 185,20

hupallattesthai, change, 116,2-3

huparkhein, attach to, belong, be present, 118,19; 157,3.22-29; 160,18; 161,8; 169,13; 177,22

huparxis, existence, 101,7; 172,12

hupekkauma, hupekkauma, 148,21; 149,15

hupenantios, opposite, reverse, 111,3; 122,30; 159,1

huperballein, exceed, 136,14; 169,17

huperbolê, excess, 138,11; 154,28; 185,29

hupêretein, serve, 116,8

hupêretikos, serving, serve, 105,32

huphistashai, subsist, exist, 117,20;

125,6; 126,19; 149,20; 155,20
hupienai, pass beneath, 132,15
hupokeisthai, hupokeimenon, (be)
subject, underlie, 101,20-27; 102
passim; 103,23-4; 106,20.21;
119,21-121,6.18; 122,12-20; 125,1-2.27;
126,17; 134,35; 138,38; 148,2.26.29;
150,4; 160,6-9; 161,10-11; 164,6;
168,25-32; 169,3; 176,14
hupokhôrein, move backwards, retreat
before, 130,25; 139,6
hupokrinesthai, profess, 180,19
hupolambanein, suppose, 110,11; 113,3;
162,34-5; 186,15
hupomenein, persist, remain, 123,36;
125,3; 138,16-36; 139,19; 176,15
hupoptôtos, fall under, 131,29
hupostasis, existence, real existence,
117,24; 120,2.20; 161,14
hupotassein/hupotattein, subordinate,
119,12; 180,2-3
hupotithesthai, make supposition, 151,3
hôs, on the assumption that, 182,25.28;
184,11

iasthai, remedy, 175,31
iatrikê, medicine, 164,29; 165,38; 166,2
iatros, doctor, 164,35-6; 165,37;
177,9-12; 185,20
idios, idiâi, kat' idian, own, proper(ly),
peculiar, on its own, individual(ly),
by themselves, in a particular way,
separately, special, 105,32;
111,10-13.28; 112,4.8; 115,9.31;
117,5.19; 121,32; 125,6-16; 126,15;
130,19; 135,21; 137,3; 148,9; 150,17;
153,8; 161,30; 165,14; 167,1; 175,8;
185,14; *idion,* property, 120,26;
121,25
ikhthus, fish, 128,6
iskhnotês, thinness, 177,12
iskhuros, strong, 128,2
iskhus, force, influence, power, 131,32;
132,13; 157,35; 158,8; 162,11; 163,3;
169,36; 175,19; 177,4; 181,3.23
isos, equal, equivalent, 104,16; 123,16.
25-9; 124,17; 129,18; 140,18-25;
141,3-20; 146,28-9; 181,12
isoun, make equal, 139,37-140,1; 141,13

kados, jar 115,20

kaiein, burn, 138,9; 149,12-13.26
kairos, occasion, time, 154,16; 179,32
kakia, vice, vicious state, wickedness,
113,30; 121,26; 123,22-23; 154,4-29;
175,22
kakodaimôn, unhappy, 154,30
kakodaimonia, unhappiness, 154,29-30
kakopatheia, persistence in troubles,
185,29-30
kakos, -ôs, bad(ly), base, evil, 154,24;
162,5; 167,22; 168,9; 175,27; 182,16;
186,11
kakotekhnia, malpractice, 180,28-9
kakourgein, engage in evil-doing, 158,35
Kallias, Callias, 185,14
Kallisthenes, Callisthenes, 186,30
kallos, beauty, 162,12
kalos, noble, 151,21-2; 154,31-6; 155,1-12.
30-1; 167,24; 174,19.22; 175,13-21;
kalôs, in a fine way, well, 167,9; 175,30
kapnos, smoke, 149,13.23.26
karterikos, enduring, 185,29
katabolê, depositing, 112,21
katabussoun, bury deep within,
135,19-20
katadêlos, clear, 148,3
katagignôskein, condemn, 175,4
katalambanein, comprehend, 106,5
kataleipein, leave, leave behind, 127,14;
136,2; 145,8; 159,19-20; 174,3; 182,4
katamanthanein, discover, learn,
101,4.12; 184,14
katanaliskein, consume, 138,20
katanankazein, necessitate, necessity,
174,33-4; 183,12; 186,20
katanoein, observe, 180,15
katantikru, opposite, 132,7; 146,11.23-4
katapherein, carry downwards, 179,1
katapheugein, flee, 180,7
kataphora, downwards motion, 179,3
katarithmein, number, 176,8
kataskeuazein, construct, establish,
153,19-20; 165,10; 168,7
kataskeuê, arrangement, constitution,
establish, 163,15; 170,10; 185,22.25
katastrophê, ending, 185,16.26
katazên, spend life, 157,1
katêgorein, apply, predicate, 101,18- 19;
104,12; 117,1; 177,30; 178,23-4
katêgoria, category, 116,27; *Katêgoriai,*
Categories, 119,22.25

khrômatizein, colour, 142,16; 144,16-17
khronikos, of time, 143,33
khrônnunai, colour, 114,11.14; 143,12;
  144,6.36; 147,22; 150,7
khronos, time, 101,8; 110,33; 130,7-8;
  137,6.12; 138,18; 139,21-2; 143,6.
  25-34; 145,12; 161,32; 186,15.18
khrôsis, colouring, 146,23
khrusos, gold, 101,21.26; 140,5
kinduneuein, risk, 177,2
kinein, move, be in motion, change,
  affect, cause movement, cause
  change, prompt, set in motion,
  106,5-17; 110,5.25; 118,22; 119,19-20;
  122,32; 123,1.3; 127,29; 129,23; 130,1.
  6-8; 131,3-19.33; 135,30; 137,12; 143,10.
  24-5; 145,31; 146,6; 147,1.8-12; 151,19;
  160,15; 171,20
kinêsis, change, movement, motion,
  move, being moved, causing change,
  101,7; 103,31; 105,2.10-14; 106,7-8.17;
  113,9.11; 115,23-8; 123,3; 128,18; 130,11.
  28; 131,2-10; 136,3; 137,12-14; 138,13;
  139,22; 143,6.24; 145,11; 147,5.14;
  170,10-14; 181,15; *kinêsin ginesthai*,
  be moved, 131,13-14
kinêtikos, affect, able to affect, set in
  motion, 142,14; 145,18; 146,?1;
  149,35-6; 160,12
kirnan, mix, 124,14
klasis, bending, 133,4.11.13; 134,25
klazein, bend, 133,6.10-12
klinê, bed, 181,33
koilia, belly, 104,2
koilos, concave, 133,33; 134,11-21; 146,10
koilotês, concavity, 134,14
koimasthai, sleep, be asleep, 103,19;
  129,8; 153,3; 161,40; 162,2; 165,25
koinônein, (have) share in, have in
  common, possess portion, 107,20;
  117,9; 125,11; 126,1.5.26; 144,10.13;
  156,26; 172,19-23
koinônia, community, 156,29-34;
  157,8.21.23.30; 158,14-28
koinônikos, communal, 156,31.34;
  157,9.17.19.22.30; 162,20
koinos, common, (in) general, share,
  104,9; 105,18; 111,8-12; 116,20-8;
  119,13; 124,30; 125,14.16.27; 126,29-30;
  127,1-2.23-5; 142,6; 144,8.30; 147,27;
  155,10; 157,37; 158,2.30; 159,1; 162,32;

  168,28; 176,3; 179,26.28; 182,18; 183,1;
  185,13
kolazein, punish, 175,5; 184,6-7
kolla, kollan, glue, 115,1-2
kôluein, hinder, prevent, 134,23;
  147,23-5; 149,22; 168,17; 170,20
kôlutikos, prevent, 153,10
koniortos, dust, 149,24
kônos, cone, 128,32; 129,12-15; 130,16;
  134,14-19; 146,17-32; <147,20>
korê, eye-jelly, jelly of eye, pupil,
  128,25; 129,2.5.10.21; 130,15.21;
  131,37; 132,3.26; 134,26; 135,9-10;
  136,14-18; 142,17.21.31; 145,16;
  146,19.25.33
koros, satiety, 168,13
koruphê, vertex, 146,19
koskinon, sieve, 129,31
kosmos, world, 131,8.11; 139,10.33;
  171,31
kotulê, measure, 141,9-18
kotuliaios, one measure, 141,13-14
kouphos, light, 126,25-8; 147,31; 148,28
kouphotês, lightness, 184,19
krama, blend, 116,11; 141,10
krasis, blending, 104,24-34; 112,15;
  170,19
kratein, prevail, 125,29; 130,6
kratunein, give force to, 183,8
kreittôn, superior, 158,21
krêpis, foundation-stone, 161,30
krêsphugeton, refuge, 180,6
krinein, decide, judge, 107,8; 134,14-18;
  143,2-3; 146,3.8.17.29.33; 148,6; 172,28.
  32; 174,1.24; 175,2
krisis, decision, judgement, judging,
  105,21.23; 107,7; 161,7; 173,14.16.
  29-30; 174,10-29; 175,28; 180,16;
  182,18; 183,33
krithê, barley, 115,35
kritikos, judging, (able to) judge,
  discerning, concerned with discernment, 106,3; 107,7; 119,3-11; 156,14.15
krounos, spring, 128,30
krustallos, ice, 132,36-7; 138,11-12
ktasthai, acquire, obtain, 163,37; 164,12.
  14; 165,20; 175,24.29
ktêsis, acquisition, possession, 159,28;
  163,31; 164,7
ktêtikos, involving acquisition, 164,12-13
kuathos, (liquid) measure, 140,22-23

179,16-17; 185,34
mantis, prophet, 186,8
marainein, weaken, 128,4-5
marturein, bear witness, provide
evidence, 175,8; 176,3; 183,3; *marturesthai*, employ as evidence, 157,19
marturion, evidence, 173,33
matên, in vain, 157,17; 163,24-9; 164,8-9.
27; 165,30; 166,11; 178,27-8; 183,26.
28; 184,16
mê on, not-being, 116,3-4; 123,34.35;
170,11-18; 171 passim; 172,3-15
Megarikoi, Megarians, 150,35
megethos, magnitude, size, 131,27-8;
135,7.10.15,22; 141,26-8; 146,17.33;
166,28
meioun, diminish, 116,2; 123,15.19; 137,8
melainein, blacken, 141,2
melania, blackness, 122,30.36; 184,19
melankholia, melancholy, 161,17
melas, black, 117,25; 124,35-7; 150,11;
168,26
melikraton, diluted honey, 116,7
mêlon, apple, 123,24-32
melos, tune, 167,5
menein, remain, abide, persist, be
stationary, survive, 112,32; 115,5;
117,24; 120,30; 123,29-30; 125,25; 126,9;
129,11.24; 134,8; 135,20-31; 136,2;
139,10.24-8.35; 140,2.32; 141,23; 147,10;
173,15; 176,21; 180,10; 184,20-1
mênusis, indication, information,
inform, 137,34; 157,12
meros, part, 104,22; 114,27-8; 115,30;
118,12; 119,34; 122,4-11; 129,13;
130,21; 131,17-21; 155,22-7; 162,14; *epi
merous*, particular, 131,9-15; *para
meros*, in turn, 118,7; 121,25-6;
147,32
mesos, centre, in between, mean,
129,18; 130,4; 131,10-21; 141,17
mestos, full, 124,14; 139,34-5
metabainein, change place, migrate,
112,8.32; 141,7
metaballein, change, 120,27-8; 125,27;
127,19-21; 180,1; 184,26
metabasis, transition, 149,19-20
metabolê, change, changing, transformation, transition, 125,35; 127,22;
143,7.17; 144,18; 182,10; 184,17.22
metadiôkein, pursue, 154,36

metaginôskein, repent, 173,32
metakineisthai, change direction,
139,26
metakomizein, move, 123,26.28
metalambanein, acquire portion,
acquire share in, 124,27-9; 125,22
metanoein, repent, 175,3
metapherein, move, transfer, 124,12;
180,8
metapiptein, change, 180,9
metaskhêmatizein, re-shape, 133,36
metaxu, between, intervening, intermediate, within, 129,16.19; 131,22;
132,8-9.27; 136,12.21; 141,34; 142,17;
145,26; 146,4.7.31-4; 147,17.19;
150,23
metekhein, (have) share (in), 105,5;
106,1; 115,29; 117,7; 142,27; 147,28;
149,2.17; 150,4.6.[12]
meterkhesthai, go away, 113,22-4
methêmerinos, of mid-day, 128,2-3
methistanai, convert, 125,29; *methistasthai*, be removed, change position,
139,5-6; 143,14-15
metousia, sharing in, 170,18-19
metrein, measure, 135,5
migma, mixture, 112,13; 141,10.16
mignunai, mix, 116,36-7; 125,7; 126,3.
20; 128,9; 135,16; 140,5-141,21;
149,22-32; 171,7
mikros, small, 124,11; 141,1; 147,30;
148,28
mikrotês, smallness, 126,2
miktos, mixed, 115,24; 116,36
mimeisthai, imitate, 108,21; 146,13;
147,5
misein, hate, 117,18
misthos, reward, 180,28
mixis, mixture, admixture, mixing,
102,10; 104,24; 112,12; 126,6; 136,32;
140,16-17.33; 148,12; 149,24; 150,5;
170,19; 171,2; 172,15
mnêmê, memory, 162,1
mnêmoneuein, mention, remember,
105,28; 119,13.25; 162,1; 186,14.21
moira, destiny, destined, 180,4; 182,15;
186,5.7
mokhthêros, bad, in bad condition,
151,17; 175,12
molibdos, lead, 120,17; 140,6
morion, part, 103,31; 104,30; 105,18;

orgizesthai, grow angry, 105,1; 118,7
orthos, right, 156,5; 167,5; (angle), 181,12
oruttein, dig, 178,20
osmê, odour, smell, 107,1; 114,16;
 123,18-24; 124,18
osphrêsis, (sense of) smell, 107,1
ostoun, bone, 128,6
ôthein, push, 123,1
ouranios, heavenly (bodies), 113,9
ouranos, heaven, sky, 129,13; 130,2;
 161,32; 171,33
ous, ear, 157,27
ousia, being, substance, essence,
 101,3-103,29; 104,27; 108,29; 110,27;
 112,10; 116,26; 117,5; 119,22-9; 120,27-
 122,24; 140,2; 168,32; 181,19; 182,35
ousiôdês, of substance, 111,15
oxus, sharp, 128,31
ozein, possess odour, 123,22

pagos, frost, 132,35; 133,2
paidion, child, 153,3
pais, child, 175,12
pakhumerês, dense, 114,37; 140,3-4
pakhunesthai, become denser, 140,33-4
pakhuntikos, making denser, 140,37
pakhus, dense, thickness, 128,33;
 129,21; 135,28; 140,3-4.29.33.38;
 141,2; 142,29; 149,9
palaiein, wrestle, 104,36-7
para, deriving from, 108,17; 125,23.26;
 126,1; from (of tradition), tradition,
 150,19; 169,33; 172,16; *para meros*, in
 turn, 121,25.26
parabainein, contravene, go against,
 158,34; 182,17; 184,33-185,1
parabasis, contravention, 158,37;
 159,5-8
paradekhesthai, receive, 130,22
paraginesthai, arrive, become present,
 come to be present, 104,26; 119,6-7;
 123,15-16
parakalein, call in, 182,28; 183,32-3;
 184,2
parakeisthai, be adjacent, be placed
 alongside, 125,30; 136,20-1;
 145,27.29; 150,10
parakomizein, bring up, 123,22
parakopê, derangement, 161,17
parakoptein, be deranged, 161,19
paralambanein, adopt, introduce,

157,21-2; 163,34
parallattesthai, differ, 107,3
paralogos, paradoxical, 132,37; 133,1;
 140,33
paraluein, release, 171,35-172,1
parapherein, remove, 138,17
paraskeuazein, prepare, 136,10
paraskeuê, endowment, 181,23; readiness, 184,22-3
paraspeirein, diffuse, 170,12; 171,7
parasurein, sweep aside, 135,33; 136,4
parathesis, juxtaposition, 115,33; 140,9
parekhein, cause, make, provide, 111,20;
 112,13; 133,13; 149,34; 168,2; 171,25
parekteinein, extend equally, extend
 throughout, 139,37; 140,9-10; 141,22-3
paremphainesthai, appear incidentally,
 106,28
parhistasthai, stand alongside, stand
 next to, 130,10; 143,13
parienai, come in, 166,11
parisoun, make equal, 141,11.21
parousia, presence, 103,8.10; 105,12;
 106,21; 118,19; 123,14; 124,27; 142,4-
 145,4; 148,16; 154,17; 160,30; 170,19
paskhein, apply to, be affected, (have
 something) happen to, undergo,
 107,13.16; 110,7.9; 111,3.8.21; 112,1.
 5; 114,31-3; 117,12.15; 122,27-31;
 128,29.33; 131,36; 133,1; 137,34;
 141,30-3; 142,2; 143,8-9; 144,15-
 145,16; 150,6; 184,25
pathêtikos, emotional, such as to be
 affected, subject to being affected,
 that can be affected, 111,2.4.7;
 144,28; 155,33.37
pathêtos, subject to being affected,
 144,33
pathos, emotion, affection, being
 affected, experience, feature, what
 applies, 104,24-5; 110,33; 111,4-5;
 115,27; 117,18; 118,8; 119,5; 131,30;
 143,3.10.16; 144,9.31-2; 145,24; 147,16;
 147,27; 155,8; 157,37; 168,25-36; 169,5-6
pauesthai, cease, 102,22; 132,34; 143,14-16
pêgnusthai, freeze, 132,38
peirasthai, try, make trial of, 117,1;
 175,1; 180,29; 183,8
peithesthai, obey, 184,6
pêkhus, cubit, 137,19.20
pelagos, sea, 140,22-3

phronêsis, practical wisdom, 156,2-13. 21-5

phronimos, with/having practical wisdom, 156,10-20; *phronimôs*, wisely, 161,20

phthartos, perishable, that passes away, 171,3-6; 185,8

phtheirein, destroy, 102,10*; 113,1; 115,4; 116,4; 120,33; 125,2.31.33; 158,28; 184,20

phtheiresthai, perish, 123,34-5; 170,17; 171,4

phthora, destruction, passing away, death, 117,24; 181,21.27; 182,32; 184,23; 185,18

phuein, be by/in nature, be endowed by nature, be natural, be of a nature to, be, naturally, 128,2; 131,36.38; 132,30; 133,30; 134,6; 140,25; 142,4-5. 10; 143,16. 20; 144,4.15; 148,8.19-26; 156,33; 157,1-7; 158,33; 171,26; 175,27.30

phulaktikos, preserving, preserve, 162,26

phulassein/phulattein, keep, defend, preserve, 120,27; 135,18-19; 145,11. 14; 147,24; 158,21-2; 161,21; 165,20; 168,8; 174,15-16; 177,23; 181,24.26; 186,3; *phulattesthai*, guard against, 182,29

phusan, inflate, 115,19

phusikos, -ôs, natural(ly), 102,1.27-8; 103,25-32; 104,6.11; 107,5; 119,28; 120,5-10; 121,16-25; 122,17.25-32; 125,14; 157,4.20; 158,16; 179,3.5; 181,22; 184,13; 185,19-24; 186,19

phusis, kata phusin, nature, natural(ly), passim; *phusis*, naturally existing thing, 182,34

phuteuein, plant, 178,1.5

phutikos, plant-like, vegetative, 105,18-22; 118,12.20-30; 119,19

phuton, plant, 104,9; 105,7-14; 140,27

phônêtikos, of speech, 105,33

pikrotês, bitterness, 122,31

piptein, fall, be subject to, occur, 126,19; 146,9; 163,33; 169,13; 179,1; 181,16

pisteuein, believe, believe in, entrust, 177,4; 181,1-2.20.23; 183,6

pistis, belief, believe, 180,17

pistoun, confirm, 122,21

pithanos, plausible, 131,35

plagios: ek plagiou, sideways on, 146,10

platunein, spread out, 128,32

plêgê, being bitten, 178,21

pleistos: hôs epi to pleiston, for the most part, 180,4; 185,24.27

plêktikos, striking, 137,17-21

pleonazein, predominate, 115,24-5; 125,8.32-3

pleon ekhein, be more than, 137,30; advantage, 154,8.11

pleonektein, take advantage, 158,20

plêrês, full, filled, 115,20; 129,9.26; 139,4.8; 140,3.30

plêroun, fill, 125,21

pleura, side, 181,11

ploutos, wealth, 166,17

pnein, blow, 135,33

pneuma, breath, pneuma, 115,6-11; 116,32.34; 118,1; 125,21-2; 131,3. 11.13.22; 132,36; 133,3.15; 134,10

pneumôn, lung, 115,19

poiein, act, do, perform, create, make, bring about, produce, explain, 107,23-108,22; 110,8-112,1; 114,31.33; 121,33; 124,33; 126,7; 129,20; 130,13. 19; 132,16.18; 135,8; 136,8; 137,5.11; 141,25-142,10; 144,5; 153,15; 155,13; 157,17; 158,7; 159,3.29-33; 160,23; 161,6.24; 163,24-5; 164,31; 166,5.37.39; 167,7; 168,6.25-9; 171,15; 172,25; 174,16-21; 175,10.20; 176,26; 177,11. 25; *anaphoran poieisthai*, refer, 174,14

poiêma, thing produced, 112,1

poiêteos, should be done, 184,6

poiêtês, poet, 182,14; 186,6; producer, 111,6

poiêtikos, productive, produce, 107,29-108,.29; 110,11-112,4; 159,34-160,10; 162,24; 166,3-5.33; 167,23-34; 169,25; 173,2.15.17; 176,11-178,9

poiotês, quality, 113,29; 114,16-17; 115,4-5.37; 116,3; 117,4-9; 122,16-25; 123 -4 passim; 169,1

poioun, qualify, 113,33; 124,21.23

polemios, enemy, 179,5

politês, fellow-citizen, 162,20

politikos, political, 162,20

polus: epi polu, for the most part, 171,34-5; 172,5

Poluzêlos, Polyzelus, 186,30

ponein, ponos, labour, 185,29.31

poros, pore, passage, 128,25; 129,9.
25-32; 139,3-16.25; 140,8; 142,32
porrô, afar off, distant, far, far away,
135,13; 136,6; 139,20; 147,3.5; *porrô-
terô*, further, further away, 137,18;
143,26; *porrôtatos, -ô*, furthest,
139,23; 148,18.22; 149,13
porrôthen, from far away, from a long
way off, distant, afar off, 135,6;
137,7.16; 145,34-5; 147,1
pôs ekhein, be in a certain state, 118,35
posotês, quantity, 116,26; 135,4; 169,1
pragma, thing, 151,14; 152,21.33;
167,6.9; 177,3; 186,11
prakteos, should be done, should do, to
be done, 156,11.18; 172,22-32; 174,18;
182,27; 183,31
praktikos, concerned with action,
productive of action, 105,31; 119,3.5;
performing, perform, 154,31; able to
do/act, capable of doing, 156,15.23;
175,17
praktos, that is done, to be done,
119,16; 154,32; 156,16.19.22
prassein/prattein, do, act, (perform)
action, 105,23-4; 119,2-3.17;
154,3-156,15; 159,2.11-14; 160,13;
161,35-6; 164,11; 165,3-8; 166,31;
172,25-174,30; 175,24-5; 177,29.32;
180,7; 183,20; 184,8
praxis, action, conduct, doing, 105,17-24;
118,38; 119,5; 155,29.33; 156,7; 160,15;
161,29-31; 163,19.22; 164,11-23;
174,9-10; 177,34; 180,34; 182,23;
183,15-23; 185,22.25
presbuteroi, elders, 158,1
pro ergou, useful, 181,5
proagein, advance, prefer,
167,15-16.31.33; 175,18
proagôgê, preferring, 167,17
probolê, projection, 130,11-12
prodêlôs, clearly, 186,27
prodotês, traitor, 154,8
proêgmenos, preferred, 163,4; 167,13-32
proeisienai, enter in beforehand, 135,18
proempiptein, enter before, enter first,
135,4; 136,14
proepinoeisthai, be conceptually prior,
111,18
proethizein, previously habituate, 158,7
progignôskein, foreknow, 180,20

prohaireisthai, choose, make choice,
106,12; 155,4; 159,1-2; 171,18.23;
172,11-12; 173,20; 177,29
prohairesis, choice, 119,17; 169,37-8;
171,17-18.27; 172,7; 173,13-17; 174,9-10;
176,28; 177,24.31-4; 178,1-16; 180,6;
181,29.35; 182,4; 185,6-9.23; 186,2
prohairetikos, capable of choosing,
175,16; [matter] of choice, 177,27
prohêgeisthai, precede, 161,12; 171,8.
13; 183,22; be conducive, 160,32-
161,2; *prohêgoumenos*, primary,
113,14; 183,26-7; *prohêgoumenôs*,
primarily, in a primary way/sense,
150,11-12; 166,18; 177,8
prohodos, progression, go on, 123,7;
125,37; 150,23; distance travelled
forth, 137,22
prohorasthai, foresee, 185,34
prohuparkhein, exist beforehand, 170,4;
171,22-5
proienai, advance, go on, proceed,
progress, 104,21; 109,23; 110,32-3;
121,15; 123,33; 127,29; 128,28;
143,25; 144,3; 150,34; 151,22
prokataballein, lay down beforehand,
170,6; 171,19.24; 173,15.22
prokhein, pour forth, 137,15
prokheirizesthai, consider, 131,7
prokheiros, ready, readily, 101,4
prokhôrein, proceed forwards, 128,29-32
prokrinein, prefer, 172,29; 173,25.35;
174,31
prolambanein, acquire already, 107,26;
conceive, suppose, 155,36; 162,34.37
prolegein, foretell, 180,26; 186,8
prolêpsis, conception, 176,3; 179,27.30
promanthanein, learn in advance, 182,29
promênuein, declare beforehand, 180,20
pronoein, forethought, 153,19
pronoia, providence, 113,15.16
proôthein, push in front, 136,13.15.21.24
propempein, send before, 136,18; send
forth, 129,21
proptôsis, ejection, 127,28
prosaporein, raise difficulty against,
134,31
prosballein, apply self to, 136,9; impact,
129,18
prosbolê, application, apply, 137,13;
impact, 143,2

sklêros, hard, 107,3; 122,29
sklêrotês, hardness, 131,23
skopos, goal, 152,19.21; 153,14; 155,6-12;
  156,7-20; 164,36; 174,13-27; 176,23-4;
  178,11
skoteinos, dark, darkened, 131,37;
  137,36-7
skotos, dark, darkness, 127,37; 128,3.8.
  11; 131,31; 132,6; 137,36-139,18; 143,28;
  144,24.26; *skotos ekhein*, be dark,
  132,8
skotôsis, clouding of judgement, 161,17
skuteus, cobbler, 154,20
smikrotês, smallness, 113,35
Sôkratês, Socrates, 185,14
sôma, body, 102,10-107,16; 112,9-
  150,6.[13] passim; 160,21.33;
  162,5-16; 163,14-23; 164,21.27;
  168,26-33; 172,18; 185,17
sômatikos, bodily, 115,3.5; 121,13;
  163,28.35; 164,19.32; 165,1.19;
  166,10-13; 168,6.16; *sômatikôs*, in the
  manner of a body, 123,1-3
sophos, wise, 163,5-8; 164,2; 165,29-30;
  166,1; 168,8
sôphronein, temperance, 175,21
sôphronikos, temperate, 159,12; 175,20
sôphronôs, temperately, 154,10
sôphrosunê, temperance, 154,9-10;
  155,22; 159,12-13
sôros, heap, 115,35
Sôsikratês, Sosicrates, 151,30
sôstikos, preserve, that preserves,
  157,21; 158,27
sôtêria, being saved, 179,5-6
sôzein, preserve, save, 133,5-6; 135,8.14.
  34; 142,24.27; 158,16.19.29; 162,21-2;
  170,8; 172,10; 179,4.6; 182,21
sperma, seed, 103,9; 112,21-2; 168,33
spoudaios, good, 161,35; 167,11
spoudê, eagerness, 185,30
stalagmos, drop, 141,19-22
stasis, rest, 147,13-14
stegein, hold, 142,23.30
stenokhôrein, cramp, 116,14
stenôpos, narrow place, 147,12
stenos, narrow, 128,28; *eis stenon
  sunagein*, make narrow, 129,15
stenoun, narrow, 128,30
sterein, deprive, 150,5; 157,7; 163,16
stereos, solid, 128,31; 129,25; 133,18.19;

142,29; 148,4; 149,36
stereotês, solidity, 136,1
sterêsis, privation, 114,13; 119,28;
  144,24; 147,15; 149,18.21
sterrotês, solidity, 142,26-7
Stoa, Stoa, Stoics, 113,13; 160,5
stoikheion, element, 118,22; 125,5.35;
  126,29; 127,4-5.12. 14.22; 182,10
Stôïkoi, Stoics, 150,28
stokhazesthai, aim, aim at, 160,13;
  186,11
stoma, mouth, 104,1
sumbainein, attach, be attribute, (attach
  as) accident, be accidental attribute
  of, 101,3-4; 109,17; 117,30; 170,13-14;
  177,8-27; *kata sumbebêkos*, acciden-
  tal(ly), incidentally, per accidens,
  109,22; 117,13; 131,30; 166,16;
  170,13-14; 171,9-13; 177-8 passim;
  sumbainein, happen, result, turn out,
  125,33-4; 131,21; 132,10; 133,24-
  13416; 183,10.15; 185,26; 186,10
sumballein, collide, 147,19; *sum-
  ballesthai*, contribute, 182,35-183,1
sumbolon, correspond, corresponding,
  126,30; 127,21-5
sumboulê, counsel, 184,3*
sumbouleuein, -esthai, advise, give
  advice, 175,3-4; 185,35
sumboulia, advice, 185,21
sumboulos, adviser, 182,28; 183,32; 184,2
summenein, endure, 158,23.25
summetaballein, change with, 104,31
summetapherein, carry/transport
  along with, 123,31-2; 124,15; 139,26
summetria, proportion, 162,13
summetros, proportionate, 166,28
summignunai, mix, 136,33; 137,10
sumpaskhein, be affected along with,
  117,10-15
sumpheron, advantageous, 151,21-2;
  174,18.22
sumphônein, agree, 176,5.6; 179,31
sumphônia, consistency, consistent,
  182,31
sumphônos, in harmony, 153,20
sumphora, misfortune, 180,24
sumphtheirein, destroy together, 116,7
sumphuesthai, coalesce, 127,32; 129,10-14
sumphutos, cognate, connate, 118,1;
  184,24

tithenai, lay down, place, make, assert, suppose, 137,17; 145,12; 152,5; 156,8; 162,33; 163,4; 168,15; 174,12-13; 177,15; 179,7.17-18; 182,8.19

tmêtikos, dissecting, dissect, 169,22.24.30

tode ti, this-something, a certain thing, this particular, 101,18.25; 102,4.8.19. 22; 106,21; 107,17; 111,17; 119,35; 120,1-9; 121,19; 122,12-13; 125,8.32; 155,1; 173,27.35

toikhos, wall, 133,15; 135,25; 144,14

tonikos, tensioned, 130,27; 131,2-6

tonos, tension, 115,10.12; 132,3

topikos, -ôs, in place, spatial, 115,25. 27; 122,32; 123,3; 130,7; 139,22

topos, place, region, 101,8; 112,6-7; 113,19-22; 116,1; 117,28; 123,18.25-30; 128,34; 132,19; 138,24.27; 139,36; 140,11-20; 141,3-5.27; 149,8; 161,32; 171,31; 178,20; 179,4; topic, 152,17

trakhutês, roughness, 131,24

trepein, modify, 142,2.4.15-19; *trepesthai*, turn, 127,20; 175,18

trephein, trephesthai, feed, nourish, nutrition, 103,37; 105,11.26; 111,21; 118,16-17.34; 138,22; 153,5

tribê, experience, 180,25

tribein, rub, 114,32

trigônos, triangle, 181,11-12

trikotulaios, three measures, 141,10

tropê, modification, 142,19; 143,5.11; solstice, 181,17

trophê, nourishment, food, 103,38; 111,20; 118,21; 138,21.23; 149,11; 179,4.5

tukhê, luck, 170,9; 171,15; 176.1-179,21; 180,5-11; 182,23; 183,6; 184,28.31; 185,3.10.36

tukhêros, due to luck, 172,6

tunkhanein, achieve, obtain, 163,10; 165,32-6; 166,1; 175,19-20; 177,29.30

tupos, outline, 186,11; stamping, 133,38; 134,10

tupôsis, stamping, 130,21; 134,1-27; 137,27

tupoun, stamp, 130,16; 133,25.28; 134,3-7.19

turannos, tyrant, 154,12

Xenarkhos, Xenarchus, 151,8

xêros, dry, dryness, 126,25.27; 127,4.13-16.26; 149,5

xêrotês, dryness, 126,11-12.17; 131,24

xulinos, wooden, 169,2

xulon, wood, piece of wood, log, 101,20; 115,6; 120,19-23; 140,38; 149,12

xunienai, come together, 129,14

zên, live, be alive, life, living, spend life, 102,35-105,23; 118,18-32; 151,32-153,26; 156,32; 162,35-6; 163,11; 164,9-10; 165,15-18; 166,22-9; 168,5; 183,3; 185,28

zêtein, enquire, enquiry, inquirer, look for, seek, 129,3; 136,8; 144,37; 150,26; 158,31; 159,23-4; 162,4; 172,22.27; 173,12.34; 177,3; 181,6; 182,12-13; 184,4

zêtêma, enquiry, 159,24-5

zêtêsis, seeking, 158,30-3

Zeus, Zeus, 168,4

zôê, life, 104,11-16; 118,18.20; 153,23; 162,33

zôigraphos, painter, 146,14

zôion, animal, (living) creature, 102,10-106,17; 114,5-118,2; 121,20-1; 128,17; 129,8; 141,6.8; 144,21; 150,29; 152,1; 157,1-10; 162,21; 168,23-169,24; 172,23-30; 173,23; 175,9; 182,9; 183,28.32; 185,13

zopheros, dark, darkened, 132,12-133,8

zophoun, darken, 132,16-17

Index of Passages Cited

89-90; **28,9**, 90-1; **28,16-31,18**,
89-90; **28,23-6**, 94; **28,23-8**, 96;
28,28-29,8, 95; **29,8-12**, 94;
29,12-30,1, 94; **29,21-31**, 98;
30,1-6.6-12, 98; **30,12-18**, 98, 142;
30,18-21, 98; **30,21-3**, 89; **30,23-5**,
89, 91; **30,25-31,1**, 93; **30,25-31,9**,
89; **31,1-3**, 93; **31,4-5**, 91; **31,6-7**, 92;
31,9-18, 89; **31,11-18**, 127; **31,19-29**,
90, 107; **31,23-5**, 108; **32,1-9**, 89;
32,1-33,25, 114; **32,25-7**, 108; **36,9**,
130; **42,26-43,1**, 127; **43,2-4.13**, 134;
43,13-14, 145; **43,17-47,30**, 143;
44,1-7, 143; **44,25-45,4**, 145; **45,2-4**,
143; **45,5-11**, 146; **45,5-6.10**, 142;
45,11-15, 144; **45,13**, 134; **45,20-21**,
144; **45,25-46,6**, 145; **45,26-46,3**,
133, 145; **46,9-12**, 146; **46,13-21**,
147; **46,20**, 242; **46,21-47,1**, 145;
46,21-47,3, 148; **46,21-47,8**, 134;
47,8-19, 149-50; **47,10**, 143; **47,13**,
145; **47,15-17**, 148; **49,28-50,3**, 142;
50,10-11, 137; **52,1.9**,134; **56,10-
58,22**, 107; **56,12**, 114; **56,17-58,22**,
107; **56,23-57,-10**, 108; **57,10-11**,
111; **57,11-12**, 108; **57,18-19**, 113;
57,19-20, 108; **57,21-58,1**, 112-13;
57,23-5, 113; **57,25-7**, 111, 113;
57,27-58,1, 113; **58,1ff.**, 109-10;
58,8-12, 109; **58,12-15**, 110; **58.15-
16**, 111; **58,16-20**, 112; **59,1-10**, 129;
59,11-14, 131; **133,24**, 127; **134,11**,
127, 132

In Metaphysica, **103,31ff.**, 159; **104,8**,
207; **115,10**, 15; **142,13-16**, 145;
153,7, 15

In Meteorologica, **6.15**, 207; **7,9**, 43;
7,10-14, 207; **14,25ff.**, 67, 81;
141,11-12, 89; **141,34**, 110

In Physica, cod. Paris. suppl. gr. 643
101r, 44; fr.1 Giannakis, 222; fr.2,
220; fr.15, 127-8; fr.16, 133

In Topica, **2,16-19**, 59; **51,5-6**, 198;
99,2-20, **100,31- 101,14**, 237;
145,23-32, 165; **166,33- 167,2**, 174;
173,14-16, 50; **173,11- 14**, 174;
183-7, 237; **190,9-11**, 165; **211,9-14**,

185; **236,10-16**, 182; **242,7**, 183

Problemata Ethica, **3**, 76; **8**, 160; **9**,
207, 214-15; **11**, 237; **18**, 214; **22**,
160; **24**, 167; **25**, 164, 178; **28**, 160;
29, 207-8, 213-14, 227

Quaestiones, **1.2**, 2, 134, 142-3, 148; **1.8**,
2, 19, 62, 65-6; **1.11**, 21; **1.13**, 113;
1.15, 75; **1.17**, 2, 62, 65, 67; **1.21**, 134;
1.25, 69, 207; **1.26**, 2, 62, 64-5, 67; **2.3**,
42-3, 207-8; **2.7**, 75, 121; **2.8**, 19, 57,
63; **2.12**, 121; **2.15**, 75; **2.17**, 67, 81;
2.19, 207; **2.20**, 67; **2.23**, 118; **2.24**,
15; **2.26**, 63; **3.2-3**, 35; **3.5**, 237; **3.7**,
61; **3.11**, 169; **3.13**, 22, 210

[ALEXANDER OF APHRODISIAS]
In Metaphysica, **699,4**, 31
ANAXAGORAS
fr. 59B17 DK, 84
ANONYMOUS
In EN (*CAG* 20), 121; **232,10**, 169, 215;
232,11-12, 169; **233.15**, 169, 215
ARISTOTLE
Analytica posteriora, **1.4 33a34ff.**, 65
Categoriae, **2 1a24-5**, 62, 65; **5 3a7**,
61, 64; **5 3a22-8**, 63; **5 3b24**, 64; **5
3b25**, 80; **5 4a10ff.**, 70; **8 10b13**, 80
De anima, **1.1 403a3-10**, 3; **1.4
408b11-15**, 21; **1.5 415b10-15**, 47;
2.1, 45; **2.1 412a6-9**, 70; **2.1 412a17**,
52; **2.1 412a18**, 62, 68; **2.1
412a22ff.**, 156; **2.1 412a27-8**,19; **2.1
412b5-6**, 18; **2.1 413a4-7**, 3; **2.2-3**,
55; **2.3 414b28-32**, 21; **2.4 415b2.20**,
157; **2.4 416a15**, 57; **2.5 417b2ff.**,
35; **2.7 417b14, 418a5**, 60; **2.7
418a26-b3**, 145; **2.7 418b6**, 142; **2.7
418b7-9**, 135; **2.7 418b9-10**, 129;
2.7 418b11, 134; **2.7 418b11-13**,
129; **2.7 418b12-13**, 133; **2.7
418b14**, 117; **2.7 418b20-6**, 133; **2.7
419a2-5**, 92; **3.1 425a4-5**, 131; **3.1
425a14-30**, 60; **3.2 425b12-25**, 61;
3.2 425b24-5, **3.3 428a15-16**, 136;
3.4 429a18-27, 25; **3.4 429b3-4**, 29;
3.4 429b5-9, 27; **3.5 430a14-15**, 42;
3.5 430a15-17, 27; **3.8 432a1-3**, 29;
3.9-11, 3; **3.10 433b15-17**, 23

Subject Index

This index is selective, and is supplementary to the specialised word-indexes and Index of Passages Cited; it should be used in conjunction with these.

Made in the USA
Middletown, DE
26 August 2022

72307465R00179